CANADIAN CRIMINAL JUSTICE HISTORY: AN ANNOTATED BIBLIOGRAPHY

The first hundred years of Canada's criminal justice system are covered in this bibliography of published and unpublished scholarly materials written between 1867 and 1984. It offers 1100 French and English citations, most accompanied by English-language abstracts. Through a distinctly interdisciplinary focus this bibliography brings together, for the first time, a broad range of secondary sources essential for advanced research on the history and development of public policing, the criminal court system, and the correctional system.

Organized into four broad subject areas, the bibliography deals first with police, including documents relating to the history and development of the RCMP, provincial and municipal policy, and the early use of the military in a policing capacity. The next chapter provides a context in which major components of the criminal justice system evolved: material on the history of crime and deviance, juvenile delinquency, and reform movements. The third chapter covers the history and development of the criminal law and the criminal courts. Finally, chapter four deals with documents relating to the development of institutions for coping with criminals, the poor, and the insane; punishment and treatment of incarcerated offenders; penal reform; and the history and development of various sentencing alternatives, such as transportation, probation, and parole.

Author and subject indexes provide ready access to the bibliography, and an appendix of sources searched is of invaluable assistance to researchers.

RUSSELL SMANDYCH is a member of the Department of Sociology, University of Manitoba.

CATHERINE J. MATTHEWS is Principal Investigator, Canadian Criminal Justice History Project, and Head Librarian, Centre of Criminology, University of Toronto.

SANDRA J. COX is Librarian and Research Associate, Canadian Criminal Justice History Bibliography Project.

Russell C. Smandych,
Catherine J. Matthews,
and Sandra J. Cox

with the assistance of
Ezzat A. Fattah and Jean Trépanier

Canadian
Criminal Justice
History

AN ANNOTATED BIBLIOGRAPHY

UNIVERSITY OF TORONTO PRESS
Toronto Buffalo London

© University of Toronto Press 1987
Toronto Buffalo London
Printed in Canada

ISBN 0-8020-5720-9

Canadian Cataloguing in Publication Data

Smandych, Russell Charles
  Canadian criminal justice history

  Includes index.
  ISBN 0-8020-5720-9

  1. Criminal justice, Administration of – Canada –
  History – Bibliography. 2. Crime and criminals –
  Canada – History – Bibliography. 3. Police –
  Canada – History – Bibliography. 4. Correctional
  institutions – Canada – History – Bibliography.
  I. Matthews, Catherine J. II. Cox, Sandra J.
  III. Title.

KE8813.A1S62 1987   016.364′971   C87-094673-0

To future students of
Canadian criminal justice history

Contents

Preface

Contemporary interest in the study of Canadian 'criminal justice history' has reached an unprecedented level. Within the academic departments and research centres of various Canadian universities, academics have begun to display considerable interest in such topics as the history of crime, the history of courts and the administration of criminal justice, and the evolution of modern institutions of social control. Although there exists a substantial body of secondary literature of potential value to researchers entering the field, access to this literature has remained scattered across a number of history, sociology, law, and criminology indexes and bibliographies. The recent increase of scholarly interest in Canadian criminal justice history has demonstrated the need for an interdisciplinary research resource to provide bibliographic control for the scattered literature. *Canadian Criminal Justice History: An Annotated Bibliography* was created to fill this void.

SCOPE AND CRITERIA

Canadian Criminal Justice History: An Annotated Bibliography consists of published and unpublished scholarly materials written between 1867 and 1984, and pertaining to the history of Canadian criminal justice to approximately 1970. It is a compendium of over 1100 English- and French-language citations, the majority of which are accompanied by English-language abstracts. Through a distinctly interdisciplinary focus this bibliography brings together, for the first time, a broad range of published and unpublished secondary sources essential for advanced research on the history and development of public policing, the criminal court system, and the correctional system.

In compiling a bibliography on such an interdisciplinary subject area the researchers have had to make some difficult decisions regarding criteria for the inclusion of materials. Clearly the potential usefulness of a document to academics and researchers interested in Canadian criminal justice history was a primary concern. The difficulty is that 'criminal justice history' as an area of academic inquiry has not been very uniformly defined, either in the literature or by the academic community. An examination of existing published reference sources, such as those compiled by Knafla ('Crime, Criminal Law and Justice in Canadian History: A Select Bibliography, Origins to 1940,' in *Law and Society in Historical Perspective*, edited by D.J. Bercuson and L.A. Knafla, pp. 157–171 [Calgary: University of Calgary, 1979]), Maddaugh (*A Bibliography of Canadian Legal History* [Toronto: York University Law Library, 1972]), and Boult (*A Bibliography of Canadian Law*, New ed. [Ottawa: Canadian Law Information Council, 1977; first supplement, 1982]), indicated that the field of Canadian criminal justice history could be defined as encompassing an immense range of substantive topics, an abbreviated list of which might include: the history of policing and law enforcement; the history of crime, deviance, and dependency; the history of the legal profession, the courts, and the administration of criminal justice; the history of forms of 'private justice' (such as duelling and vigilantism); the history of civil disobedience, labour unrest, and rebellion (such as the Winnipeg General Strike or the Riel Rebellion). In addition, we recognized that the history of Canadian corrections could be taken to include not only the history of prisons and penitentiaries, but also that of other institutions such as insane asylums and poorhouses, which were created to deal with the deviant and dependent in early Canadian society. Clearly the breadth of these areas was considerable, and we had to focus our search into a manageable yet meaningful picture of criminal justice history.

In Chapter 1, under the general heading 'Police,' the bibliography includes documents relating to the history and development of the RCMP and provincial and municipal police forces, and the early use of the military in a policing capacity. We have excluded materials on the history of private policing and private security systems. We have excluded many popular accounts of police history, as many were autobiographical or biographical, or descriptive and based on personal reminiscences rather than scholarly research of primary and secondary sources. While these are interesting and contribute to a picture of history, they do not meet the criteria of the present bibliography. Some, however, have been included, and are to an extent indicative of the nature of much historical writing on this subject area.

Chapter 2 focuses on the realization that the historical development of the major components of our criminal justice system (i.e., the police, the courts, and corrections) did not evolve in a vacuum. Rather, the historical development of the Canadian criminal justice system occurred within the context of broader nineteenth-century social developments and was influenced by a number of external factors, including changes in the criminal law, the perceived seriousness of criminal behaviour, and the structure of Canadian society itself. Chapter 2, therefore, includes materials on the history of crime and deviance in Canadian society, juvenile delinquency, and reform movements such as public-health reform, urban reform, and temperance. In Chapter 2 generally we have not included descriptive and popular accounts of criminal events unless they were serious scholarly works.

Chapter 3 covers the history and development of the criminal law and courts of law which have historically had jurisdiction over criminal matters. This excludes such topics as the history of the civil courts and judicial review, but includes selected material on the history of the family courts as they pertain to the development of juvenile courts. Chapter 3 generally excludes descriptions of the architecture and physical premises of courthouses and most memoirs and biographies of judges. The existence of such superior biographical and social-history scholarship in the form of the *Dictionary of Canadian Biography*, and knowledge of the Canadian content of the forthcoming *Dictionary of Legal Biography* (see *Now and Then*, 2: 2, September 1982), assured us of the availability of thorough coverage of biographical history for the researcher.

In Chapter 4, on 'Prisons and Social Welfare Institutions,' are documents relating to the development of institutions for coping with the criminal, the poor, and the insane; the punishment and treatment of incarcerated criminals; penal reform; and the history and development of various sentencing alternatives, such as transportation, probation, and parole. We have included items dealing with developments occurring within the federal realm, as well as regional, provincial, and local developments.

Originally the compilers intended to annotate all entries in the bibliography. However, when it became apparent that the bibliography would be more than double its estimated size, that intention was modified. Where no annotation is provided, the compilers have relied on various criteria for the vetting of inappropriate documents, such as: author's academic credibility, status of publisher, article or book content as derived from article or book title, and document 'description' (e.g., a one-page article, an unknown journal, a 'popular' account), as well as the academic credibility of the source from which our citation was derived.

The primary aim of the compilers was to include documents which are a scholarly historical-research effort. While this aim readily eliminates consideration of fictional accounts, descriptive narratives and commentaries, and popular editorials, it does not facilitate decision-making about earlier works which do not meet contemporary 'scholarly' standards.

In our extensive search of over one hundred indexes, catalogues, checklists, and previously published bibliographies (listed in the Appendix) we cast a wide net to permit ourselves a broad perspective on our subject. Our months of searching yielded over 3000 entries which have been 'distilled' to more than 1100.

Throughout the process we strove to maintain a delicate balance between loyalty to our main selection criteria and knowledge that we were, by virtue of those criteria, eliminating some bibliographic references likely to be of some value to some people. As a group we excluded reports of royal commissions, annual reports, and other government publications which were not exclusively historical studies. These are more properly 'primary' rather than 'secondary' sources. We have retained, however, criminal justice histories, penitentiary histories, etc., funded by government but carried out by independent researchers.

Bibliography is a task without end. We continue to find new and interesting references, but have to stop somewhere in order to ever publish. We believe that we have achieved our objective of bringing together the interdisciplinary literature, and trust that users of this bibliography will find it of some assistance in their research.

C.J.M.
R.C.S.
S.J.C.

Acknowledgements

A bibliography of this scope is a task of great proportions, a task which could not have been undertaken without the support of many individuals and organizations. In particular we acknowledge the generous funding for this project provided through the Canadian Studies–Research Tools Strategic Grants Program, Social Science and Humanities Research Council of Canada (Grant No. 491–82–1115), Osgoode Society, and Humanities and Social Sciences Committee of the Research Board of the University of Toronto. Furthermore, funds awarded to the Centre of Criminology through the Contributions Program of the Solicitor General, Canada, indirectly and directly, contributed to our ability to complete this research.

Our early work on the project in 1981 benefited from the support of Professor Tony Doob, director of the Centre of Criminology, who made the many resources of the centre available to us from the start. We thank Professor John M. Beattie, acting-director (1986–7), for extending that support right through until publication. As well, we appreciate the assistance of the centre's administrative personnel, Rita Donelan and Elizabeth Burgess, and the library staff, Jane Gladstone, Pearl Hsing, and Anne Bright. The word processing wizard was the ever-cheerful Marie Pearce, who worked her way through many drafts and corrections, assisted in the early stages by Wendy Burgess. The intellectual support of our colleagues at the centre has contributed in many unseen ways to our work.

We were very fortunate to be assisted by several individuals, foremost of whom are Dr. Jean Trépanier, of Ecole de Criminologie, Université de Montréal, and Professor Ezzat Fattah of the Department of Criminology, Simon Fraser University. Dr. Trépanier provided consultation on the selection and inclusion of French-language documents, and Professor Fattah prepared English-language annotations of French source documents.

Additional 'French to English' abstracting was performed by Dany Lacombe and Bruno Théorêt. Bibliographic verification was very capably assisted by the work of three students in the Faculty of Library and Information Science: Lester Webb, Martha Scott, and Darrel Reid.

In compiling a bibliography the authors rely on the work of earlier bibliographers, and collect and evaluate references from indexes, catalogues, abstracts, and other bibliographies. We appreciate Dr. J.G. Woods, director, Research Division, Solicitor General of Canada, having made available to us the unpublished manuscript of his *Corrections History Bibliography*, a valuable part of the Corrections History Project of the Solicitor General of Canada. (This work has since been published as *Bibliography of Canadian Criminal Justice History* [Programs Branch User Report no. 1984–71; Ottawa: Ministry of the Solicitor General, Programs Branch, 1984].) William Beahen, historian, Royal Canadian Mounted Police, provided some useful suggestions for Chapter 1. Professor Allan Moscovitch, School of Social Work, Carleton University, kindly provided access to his (then unpublished) bibliography *The Welfare State in Canada: A Selected Bibliography, 1840–1978* (Waterloo: Wilfrid Laurier University Press, 1983).

Intellectual and moral support has been valuable to us through the course of the project. Thanks go to Professor Balfour Halévy, chief librarian, Faculty of Law, York University, for his helpful suggestions early in the project. Dr. Peter Oliver, of York University and the Osgoode Society, has offered valuable suggestions. Our special thanks go to Professor Graham Parker, Osgoode Hall Law School, York University, for his many suggestions based on his detailed reading of the manuscript.

The assistance of the book selectors and reference librarians of the John P. Robarts Research Library, University of Toronto, who carefully reviewed our 'Methodology/Sources to Be Searched Bibliography' and made many helpful suggestions, especially Dr. M. Distad, Jane Clark, Mary McTavish, and C. Blackstock, is gratefully acknowledged. Other unnamed staff of the Robarts Library in the Reference, Microtext, and Interlibrary Loan departments deserve acknowledgement and thanks.

We have engaged in correspondence with many academics, researchers, and authors from coast to coast, and would like to thank them collectively for the many citations and documents supplied to us in the course of our research. Our only regret is that we have been unable to include all of their work, particularly their 'forthcoming' papers, theses, and books. We are encouraged to know of such vital research work in progress, and only hope that other researchers in this vastly interdisciplinary field will locate their future works.

We would like to acknowledge the assistance of Heather Moore, chief librarian, and the staff of the Library of the Solicitor General of Canada; librarians and staff of the Faculty of Law Library, Osgoode Hall, York University; University of Toronto Libraries, including the Centre of Criminology Library and the Faculty of Law Library; Glendon College (York University) Library;

University of British Columbia; Simon Fraser University; Queen's University; the University of Western Ontario; University of Ottawa; Carleton University; Université de Montréal (and particularly Jacqueline de Plaen); Metropolitan Toronto (Reference) Library; and the National Library of Canada. Further assistance, primarily interlibrary loan co-operation, was received from numerous libraries including the Law Society of Upper Canada Great Library, the Legislative Library and Reference Service of the Ontario Legislature, the Legislative Library, Fredericton, N.B., the Legislative Library, Victoria, B.C., the Royal Canadian Mounted Police Headquarters and College Library, the Ontario Provincial Police Library, the Glenbow-Alberta Institute, and dozens of others.

We are grateful to Mr. Virgil Duff, managing editor, University of Toronto Press, for his interest and support in bringing this project to publication, to Mr. Peter Scaggs, production manager, for his many helpful suggestions, and to Lorraine Ourom and Beverley Beetham-Endersby for their editorial suggestions and advice.

We are grateful for the support and encouragement of our families who have shared the trials and tribulations of this interesting project.

Without the support and assistance of these dozens of people, plus others unnamed who have given feedback at many points, reviewed early drafts, debated the merits of various documents, responded to questions, and so on, we are truly appreciative. The final responsibility rests with us, and we duly acknowledge that. Users of the bibliography may challenge our decisions to include or exclude certain documents, but be it known that we assume responsibility for those decisions, and welcome continuing debate and scholarship in that exciting and challenging area of interdisciplinary study, Canadian criminal justice history.

C.J.M.
R.C.S.
S.J.C.
11 November 1986

Instructions to Users

As noted in the Preface, this bibliography is divided into four broad chapters. Within each chapter entries are arranged alphabetically by author or editor. Where authors have more than one publication they are arranged chronologically from earliest to latest work.

At the end of the bibliography users will find a complete Author Index covering the names of all authors, editors, co-authors, etc. References are to document entry number rather than page number. Document entry numbers run down the left margin of each page of the text.

A Subject Index follows the Author Index. 'See' references and 'See also' references are provided to guide the user to preferred terminology. Certain exigencies have been allowed to bring like matters together and promote ease of indexing. For example, materials on the North West Mounted Police, the Royal North West Mounted Police, and the Royal Canadian Mounted Police have been brought together under the last-cited name. This is not to deny the historical significance of the three names and time frames of the force, but as many documents cover the force from its early days to the present, we would have to end up with a more cumbersome multiple-entry listing to reflect this.

Another area where 'historical' concessions were made for ease of index creation (and, we hope, use) concerns the naming of the political and geographic concepts of Upper Canada, Lower Canada, New France, Western Canada, etc. Many documents clearly specify where discussion of Upper Canada leaves off and Ontario begins, whether Western Canada includes Manitoba or British Columbia, etc., while others are more vague. We have taken the liberty of using the names of the present provinces as geographic subdivisions, and tried to ascertain as closely as possible the geographic area to which the documents refer. The only broad geographic heading used is 'Northern Frontier,' which could include any or all of northerly Manitoba, Saskatchewan, Alberta, British Columbia, and the Yukon, the Northwest Territories, and occasionally even the northernmost reaches of Ontario or Quebec.

In creating the subject index we have tried to maintain a balance between creating highly specific headings on the one hand and classifying like concepts together on the other. We hope that the user is satisfied. We could not highlight all the aspects of each document in the index, and have therefore allowed an average of two or three headings per entry, although some have one and others four or five.

As a record of the intellectual boundaries of our bibliographic search we have included an Appendix: Sources Searched. Divided into five sections covering 'General and Regional Bibliographies,' 'Subject Bibliographies,' 'Periodical Indexes,' 'Dissertation Indexes,' and 'Journals Comprehensively Searched,' this documents the breadth of our coverage. Researchers wishing to update certain indexes should do so from the dates indicated.

Researchers wishing to obtain copies of documents cited in the bibliography are best directed to large university libraries where the major journals and monographs can most likely be obtained. We are fortunate to have accessed most items in the libraries of the University of Toronto (including the Centre of Criminology Library and the Faculty of Law Library), with additional documents close by at York University Law Library and the Law Society of Upper Canada Great Library. If individuals are not able to locate an item, and a major library participating in interlibrary loans is not able to verify a holding location through inquiry to the National Library, then users could contact the Library of the Centre of Criminology, University of Toronto, which could assist in location and document delivery.

CANADIAN CRIMINAL JUSTICE HISTORY:
AN ANNOTATED BIBLIOGRAPHY

1

Police

1. Addington, Charles H.

A History of the London Police Force: 125 Years of Police Service. London, Ont.: Phelps Pub. Co., 1980.

The police force of the city of London, Ont., created in 1855, evolved from earlier forms of police organization, as official records of the judicial district show constables in 1831 and 1832. The author recounts early political and legislative factors influencing the establishment of the City of London Police Force in 1855. Investigation of police court records as well as the local newspaper, the London *Free Press*, was used to provide a picture of law enforcement in nineteenth-century London. There is information provided on London's police chiefs, police stations, and developments in transportation and communications. There are numerous photographs, a chronology of events in the history of the police from 1855 to 1980, and various appendices of city-council minutes, police regulations, organizational charts, budget estimates (1901), a list of police commissioners, and a selective bibliography of primary and secondary sources.

2. Addington, Charles H.

A History of the Police Association of Ontario. London, Ont.: Phelps Pub. Co., 1982.

3. Allan, Iris.

White Sioux – Major Walsh of the Mounted Police. Sidney, B.C.: Gray's Publishing, 1969.

4. Allen, Robert S.

'The Mounties and the North. "One Hundred Years".' *North/Nord* 20 (3, May–June 1973): 2–8.

5. Anderson, Frank W.

Saskatchewan's Provincial Police. Calgary: Frontier Publishing, 1972.

In this booklet, Anderson provides a popular account of the history of the Saskatchewan Provincial Police (SPP). Drawing on files of the SPP held in the Saskatchewan Provincial Archives, Saskatoon, the author discusses the circumstances leading to the establishment of the force in 1917, and the various law-enforcement and social-service duties assumed by its members. The author also recounts a number of sensational criminal cases investigated by the SPP prior to its disbanding in 1928.

6. Artigue, Jean D.

Six Years in the Canadian North West. Toronto: Hunter, Rose, 1882.

This is the first book published on the NWMP. It was translated from the French by L.C. Corbett and S. Smith. It was reprinted in 1973 by Mika Publishing in Belleville, Ont., as part of the Canadian Reprint Series.

7. Atkin, Ronald.

Maintain the Right: The Early History of the NWMP, 1873–1900. Toronto: Macmillan, 1973.

This book describes the early history of the NWMP, from 1873 to 1900. It is an attempt to present the story of the first quarter-century of the NWMP from its foundation in 1873 until the end of the nineteenth century when settlement of the lonely lands its officers had patrolled and the more sophisticated methods of transportation had vastly changed their duties. The book covers four periods which coincide with the tenures of four commissioners: (1) G.A. French, (2) J.F. Macleod, (3) A.G. Irvine, (4) L.W. Herchner. The account is composed mainly from the reports, diaries, and memoirs of men who lived through those harsh historic years, and includes an excellent bibliography of primary and secondary sources located at the Public Archives of Canada, the Glenbow-Alberta Institute Archives, and the RCMP Headquarters Archives.

8. Barot, Danielle, and Bérard, Nicole.

Etude historico-juridique, organisation et pouvoirs de la police: Rapport soumis au Solliciteur Général du Canada dans le cadre de la recherche sur le rôle, les fonctions, et l'efficacité de la police. Montréal: Université de Montréal, Centre International de criminologie comparée, 1972.

This report, one of several issued by the International Centre of Comparative Criminology on police in Canada, examines the historical evolution of police powers through an analysis of pertinent legislation and jurisprudence. The first part of the report traces the origin of police organization in England and Canada. This is followed by the history of professional police under the influence of ideas put forward by John and Henry Fielding and Patrick Colquhoun and reforms undertaken by Sir Robert Peel. Police organization in Canada is examined prior to and after Confederation. The pre-Confederation period is divided into several sub-periods: 1759–64; 1764–74; 1774–91; 1791–1837/8; 1841–67. Under the post-Confederation period, the authors discuss the constitutional division of power in Canada and the historical origins of the various police forces: federal, provincial, municipal, and others. The last part of the report examines police powers, in particular, the powers of arrest.

9. Bayley, David H.

'Police Function, Structure, and Control in Western Europe and North America: Comparative and Historical Studies.' In *Crime and Justice: An Annual Review of Research*, vol. 1, pp. 109–143. Edited by Norval Morris and Michael Tonry. Chicago: University of Chicago Press, 1979.

This article examines comparative and historical studies of the function, structure, and control of the police in Western Europe and North America, assessing what is known about variations in each and whether explanations for these variations have been convincingly demonstrated. The author categorizes the studies according to whether they focus on explaining (1) 'the scope of the police function,' (2) 'the structure of policing,' and (3) 'the control of police.' Within each category the findings stemming from comparative and historical research on the police in several western countries, including Canada, are discussed. In a concluding section, the author considers the state of comparative and historical research on the police, and provides a list of topics needing research attention. Overall, he concludes that 'the field of comparative and historical research on the police in Western Europe and North America is still in its infancy,' and that authors have yet to adequately explain variations in the function, structure, and control of the police in various western countries.

10. Beahen, William.

'Mob Law Could Not Prevail.' *Alberta History* 29 (3, Summer 1981): 1–7.

In this article, the author discusses the role of the NWMP in maintaining law and order in Calgary after the outbreak of a smallpox epidemic and ensuing racial tensions between Anglo-Saxon and Chinese residents of the town that occurred during the summer of 1892. According to the author, the spread of the disease engendered considerable anxiety in Calgary, manifesting itself in outbreaks of hostility towards the town's Chinese residents, who were viewed as being responsible for transmitting the disease. The article notes that the participation of the NWMP in establishing a quarantine for individuals exposed to the disease and suppressing mob violence directed against the Chinese resulted in a conflict over jurisdiction between the federal police force and the then existing Calgary Police Department. The author concludes that the smallpox incident in Calgary is evidence of the impact of federal authority exercised in the West during the territorial period.

11. Beahen, William.

'Tribulations of a Frontier Police: The R.N.W.M.P. Detachment at Edson, Alberta, 1910–1913.' *RCMP Quarterly* 47 (4, Fall 1982): 25–29.

12. Bellemare, J.; Beaudoin, J.L.; and Fortin, J.

Historico-Legal Study: Organization and Powers of the Police. First Progress Report. Montreal: University of Montreal, International Centre of Comparative Criminology, 1972.

13. Bellomo, J. Jerald.

The Liquor Question and the North West Mounted Police, 1874–1905. Ottawa: RCMP Historical Section, n.d.

14. Benn, G.H.

'Frontier Law Enforcement.' *RCMP Quarterly* 35 (4, April 1970): 27–30.

This article discusses the provisions made for the maintenance of law and order in the region around Farwell (now Revelstoke), B.C., during the time of the building of the railway, between 1884 and 1899. Particular attention is given to recounting the dispute which arose in 1885 between members of the NWMP and the B.C. Provincial Police force, over the enforcement of conflicting federal and provincial liquor legislation.

15. Betke, Carl F.

'The Mounted Police and the Doukhobors in Saskatchewan, 1899–1909.' *Saskatchewan History* 27 (1, Winter 1974): 1–14.

With the increase in settlement and agricultural development on the Canadian prairies after 1885, the Mounted Police took on the task of dealing with immigrant groups whose cultural habits and religious beliefs brought them into conflict with Canadian law and settlement policy. An extreme case of such conflict occurred in Saskatchewan after the arrival of Doukhobor settlers from Russia, who insisted on living on a communal basis rather than taking up individual homesteads as required. This article provides an account of Mounted Police confrontations with Doukhobors in Saskatchewan in the period 1899–1909. The author maintains that the manner in which the police dealt with fanatical members of the religious sect illustrates the tolerance with which settlers of diverse habits were treated, if they were seen to be hardworking and potentially successful farmers.

16. Betke, Carl F.

'Pioneers and Police on the Canadian Prairies, 1885–1914.' Canadian Historical Association. *Historical Papers* (1980): 9–32.

17. Betke, C.; Thompson, D.; and Gordon, G.

Selected Aspects in the Historical Role of the Mounted Police in Canada. Ottawa: RCMP Historical Section, 1977.

18. Bindloss, Harold.

The Prairie Patrol. New York: Frederick A. Stokes Company, 1931.

19. Boston, J.

'Saga of the Yukon.' *RCMP Quarterly* 31 (3, January 1966): 4–7.

   This article recounts the trials and hardships experienced by members of the Mounted Police posted to the Yukon in the years following the Klondike gold rush of the 1890s. Particular attention is given to describing the heroic manner in which John Duncan Dempster, who was posted in the Yukon for more than 36 years, led a search party to find the whereabouts of an overdue police patrol in 1911.

20. Brazill, A.R.

'The Newfoundland Police Force.' *The Newfoundland Quarterly* 61 (4, Winter 1962): 13, 35–36; 62 (1, Spring 1963): 36.

21. Breen, David H.

'The Mounted Police and the Ranching Frontier, 1875–1905.' In *Men in Scarlet*, pp. 115–137. Edited by Hugh A. Dempsey. Calgary: McClelland and Stewart West, 1974.

   The author discusses how the advance of railways in the West provided cattlemen with access to eastern markets. When the NWMP arrived they also were a market, and they brought security from the threat of Indians. Many policemen also became ranchers themselves and hence formed a core around which the later ranching industry grew. The police also had a task in patrolling borders to prevent Canadian-fattened cattle from being herded across the border to be sold in Chicago.

22. Brinkworth, George Walter.

Royal Northwest Mounted Police, Canada. Regina, 1910.

23. Brown, Lorne, A., and Brown, C.

An Unauthorized History of the RCMP. Toronto: James Lorimer, 1973; 2nd ed., 1978.

Written for the purpose of exposing the mythical character of accounts that have tended to glorify the history of the RCMP, this book undertakes a critical re-examination of the origin and history of the force. In succeeding chapters, the authors attempt to document the 'misdeeds' of the RCMP and its predecessors, the NWMP and the RNWMP. Particular attention is given to exposing the force's racist attitude towards native Indians, its traditional strike-breaking role, and its violation of the civil liberties of individuals (such as communists, students, and draft dodgers) who, at one time or another, were seen to pose a threat to the status quo. Attention is also given to criticizing much of the literature that has been written about the RCMP, for its tendency to accept and perpetuate 'RCMP versions of history.' In attempting to substantiate their thesis, the authors draw on a range of primary historical documents, secondary historical literature, and previous popular exposés of the RCMP.

24. Brownhill, H.E.

'50 Years of Fingerprinting.' *RCMP Quarterly* 26 (3, January 1961): 155–167.

25. Bush, Edward F.

'The North West Mounted in Klondike Days.' *Canadian Geographic Journal* 92 (1, 1976): 22–27.

26. Bush, Edward F.

'Policing the Border in the Klondike Gold Rush.' *Canadian Geographic Journal* 100 (October–November 1980): 70–73.

27. Bushley, L.C.

'The History of Criminal Intelligence Service Canada.' *Canadian Police Chief* 69 (2, 1980): 29–33.

28. Cameron, Agnes D.

'The North West Mounted Police.' *Cornhill Magazine* 34 (January 1913): 87–97.

29. Campbell, Marjorie Freeman.

A Century of Crime: The Development of Crime Detection Methods in Canada. Toronto: McClelland and Stewart, 1970.

This is a descriptive history of crime detection methods in Canada, which attempts to illustrate the increasing sophistication of police investigation techniques from the middle of the nineteenth century to the middle of the twentieth century. There is biographical information on John Wilson Murray (a well-known Canadian detective of the late nineteenth century) and descriptions of some of the cases he 'solved.' Although there is acknowledgement of events in other parts of Canada, the emphasis is clearly on cases and developments in Ontario. Developments in fingerprinting and blood-typing and other forensic achievements are illustrated through case examples. There are almost 20 pages of notes (citing primary and secondary research sources), a 7-page bibliography, and an index of names.

30. Campbell, Peter A.

'The Formation and Development of the Security and Intelligence Branch of the Royal Canadian Mounted Police.' M.A. thesis, Concordia University, 1978.

The amassing and analysis of intelligence was one of the permanent functions of the RCMP. This thesis examines the development of the intelligence system in Canada and the various political demands which dictated the direction of intelligence-gathering and its eventual utilization. For the purposes of the study the development of intelligence in Canada is classified in four periods in which intelligence was employed by the federal government as a basis for the institution of defence policies against a perceived threat: 1864–74; 1914–18; 1919; and 1920–38. Through analysing the manner in which intelligence-gathering was utilized during each of these periods the author attempts to determine whether it was used to counteract foreign intrusion into Canadian affairs or to ensure the protection and continuity of the existing ruling order within Canada. He concludes that although intelligence-gathering during the period 1864–74 was clearly used to counteract foreign intrusion into Canadian affairs, in subsequent periods the distinction between counter-intelligence and intelligence-gathering for the purpose of protecting the existing ruling order became increasingly unclear. The basic documentation for the study comes from government publications, legislation, and correspondence; police files containing information on intelligence-gathering; and interviews with ex-members of the Security and Intelligence Branch of the RCMP.

31. Cannings, K.L.

'An Image of the Police within Discussions of the Canadian Bail System, 1960–1975.' M.A. thesis, University of Toronto, Centre of Criminology, 1977.

The first major overhaul of the bail system in Canada occurred with the introduction of the *Bail Reform Act* in 1972. This study examines the question of whether the image of the police in discussions of the Canadian bail system changed after the enactment of the 1972 legislation. Canadian newspaper articles published in the period 1960–75 form the major data source for the author's exploratory historical analysis.

32. Carpenter, James Harold.

The Badge and the Blotter: A History of the Lethbridge Police. Lethbridge: Historical Society of Alberta, Whoop-up Country Chapter, 1975.

The author, who was a member of the Lethbridge Police Force for 17 years before becoming its chief (1957–71), provides a history of a municipal police force based on research of primary and secondary sources as well as personal reminiscences. The book describes the early policing of the Lethbridge area, from the time of the NWMP, to the creation of the Lethbridge Police Force in 1902, to the years in which Carpenter was the chief constable. The book contains interesting photographs and illustrations, and has several appendices such as 'Excerpts from the General Ledger, 1909,' 'A Chronology of Police Officers,' 'A Chronology of Police Commissioners,' and 'Bylaws Relating to the Police.'

33. Chambers, Ernest J.

The Royal North West Police: A Corps History. Toronto: Coles Publishing Co., 1972. (Originally published, Montreal: Mortimer Press, 1906)

Undertaken as an attempt to produce an 'authentic account' and 'a volume of some sort of historical significance,' this book examines the origin, development, and work of the Mounted Police from 1872 to 1906.

34. Chapman, Brian.

'The Canadian Police: A Survey.' *Police Studies* 1 (1, 1978): 62–72.

35. Charters, Dean.

Mountie, 1873–1973: A Golden Treasury of Those Early Years. Don Mills, Ont.: Collier-Macmillan Canada, 1973.

Through the presentation of more than 200 black and white photographs this book documents the early years of the Mounties, from the early 1870s until approximately 1912. Prepared to mark the centennial anniversary of the RCMP, it offers insight into social conditions in the West at the time the force came into being, provides glimpses of well-known and lesser-known Mounties of the era, provides a visual record of the Mounties' uniforms, etc. The years 1873–1973 in the book's title refer to the centenary of the force, not to the scope of the book. There is a chronology of major events from 1873 to 1920. The bulk of photographs in the book are from the Glenbow-Alberta Institute.

36. Clark, Cecil.

Tales of the British Columbia Provincial Police. Sidney, B.C.: Gray's Publishing Co., 1971.

This book contains revised versions of articles originally published in *The Islander* and the Sunday Magazine of the *Victoria Daily Colonist*.

37. Cooper, H.S.

'The Evolution of Canadian Police.' In *The Police Function in Canada*, pp. 37–52. Edited by W.T. McGrath and M.P. Mitchell. Toronto: Methuen, 1971.

This is one of 15 chapters in the book, and as such gives a brief history of the development of policing in Canada. The author, a former deputy commissioner of the RCMP, discusses the establishment of selected police forces at the municipal, provincial, and federal levels, looks briefly at statutory powers of police and police forces, and provides a cursory introduction for readers with no previous background on policing. A short list of items for further reading is included.

38. Crevel, Jacques.

'Nécessité d'une police en Gaspésie au 17e siècle.' *Revue d'histoire de la Gaspésie* 4 (4, October–December 1966): 170–174.

In the second half of the seventeenth century the shores of Gaspésie were invaded by fishing boats and trading ships that stopped there on their way to Quebec, and a settlement soon began. The administrators of this fishing region were concerned with surveillance of the shores and protection of fishermen, traders, colonists, and settlers. Policing the shores proved to be a difficult task because of the lack of means, while maintaining order on land was not much easier. Alcohol consumption led to disputes, quarrels, and altercations; deserters and fugitives from the colony came to seek refuge in Gaspésie where they could find a ship to take them back to Europe. In 1673 Frontenac wrote to Colbert asking for resources to police Gaspésie but without success. Furthermore, it was not easy to send soldiers from the colony to Gaspésie, as the round trip took almost two months. This left the authorities helpless and unable to chase all kinds of wrongdoers.

39. Crockett, Wayne.

'The Uses and Abuses of the Secret Service Fund: The Politics of Police Work.' M.A. thesis, Queen's University, 1982.

40. Croft, William F.

'Sidelights on the Hamilton Police Force.' *Wentworth Bygones* 7 (1967): 64–66.

The author provides a brief account of the history of the Hamilton Police Department from 1833 to around 1920. Note is made of the growth in the size of the force, the establishment of various police stations, and the types of horse-drawn, and later motorized, vehicles used during the period.

41. Daw, Ruth M.

'Sgt.-Major J.H.G. Bray, the Forgotten Horseman.' In *Men in Scarlet*, pp. 152–162. Edited by Hugh A. Dempsey. Calgary: McClelland and Stewart West, 1974.

The author provides some biographical information on John Bray, who as an ex-sergeant of the NWMP was a pioneer soldier-settler in southern Alberta in the later part of the nineteenth century.

42. Deane, R. Burton.

Mounted Police Life in Canada: A Record of Thirty-One Years' Service. Toronto: Coles Publishing Co., 1973. (Facsimile reprint of the 1916 edition)

This book describes one individual's life as a member of the NWMP. It was originally published by Cassell in 1916 and has been reprinted as part of the Coles Canadiana Collection.

43. Dempsey, Hugh Aylmer.

Jerry Potts, Plainsman. Calgary: Glenbow Foundation, 1966. (Occasional Paper no. 2)

This paper outlines the legend of Jerry Potts's life, first as a guide, interpreter, and adviser to the young NWMP force, and later as one of the force's most valuable employees. The facts of his career, which have never before been written, are told here by his mother's people, the Blackfoot, and by his friends. This occasional paper was reprinted in *Montana, the Magazine of Western History*, 17 (4, 1967): 2–17.

44. Dempsey, Hugh Aylmer.

'The North-West Mounted Police – A Brief History.' *Alberta Historical Review* 15 (3, Summer 1967): 1–7.

This article provides highlights of various events associated with the history of the Mounted Police from 1873 to 1920. The author notes that during this period 'the field of usefulness of the Force was continually broadened,' and that it came to gain 'profound respect' for its 'brilliant and steadfast services.'

45. Dempsey, Hugh Aylmer.

'The "Thin Red Line" in the Canadian West.' *The American West* 7 (1, January 1970): 24–30.

In this article, the author describes aspects of the early history of the Mounted Police which have contributed to fostering the legend that the force was made up of heroic and loyal British subjects who personified the best in the 'thin red line' tradition. He maintains that the image of the mounted policeman as a hero figure of the Canadian West is not entirely without foundation, even though many modern police officers are understandably embarrassed by the overly glorified and romantic manner in which the history of the force has been portrayed.

46. Dempsey, Hugh Aylmer.

William Parker: Mounted Policeman. Calgary: Glenbow-Alberta Institute, 1973.

William Parker's previously unpublished letters and diaries have been brought together here by Dempsey to document and illustrate life in the NWMP from 1874 until the early twentieth century. There is a lengthy section called 'Reminiscence,' published virtually intact and documenting Parker's 38½ years' service in the Mounties, then the letters, which are heavily edited to remove ephemeral comments. The diaries of Parker are not included, but are an excellent source of primary data; they are owned by the Glenbow-Alberta Institute in Calgary.

47. Dempsey, Hugh Aylmer.

'Writing-on-Stone and the Boundary Patrol.' In *Men in Scarlet*, pp. 138–151. Edited by Hugh A. Dempsey. Calgary: McClelland and Stewart West, 1974.

Writing-on-Stone is the name of a place southeast of Lethbridge on the Milk River, just north of the Montana border. The area had pictographs on the dried walls of deep ravines and was revered and feared by Indians who believed they were done by spirits or bluebirds (at the direction of spirits). As a result of the effect of these pictographs and myths on the behaviour of the Indian tribes, the NWMP came to be involved in many ways near the area.

48. Dempsey, Hugh Aylmer, ed.

Men in Scarlet. Calgary: McClelland and Stewart West, 1974.

As a tribute to the centennial celebrations of the RCMP, the Historical Society of Alberta and the University of Lethbridge organized a RCMP Conference in 1974, inviting Canada's foremost historians in the field of Mounted Police history to present a paper and to contribute a chapter in this book. The book begins with the great march west and deals with Indians, politics, and ranching. It looks at the career/biography of one policeman and concludes with chapters on various aspects of the force's early history. (Annotated references to individual contributions are included at entries 21, 41, 47, 68, 84, 96, 106, 121, 137, 151, 164, 191, and 215.)

49. Denny, Cecil Edward, Sir.

The Law Marches West. Toronto: Dent, 1939.

The author of this book was a NWMP inspector from 1874 to 1882. The book provides a personal account of the force's early history, and its success in bringing law and order to the

Northwest Territories. It was originally published in 1924 under the title *The Birth of Western Canada: A History* at 499 pages in length. A copy of the 1924 publication is available at the RCMP Museum, Regina.

50. Denny, Cecil Edward, Sir.

'The Early North-West Mounted Police.' *RCMP Quarterly* 30 (3, January 1965): 7-12.

This article provides a brief personal account of the author's experience with the NWMP from 1873 to 1875. The manuscript was not found until the early 1960s, which explains its belated publication.

51. Donaghey, Sam.

A History of the City of Edmonton Police Department: Blue, Red and Gold, 1892–1972. Edmonton: City of Edmonton Police Department, 1972.

52. Donkin, John G.

Trooper and Redskin in the Far North-West: Recollections of Life in the North-West Mounted Police, Canada, 1884–1888. Toronto: Coles Publishing Co., 1973. (Facsimile reprint of 1889 edition published in London by Sampson, Low, Marston, Searle and Rivington)

This book, published as part of the Coles Canadiana Collection, presents recollections of life in the NWMP between 1884 and 1888.

53. Dorrance, James French.

Never Fire First: A Canadian Northwest Mounted Story. Toronto: Goodchild, 1924.

54. Douthwaite, Louis Charles.

The Royal Canadian Mounted Police. London: Blackie and Son, 1939.

This is a descriptive history of the RCMP from its creation until the late 1930s, written to dispel some of the romantic myth surrounding the Force. There are no notes, bibliography, or index.

55. Dwight, Charles P.

Life in the North West Mounted Police, and Other Sketches. Toronto: The National Publishing Co., 1892.

56. Edmonds, W.E.

'The Establishment of the North-West Mounted Police in Northern Alberta.' *Alberta Historical Review* 2 (4, Autumn 1954): 4–10.

This article describes events surrounding the establishment of the NWMP and its famous march west in 1874. The author argues that while plans for the creation of a mounted police force dated back to 1870, it is doubtful that the NWMP would have been established when it was 'had not the public conscience been stirred into activity by the hideous massacre of Canadian Indians at the hands of American whiskey traders.'

57. Edmonton Police Department.

Pride in the Past, 1894–1982. Edmonton: Edmonton Police Department, 1982.

This commemorative booklet describes the development of policing in Edmonton from the time of the arrival of the NWMP in 1875 to the date of the opening of the new Edmonton City Police Department headquarters in 1982. The narrative text is interspersed with numerous photographs highlighting notable features of the history of policing in Edmonton.

58. Elliot, Marie.

'Policing the Gulf Islands, 1866–1916.' *British Columbia Historical News* 15 (1, Fall 1981): 15–18.

Based primarily on a reading of incoming correspondence and superintendents' letterbooks contained in the B.C. Provincial Police files, this paper documents the experiences encountered by constables assigned to police the Gulf Islands between 1893 and 1905. The author provides information regarding the types of crimes constables had to investigate, the hardships experienced in the course of their efforts, the establishment of local lockups, and the backgrounds of individual officers. The author concludes that the police constables assigned to the Gulf Islands were self-reliant individuals who quickly gained the respect of the Islands' residents.

59. Fergusson, Charles Bruce.

'A Glimpse of 1885.' *Saskatchewan History* 21 (1, Winter 1968): 24–29.

60. Fether, R.C.

The Yukon Field Force. Montreal: Gazette Printing Company, 1936.

61. Fetherstonhaugh, Robert Collier.

The Royal Canadian Mounted Police. New York: Carrick and Evans, 1938.

This is a history of the RCMP based on the force's own records and documents which emphasizes the adventures of the men rather than the details of organization and administration.

62. Fisher, Robin.

'Indian Warfare and Two Frontiers: A Comparison of British Columbia and Washington Territory during the Early Years of Settlement.' *Pacific Historical Review* 50 (1, February 1981): 31–51.

Although several historians have sought to compare the manner in which law and order were maintained on the Canadian prairies and in the midwestern United States, little comparative-historical work has been carried out in relation to the situation that existed on the Pacific slope of the Rockies. The present study attempts to compensate for this by undertaking a comparison of Indian warfare and the treatment of Indians in British Columbia and Washington Territory during the nineteenth century. An effort is made to explain why B.C. Indians responded in a less violent manner to the intrusions of European settlers than did Indians in Washington Territory. Differences in the indigenous cultures of the west-coast Indians, the effect of the fur trade in promoting cordial relations between Indians and Europeans in British Columbia, and the differing policies of Canadian and U.S. governments with respect to the treatment to be afforded Indians are examined as possible explanations. The author's findings indicate that the Indians of British Columbia and Washington Territory responded differently to European settlement 'not so much because of differences in the indigenous cultures, but because of the differences in the attitudes and policies adopted towards them.'

63. Fitz-Gerald, W.G.

'Policing the Wilderness.' *Outlook* 87 (October 26, 1907): 431–439.

64. Forbin, Victor.

'La gendarmerie du pôle nord.' *Revue des deux mondes* (September 15, 1930): 402–430.

This study is devoted to the history of the 'Mounted Police of the North Pole.' It was in 1873 that an élite corps was created following Canada's acquisition of the vast territory that belonged to the Hudson's Bay Company. To hasten the pacification of the prairies, the young confederation, founded in 1867, constituted a corps of police which received the name 'Northwest Mounted Police.' In the year following its creation, the 300 officers who constituted the force were exploring a vast unknown and virgin territory. In 1905 the exploits of the force justified the addition to its name of the prefix 'Royal.' In 1920 the force absorbed the Dominion Police (small corps of federal mounted police) and became known as the Royal Canadian Mounted Police. This historical review discusses the complicated functions that the force performed; its dealings with a population with very different customs, the Eskimos; certain acts of courage by its members; the problems posed by the harsh weather conditions and by arctic wolves; the means of transportation; and the history of some of the force's detectives. The study ends with a detailed account of the disappearance of two French priests, Father Rouvier and Father Le Roux, in 1915; their murder by the Eskimos; and the role of the RCMP in solving the case.

65. Fox, Arthur.

The Newfoundland Constabulary. St. John's: Robinson-Blackmore, 1971.

Early colonization of Newfoundland was related to the fishing industry. The appointment of a British governor in Newfoundland in 1729 was an early step towards government and a justice system, as he had the authority to appoint 'Justices of the Peace and other Ministers of Justice.' The appointment of constables by Governor Osborne in 1729 gave the Newfoundland Constabulary the distinction of being the oldest police force in Canada. An account of the early role of the police constable in the administration of justice is provided, as well as informative commentary on social and political conditions in Newfoundland. When Newfoundland joined Confederation in 1949, policing of all of Newfoundland and Labrador, with the exception of St. John's, was taken over by the RCMP.

66. Gardiner, Paddy.

'Winged Mounties.' *RCMP Quarterly* 35 (3, January 1970): 4–12.

This article chronicles the development of the Aviation Section (or Air Division) of the RCMP from the time of the RCMP's first request for an air patrol in 1928 until 1968.

67. German, Peter M., and McIvor, Alan A.

'The Prince Edward Island Provincial Police.' *RCMP Quarterly* 46 (1, Winter 1981): 30–37.

Prince Edward Island's first provincial police force was created in 1930. Less than two years later it was disbanded, and the provincial government entered into a contract to have the RCMP assume law enforcement duties across the province. This paper recounts the brief history of the Prince Edward Island Provincial Police force, noting its role in traffic, prohibition, and criminal law enforcement as well as the many other functions (such as tax collection) performed by its members. After being disbanded in 1932, 9 of its 30 members (a list of which is provided) stayed on to become RCMP officers.

68. Getty, Ian A.L.

'The Role of the Mounted Police Outposts in Southern Alberta.' In *Men in Scarlet*, pp. 187–197. Edited by Hugh A. Dempsey. Calgary: McClelland and Stewart West, 1974.

The author comments on the lack of accessible or reliable historical information on NWMP outposts and the lack of recognition of the importance of these outposts in the history of law and order in southern Alberta before the days of provincial status. Getty goes on to provide the reader with a brief historical description of outposts. The chapter has detailed footnotes for further links with bibliographic and archival materials.

69. Gilkes, Margaret, and Symons, Margaret.

Calgary's Finest: A History of the City Police Force. Calgary: Century Calgary Publications, 1975.

70. Gilling, William, and Blucher, Frederick R.

Ontario Provincial Police 60th Anniversary, 1909–1969. Toronto: Ontario Provincial Police, 1969.

71. Glendinning, T.S.

'The Newfoundland Rangers.' *RCMP Quarterly* 16 (3, January 1951): 212–217.

72. Goldring, Philip.

'The Cypress Hills Massacre: A Century's Retrospect.' *Saskatchewan History* 26 (3, Autumn 1973): 81–102.

   In June 1873 more than twenty Assiniboine Indians were killed by a small party of American frontiersmen in the Cypress Hills, near the juncture of the present-day borders of Alberta, Saskatchewan, and Montana. In the years following this unique event in Canadian history, numerous accounts have been written about the 'Cypress Hills Massacre.' Drawing on a wide range of archival data not examined by previous writers, this article attempts to reconstruct the sequence of events leading up to and following the massacre, as well as reinterpret the consequences it had for federal government – North-West Mounted Police – Indian relations in western Canada. In doing this, the author dispels several widely accepted myths and legends surrounding the reasons for an outcome of the massacre.

73. Goldring, Philip.

'The First Contingent: The North-West Mounted Police, 1873–74.' *Canadian Historic Sites: Occasional Papers in Archaeology and History*, no. 21. Ottawa: Parks Canada, 1979, pp. 5–40.

74. Goldring, Philip.

'Whisky, Horses and Death: The Cypress Hills Massacre and Its Sequel.' *Canadian Historic Sites: Occasional Papers in Archaeology and History*, no. 21. Ottawa: Parks Canada, 1979, pp. 41–69.

   This is a modified version of the author's 1973 account (see entry 72 above).

75. Gough, Barry M.

'Keeping British Columbia British: The Law-and-Order Question on a Gold Mining Frontier.' *Huntington Library Quarterly* 38 (3, May 1975): 269–280.

The Fraser River gold rush of 1858 attracted numerous prospectors from the gold fields of California who at the start had little respect for the institutions of law and order being applied on the B.C. frontier. The initial unwillingness of American miners to submit to the type of legal and judicial system established by James Douglas, the governor of the colony, and Matthew Baillie Begbie, who became known as 'the hanging judge,' is reflected in letters sent by prospectors back to the United States voicing their opposition to such restrictions as mining licences and fees. Despite the fact that after 1858 the colony of British Columbia was populated largely by potentially hostile foreigners, officials managed to maintain law and order and win the confidence and respect of the miners. On the basis of this evidence, the author concludes that the administration of law and order on the gold mining frontier did much to develop both the non-American nature and truly British character of British Columbia.

76. Gough, Barry M.

'Official Uses of Violence against Coast Indians in Colonial British Columbia.' In *Pacific Northwest Themes: Historical Essays in Honour of Keith A. Murray*, pp. 43–69. Edited by James W. Scott. Bellingham, Wa.: Centre for Pacific Northwest Studies, 1978.

77. Gough, Barry M.

'Send a Gunboat! Checking Slavery and Controlling Liquor Traffic among Coast Indians of British Columbia in the 1860's.' *Pacific Northwest Quarterly* 69 (4, October 1978): 159–168.

From the mid-nineteenth until the early twentieth century the British navy policed the west coast of British Columbia. During the 1860s, the police work of Her Majesty's ships in B.C. waters extended to two social matters that concerned the northwest-coast Indians and preyed on the Victorian conscience – slavery and liquor. This study, based on admiralty, fur trade, and colonial papers, suggests that while neither antislavery nor prohibition work was easy, the efforts of British naval officers did help to reduce the amount of indigenous slavery among northwest-coast Indians and diminish the liquor traffic to natives.

78. Grant, Philippe.

'Une plume à la casquette de la gendarmerie.' *RCMP Quarterly* 39 (3, July 1974): 23–26.

The author outlines the important role the Mounted Police played in the settlement of the Canadian West. It was Sir John A. Macdonald, prime minister of Canada, who understood that in addition to the treaties signed with the Indians there was a need for a paramilitary force composed of young resourceful men possessing the qualities of both soldiers and policemen, a force capable of maintaining peace while at the same time aiding Indians and whites to improve their lot.

79. Grierson, Anne Irene.

The Mounties. Toronto: Ryerson, 1947.

80. Hall, Frank.

'Manitoba's Own Mounties.' *Manitoba Pageant* 52 (Autumn 1973): 4–9.

81. Hamilton, Charles Frederick.

Royal Canadian Mounted Police. Ryerson Canadian History Readers. Toronto: Ryerson, [1929].

82. Haney, Reginald Arthur.

'Police Labour Relations in Ontario under the Police Act, 1946–1973.' LL.M. thesis, York University, 1974.

83. Hanson, Stan D.

'Policing the International Boundary Area in Saskatchewan, 1890–1910.' *Saskatchewan History* 19 (1966): 61–73.

During the period of pioneer settlement in the Northwest, the international boundary area in Saskatchewan presented a considerable potential for lawlessness. Drawing on annual reports of the NWMP and court records, the author examines the extent of crime in the area and the steps taken to cope with it. His findings indicate that although the police were called upon to deal with a variety of crimes (the most frequent being horse-stealing and cattle-rustling), the extent to which lawlessness was a problem was lessened by the persistent law enforcement efforts of the NWMP.

84. Harrison, Dick.

'The Mounted Police in Fiction.' In *Men in Scarlet*, pp. 163–174. Edited by Hugh A. Dempsey. Calgary: McClelland and Stewart West, 1974.

Harrison analyses the fictional works written about the Mounted Police and concludes that while some early authors, such as Ralph Connor, Harwood Steele, and Philip Godsell, had good historical information, many other authors capitalized on the force's success and the public myths that have grown up around it. Harrison describes and gives examples of specific authors' treatments of the Mounties, and goes on to examine more recent works and trends.

85. Harvison, C.W.

The Horsemen. Toronto: McClelland and Stewart, 1967.

The horses and scant equipment of the early days of the RCMP have been replaced by cars, planes, and launches. The strength of the force has multiplied many times over, and the annual budget has increased from a few thousand dollars to more than a hundred million. This book attempts to recount some of these changes and emphasizes that the strong *esprit de corps* and legendary devotion to duty that the RCMP force has engaged since its inception are still with it today. The story is the author's autobiography as a member (and in 1960, the commissioner) of the RCMP.

86. Hatch, Frederick John.

'The British Columbia Police: 1858–1871.' M.A. thesis, University of British Columbia, 1955.

The British Columbia Police was established in September 1858. From 1858 to 1871 the force was not an organized police force in the modern sense, but rather a modified form of the English system of police officers, composed of stipendiary magistrates and paid constables, established in London in 1792. This thesis examines the history of the British Columbia Police and its role in the administration of justice in the province. Substantive chapters deal with: the creation of the force, the role it played in maintaining law and order during the Fraser River gold rush, the early attempts made to reorganize the force along the lines of the Irish Constabulary, the jurisdiction and duties of magistrates and police constables, crime in the colony, the education of Indians in the ways of 'the white man's law,' the Victoria Police Force and its relation to the British Columbia Police, and the reasons for the delay in reforming the force in accordance with the Irish Constabulary model. The author maintains that the main reasons for this delay reside in 'the tradition inherited from the police system of the colonial period,' and the fact that from 1858 to 1871 'the British Columbia Police gave satisfactory service in spite of the handicaps under which the constables worked.'

87. Hatch, Frederick John.

'British Columbia's First Policeman.' *RCMP Quarterly* 37 (3, July 1972): 37–43.

This article is a history of Chartres Brew and how he came to be British Columbia's first policeman, in an effort to ensure British authority during the gold rush in British Columbia and to provide policing of the gold fields.

88. Haydon, Arthur Lincoln.

The Riders of the Plains: A Record of the Royal North-West Mounted Police of Canada, 1873–1910. London: Melrose, 1910; Toronto: Copp Clark, 1910; Edmonton: Hurtig, 1971.

The author provides a glowing account of the origin and early development of the NWMP. He argues that the force was established to suppress the whiskey trade, protect the Indians, and bring law and order to the Northwest Territories.

89. Higgins, E.G.

Twelve O'Clock and All's Well: A Pictorial History of Law Enforcement in the Sudbury District, 1883–1978. Sudbury, Ont.: The Sudbury Regional Police Association, 1978.

This book contains much local political and social history of Sudbury, as well as the evolution of law enforcement and policing in the area. It starts with a brief note on law enforcement in nineteenth-century Upper Canada, and follows through the settlement period, incorporation of the Town of Sudbury in 1893, the two world wars, and the development of the city in the 1970s. The town was created along the railway line and the need was soon felt for a constable, especially for liquor control. The construction of a court house and prison facilities is described along with an increase in the number of local constables. The first OPP detachment was established in Sudbury following the First World War, and the RCMP arrived in 1931. Major crimes and disasters are related. The book contains 215 photographs in a total of 123 pages, and a small bibliography.

90. Higley, Dahn D.

O.P.P.: The History of the Ontario Provincial Police Force. Toronto: Queen's Printer, 1984.

This is a chronological history of the development of provincial policing in Ontario, from the days of frontier police to the actual creation of the Ontario Provincial Police force in 1909, to the current history of the force in the 1980s. In the course of this development the author recounts some social and political elements of early Ontario which related to policing, and describes police handling of notorious crimes. The author's research resources include primary and secondary materials from private collections, provincial archives, and other sources. Information on various districts and detachments, constables, and commissioners contributes to a more descriptive than analytical picture of the history of the Ontario Provincial Police. This 688-page book has a detailed 37-page index and 10 pages of notes, and is illustrated with black and white photographs.

91. Horrall, Stanley W.

'Historic Document Recalls Establishment of the Force.' *RCMP Quarterly* 36 (3, January 1971): 28.

This one-page note consists mainly of a reprinted copy of the original order-in-council, signed by Sir John A. Macdonald and Governor-General Lord Dufferin, which authorized the establishment of 'a police force in and for the North-West Territories' on August 30, 1873.

92. Horrall, Stanley W.

'Sir John A. Macdonald and the Mounted Police Force for the Northwest Territories.'
Canadian Historical Review 53 (2, June 1972): 179–200.

In this article, the author sets out to reconsider the origin of the NWMP in light of recent historical research. Particular attention is given to documenting the important, though previously overlooked, part played by Sir John A. Macdonald in creating the NWMP. The author points out that Macdonald began organizing a mounted police force in 1869 as part of the preparations for assuming sovereignty over the lands granted by charter to the Hudson's Bay Company. The motives and plans that guided Macdonald in his attempt to organize a mounted police force between 1869 and 1874 are considered at length, as are the political and practical problems he encountered in the course of his efforts. Contrary to earlier historians of the NWMP, the author concludes that the creation of the force was primarily the work of Macdonald, who, in seeking a practical means to oversee the orderly settlement of Canada's frontier, recognized the need for a federal force of soldier-policemen trained and equipped for warfare on the plains and having wide judicial powers and responsibilities.

93. Horrall, Stanley W.

'La filière française.' *RCMP Quarterly* 38 (3, July 1973): 30–31.

There is little awareness of the contributions French Canadians made to the RCMP since the force was created in 1873. The law of May 23, 1873, authorizing the foundation of the Mounted Police, stipulated that the recruits be able to read and write English or French and this requirement was never changed. Among the first members hired by the force in 1873, 50 came from the Province of Quebec. Many of them were bilingual and approximately 15 spoke only French. The contributions of some French-Canadian officers are outlined.

94. Horrall, Stanley W.

The Pictorial History of the Royal Canadian Mounted Police. Toronto: McGraw-Hill Ryerson, 1973. (*L'histoire illustrée de la Gendarmerie royale du Canada.* Toronto: McGraw-Hill Ryerson, 1974)

The year 1973 marked the hundredth anniversary of the formation of the NWMP, a small force established to uphold law and order in the Northwest Territories. From these small beginnings has grown the RCMP, one of the world's best-known police organizations. In this book, the official historian of the force outlines its history from the early days and interweaves it with the history of Canada. The book is illustrated with photographs, engravings, paintings, and documents from the RCMP archives, the Public Archives of Canada, and numerous other sources, and is published in English and French editions.

95. Horrall, Stanley W.

'A Policeman's Lot Is Not a Happy One: The Mounted Police and Prohibition in the North-West Territories, 1874–1891.' *Transactions of the Historical and Scientific Society of Manitoba*, Series 3 (30, 1973–74): 5–16.

In this article, the author discusses the formation of the romantic and heroic myth of the NWMP, which stemmed from its success in creating law and order in the Canadian West during the 1870s, and the reversal of its reputation after 1880. According to the author, the reputation of the force suffered from its having to enforce stringent territorial liquor laws against the wishes of white settlers. He notes that the rigorous enforcement of prohibition laws threatened the survival of the force until as late as 1900, around which time provincial police forces assumed responsibility for the task.

96. Horrall, Stanley W.

'The March West.' In *Men in Scarlet*, pp. 13–26. Edited by Hugh A. Dempsey. Calgary: McClelland and Stewart West, 1974.

Horrall describes the expedition of 275 members of the NWMP from Fort Dufferin in Manitoba to the foothills of the Rocky Mountains in 1874.

97. Horrall, Stanley W.

'The Maritime Provinces District.' *RCMP Quarterly* 42 (1, Winter 1977): 5–9.

In 1932 the RCMP attempted to establish a regional command in the Atlantic provinces similar to that which had existed in Saskatchewan and Alberta from 1905 to 1917. This article examines the efforts made by Commissioner James H. MacBrien to establish a permanent Maritime Provinces District, the specific plans he proposed for reorganizing the command of the force, and the circumstances which caused him to change his proposals. Major events that prevented the establishment of a permanent Maritime Provinces District in the 1930s included the requests made by the Maritime provinces that the RCMP take over existing provincial police forces, and the insistence of certain provincial authorities that the RCMP contracted to do provincial policing be responsible to the province's attorney-general.

98. Horrall, Stanley W.

'The Royal North-West Mounted Police and Labour Unrest in Western Canada, 1919.' *Canadian Historical Review* 61 (June 1980): 169–190.

The RNWMP was initiated into the world of secret agents and espionage in 1914 when it became a part of the intelligence network organized under the Dominion Police to protect national security. With the rise of labour unrest in western Canada in 1919, the RNWMP took on a greater intelligence role, which involved having undercover agents take up positions in radical labour organizations, and the use of informants to gain information about alleged 'Bolshevik' plotting to overthrow the government. This article documents the intelligence efforts undertaken by the RNWMP in the months leading up to the Winnipeg General Strike. The author maintains that while the Mounted Police developed an effective intelligence service which provided officials in Ottawa with reliable information about the aims and plans of union leaders, this information was not subjected to careful assessment. As a consequence, federal politicians continued to believe that western Canadian labour unions were involved in a conspiracy to launch a Russian-inspired socialist revolution. The author concludes that in the aftermath of the Winnipeg General Strike, concern with the recurrence of labour unrest led to radical changes in the federal system of security and policing, the most important one being the expansion of the role of the renamed Royal Canadian Mounted Police to include responsiblity for federal law enforcement and national security throughout the country.

99. Horrall, Stanley W.

'Foster's First Case.' *RCMP Quarterly* 46 (2, Spring 1981): 25–30.

100. Horrall, Stanley W., ed.

A Chronicle of the Canadian West: North-West Mounted Police Report for 1875. Calgary: Historical Society of Alberta, 1974.

Towards the end of 1874, the commissioner of the NWMP, Lieutenant Colonel G.A. French, began preparing an official report on the operation of the force which he had commanded during the previous year. The 1874 report became the first of a valuable collection of annual reports documenting the history of the Mounted Police in Canada. This publication includes the text of the report, originally printed in the *Sessional Papers of Canada* for 1874, along with an introduction by G.S. Horrall.

101. Howard, G.S.

'Stampede!' *RCMP Quarterly* 39 (4, October 1974): 3–11.

This article recounts the dramatic incident of a stampede of 250 horses that occurred in 1874 as the newly created NWMP was preparing to move west from a temporary camp established near the international boundary at Dufferin (now Emerson), Manitoba. Drawing on the reports and diaries of witnesses, the author describes the prairie lightning storm that caused the stampede, the havoc that it raised, and the heroic and successful efforts made by members of the force to round up the escaped horses. He concludes that perhaps no single incident in the early history of the NWMP served more effectively to weld its members into a more solid, loyal organization.

102. Hutchinson, Robert.

A Century of Service: A History of the Winnipeg Police Force, 1874–1974. Winnipeg: City of Winnipeg Police Force, 1974.

This book covers Winnipeg's police history from the outpost days of 1874 up to the modern progress of 1974. The book is illustrated with photographs and presents statistical tables based on the Winnipeg police services.

103. Huxter, K.G.

'The Lyalls of the North.' *RCMP Quarterly* 38 (4, October 1973): 22–24.

The author discusses the manner in which Ernie Lyall, a long-time resident of the Northwest Territories, has on many occasions assisted RCMP officers in the performance of their duties. Specific instances in which Lyall assisted officers as an interpreter at trials and in investigating homicides, dating from the 1930s to the 1960s, are recounted.

104. Jackson, Basil.

'To Serve and Protect: The Remarkable and Exciting History of the Metropolitan Police Force.' Unpublished manuscript. Toronto City Archives, City Hall, Toronto, n.d.

The author of this 600-page typescript manuscript provides a detailed narrative account of the development of policing in Toronto from the 1830s to the 1970s.

105. Jamieson, F.C.

The Alberta Field Force of '85. Canadian North-West Historical Society Publications, vol. 1, no. 7, 1931.

106. Jennings, John Nelson.

'The Plains Indians and the Law.' In *Men in Scarlet*, pp. 50–65. Edited by Hugh A. Dempsey. Calgary: McClelland and Stewart West, 1974.

In this chapter the author considers the fact that the frontier of western Canada is one of the few examples of an area settled with comparatively little racial friction. He contrasts this type of settlement and the role of the Mounted Police in bringing it about with the role of the American Army in bringing law and order to the American West.

107. Jennings, John Nelson.

'Policemen and Poachers: Indian Relations on the Ranching Frontier.' In *Frontier Calgary: Town, City, and Region, 1875–1914*, pp. 87–99. Edited by Anthony W. Rasporich and Henry C. Klassen. Calgary: McClelland and Stewart West, 1975.

In many areas there were good relations between the Indians and the ranchers, but in towns like Calgary the anti-Indian sentiment was strong and the NWMP played an important role in smoothing out relations. There is clear evidence of cattle killings by Indians in the writings of early ranchers, but certainly not as many as the local newspapers purported. The author suggests that a 'surprising aspect of Indian history during the period of the cattle frontier from the late 1870s to the mid-1890s is the very low rate of Indian crime.' The two major factors relating to the success of the NWMP were their strict enforcement of liquor laws thereby almost completely eliminating the liquor trade to the Indians, and their very thorough patrol system. While members of the Mounted Police had a strong community of interest with the ranchers, Commissioner Macleod gained the friendship and confidence of the Indian chiefs and their tribes. The article also documents the NWMP's relations with the Indians as the reserve system came into effect, and notes the changes in social and bureaucratic circumstances, and the role of the Indian Affairs department.

108. Jennings, John Nelson.

'The North West Mounted Police and Indian Policy, 1874–1896.' Ph.D. dissertation, University of Toronto, 1979.

In contrast to more general histories of the force, Jennings' dissertation examines the more specific topic of Indian relations with the NWMP, during the two decades following its arrival in western Canada. The relatively harmonious and peaceful nature of police/Indian relations from 1874 to around 1885 resulted from the ability of the NWMP to capitalize on the legacy of fair dealing towards Indians insisted upon by the Hudson's Bay Company after 1821, and the absolute power of the NWMP in matters relating to the arrest, prosecution, and sentencing of criminal offenders. After 1885, however, the involvement of the NWMP in implementing the federal government's policy of coercive assimilation and separation of Indians on reserves led to a severe deterioration in the early mutual respect shared by Indians and the police.

109. Johnson, J.K.

'The Social Composition of Toronto Bank Guards, 1837–1838.' *Ontario History* 64 (2, June 1972): 95–104.

In this article, Johnson attempts to place the body of men who guarded the two banks of Upper Canada during the 1837 rebellion into the social context of the era. While prior studies by Charles Lindsay, Donald Creighton, and W.G. Ormsby have stated that the loyalist militia came from the same socio-economic level as the rebels themselves, being 'yeomen' and 'labourers,' Johnson suggests that the bank guards were an élite group of bank and government employees, merchants, doctors, lawyers, and gentlemen. Evidence is found in British muster rolls and pay lists held at the Public Archives of Canada. Lists of two units of guards totalling 81 names are analysed by occupation and reproduced in the article. Explanation for the composition of this distinguished group is offered in two main points: first, the proximity of the workplaces of these men to the Bank of Upper Canada and the Toronto branch of the Commercial Bank of the Midland District; and second, the contemporary belief that these institutions of substantial social importance were in great danger.

110. Johnston, J.R.

'A Brief History of the Canadian Pacific Police.' *RCMP Quarterly* 28 (4, 1963): 255–263.

This article surveys the history of the Canadian Pacific Police, a department of the RCMP responsible for the safety of people travelling with the CPR, the protection of the company, and law enforcement on the company's premises.

111. Jones, Gerald.

'The Newfoundland Rangers.' *Newfoundland Quarterly* 70 (2, November 1973): 7–9.

Jones recounts the creation, growth, and final absorption into the RCMP of the Newfoundland Ranger Force. The force emerged as a result of the 1933 Royal Commission which explored the financial and social conditions of Newfoundland. The report of the commission recommended that a law enforcement agency be established in Newfoundland, after the fashion of the RCMP in Canada. The mandate of the force at its organization in 1935 is specified, and early duties are listed as: law enforcement, social services, and court reporting. Police training, uniforms, and detachments are described. The impact of the Second World War on the supply of police officers is considered. In 1949 Newfoundland became Canada's tenth province, and in 1950 the Newfoundland Ranger Force ceded their role to the RCMP. Jones also points out the aims of the Newfoundland Ranger Force Association in the compilation of the history of the force. Black and white illustrations of police officers are included.

112. Juliani, T.J.; Talbot, C.K.; and Jayewardene, C.H.S.

Urban Centurions: A Developmental Perspective of Municipal Policing in Canada. Ottawa: Crimcare, Inc., 1984.

Only in recent years have Canadian authors begun to produce historical studies of different provincial and municipal police forces. Most of these studies have concentrated on the development of the organizational structure of such police forces, rather than on the development of their duties and functions. Undertaken as the second part of a larger study aimed at ascertaining the future of policing in Canada (see entry 202 below) this book provides a historical overview of the duties and functions assumed by municipal police forces across the country. Divided along chronological lines, substantive chapters focus on examining: (1) the origins of municipal policing in Canada, 1651–1900, (2) Canada's municipal police in the early twentieth century, (3) municipal police in the 'Boom-Bust' years, 1921–45, and (4) post-war municipal policing in Canada, 1946–84. The authors' findings indicate that throughout their history municipal police forces in Canada have been called on to perform three basic functions: to intervene and prevent open conflict between groups, to establish moral order, and to apprehend criminals to have them punished.

113. Kavanaugh, K.W.

'The Alberta Provincial Police.' *RCMP Quarterly* 38 (1, January 1973): 28–31.

The Alberta Provincial Police (APP) was established in 1917 because of the shortage of manpower experienced by the RNWMP during the First World War. The APP assumed responsibility for provincial policing in Alberta until 1932, when it was disbanded and replaced by the RCMP. This article provides an overview of the history of the force. Attention is given to discussing the 'acute growing pains' of the force (differences of opinion, resignations, and the shortage of manpower), the jurisdiction and duties of officers, the force's esteemed record in reducing crime, and the objections expressed by Alberta citizens upon learning that the APP was to be disbanded. The article is based on annual reports of the APP and items printed in local newspapers.

114. Kehoe, Mary.

'History of Strike-Breaking.' *Canadian Labour* 17 (10, October 1972): 2–8.

Kehoe lists and briefly describes in this article major examples in Canadian history of public police involvement in strike-breaking. She argues that such activity promotes violence on the picket line, and that strike-breaking is, in reality, union-breaking by the employer. The discussion begins with the Montreal longshoremen's strike of 1903 in which armed forces from Quebec and Toronto were called in to assist the Montreal militia. Examples are given of violent attacks on strikers by strike-breakers, such as during the Winnipeg General Strike of 1919 and the Asbestos Strike following the Second World War. Kehoe alleges that intervention involved intimidation and political oppression against union organization. It is also argued that the perpetrators of such violence were not brought to justice, whereas strikers were often jailed. Kehoe points out that at present private security services may be hired as policemen for 'anti-union employers.' Primary sources are used but not fully cited in footnotes.

115. Kelly, Nora.

The Men of the Mounted. Toronto: Dent, 1949.

In compiling this history of the RCMP the author has relied on primary and secondary materials, taking the reader from 1873 to 1948 through a series of anecdotal and descriptive chapters. There is a chronological index of major events in the history of the force from 1871 to 1949, an alphabetical index, and maps and photographs.

116. Kelly, Nora.

'The Evolution of the R.C.M.P.' *Canadian Geographic Journal* 86 (4, April 1973): 168–181.

In a special issue to salute the RCMP centennial, Kelly covers the twentieth-century evolution of the force. In 1900, the force numbered 750, one-third of whom were stationed in the Yukon. In 1905, King Edward VII honoured the North-West Mounted Police by allowing it to use the prefix 'Royal.' At this time the force took over the duty of law enforcement in the two new provinces of Alberta and Saskatchewan. The First World War depleted the ranks to a total of 303 in 1918, only 3 more than the original number in 1873. However, it was ordered in 1918 that the force be recruited to a strength of 1200. Involvement in suppression of the 1919 Winnipeg General Strike is related, as well as growth of the force in the 1920s, especially in eastern Canada. Means of training, transportation, communication, crime control, and organizational developments are described. Second World War duty is related, including marine work and spy investigation. Kelly follows the evolution of the force to the early 1970s, involving developments in technology, staff education, crime-detection methods, and organizational structure. This article has no footnotes or bibliography. (See entries 159 and 169 below.)

117. Kelly, Nora, and Kelly, William.

The Royal Canadian Mounted Police: A Century of History, 1873–1973. Edmonton: Hurtig, 1973.

This book combines the recognized historical expertise of Nora Kelly, author of two previously published works on the RCMP, and the first-hand knowledge of William Kelly, a former deputy commissioner of the force. Together they have produced a history documenting the courage, drama, occasional frustration, and humour that marked the establishment of law and order in the Canadian West. The book is illustrated with over 60 photographs and 4 maps. A bibliography and indexes are also included.

118. Kelly, William, and Kelly, Nora.

Policing in Canada. Toronto: Macmillan/Maclean-Hunter, 1976.

Written mainly from the police point of view, this is a major source of information on policing in Canada, both historical and contemporary. Part one addresses the history of police and the legal system in New France and Upper Canada. Developments in Newfoundland, Halifax, Manitoba, Winnipeg, Saskatchewan, Alberta, Edmonton, Calgary, British Columbia, and Vancouver are briefly treated, providing some background to policing by municipal, provincial, and federal forces. The book is based on primary and secondary sources, and has a subject index.

119. Kemp, V.A.M.

Scarlet and Stetson: The Royal North-West Mounted Police on the Prairies. Toronto: Ryerson, 1964.

This book is divided into two parts. The first part, 'Personality,' deals with life in the NWMP based on historical anecdotes of the personnel of the force. The second part, 'Performance,' describes duties and documents developments in police service. The emphasis throughout is on the prairie provinces. The author describes the policing of the Prairies from the start of the twentieth century up until 1917 when local police departments assumed responsibilities previously handled by the NWMP, and when the NWMP ranks dwindled as men left for military service in the First World War. The book documents 'the Perry era' during which Commissioner Perry headed the force. The author, a former assistant commissioner in the RCMP, provides no footnotes or bibliography, but in the Preface acknowledges access to some archival as well as selected secondary sources used in this descriptive history.

120. Kennedy, Ross D.

'The Lost Patrol.' *Canada West Magazine* 6 (3, Summer 1976): 17–28.

Kennedy relates 'one of the most tragic episodes in the annals of the Mounted Police.' This episode took place in 1910 when Inspector Francis Fitzgerald and three constables, Carter, Taylor, and Kinney, set out on the Fort McPherson–Dawson City patrol. Kennedy describes the unfortunate choice of these inexperienced constables, and the severity of the winter conditions with which the party was faced. Also significant were the change of route and reduced rations initiated by Fitzgerald, with the aim of shortening the duration of the trip. The expedition is described day by day, with the occasional documentation of Fitzgerald's diary. As supplies ran out fingers and toes began to freeze, and the party lost its way. They started to eat the sled dogs, which in turn hampered their progress. Finally, only 25 miles from the refuge of Fort McPherson, having left behind the three constables dead in the snow, Fitzgerald wrote a short will and died. Kennedy provides a photograph of the 1911 search patrol, but does not describe the progress of the search. The article is a tribute to the bravery of the Mounties.

121. Klassen, Henry C.

'The Mounties and the Historians.' In *Men in Scarlet*, pp. 175–186. Edited by Hugh A. Dempsey. Calgary: McClelland and Stewart West, 1974.

Klassen appraises a number of books that are representative of historians' opinions and writings about the Mounted Police in their first hundred years of operation, noting that there are more positive works than negative.

122. Knowles, Valerie.

'Early Guardians of Montreal's Waterfront [the Montreal River Police].' *RCMP Quarterly* 30 (2, October 1964): 3–8.

On October 19, 1864, during the American Civil War, a band of Confederate soldiers who had found security on Canadian soil charged over the Canadian-American border and raided the town of St. Alban's, Vermont, plundering three banks and killing a bystander. The St. Alban's Raid strained relations between the American and Canadian governments because the Montreal judge before whom the 'captured culprits' were brought refused to extradite the prisoners to the United States. The author of this article maintains that while the American government was understandably irate about the St. Alban's Raid, it neglected to take into consideration the rather elaborate preparations made by the Canadian government to counter or suppress such raids. These preparations involved the extension of the jurisdiction of the Government Police (also known as the Water Police or River Police) at Montreal to the American border. In addition to discussing the efforts made by the Government Police to guard against disturbances by Canadian-based Confederate soldiers during the American Civil War, the author examines the reasons for the establishment of the force in 1851, and the various law enforcement duties carried out by its members while acting as guardians of Montreal's waterfront during the nineteenth century.

123. LaChance, Vernon.

'The Mounted Police Detachment at Wood Mountain and Its Activities from the Organization of the Force in 1873 until 1882.' *Canadian Defence Quarterly* 6 (4, July 1929): 493–500.

While on its march west in 1874, a contingent of the NWMP travelled to the settlement of Wood Mountain near the U.S.-Canadian border to obtain supplies. In subsequent years a supply depot was established at Wood Mountain, and members of the NWMP visited periodically. This article describes the activities of the NWMP in the Wood Mountain area from 1874 to 1882. The author notes that one of the major problems encountered by the NWMP in the area was that of dealing with the many U.S. Indians who crossed the border into Canada to avoid being captured by American troops seeking revenge for the destruction of General Custer's forces in 1876.

124. LaNauze, C.D.

'Police Patrol in the Northwest Territories of Canada.' *Geographical Journal* 51 (May 1918): 316–323.

125. Lefèbvre, Fernand.

'L'histoire du guet à Montréal.' *Revue d'histoire de l'Amérique française* 6 (1952): 263–273.

The author gives a brief description of Montreal at night at the beginning of the nineteenth century then follows it by tracing the origins of the Montreal Police. Before 1800, the task of looking after the security of the citizens and the cleanliness of the streets fell upon the justices of the peace who were assisted by sheriffs and ushers. In serious cases they were helped by the garrison troops. A law passed in 1787 authorized the nomination of peace officers who at the time were not paid for their services. In 1818 the police corps in Montreal consisted of a chief, an assistant chief, and 24 watchmen who may be considered the forerunners of present-day constables. The watch was practised from 7:00 p.m. to 5:00 a.m. By 1845 there were 3 police stations with 45 policemen. The daily pay for a policeman was $0.50 and was raised to $1.00 in 1857. John Molson, founder of the famous brewery, was appointed director general of Montreal Police from 1830 to 1836. The diary of the watch corps for the year 1836 is kept in the judicial archives of Montreal. It has 76 pages, 46 of which are blank and another 3 have been removed. It contains the results of the rounds made in both the east and west parts of the city and these are recorded in French and English respectively. Several extracts of the day-book are reproduced.

126. Lodhi, Abdul Qaiyum; Munger, F.; and Tilley, C.

Policing and the Visibility of Crime in Nineteenth Century Canada, England and France. Ann Arbor, Mich.: Center for Research on Social Organization, University of Michigan, 1974. (CRSO Working Paper, no. 93)

This paper concentrates on the nineteenth century and deals with the effect of expanded policing on criminal trends. It considers an apparent increase in property crime as being mainly the result of expanded reporting, and a long-run decline in property crime as the result of rising effectiveness of surveillance and apprehension. The work contains some statistical material but the primary focus is on the social organization of policing.

127. Long, Harold G., ed.

Fort Macleod: The Story of the North West Mounted Police 1874–1904, Royal North West Mounted Police, 1904–1920, Royal Canadian Mounted Police, 1920 to the Present Time. Lethbridge: Fort Macleod Historical Association, 1958.

This is a collection of articles on the history of the RCMP, particularly as they relate to Fort Macleod and former commissioner James F. Macleod (1876–80). Individual authors include John Peter Turner (historian of the RCMP from 1939 to 1948 and author of a major two-volume history of the force, *The North-West Mounted Police 1873–1893*), Hugh A. Dempsey (author of several works on the RCMP), and others. While the Turner paper is 27 pages in length, the others are much briefer; the complete booklet is only 96 pages in length.

128. Longstreth, Thomas Morris.

The Silent Force: Scenes from the Life of the Mounted Police of Canada. New York: Century Company, 1927; London: Philip Allan and Co. Ltd., 1928.

This is a history of the RCMP divided into parts according to the terms of service of the past commissioners from 1873 to 1922.

129. Longstreth, Thomas Morris.

In Scarlet and Plain Clothes: The History of the Mounted Police. Toronto: Macmillan Co., 1933.

This history of the first six decades of the RCMP's work concentrates on various episodes the author considered noteworthy, such as the building of the Canadian Pacific Railway, the Rebellion of 1885, and the conquest of the Yukon.

130. Longstreth, Thomas Morris.

The Scarlet Force. Toronto: Macmillan, 1954.

131. Luckhurst, Margaret.

North West Mounted Police: Early History of the R.C.M.P. Lethbridge: Southern Printing Co. Ltd., 1973; Lethbridge Division RCMP Veteran's Association, 1974.

132. MacBeth, R.G.

Policing the Plains: Being the Real Life Record of the Famous Northwest Mounted Police. Toronto: Hodder and Stoughton, 1922; Toronto: Musson Book Co., 1926; Toronto: Musson, 1931.

Relying mainly on personal accounts offered by early members of the NWMP, the author examines the circumstances surrounding the establishment of the force and its outstanding record in policing the Northwest Territories.

133. McDonald, Kelly.

The R.C.M.P. Toronto: Macmillan, 1973.

134. MacDonald, W.E.G.

'Commissioners from French 1873 to McClellan 1964.' *Scarlet and Gold* 46 (1964): 9–23.

The author's concern in this article is to highlight the individual contributions RCMP commissioners have made to the success of the force, and to pinpoint some of the developments that occurred during the tenure of office of commissioners from French to McClellan.

135. McLeod, D.M.

'Liquor Control in the North-West Territories: The Permit System, 1870–1891.' *Saskatchewan History* 16 (Autumn 1963): 81–89.

McLeod treats the problem of the control of liquor consumption faced by the administration in the Northwest Territories during the three decades before the turn of the century. The author observes the constant conflict between the prohibitionists and the 'drinking people' over policies on liquor established in the early West. McLeod begins in the early 1870s with legislation intended to prohibit the Indians' access to liquor, and at the same time to allow consumption by white settlers. The permit system is described, as well as the resulting bribery, smuggling, fraud, and the abuse of other intoxicating liquids. A new administration in the 1880s responded by establishing a licensing system for beer sales in hotels, but illegal liquor consumption continued. McLeod points out the difficulty of the enforcement of liquor laws in the West and along the border, particularly when many citizens and police opposed the regulations and resented interference from Ottawa. McLeod concludes by summarizing the weaknesses of the permit system, and the movement for self-government in the West.

136. MacLeod, J.E.A.

'Mounted Police Beginnings.' *RCMP Quarterly* 3 (1, July 1935): 10–20.

137. Macleod, Roderick Charles.

'The Mounted Police and Politics.' In *Men in Scarlet*, pp. 95–114. Edited by Hugh A. Dempsey. Calgary: McClelland and Stewart West, 1974.

The author considers the NWMP as an arm of the central government and the fact that the NWMP took no part in either municipal or territorial politics. This is not to say that the NWMP didn't affect local politics by its presence, but that in being answerable to the Canadian government it could avoid involvement in local issues. The chapter goes on to consider the role of the Canadian government and politics in the future of the NWMP and the territory it patrolled.

138. Macleod, Roderick Charles.

'The Problem of Law and Order in the Canadian West, 1870–1905.' In *The Prairie West to 1905: A Canadian Sourcebook*, pp. 132–216. Edited by Lewis G. Thomas. Toronto: Oxford University Press, 1975.

139. Macleod, Roderick Charles.

The North West Mounted Police and Law Enforcement, 1873–1905. Toronto: University of Toronto Press, 1976.

Written originally as a doctoral dissertation, this book provides an original and well-documented account of the history of the NWMP. Divided into two major parts, the book covers: (1) the growth and development of the NWMP from 1873 to 1905 (i.e., origins, leaderships, and organization), and (2) specific problems confronted and responded to by the force prior to 1905 (i.e., patronage and politics, crime and criminals, the enforcement of liquor laws, and minority groups). Through his examination the author attempts to establish the reasons for the success of the Mounted Police, both in 'policing the frontier' and 'in making the transition to maintaining the law in a settled and developed community.'

140. Macleod, Roderick Charles.

The North-West Mounted Police, 1873–1919. Canadian Historical Association Booklets, no. 31. Ottawa: Canadian Historical Association, 1976.

This booklet of the Canadian Historical Association provides a concise history of the NWMP from 1873 to 1919, by the author of a major history of the force. In the booklet he summarizes the formation of the force, relations with Indians and ranchers (1874–84), the 1885 Riel Rebellion, matters of reform and administration of the force, particularly under Commissioner L.W. Herchmer, the expansion of the force into the North, and the impact of the First World War and Security and Intelligence operations. The author concludes that the 1919 amendment to the RNWMP Act, which brought about the merger of the RNWMP with the Dominion Police and the new name Royal Canadian Mounted Police, gave the force a nation-wide role and enhanced its standing as the senior police force in the country.

141. Macleod, Roderick Charles.

'Canadianizing the West: The North-West Mounted Police as Agents of the National Policy, 1873–1905.' In *Essays on Western History*, pp. 101–110. Edited by L.H. Thomas. Edmonton: University of Alberta Press, 1978.

142. Marquis, Gregory.

'The Police Force in Saint John, New Brunswick, 1860–1890.' M.A. thesis, University of New Brunswick, 1982.

The Saint John police force was organized in 1849 in the wake of decades of sectarian violence. In the decades subsequent to the establishment of the force, violence and crime became less of a problem for public order than 'lower class leisure activities.' This thesis examines the development and role of the Saint John police in the period 1860–90. An attempt is made to assess the adequacy of competing 'liberal' and 'social control' interpretations of the purposes served by the establishment of public police forces, and clarify the 'class nature of nineteenth-century law enforcement.' The author concludes that despite the noble principles handed down by Peel in 1829, law enforcement in Saint John was accompanied by a class bias, and that the actions of the police support the theory that they were exercising 'new standards of social control in the mid-nineteenth-century city.'

143. Martin, A.

'The Sheriffs of Assiniboia.' *Western Law Times* 1 (8, November 1890): 153–163.

144. Massicotte, E.-Z.

'La maréchaussée à Montréal.' *Bulletin des recherches historiques* 22 (1, January 1916): 16–18.

145. Massicotte, E.-Z.

'Couvre-feu et rondes de nuit.' *Bulletin des recherches historiques* 36 (5, May 1930): 266–269.

146. Mayfield, Barbara.

'The Northwest Mounted Police and the Blackfoot.' M.A. thesis, University of Victoria, 1979.

147. Mitchell, V.W.

'Halifax Police Department: A Brief History of Canada's Oldest Constabulary.' *RCMP Quarterly* 30 (4, April 1965): 3–8.

This article examines the origins and development of the Halifax Police Department. The author traces the origins of the Halifax police back to a proclamation dated July 17, 1749, in which the governor in council called all settlers to assemble in separate companies and appoint a constable. Drawing on early records of the City of Halifax, he discusses the specific duties entrusted to early constables by justices of the peace, and changes that affected the system of policing that existed in Halifax during the eighteenth and nineteenth centuries. Brief attention is also given to noting many changes that have affected the Halifax Police Department since the beginning of the twentieth century.

148. Morgan, Edwin Charles George.

'The North West Mounted Police, 1873–1883.' M.A. thesis, University of Saskatchewan, 1970. Also published as Manuscript Report Series, no. 113. Ottawa: Parks Canada, 1970.

This thesis examines the reasons for the creation of the NWMP, the main outlines of its organizational and administrative structure, its principal activities, and the performance of its duties in the period 1873–83. It assesses its relations with the population of the Northwest Territories, its contribution to the settlement of the area, and the degree to which it furthered the aims of the Dominion government. Departing from 'unreservedly complimentary' interpretations of the history of the NWMP, the author concludes that in its early years the police force had to overcome a number of problems, including financial stringencies, poor recruiting methods, and problems of morale and desertion, in order for it to successfully carry out its duties.

149. Morgan, Edwin Charles George.

'The North-West Mounted Police: Internal Problems and Public Criticism, 1874–1883.' *Saskatchewan History* 26 (Spring 1973): 41–62.

This article draws on the author's 1970 M.A. thesis and reiterates his earlier conclusions (see entry 148 above).

150. Morrison, William Robert.

'The Mounted Police on Canada's Northern Frontier, 1895–1940.' Ph.D. dissertation, University of Western Ontario, 1973.

Between 1895 and 1949 the Mounted Police established their presence in five separate regions of the Canadian Arctic and sub-Arctic. In each region, the primary duties of the police were to assert Canadian sovereignty and establish and maintain law and order. It also provided almost the entire range of government civil services to the frontier. This study examines the broad role played by the Mounted Police in the development of the Canadian North. The author's findings indicate that because the police shared a strongly defined conception of their role – 'to catch criminals and maintain the law' – they approached their civil-service duties with less enthusiasm. Nevertheless, he concludes that 'despite some occasional failures and derelictions of duty, the jobs which the police disliked were done well, while those they found to their taste could not have been done better.' Major sources of primary data used in the study include the Royal Canadian Mounted Police Papers held in the Public Archives of Canada, newspapers and periodicals, and published government documents.

151. Morrison, William Robert.

'Native Peoples of the Northern Frontier.' In *Men in Scarlet*, pp. 77–94. Edited by Hugh A. Dempsey. Calgary: McClelland and Stewart West, 1974.

The author considers the differences between the 'noble redskin' Indians of the prairies and the Yukon Indians who lacked a cohesive social structure and who were facing starvation. From the early days of white settlement the Yukon Indians had problems with liquor and disease, and because of a lack of government policy with regard to the Indians and other factors, by 1925 there had been significant changes in the relationship between the police and Eskimos.

152. Morrison, William Robert.

'The North-West Mounted Police and the Klondike Gold Rush.' *Journal of Contemporary History* 9 (2, 1974): 93–105. Also in *Police Forces in History*, pp. 263–276. Sage Readers in 20th Century History, vol. 2. Edited by George L. Mosse. London: Sage Publications, 1975.

The author examines the activities of the NWMP in the Yukon during the Klondike gold rush from 1897 to 1899. He maintains that through examining this episode in the history of the force, one can learn a great deal about its methods of operation, as well as its strengths and weaknesses. Incidents of crime and lawlessness dealt with by the NWMP after its arrival in the Yukon are used to illustrate the manner in which the force was able to replace the pre-existing 'American-style' system of frontier justice with one based on the British model.

153. Morton, Desmond.

'Aid to the Civil Power: The Canadian Militia in Support of Social Order, 1867–1914.' *Canadian Historical Review* 51 (4, December 1970): 407–425.

Throughout the nineteenth century, the Canadian militia was regularly called into service to meet threats to public order. In the absence of effective local or provincial police forces, the militia was frequently the only available support for a magistrate confronted by rioting sectarian groups and defiant strikers. Drawing on the records of the Department of National Defence, the author identifies 48 separate occasions between 1867 and 1914 when the militia was called to the aid of the civil power. Included among these are 5 occasions when troops were called to prevent Orange-Catholic riots, 33 different interventions in strikes, 2 summonses to prevent illegal prize-fighting, and one occasion when troops were placed on guard at a hanging. An attempt is made to determine how it was that the militia came to be used in a police role, how it functioned, and how its role was regarded by the rest of Canada and the troops themselves. The author concludes that the militia found in strike-breaking and other police functions 'a chance for excitement, an opportunity to exercise their power and a justification for an otherwise insubstantial social role.'

154. Morton, Desmond.

'Cavalry or Police: Keeping the Peace on Two Adjacent Frontiers, 1870–1900.' *Journal of Canadian Studies* 12 (2, Spring 1977): 27–37.

Departing from more popular interpretations, Morton questions the extent to which the superior character and quality of the NWMP, as compared to the U.S. cavalry, was responsible for the orderly settlement of the Canadian West. Drawing on both secondary literature and primary sources, he re-examines the circumstances which led to the creation of the NWMP, and mythical aspects of the force's early history that contributed to making it a source of national pride for Canadians. Substantive differences in the role and outlook of the NWMP and their U.S. counterparts are considered, along with various possible reasons why the process of settlement and Indian policy differed between the two frontiers. The author maintains that although the inventiveness shown by the Canadian government in creating the NWMP allowed for the more peaceful settlement of the Canadian West, the impact of western settlement on the indigenous population of Canada and the United States was depressingly similar.

155. Mowery, William Byron.

The Long Arm of the Mounted. New York and Toronto: McGraw Hill, [1948].

156. Mowery, William Byron.

Sagas of the Mounted Police. New York: Bouregy and Curl, 1953.

157. Neering, Rosemary.

North-West Mounted Police. Growth of a Nation Series. Toronto: Fitzhenry and Whiteside, 1974.

158. Neuberger, R.

Royal Canadian Mounted Police. New York: Random House, 1953.

159. Nicholson, L.H.

'North-West Mounted Police, 1873–1885: "Highlights of the First Years".' *Canadian Geographic Journal* 86 (4, April 1973): 142–154.

This article may be seen as the background to articles by Kelly and Rivett-Carnac, also included in this special issue of the journal which salutes the RCMP centennial (see entry 116 above and 169 below). As the title implies, Nicholson intends to outline the early period of the existence of the Mounties. The article begins by setting the scene in the West, considering the activities of the Indians both in Canada and in the United States. It continues to describe the origin of the force, and its establishment of posts in the West. Activities in liquor control and policing the building of the railway are related, within the context of changes in the West and the administration of the force. The article culminates with a consideration of Mountie involvement in the 1885 Rebellion. Nicholson argues that by this time, 'peace, settlement, and progress were at hand in the prairie country, and for the N.W.M.P., its golden years were just ahead.' Primary sources used are not fully cited.

160. Nish, Elizabeth, and Hagan, William T.

'Indian Police and Judges – Experiments in Acculturation and Control.' *Revue d'histoire de l'Amérique française* 20 (2, September 1966): 308–310.

161. Osipoff, Fred.

'The S.P.P. 1910–1928.' *Canadian Journal of Arms Collecting* 4 (1, February 1966): 5–11.

This article provides a brief survey of the history of the Saskatchewan Provincial Police. The author, a gun collector, notes that his interest in the activities of the force stemmed from his coming across various arms bearing the stamp 'S.P.P.' The article describes the efforts carried out by the SPP in attempting to enforce prohibition legislation, and the various arms and equipment used by the force during its 18-year history.

162. Penner, Norman.

'How the RCMP Got Where It Is.' In *RCMP vs the People: Inside Canada's Security Service*, pp. 107–121. Edited by Edward Mann and John Alan Lee. Don Mills, Ont.: General Publishing, 1979.

The author suggests that since its creation in 1873 the Mounted Police have had two missions – one public and one hidden. The public role has been to maintain law and order. The hidden agenda, suggests Penner, has been 'the surveillance and sometimes forceful control of all minorities that do not fit into the Canadian establishment's model of public order.' He goes on to link this to similarities with the Irish Mounted Constabulary, Mountie links with corporate interests in labour disputes, and discusses the political and legislative impacts on the force.

163. Phillips, Roger F., and Klancher, Donald J.

Arms and Accoutrements of the Mounted Police, 1873–1973. Bloomfield, Ont.: Museum Restoration Service, 1982.

This substantial reference text found its beginnings in a pamphlet by Phillips with S.J. Kirby entitled *Small Arms of the Mounted Police*, Historical Arms Series no. 6 (Ottawa: Museum Restoration Service, 1965). Chapters 1 to 5 in the 1982 text cover chronological periods which reflect eras in the evolution of arms used by the Mounties, such as 'The Quest for an Improved Arm, 1875–1904.' Chapters 6 to 10 contain information on different types of arms, such as machine guns, ammunition, artillery, swords, and lances. Chapter 11 considers accoutrements such as holsters and saddles. Commemorative arms, such as engraved rifles, are covered in Chapter 12. The book provides historical background and describes the nature, source, and use of arms. Over 400 black and white plates of photographs and illustrations, well identified, support the text. Appendix I provides a list of serial numbers located for a variety of arms, which assists the collector and exhibitor. Appendix II discusses arms training, and includes reproductions of paragraphs from original training manuals. The many primary sources used are clearly identified in notes, but a bibliography is lacking. The text is well indexed.

164. Poole, Colin.

'Identification of Mounted Police Outposts in Southern Alberta.' In *Men in Scarlet*, pp. 198–211. Edited by Hugh A. Dempsey. Calgary: McClelland and Stewart West, 1974.

The author reports on a project initiated to record locations and descriptions of Mounted Police outposts which existed in southern Alberta. The chapter includes a table 'NWMP Outposts in Southern Alberta, 1874–1904' which reports the names of outposts, the related headquarters post, the period during which it was occupied, the average strength, type of accommodation and the location, and remarks. The author expresses the hope that when the project is finished a program of historical preservation can be undertaken.

165. Porter, W.

'Newfoundland Rangers – Its History from 1935–1950.' Unpublished manuscript, Maritime History Collection, Memorial University, 1973.

In 1935 the Newfoundland Ranger Force was established to take over the law enforcement duties of the Newfoundland Constabulary, and assume responsibility for a wide range of civil-service duties on the island. It existed as the only police force in Newfoundland until the RCMP took over the policing of the province in 1949. This paper provides information on the reasons for the establishment of the force, the training program followed by officers, and the many duties that the officers carried out, which included acting as game wardens and welfare and customs officers as well as enforcing the criminal law. The paper draws exclusively on archival material held in the Newfoundland Provincial Archives.

166. Provost, Honorius.

'Les premiers règlements de police à Québec.' *Revue de l'Université Laval* 17 (3, 1962–3): 284–289.

Jean Talon was the first administrator (intendant) in New France. Although he received an order from the Council of State in France signed by Colbert and dated June 4, 1672, to establish regulations for the police, he never did. It was Frontenac who formulated the first rules for the police in the city of Quebec. The rules were registered with the Supreme

Council (Conseil Souverain) on March 27, 1673. The rules consisted of 31 sections governing the market, the bakers, the butchers, the blacksmiths, the weights and measures, house construction, cleaning of the streets, the keeping of animals, and so on. New regulations were sanctioned by the council on May 11, 1676; this time they contained 42 sections. It was a real police code that applied to the whole colony. These regulations remained in force until the end of the French regime although there were some modifications and several additions over the years. Restrictions on the sale of alcoholic beverages were introduced in August 1684 and modified in February 1686.

167. Rico, José M., and Sarrazin, M.

Une approche socio-historique de la police à Montréal et en Ontario. Montréal: Université de Montréal, Centre international de criminologie comparée, 1975.

Using the Montreal police and Ontario police the authors examine their history, evolution of powers, and selection and hiring practices and evaluate police action and function. An earlier version was released as a progress report in March 1972 called 'La Police de Montréal: aspects socio-historiques.'

168. Ritchie, Mary Edna.

Royal Canadian Mounted Police. Toronto: Copp Clark, 1946.

169. Rivett-Carnac, Charles.

'Establishment of the R.C.M.P. Presence in the Northwest Territories and the Arctic.' *Canadian Geographic Journal* 86 (4, April 1973): 155–167.

This article complements those by Nicholson and Kelly from this special issue which is a tribute to the centennial of the RCMP (see entries 116 and 159 above). The author commences in the decade before the turn of the century, describing the first northern patrol which crossed Lake Winnipeg en route to York Factory. He proceeds through various expeditions such as a 1903 trip to the Arctic Ocean, and Fitzgerald's 1911 Fort-McPherson-to-Dawson-Patrol, in which the participants died. Selected exploration expeditions are described, as well as travels for law enforcement and the escort of prisoners. Rivett-Carnac notes that murder was not infrequent among the Eskimos of the North who 'had to be taught the necessity of the white man's law.' The relative lack of information about early expeditions is lamented, and some speculation is made about the hardships faced. Primary sources are not cited. There are several black and white photographs included, as well as a map indicating the various expeditions.

170. Robertson, Duncan Francis.

'The Saskatchewan Provincial Police 1917–1928.' M.A. thesis, University of Saskatchewan, 1976.

This thesis chronicles the brief history of the Saskatchewan Provincial Police force, from its inception in 1917 until it was disbanded in 1928. The study begins with an overview of policing (by the RNWMP) in Saskatchewan from the formation of the province in 1905 until the takeover of police duties by the SPP in 1917. Ensuing chapters discuss the reasons for the establishment of the force, and the work of the SPP in three areas: the enforcement of liquor legislation, the investigation of major cases and daily police routine, and the enforcement of school attendance. The study concludes with an examination of the reasons given for disbanding the force and a subsequent investigation carried out in relation to various activities of different members of the force during the period of its existence.

171. Robertson, Duncan Francis.

'The Saskatchewan Provincial Police, 1917–1928.' *Saskatchewan History* 31 (1, Winter 1978): 1–11.

This article draws on the author's 1976 M.A. thesis, and presents similar findings (see entry 170 above).

172. Robertson, R.W.W.

The Law Moves West: The North-West Mounted Police, 1873–1878. Toronto: Burns and MacEachern, 1970.

173. Rogers, Nicholas.

'Serving Toronto the Good: The Development of the City Police Force, 1834–1880.' In *Forging a Consensus: Historical Essays on Toronto*, pp. 116–140. Edited by Victor L. Russell. Toronto: University of Toronto Press, 1984.

Although a good deal of research in Canada has been devoted to the history of the RCMP, the history of municipal police forces has not been subjected to the same scrutiny. In the case of Toronto, historians have tended to assume that the development of the city police force, 135 strong by 1881, was a natural concomitant of urban expansion. Departing from this interpretation, the author examines the organization and early role of the Toronto police force within the context of broader questions concerning ideology, political partisanship, and class. Relying mainly on Toronto City Council minutes, Toronto Police Board records, and accounts provided in local newspapers, particular attention is given to documenting the influence of sectarian politics and conservative ideology on the development of the police force and the role played by its members in policing the lower classes. The author points out that rather than being simply the result of urban expansion, the development of the Toronto city police force was a product of changing and sometimes competing political and social forces. He concludes that by the 1880s the Toronto police 'had become integrated into the authority structures of Victorian Toronto, alongside schools, charities, prisons, asylums, and benefit societies.' By this time it had also assumed the role of being a 'coercive agency of moral reform.'

174. Routledge, Penelope Dawn.

'The North-West Mounted Police and Their Influence on the Sporting and Social Life of the North-West Territories, 1870–1904.' M.A. thesis, University of Alberta, 1978.

The march west in 1874 of the newly formed NWMP force marked the beginning of a new era in the history of Canada's western frontier, an era of law and order. The purpose of this thesis is to show how the members of the force, during their leisure time, influenced early social and sporting life on the prairies. Drawing on diaries, personal papers, correspondence, daily journals, and pamphlet material held in the Glenbow-Alberta Institute Archives, the author points out that through participating in such events as dances, dinners, drama presentations, and band concerts, the NWMP interacted with local Indians and settlers on an ongoing basis. They also organized a variety of individual and team sporting events. The author concludes that the NWMP had a significant and unique influence upon social life and the development of sport in the Northwest Territories.

175. Roy, Pierre Georges.

'Les shérifs de Québec.' *Bulletin des recherches historiques* 40 (1934): 433–446.

Following a brief summary of the history and tasks performed by the sheriff in England, the article traces the careers of several sheriffs in Quebec starting with James Shepherd who was nominated sheriff for the district of Quebec on May 1, 1776, and ending with Lauréat Lapierre, nominated May 3, 1934. Other sheriffs whose careers are discussed are: Philippe-Joseph Aubert de Gaspé, William Smith-Sewell, Thomas Ainslie Young, Charles Alleyn, Ethienne-Théodore Paquet, Charles-Antoine Ernest Gagnon, Charles Langelier, Jean Cléophas Blouin. A short biographical history is provided for each of these sheriffs.

176. Sage, Walter N.

'The North-West Mounted Police and British Columbia.' *Pacific Historical Review* 18 (1949): 345–361.

Sage describes the source, mandate, creation, and evolution of the Mounties in Canada, as a means by John A. Macdonald of securing the West. The force only operated continuously in British Columbia after its reorganization in 1920 as the RCMP. However, they did work prior to this in British Columbia on special projects. The role played by the Mounties in law enforcement during the building of the railway is related. The rebellions of 1870 and 1885 are also summarized. Sage focuses on the actions of the NWMP in dealing with B.C. Kootenay Indian concerns about the arrival of the railway. Details of travel, supplies, and accommodations are offered by Sage in a narrative style. This article is an attempt to 'study in miniature the workings of the "silent force",' and is strongly supported by substantial texts of annual official statements submitted to the government of Canada by the commissioner of the NWMP.

177. Sawatsky, John.

Men in the Shadows: The R.C.M.P. Security Service. Toronto: Doubleday Canada, 1980.

178. Sawatsky, John.

For Services Rendered: Leslie James Bennett and the R.C.M.P. Security Service. Toronto: Doubleday Canada, 1982.

179. Senior, Elinor.

'The Provincial Cavalry in Lower Canada, 1837–1850.' *Canadian Historical Review* 57 (1, March 1976): 1–24.

180. Senior, Elinor.

'The Influence of the British Garrison on the Development of the Montreal Police, 1832–1853.' *Military Affairs* 43 (2, April 1979): 63–68.

This article discusses the frequent use of imperial troops as an aid to the civil power in Montreal from 1832 to 1853. British military authorities actively encouraged the development of rural and municipal police systems in the 1840s, as a result of the military's participation in the maintenance of law and order in the city. The British military command was anxious to leave the role of law enforcement to local police as civilians and the press often criticized the actions of the British. However, in the midst of civil disorder in 1837, the small police force which had been created was dissolved when funds ran out. Senior relates the activities and administration of the British garrison during the 1840s and 1850s, and efforts to organize police at this time. Arms, ammunition, saddlery, and personnel were provided by the garrison in the establishment of a mounted constabulary in 1849. Senior argues that 'the discipline of the garrison set the tone of the force, imposing standards of service and conduct where standards were needed.' The article is well documented by primary sources, including contemporary reports from the media.

181. Shanes, Mary A.

'The Police Organization as a Mechanism of Social Control in Nineteenth-Century Hamilton.' M.A. thesis, McMaster University, 1975.

This study examines the police organization of Hamilton, Ont., and the nature of its relationship with its urban environment during the nineteenth century. The central theme of the thesis is that with increasing urbanization there occurs a corresponding increase in society's reliance upon formal mechanisms of social control. The author pursues this theme through examining historical literature that supports the view that the development of the Hamilton police force paralleled the growth of the city, and that changes in the police organization stemmed from its effort to adapt to 'crisis situations in the urban environment.' The thesis is based mainly on sociological literature concerned with modern police organizations and published material on the social history of Hamilton.

182. Sharp, Paul Frederick.

Whoop-up Country: The Canadian-American West, 1865–1885. Minneapolis: University of Minnesota Press, 1955.

The author attempts to account for the establishment of the NWMP in 1873. Departing from the interpretations of other historians, he argues that the force was created as a result of economic conflict over the American-based whiskey trade. Details concerning the cross-border whiskey trade and its impact on social life in the Northwest Territories are discussed, along with the differences that characterized early settlement north and south of the border.

183. Sharp, Paul Frederick.

'Three Frontiers: Some Comparative Studies of Canadian, American, and Australian Settlement.' *Pacific Historical Review* 24 (1955): 369–377.

In this article, the author contrasts relations between the Canadian government and Indians in the Northwest Territories with comparable developments in the United States and Australia. He maintains that unlike in the United States, where Indian policy was devised by unconcerned politicians and carried out by venal Indian agents and rash army officers, the Canadian government conceived a 'well-planned and honourable policy' which was executed in an orderly manner by the NWMP.

184. Shaw, T.E.G.

'Murder at Belly Butte.' *RCMP Quarterly* 26 (1, July 1960): 18–29.

185. Shepstone, H.J.

'Work of the Famous Canadian Police in Pacification and Exploration.' *World's Work (London)* 35 (December 1919): 32–43.

186. Shipley, N. LaVerne.

Municipal Police History of the City of London, Ontario. [London, Ontario: 1969?]

187. Shirley, Glen.

Law West of Fort Smith: Frontier Justice in the Indian Territory, 1834–1896. Toronto: Collier, 1961.

188. Smith, George.

'Early Police in Manitoba.' Paper presented to the Manitoba Historical Society, March 11, 1947. (Provincial Archives of Manitoba)

189. Sookdesosingh, Bose.

'The Role of the R.N.W.M.P. in the Winnipeg General Strike, 1919.' M.A. thesis, University of Toronto, Centre of Criminology, 1973.

The Winnipeg General Strike was very political in nature. What began as a conflict between employers and workers quickly became a contest between the state and workers. The machinery which the federal government used most successfully to break the strike was the RNWMP. Divided into three parts, this thesis examines: (1) the industrial, social, and political climate within which the strike occurred; (2) the role played by the RNWMP in ending the strike; and (3) police attitudes towards protest and protesters as reflected in the strike-breaking activity of the RNWMP. The author concludes that the role played by the RNWMP in the Winnipeg General Strike brings into question whether police forces should not be better trained in policing industrial disputes.

190. Stan, Jerome.

'The Clash of Cultures, the Collision of Gods: A Study of Missionary, Police and Indian Affairs Officials' Attitudes towards Indians in the North-West Territory, 1870–1900.' M.A. thesis, Trent University, 1978.

This thesis attempts to gain an understanding of Indian-white relations in the Canadian Northwest during the period in which the region was changed from an Indian territory to a white domain. Emphasis is placed on examining how white settlement and civilization acted upon the Indians and their way of life, as reflected in the attitudes and actions of missionaries, the NWMP, and government officials involved with Indian affairs. The author concludes that in the period 1870–1900 'the Indian-white relationship steadily became a relationship of greater imbalance, inequality, and dominance, with the scales most often tipped towards white society.' Historical data sources used to substantiate this thesis include the reports of missionary societies, government reports, correspondence, secondary literature relating to the history of the NWMP, and the records of the federal Department of Indian Affairs.

191. Stanley, George F.G.

'The Man Who Sketched the Great March.' In *Men in Scarlet*, pp. 27–49. Edited by Hugh A. Dempsey. Calgary: McClelland and Stewart West, 1974.

Stanley's description of the great march west of the NWMP from Fort Dufferin in Manitoba to the foothills of the Rockies is colourfully written and provides informative historical details. The chapter is illustrated with drawings of a young French-Canadian artist, Henri Julien, who had been assigned to cover the activities of the Mounted Police for the *Canadian Illustrated News*, Canada's leading picture periodical. The chapter concludes with a list of 40 of Julien's sketches of the great march which appeared in the *Canadian Illustrated News*.

192. Steele, Harwood.

Policing the Arctic:The Story of the Conquest of the Arctic by the Royal Canadian (formerly North-West) Mounted Police. Toronto: Ryerson, 1936.

The author, historian of the Canadian government Arctic Expedition of 1925, writes of the 'peaceful, adventurous conquest of Arctic and sub-Arctic Canada' by the RCMP. The book is well documented with references to both primary and secondary sources. There is a very detailed name and subject index.

193. Steele, Harwood.

The R.C.M.P. Toronto: Clarke, Irwin, 1968.

194. Steele, Samuel B.

Forty Years in Canada:Reminiscences of the Great North-West with Some Account of His Deviance in South Africa. Toronto: McClelland, Goodchild and Stewart Limited, 1915; Toronto: McGraw-Hill Ryerson Limited, 1972.

This is a personal account of the author's experiences as a member of the NWMP and as a military colonel in the South African War.

195. Stenning, Philip C.

Police Commissions and Boards in Canada. Toronto: University of Toronto, Centre of Criminology, 1981.

196. Stenning, Philip C.

'The Role of Police Boards and Commissions as Institutions of Municipal Police Governance.' In *Organizational Police Deviance:Its Structure and Control*, pp. 161–208. Edited by Clifford D. Shearing. Toronto: Butterworth, 1981.

Until recently, little research has focused on the various structures which have been established to provide for the government of police forces, the relationship between the police themselves and these governing authorities, and the influence of politics on their operations. This essay takes a first step in filling this gap in existing knowledge about police accountability by examining the historical and modern development of police boards and commissions established to govern municipal police forces in Canada. Specific attention is given to : (1) outlining the historical origins of modern municipal police forces in Canada, (2) describing the development of modern municipal police boards, (3) discussing the current variety of municipal police boards found in Canadian jurisdictions, and (4) considering recent Ontario-based controversies surrounding the accountability of police boards themselves. The author's findings indicate that the history of police boards in Canada has been marked by persistent controversy, and that in recent years this controversy has shown no signs of abating.

197. Stenning, Philip C.

'Trusting the Chief: Legal Aspects of the Status and Political Accountability of the Police in Canada.' S.J.D. thesis, University of Toronto, 1983.

Of particular interest in this thesis on the political control and accountability of the police are Chapter 2, 'English Origins of the Office of Constable' (pp. 110–173) and Chapter 3, 'Police in Early Canada' (pp. 174–241). In the latter, Stenning describes how the common-law status of the constable developed in Canada, with references to statutes and ordinances in the provinces from the eighteenth to the twentieth century. Chapter 4, 'Current Legislation Defining the Legal Status of the Police in Canada,' includes a legal analysis of the reform of police legislation between 1946 and 1977. There are extensive notes and a lengthy bibliography.

198. Stevenson, Alex.

'Lawless Land.' *North/Nord* 16 (1, January–February 1969): 22–30.

199. Stewart, Chris, and Hudson, Lynn.

Mahony's Minute Men: The Saga of the Saskatchewan Provincial Police, 1917–1928. Riverhurst, Sask.: Stewart and Hudson Books, 1978.

This self-published book includes 121 pages of history from a personal perspective. The authors show their enthusiasm in recording the interesting history of this short-lived force. Anecdotal chapters describe the creation and demise of the force and its personnel and organization. However, most chapters relate events in law enforcement and crime solving. Difficulty was found in the control of liquor in the new West. The authors suggest that the influx of European immigration early in this century resulted in increased crime, especially murder and theft. It is argued that the policing of Saskatchewan was handed back to the

RCMP in 1928 not only for economy, but also because the provincial government preferred to have an outside agency enforce unpopular laws such as liquor control. The book is augmented by snapshot-style photographs but lacks bibliography, footnotes, and index.

200. Stone, Thomas.

'The Mounties as Vigilantes: Perceptions of Community and the Transformation of Law in the Yukon, 1885–1897.' *Law and Society Review* 14 (1, Fall 1979): 83–114.

Stone discusses the transformation of law in the Yukon in the 1890s which was caused by the arrival of the Mounties. He treats the acceptance by the inhabitants of the fundamental change in local legal institutions. The miners' meeting, an informal collective of locals, determined justice when crime occurred. Decisions were based on a 'forward-looking' system, in which the likelihood of future disturbances by the person was debated, and the sole purpose of justice was to keep peace in the camp. Therefore, the moral fibre of the offender was considered more important than the offence. In 1894 Canadian law began to displace American lawlessness with the arrival of the Mounties and their successful attempt to eliminate the miners' meeting. However, Stone observes that the administration of justice by the new police was as pragmatic as before, and concentrated on the elimination of undesirable elements. The difference lay in the respect accorded the Mounties in the community, as the police strongly symbolized law and order. It is in relation to this symbol that Stone argues a parallel in the image of the Mounties in the Yukon and that of the vigilantes in the United States. Numerous examples of cases are related in this informative article. A substantial list of primary and secondary references is included.

201. Stotyn, Keith.

Policing the CPR. Calgary: Glenbow-Alberta Institute, 1972.

202. Talbot, Charles K.; Jayewardene, C.H.S.; and Juliani, Tony J.

The Thin Blue Line: An Historical Perspective of Policing in Canada. Ottawa: Crimcare, Inc., 1983.

Undertaken as a first step of a larger study designed to ascertain the future role of police in Canada, this book provides a historical overview of the origins and development of various federal, provincial, and municipal police forces. Attention is also given to tracing the development of private security and special police agencies.

203. Tallant, Clive.

'The North-West Mounted Police and the Barr Colony.' *Saskatchewan History* 7 (Spring 1954): 41–46.

Tallant sets out to document the role played by the NWMP during the first year (1903–4) of the Barr settlement in Saskatchewan. The settlement had been initiated by the Reverend Issac M. Barr, assisted by Reverend George Exton Lloyd, who promoted emigration to western Canada from the British Isles. Barr had sold land to these settlers sight unseen, and had not provided for their needs on arrival. Eventually he fled to the United States, fearing threats from the angry settlers. Fortunately, the Mountie detachment at nearby Battleford saw to their needs with food and accommodation. The Mounties were well liked and the relative lack of crime in the area allowed them time for social service and welfare duties. The NWMP are described as efficient and considerate. The article is well documented with primary sources, including correspondence and newspaper accounts.

204. Taylor, John Leonard.

'Law and Order and the Military Problem in Assiniboia, 1821–69.' M.A. thesis, Carleton University, 1967.

Prior to 1870, the Hudson's Bay Company retained responsibility for the maintenance of law and order in the colony of Assiniboia. Although crime and lawlessness were not a serious problem in the settlement, threats of disorder stemming from commercial rivalry and dissatisfaction existed throughout the 1830s and 1840s. This thesis examines the provisions made for the maintenance of law and order in the colony from 1821 to 1869. Substantive chapters deal with: (1) the structure of the legal system of Assiniboia, (2) law and order and the working of the courts, (3) law and order and the Metis, (4) the Indians and the military problem, and (5) the breakdown of order in the 1860s. The author maintains that although residents of the colony were generally satisfied with the courts and legal system, they were not satisfied with the volunteer system of policing that was established. This dissatisfaction was reflected in 'the changes made in the provisions for a police force and the repeated demands for a garrison to support the police' that were made during the period.

205. Toner, R.C., and Perrier, D.C.

'Nova Scotia Police.' *RCMP Quarterly* 47 (3, Summer 1982): 33–45.

206. Toronto Metropolitan Police.

A Brief History. Toronto: Toronto Metropolitan Police, 1978.

207. Torrance, Gordon V.

'Hamilton Police Department: Past and Present. The History of Law Enforcement in Hamilton, 1833–1967.' In *A Centennial Profile of the Hamilton Police Department 1867–1967*, pp. 1-68. Hamilton: The Corporation of the City of Hamilton, 1967.

This 68-page illustrated chapter chronicles the history of law enforcement in Hamilton from 1833 to 1967. Particular attention is given to describing the growth of the department and the establishment of new policing facilities in the twentieth century.

208. Torrance, Gordon V.

'The History of Law Enforcement in Hamilton from 1833 to 1967.' *Wentworth Bygones* 7 (1967): 67–78.

This is a condensed version of the author's chapter which appeared in *A Centennial Profile of the Hamilton Police Department* (see entry 207 above).

209. Tousey, S.

The Northwest Mounted Police. Chicago: Rand McNally and Co., 1941.

210. Trainer, Mary D.

A History of Policing in Burnaby, 1892–1950. Burnaby: RCMP, 1975.

Prepared for members of the RCMP Burnaby Detachment in honour of the centennial of the RCMP, this paper deals with the history of policing in Burnaby from its incorporation in 1892 to 1950. Although note is made of the fact that the history of policing in Burnaby can be divided into three distinct periods – (1) Burnaby municipal police to 1935, (2) the British Columbia Provincial Police to 1950, and (3) the RCMP from 1950 to the present – the research material presented deals mainly with the period to 1935. Particular attention is given to chronicling the early development of the Burnaby municipal police force and the types of law enforcement work engaged in by its members. Lengthy extracts from local newspapers, police court records, and the diaries of members of the Burnaby municipal police force are cited.

211. Turmel, Jean.

Police de Montréal: Historique de service, vol. 1, 1796–1909. Montréal: Section de recherche et planification, Service de la police de Montréal, 1971.

This is a lengthy and detailed history of the police and quasi-police forces in Montreal between the years 1796 and 1909. The author researched the Municipal Archives extensively to present budgets, maps, and statistics of the period.

212. Turmel, Jean.

Police de Montréal: Historique de service, vol. 2: 1909–1971. Montréal: Section de recherche et planification, Service de la police de Montréal, 1974.

This study examines the development and organization of the police in Montreal during the period 1909 to 1971. The period covered in the study corresponds to the beginning of an inquiry that resulted in significant changes in police organization (the Canon inquiry of 1909), and the integration of the Montreal police force in the Urban Community of Montreal (1972). Data sources examined include government documents held in municipal archives, trial transcripts, resolutions, statutes, and annual reports of the city treasurer. The author cautions the reader that because of the type of sources used, the study presents only a formal description of the police organization, and that care should be taken in interpreting the information.

213. Turmel, Jean.

'Etude rétrospective de l'organisation du service de police de la cité de Montréal, 1909–1971.' M.A. thesis, Université de Montréal, 1974.

This thesis presents an overview of the organizational development of the Montreal police department since 1909. Relying on primary and secondary sources, the author presents a qualitative analysis of official documents and newspapers pertaining to the department's organization as well as a quantitative study of its human, material, and financial resources. The author examines the relevance of five much debated themes in the historical study of police organizations for the study of the Montreal police department: public control over police services, the independence of police chiefs, the presence of police unions, recruitment problems, and the impact of official inquiries and experts' reports.

214. Turner, C. Frank.

Across the Medicine Line. Toronto: McClelland and Stewart, 1973.

This book describes the confrontations between the Mounties and the Indians in the mid-1800s in the hills of southern Alberta and Saskatchewan. The author relied on personal reminiscences, memoranda, and notes of distinguished Mounties, as well as other archival materials. The book is illustrated with photographs, has maps on the end papers, and has a bibliography.

215. Turner, C. Frank.

'Sitting Bull Tests the Mettle of the Redcoats.' In *Men in Scarlet*, pp. 66–76. Edited by Hugh A. Dempsey. Calgary: McClelland and Stewart West, 1974.

In this chapter Turner surveys the problems presented to the Canadian government and the Mounties by the presence of Sitting Bull and his tribe.

216. Turner, John Peter.

'A Short History of the Force: 1873–1948.' *RCMP Quarterly* 14 (2, October 1948): 56–81.

217. Turner, John Peter.

'When the Mounted Police Went West – Part 1.' *Canadian Geographic Journal* 10 (1, January 1935): 53–61. And 'When the Mounted Police Went West – Part 2.' *Canadian Geographic Journal* 10 (3, March 1935): 107–114.

These two articles provide a romantic and graphic description of the first march west by the Mounties in 1874. Hardships are related in an attempt to establish a clear image of the men and their personal expectations. The physical environment is also portrayed. The articles do not cite primary or secondary materials. Black and white photographs are included.

218. Turner, John Peter.

The North-West Mounted Police 1873–1893, Inclusive of the Great Transition Period in the Canadian West, When Law and Order Were Introduced and Established. 2 vols. Ottawa: King's Printer, 1950.

This two-volume history of the NWMP provides a favourable picture of the origin, establishment, and early work of the force. The origin of the NWMP is seen to have been a result of the efforts of an enlightened and humanitarian government concerned with suppressing the whiskey trade, protecting the Indians, and bringing law and order to the Northwest Territories.

219. Van Houtte, J.C.

Historique du service de police de la ville de Québec. Québec: Service de police de la ville de Québec, 1976.

220. Villa-Arce, Jose.

'Alberta Provincial Police.' *Alberta Historical Review* 21 (4, Autumn 1973): 16–19.

Villa-Arce intends in this article to remind the reader that the Mounties were not the only officers of law enforcement in the West. The RNWMP policed Alberta and Saskatchewan by federal contract to 1917, when wartime demands led the federal government to terminate such contracts. The services of the RNWMP had been an economical means of ensuring law enforcement and Alberta chose to retain many of the disbanded Mountie officers in the new provincial police force. The APP was modelled after the federal predecessor. While the difficulties are not specified, we are told that the first superintendent, a former Mountie, resigned over criticism of the force. Much of the time of the APP was spent in enforcing prohibition legislation, often leading to conflict with municipal forces, who were less diligent in liquor control. Management of labour unrest was also a demanding occupation. In 1932 the RCMP reassumed the contracts for policing Alberta and Saskatchewan, as their aim was to gain a wider mandate and to reduce the financial burden of the provincial governments. This is a survey article and lacks footnotes and bibliography.

221. Waiser, W.A.

The North-West Mounted Police, in 1874–1889: A Statistical Study. Research Bulletin, no. 117. Ottawa: Parks Canada, 1979.

222. Walden, Keith.

'The Symbol and the Myth of the Royal Canadian Mounted Police in Some British, American and English Canadian Popular Literature, 1873–1973.' Ph.D. dissertation, Queen's University, 1980.

This dissertation serves as the basis for the author's 1982 book (see entry 223 below).

223. Walden, Keith.

Visions of Order: The Canadian Mounties in Symbol and Myth. Toronto: Butterworth, 1982.

Walden's book explores the image of the RCMP reflected in British, American, and English-Canadian popular literature during the first century of the force's existence. He contends that on viewing the force, its admirers saw not an objective reality which actually existed, but rather a symbol which they themselves moulded to suit their own anxieties and concerns. He maintains that by understanding what admirers said about the force, something can be learned about the age in which they lived. Specifically, Walden attempts to show that many Britons, Americans, and Canadians saw in the Mounted Police a reflection of values and desires of their own age, such as honesty, integrity, courage, strength, compassion, and intelligence. In an age of unsettling changes, the disappearance of faith in God, and the steady growth of relativism in science, the Mounted Police also came to symbolize 'the indisputable progress of mankind, of the possibility of an escape from the evils of urban, industrial society to the serenity and health of God's wilderness, and of the existence of a just and harmonious order which permeated all civilization.'

224. Ward, L.H.

'The Growth and Progress of the RCMP Fingerprint Bureau.' *RCMP Quarterly* 21 (2, October 1955): 93–101.

225. Warner, I.

'One Hundred Proud Years: Royal Canadian Mounted Police.' *Alaska* 39 (11, November 1973): 18–

226. Wellman, G.V.

'The Recruit: Half a Century Ago.' *RCMP Quarterly* 38 (4, 1973): 45–50.

In this article, a retired RCMP officer recalls his experience as a recruit training at Regina in 1923.

227. Whittingham, M.D.

'The Evolution of the Public Police – A Social History.' *Canadian Police Chief* 70 (2, 4, Spring and Summer 1981): 27–29, 67–70.

228. Young, David John.

'The Vancouver City Police Force, 1886–1914.' B.A. essay, University of British Columbia, 1976.

The prominent national role played by the federal police since 1873 has meant that most of the literature on law and order or police work generally has focused on the RCMP. However, another institution which played an important role in stabilizing social conduct and settling early areas of unrest in Canada was the municipal police force. This essay explores the history and role of the Vancouver City Police Force during the early years of the development of the city. Divided into three chapters, the essay provides: (1) a concise account of the early history of the force, (2) a discussion of the administrative problems confronted by police boards and chief constables, and (3) a brief examination of the law enforcement work and types of crime dealt with by the police. From his preliminary analysis of available source materials, which include Board of Police Incoming Correspondence (1905–16), Police Commission Minutebooks (1908–20), and City Council Minutes (from 1886), the author concludes that during its first years of existence the Vancouver police force was more concerned with the regulation of public behaviour than with internal reform, and that it remained fundamentally unchanged for over two decades.

229. Young, Delbert A.

The Mounties. Toronto: Hodder and Stoughton, 1968.

This book covers events in the history of the RCMP from the march west in 1874, through RCMP relations with the Indians, the Riel Rebellion and the Yukon gold rush, up to more contemporary activities and achievements of the force such as narcotics control and the Igor Gouzenko affair. The bibliography cites only secondary source material.

2

Crime, Deviance, and Dependency

230. Allen, Richard.

'The Crest and Crisis of the Social Gospel in Canada, 1916–1927.' Ph.D. dissertation, Duke University, 1967.

Although Allen's pioneering study of the social gospel reform movement in Canada is more concerned with examining the impact the movement had in moulding the attitudes of labour, it also deals with the prohibition movement in Canada. In the chapter devoted to prohibition, the author indicates the leading role played by social gospel reformers in the crusade for temperance and prohibition in central and western Canada.

231. Allen, Richard.

'The Social Gospel and the Reform Tradition in Canada, 1890–1928.' *Canadian Historical Review* 49 (4, December 1968): 381–399. Also in *Prophecy and Protest: Social Movements in Twentieth Century Canada*, pp. 45–61. Edited by Samuel D. Clark, J. Paul Grayson, and Linda M. Grayson. Toronto: Gage, 1975.

A sizeable movement of reform was abroad in Canada from the 1890s to the 1930s. Underlying and accompanying various organized attempts at bringing about the reform of society through the political system was the social gospel, a movement which functioned to forge links between proposed reforms and the religious heritage of the nation. This article examines the development, success, and eventual decline of the social gospel movement in Canada. Attention is given to exploring the premises on which it was based, the impetus it gave to reform efforts aimed at dealing with urban social problems and concerns such as poverty, immigration, and prohibition, and the reasons why it began to lose support in the 1920s.

232. Allen, Richard.

'The Triumph and Decline of Prohibition.' In *Documentary Problems in Canadian History*, vol. 1: *Post-Confederation*, pp. 185–188. Edited by J.M. Bumstead. Georgetown, Ont.: Irwin-Dorsey, 1969.

233. Andrieux, Jean-Pierre.

Prohibition and St. Pierre: When Distillers and Rum Runners Made France's Colony off Newfoundland a Principal Centre for the Liquor Trade. Lincoln, Ont.: W.F. Rannie, 1983.

The author examines the history of alcohol-smuggling in the Atlantic provinces and St. Pierre and Miquelon during the prohibition era of the twentieth century.

234. Anonymous.

'Une affaire criminelle au début de la Nouvelle France.' *Bullet des recherches historiques* 50 (8, August 1945): 396–398.

This is a brief account of a conspiracy to kill Samuel de Champlain in 1608 to which Champlain himself devoted several pages in his diaries. The four conspirators were Basque fishermen who feared the loss of their business as a result of the French implantation in their territory. The chief conspirator, Jean Duval, was hanged and his head was prominently displayed.

235. Aultman, Madeline G., and Wright, Kevin N.

'The Fairness Paradigm: An Evaluation of Change in Juvenile Justice.' *Canadian Journal of Criminology* 24 (1, January 1982): 13–24.

In this article, the authors apply the model of paradigm evolution developed by Thomas Kuhn in order to analyse shifts in prevailing ideology with respect to juvenile justice philosophy and policy. Relying on this approach, the authors trace the historical shift from a 'reformative paradigm' (exemplified in the *Juvenile Delinquents Act* of 1908 and the early operation of the juvenile court) to a 'fairness paradigm' (exemplified in more recent efforts made to reform the juvenile justice system to afford young offenders more adequate procedural safeguards).

236. Babcock, Kathy.

'The Development and Implementation of the Juvenile Delinquents Act of 1908: A Study in Social Policy Formation.' Graduate essay, Carleton University, School of Social Work, 1977.

This research paper provides a critical analysis of the development and implementation of the *Juvenile Delinquents Act* (1908), within the socio-economic context of the late nineteenth and early twentieth centuries. In separate chapters, the author examines: Marxist theories of the state and social welfare, socio-economic conditions in Canada from 1880 to 1908, the importance of 'new ideologies' and the 'child saving' movement in the development of the *Juvenile Delinquents Act*, the implementation of the legislation, and the effect of the legislation on the treatment of juvenile delinquents from 1908 to 1936. The author concludes that the 1908 juvenile delinquency legislation provided the dominant class – via the state – with a vehicle for securing existing social and economic arrangements through the integration of working-class children into established social order.

237. Bain, Ian.

'The Role of J.J. Kelso in the Launching of the Child Welfare Movement in Ontario.' M.S.W. thesis, University of Toronto, 1955.

238. Baker, Walter.

'The Place of the Private Agency in the Administration of Government Policies; A Case Study: The Ontario Children's Aid System, 1893–1965.' Ph.D. dissertation, Queen's University, 1966.

239. Balikci, Asen.

'Female Infanticide of the Arctic Coast.' In *Perspectives on the North American Indians*, pp. 176–189. Edited by Mark Nagler. Toronto: McClelland and Stewart, 1972.

240. Barron, F.L.

'The Genesis of Temperance in Ontario, 1828–1850.' Ph.D. dissertation, University of Guelph, 1976.

241. Barron, F.L.

'The American Origins of the Temperance Movement in Ontario, 1828–1850.' *Canadian Review of American Studies* 11 (2, Fall 1980): 131–150.

Mid-nineteenth-century Ontario saw the emergence of several temperance crusades. This article shows that temperance became a political cause at the instigation of the Ontario middle class, who derived inspiration and support from similar temperance crusades in the United States. The article draws on the writings of mid-nineteenth-century temperance advocates and related secondary sources, which are examined in more detail in the author's 1976 Ph.D. thesis (see entry 240 above).

242. Bartlett, W.

'Prohibition in Newfoundland.' Unpublished manuscript. Maritime History Collection, Memorial University, n.d.

In 1915 the people of Newfoundland voted in a plebiscite to prohibit the importation, manufacture, and sale of alcoholic beverages. Two years later the province's *Prohibition Plebiscite Act* was passed. In 1924, the *Prohibition Act* of 1917 was repealed and the

Alcoholic Liquor Act was brought into being. Drawing exclusively on primary historical documents, this paper examines the background leading up to the 1915 plebiscite, the enforcement of the *Prohibition Plebiscite Act* from 1917 to 1924, and the reasons underlying the repeal of the act within a decade after its enactment. The major reason cited for the repeal of the 1917 act was the growing realization among politicians and law enforcement officials that it was impossible to enforce prohibition laws.

243. Bate, J.P.

'Prohibition and the U.F.A.' *Alberta Historical Review* 18 (4, Autumn 1970): 1–6.

Bate attempts to account for the rise of the prohibition movement in Alberta and the reasons why it was supported by the United Farmers of Alberta. The author maintains that the efforts of various temperance organizations to do away with 'the evils of drink' coincided closely with the UFA's objective of 'promoting, fostering, and advancing the moral, material, financial and business interests' of Alberta farmers. This connection, combined with other circumstances, justified the UFA's support for 'the campaign for a dry Alberta.'

244. Bator, Paul Adolphus.

'"The Struggle to Raise the Lower Classes": Public Health Reform and the Problem of Poverty in Toronto, 1910–1921.' *Journal of Canadian Studies* 14 (Spring 1979): 43–49.

245. Beattie, John.

Attitudes towards Crime and Punishment in Upper Canada, 1830–1850: A Documentary Study. Toronto: University of Toronto, Centre of Criminology, 1977.

Although serious crime was not a problem in Upper Canada in the 1830s and 1840s, Upper Canadians perceived crime to be a serious problem and devoted considerable public discussion to criminal behaviour and its punishment. Beattie's study, which consists of an introductory essay followed by a series of documents extracted mainly from newspapers and provincial legislative journals, is designed to exemplify the attitudes towards crime and punishment expressed by Upper Canadians, and illuminate the reasons underlying the striking departure in penal practice that took place in the period from 1830 to 1850. The documents included in the volume are arranged around five broad themes: the origins and nature of crime, the debate on capital punishment, the problem of local gaols, the origins of Kingston Penitentiary, 1835–49, and the Brown Commission, 1848–9. Drawing on these sources, Beattie argues that in the 1830s criminality came to be viewed as 'evidence of much deeper and more serious evils ... that threatened the moral and social fabric of society, and that called for powerful measures of defence.' This conviction, according to Beattie, underlay a number of striking changes in criminal law and in penal practice in Upper Canada, the most significant being the establishment of the penitentiary at Kingston in 1835.

246. Beaupré, Henri.

'La délinquance juvenile à Québec.' *Culture* 14 (1953): 385–405.

In this article, Beaupré sets out to re-examine Everett C. Hughes's argument that the parish system, which is typical of Quebec City and which is absent in almost all American cities, constitutes an exemplary model for the study of juvenile delinquency. In this effort, Beaupré undertakes a study of delinquents of Quebec City, their families, and their environment. In order to determine if the observations of foreign scholars on delinquency are applicable to Quebec City, the author retraces the origin of the juvenile court in the United States, Europe, and Canada, and reviews what are thought to be the principal causes of delinquency, particularly in urban areas. Attention is then turned to a study of the growth and actual composition of the population of Quebec City, the characteristics of its parish system, and federal and provincial legislation concerning juvenile delinquency that existed prior to the creation of the juvenile court in Quebec City.

247. Bédard-Lévesque, Claire.

'La tempérance au Québec.' M.A. thesis, Université Laval, 1980.

The author is interested in finding out how, under the influence of the clergy, the temperance movement developed in the Catholic French-Canadian environment of the province of Quebec in the nineteenth and early twentieth centuries. Her main focus is on examining the propaganda used by the clergy to convince the people of the need for temperance, and showing how the temperance movement came to be accepted. The author presents a historical account of the three main crusades which occurred in Quebec and of the organization of the temperance societies. This account shows that although the temperance movement was initiated by religious people, on the eve of the First World War it was taken over by lay reformers. She then describes the oral and written forms of temperance propaganda used by the clergy. In addition to the direct use of school instruction to convince youth of the evils of intemperance, more subtle ways of influencing popular attitudes towards alcohol, such as songs and images (paintings), permitted the movement to render its message accessible to the whole population. The thesis is based mainly on secondary sources.

248. Bedford, Judy.

'Prostitution in Calgary, 1905–1914.' *Alberta History* 29 (2, Spring 1981): 1–11.

This paper examines the manner in which prostitution, as 'the oldest profession of crime,' was dealt with by law enforcement agencies in Calgary from 1905 to 1914. The author identifies two distinct periods within this time frame, the first – from 1905 to 1909 – in which prostitution was apparently openly recognized and tolerated, and the second – from 1910 to 1914 – in which a more concerted effort was made to rid the city of 'the vices caused by rapid urbanization, liquor, drugs, and prostitution.' Despite the efforts of social reformers to find a solution to the 'moral problem' of prostitution – which was linked directly to intemperance – the author concludes that 'western Canadians of the early twentieth century achieved no more success than had their predecessors.'

249. Bellomo, J. Jerald.

'Upper Canadian Attitudes towards Crime and Punishment (1832–1851).' *Ontario History* 64 (March 1972): 11–26.

The article discusses general attitudes towards law and order as revealed in contemporary newspapers and government documents, thereby offering a broad spectrum of Upper Canadian opinion on crime and punishment. Evidence is put forth to show that in the early decades of the nineteenth century Upper Canadians were generally lenient in their attitudes towards crimes of violence such as assault. With the influx of immigrants to the province in the 1830s this attitude changed dramatically, and a collective alarm permeated society over the great 'increase in crime' that had supposedly taken place. According to Bellomo's account, the apparent breakdown in law and order in Upper Canada during the 1830s was seen to stem from a distinct 'criminal class' composed largely of immigrants who did not share the dominant value system of society, lacked proper moral and religious principles, and were prone to intemperance and idleness. As well as pointing to what were considered to be the 'major causes of crime' in Upper Canada, the article examines the 'intense debate' which ensued in the province over the question of how individual offenders were to be dealt with. Basic penological theories on the purpose of punishment in vogue during the 1830s and 1840s are discussed and the views of prominent Upper Canadian penal reformers are considered. According to the author, the chief unifying factor among penal reformers during the 1830s and 1840s was their emphasis on the need to bring about the 'reformation' of criminals by teaching them proper moral and religious principles and the virtue of hard work and discipline. Ultimately, the aim of the penal reform movement in the province, according to Bellomo, was to instil the social values of the dominant group in society in the criminal population, and thus re-establish law and order in the province.

250. Bertrand, Réal.

'L'affaire Blanche Garneau.' *Revue d'ethnologie du Québec* 6 (1, 1980): 21–34.

In 1954, 34 years after the incident, the case of the young Blanche Garneau, murdered at age 20, whose body was discovered on July 28, 1920, in Victoria Park in the city of Quebec, still occupies the top place in the judicial annals of the province. An extremely long investigation by the coroner and an inquiry on discovery revealed absolutely nothing. The preliminary hearing of two accused, their sensational trial, and their subsequent acquittal made the headlines of the newspapers in the province. Certain rumours link the murder to sons of influential political figures, and several questions on the case were asked by the leader of the opposition in the legislative assembly. The unsolved murder is likely to remain famous and unique in the history of crime in Canada.

251. Birrell, A.J.

'D.I.K. Rine and the Gospel Temperance Movement in Canada.' *Canadian Historical Review* 58 (1, March 1977): 23–42.

The Gospel Temperance movement was one of the many temperance movements founded in the United States and Canada in the mid- nineteenth century. Its leader, Francis Murphy, attracted numerous followers, who, moved by his evangelical approach, pledged to abstain from drinking alcohol. David Isaac Kirwin Rine, an alcoholic and ex-convict, was one of Murphy's leading disciples. In 1877 Rine accepted an offer to 'commence the work of the Gospel Temperance movement' in St. Catharines and Toronto. This article examines Rine's career as leader of the Gospel Temperance movement in Canada. It attempts to account for Rine's amazing success in attracting followers during his first two years in Canada, and the circumstances that led to the movement's equally sudden decline. The author maintains that Rine's support was seriously undermined by his being arrested and placed on trial for indecently assaulting a 15-year-old girl. Although he was eventually acquitted, the psychological impact of the trial on Rine, and the refusal of followers to forgive him for his moral 'indiscretion,' apparently contributed to the movement's decline.

252. Bizier, Hélène-Andrée.

Crimes et châtiments: La petite histoire du crime au Québec. Nouv. édition [Montréal]: Libre Expression, 1983.

253. Blackwell, John D.

'Crime in the London District, 1828–1837: A Case Study of the Effect of the 1833 Reform in Upper Canadian Penal Law.' *Queen's Law Journal* 6 (2, Spring 1981): 528–567.

In 1833 major reforms in the criminal law of Upper Canada were enacted. The new legislation reduced the number of crimes punishable by capital punishment, abolished the privilege of the benefit of clergy, and made other alterations to certain criminal proceedings before and after conviction. This study examines the background to and outcome of the 1833 reform in Upper Canadian penal law. In establishing the background to reform, the author describes the English system of criminal law formally introduced into Upper Canada in 1800, provincial modifications to the law in the early nineteenth century, and the influences that affected the movement towards penal reform in Upper Canada prior to 1833. The outcome of the 1833 reform in Upper Canadian penal law is then subjected to preliminary investigation through a case study of the administration of justice in the London District between 1828 and 1837. Relying mainly on the 'Returns of the Sessions of Oyer and Terminer and General Gaol Delivery for King's Bench' (also known as the assizes) the author attempts to establish the impact that the penal reform of 1833 had on the type of punishment meted out to convicted offenders. Findings indicate that while prior to 1833 the harsh English criminal law was not enforced in Upper Canada for many petty offenders, the court followed a strict interpretation of serious offences. After 1833, there was a definite change in the punishment of serious crime, with offenders, formerly subject to execution, instead being sentenced to terms of imprisonment. The author concludes that, at least in the case of the London District, the Upper Canadian penal law reform of 1833, which was accompanied by the establishment of the penitentiary, brought about real and long-overdue changes in the system of criminal punishment.

254. Blain, Jean.

'La moralité en Nouvelle-France: Les phases de la thèse de l'antithèse.' *Revue d'histoire de l'Amérique française* 27 (3, December 1973): 408–416.

Some of the early history books have tried to idealize the colonial society of New France and tried to create an image of virtue, piety, and heroism, of conduct conforming to the precepts of religion and law. The same tendency still persists in some of the more recent books. The article is a critique of these books focusing on three of them: (1) Gustave Lanctot's book *Filles du joie ou Filles du Roi, étude sur l'émigration féminine en Nouvelle-France*, published in 1952; (2) Silvio Dumas's book *Les Filles du Roi en Nouvelle-France: Etude historique avec répertoire biographique*, published in 1972; and (3) Robert- Lionel Séguin's book *La vie libertine en Nouvelle-France au dix-septième siècle*, published in 1972.

255. Blais Hildebrand, Ghislaine.

'Les débuts du movement de tempérance dans le Bas-Canada: 1828–1840.' M.A. thesis, McGill University, 1975.

Referring to newspapers and other temperance publications, this paper attempts to understand the rise of the temperance movement in Lower-Canada from 1828. The author studies (1) the consumption and the social function of alcoholic beverages as well as the groups who became the objects of the corrective fervour, (2) the formation of the first temperance societies and the role played by the church within, and (3) the main lines of propaganda directed towards the inculcation of sobriety and to the development of a bourgeois conscience among drinkers and vendors of alcoholic intoxicants. The author concludes that the temperance movement appears as an attempt on the part of the dominant culture to create a social climate more favourable to production and to bring under its control an aspect of popular behaviour which it felt threatening.

256. Bliss, Michael.

'A Living Profit: Studies in the Social History of Canadian Business, 1883–1911.' Ph.D. dissertation, University of Toronto, 1972.

Using business journals, government investigations, and private papers, this dissertation explores the collective response of the business community to major problems arising from business life and outlines its perceptions of the relations of business to the wider Canadian community. According to the author, during the last two decades of the nineteenth century, competition was viewed as 'the greatest hazard of business life.' Increasingly in the 1880s, businessmen responded to this 'hazard' by entering into price-fixing agreements, combinations, trade associations, mergers, and attempts to establish legislative restrictions on competition. He concludes that the weak anti-combines policy of Canadian governments during the period 'reflected political concurrence in the right of businessmen to combine together to achieve a "living profit".'

257. Bliss, Michael.

'"Pure Books on Avoided Subjects": Pre-Freudian Sexual Ideas in Canada.' In *Studies in Canadian Social History*, pp. 326–346. Edited by Michiel Horn and Ronald Sabourin. Toronto: McClelland and Stewart, 1974.

Books purporting to contain facts and wisdom about human sexuality were widely read in late-Victorian and Edwardian Canada. The major concerns addressed in these so-called self and sex books were also taken up by leading Canadian 'purity reformers,' who lectured widely on such 'evils' as masturbation, premarital sex, and excessive sexual indulgence. This paper attempts to outline the fundamental ideas expressed in self and sex books of the late nineteenth and early twentieth centuries, and explain the background of these ideas in North American medical and popular thought. Note is made of the fact that leading North American purity reformers believed that destructive sexual practices were most common among the lower classes of society, in particular, the class of ungodly, intemperate, dishonest, and law-breaking individuals who filled up almshouses, asylums, prisons, and reformatory institutions.

258. Boyd, Neil.

'The Dilemma of Canadian Narcotics Legislation: The Social Control of Altered States of Consciousness.' *Contemporary Crises* 7 (July 1983): 257–269.

Boyd contends that 'in a society that has an amused tolerance for the ritual of alcoholic excess, the criminalization of other modes of consciousness alteration' appears rather paradoxical. Given this seeming paradox, the author undertakes a critical examination of the origins of Canadian narcotics legislation in the late nineteenth and early twentieth centuries. His findings lend support to the need for further interpretation of the reasons underlying the emergence of such legislation, and the continuing efforts being made to control narcotic-induced altered states of consciousness.

259. Boyd, Neil.

'The Origins of Canadian Narcotics Legislation: The Process of Criminalization in Historical Context.' *Dalhousie Law Journal* 8 (January 1984): 102–136.

260. Boyer, Raymond.

Les crimes et les châtiments au Canada français du XVIIe au XXe siècle. Montréal: Cercle du livre de France, 1966.

This book is a study of crime and punishment in French Canada from the seventeenth to the twentieth century. The book is divided into eight chapters. Chapter 1 deals with the laws from ancient times to the English regime, reviewing successively the laws of France, England, the influence of the thinkers of the eighteenth century, the Indians, the Eskimos, and the laws in New France. Chapter 2 is a historical review of the death penalty from ancient times to the time of French rule in New France, the offences that were punishable by death, the views of the philosophers of the eighteenth century, and the history of abolition. In Chapter 3 the author examines other punishments: corporal punishments, monetary penalties, banishment, transportation, and so on. Chapter 4 is a study of the executioner in history, in New France and under the English regime. Chapter 5 is a historical study of torture in Greece, Rome, France, England, and Canada. Chapter 6 is a study of sorcery and witchcraft in the old and new worlds, among the Eskimos and the Indians, and among Canadians. Chapter 7 is a historical study of crime in New France, examining offences against morality, against the state, and against religion. The final chapter is a study of the history of prisons in Rome, France, England, the United States, New France, and under the English regime in Canada before and after Confederation.

261. Bradbury, Bettina.

'The Fragmented Family: Family Strategies in the Face of Death, Illness and Poverty, Montreal, 1860–1885.' In *Childhood in Canadian History*, pp. 109–128. Edited by Joy Parr. Toronto: McClelland and Stewart, 1982.

Working-class families in mid- to late-nineteenth-century Montreal lived in fairly constant contact with disease, poverty, and death. With the advent of industrial capitalism, and the increasing dependence of families upon an uncertain and very seasonal labour market, keeping a family sheltered, clothed, healthy, and together was a difficult task. This article examines the strategies employed by Montreal working-class parents in order to cope in difficult times. These strategies included the abandonment of newborn babies and the permanent or short-term placement of children in city orphanages. Particular attention is given to discussing the role played by the Catholic church in operating orphanages and caring for abandoned children.

262. Brooking, Lucy W.

'Prostitution in Toronto, 1911.' In *The Proper Sphere: Women's Place in Canadian Society*, pp. 241–249. Edited by Ramsay Cook and Wendy Mitchinson. Toronto: Oxford University Press, 1976.

263. Buckley, Suzann, and McGinnis, Janice Dickin.

'Venereal Disease and Public Health Reform in Canada.' *Canadian Historical Review* 63 (3, September 1982): 337–354.

In Canada, the so-called social hygiene campaign originated in the urban-reform movements of the late nineteenth century. During that period urban reformers increasingly stressed the need for measures to deal with such urban-associated ills as infant mortality and the vice of prostitution. Prior to 1914, however, none of the urban-reform campaigns centred on venereal disease. This article examines the reasons underlying the growing concern with venereal disease among Canadians overseas and at home after 1914, and the measures taken to prevent its spread. Note is made of the fact that in Canada much of the work was directed against prostitutes and 'loose women,' who, according to middle-class reformers, 'sacrificed themselves for mercenary or physical gain.' The authors maintain that 'because prostitutes and loose women had been regarded as the main source of infection,' reformers of the period from 1914 to 1935 viewed venereal disease as being inseparable from immorality.

264. Burnet, J.R.

'The Urban Community and Changing Moral Standards.' In *Studies in Canadian Social History*, pp. 298–325. Edited by Michiel Horn and Ronald Sabourin. Toronto: McClelland and Stewart, 1974.

This article traces the 'advance' and 'retreat' of temperance and sabbatarian reform movements in Toronto from the 1830s to the 1950s. Attention is given to examining the rise of temperance and Sabbath observance movements in the 1830s, the ethnic, religious, and political affiliations of leading Toronto-based moral reformers, the puritanical reputation Toronto gained during the nineteenth century, and the reasons for the decline in popular support for temperance and sabbatarian organizations and activities after the 1930s. The author maintains that although Toronto served as 'a centre for moral reform movements' for more than 130 years, by the 1950s previously staunch middle-class supporters had 'ceased to uphold themselves and to impose upon others with fervour the norms of temperance and sabbatarianism.'

265. Butt, William Davison.

'The Donnellys: History, Legend, Literature.' Ph.D. dissertation, University of Western Ontario, 1977.

The story of the murder of five members of the Donnelly family of Biddulph Township, Ontario, in 1880 has become widely known through popular histories, novels, dramas, songs, and movies based on the sensational case. However, there has been little scholarly research into the history of the Donnelly family and the events which led to the murder of five of its members. This dissertation attempts to develop a more accurate account of the lives of the Donnellys and the factors that precipitated their being murdered at the hands of their neighbours. The author approaches this task by undertaking an investigation of the factual accuracy of popular and fictional accounts of the case found in private lore, history and literature, newspapers, plays, and songs and movies.

266. Carter, John.

'Temperance and Local Opinion in Bruce and Grey Counties: A Summary of Events and Reactions up to 1916.' *Bruce County Historical Society Yearbook* (1976): 21–25.

267. Chapman, J.K.

'The Mid-Nineteenth Century Temperance Movement in New Brunswick and Maine.' *Canadian Historical Review* 35 (March 1954): 43–60. Also in *Canadian History before Confederation – Essays and Interpretations*, pp. 444–461. Edited by J.M. Bumstead. Georgetown, Ont.: Irwin-Dorsey, 1972.

The attempt to introduce temperance into New Brunswick aroused considerable political controversy. Although having begun as a religious movement of moral reform, during the 1840s and early 1850s the New Brunswick temperance movement became a powerful political force seeking to impose its will on the community. This article examines the connection linking temperance campaigns in New Brunswick and Maine. The author maintains that while a provincial temperance society had been established in New Brunswick in 1830, two years before the founding of a state temperance society in Maine, it was from Maine that provincial advocates of enforced abstinence drew much of their inspiration and support.

268. Chapman, Terry L.

'Drug Use in Western Canada.' *Alberta History* 24 (4, Autumn 1976): 18–27.

269. Chapman, Terry L.

'"The Drug Problem" in Western Canada, 1900–1920.' M.A. thesis, University of Calgary, 1976.

While studies of early-twentieth-century western Canadian social history have concentrated upon the impact of prostitution and prohibition on society, the equally prevalent social vice of opium usage has largely been ignored. In an attempt to compensate for this gap in historical knowledge, the author undertakes an analysis of 'the problem of opium abuse' in western Canada from 1900 to 1920. As seen by early-twentieth-century social reformers, 'opium abuse formed the tip of a pyramid that had as its two foundations, alcohol and prostitution.' Consequently, Chapman argues that as reformers came to demand an end to deviance in moral behaviour, success was dependent upon legislation of morality on three fronts. Through her analysis of attempts made to deal with the opium problem in western Canada, the author demonstrates that while the anti-drug crusade which swept the West in the early twentieth century ended in a dismal failure, the movement none the less instilled in the Canadian public a firm belief in the legislation of morality.

270. Chapman, Terry L.

'Drug Usage and the Victoria Daily Colonist: The Opium Smokers of Western Canada.' In Louis A. Knafla, ed., Canadian Society for Legal History, *Proceedings*, 1977, pp. 60–75.

271. Chapman, Terry L.

'The Anti-Drug Crusade in Western Canada, 1885–1925.' In *Law and Society in Canada in Historical Perspective*, pp. 89–116. Edited by D.J. Bercuson and Louis A. Knafla. Calgary: University of Calgary, 1979.

Considered as part of a broader Anglo-Saxon middle-class social- reform movement, this paper traces the growth and outcome of the anti-drug crusade in western Canada from the mid-1880s to the mid-1920s. Although temperance and the demand for prohibition formed the basis of the western Canadian reform movement, moral reformers campaigned vigorously for the enactment of federal legislation making the non-medical use of drugs a criminal offence. The government reacted to the reformers' demands during the period by enacting anti-drug legislation in 1908, and periodically amending the legislation in response to public pressure. Chapman concludes that although the efforts of reformers acted to encourage a belief in the legislation of morality, in practical terms the reform movement was a dismal failure.

272. Chapman, Terry L.

'The Measurement of Crime in Nineteenth-Century Canada: Some Methodological and Philosophical Problems.' In *Crime and Criminal Justice in Europe and Canada*, pp. 147–156. Edited by Louis A. Knafla. Waterloo, Ont.: Wilfrid Laurier University Press, 1981.

The historian who studies the history of crime in nineteenth-century Canada immediately confronts a multitude of problems, one of the more complex being that of deciding the most appropriate approach to adopt (i.e., sociological, historical, legal, or interdisciplinary). In this article, the author maintains that in order to add greater dimension to the study of crime in Canada, sociologists, historians, and lawyers should break through the invisible barriers that exist between the fields, and thereby broaden the parameters of their respective disciplines. In particular she contends that the writings of E.P. Thompson, *Whigs and Hunters: The Origin of the Black Act* (1975), and Douglas Hay, 'Property,

Authority and the Criminal Law' in *Albion's Fatal Tree* (1975), suggest the need for further study of crime in nineteenth-century Canada. Citing illustrative Canadian data, the author points out possible areas where studies that parallel those of Thompson and Hay could be undertaken in the Canadian context.

273. Chapman, Terry L.

'"An Oscar Wilde Type": "The Abominable Crime of Buggery" in Western Canada, 1890–1920.' In *Criminal Justice History: An International Annual*, pp. 97–118. Westport, CT.: Meckler Publishing, 1983.

This article attempts to place Canadian social and legal attitudes towards homosexuality in a historical context. The author argues that late–nineteenth-century Canadian attitudes towards acts of sodomy, buggery, and bestiality as sinful, immoral, and perverse were influenced by the publicity which surrounded the trials of Oscar Wilde during the mid-1890s in England. Through examining reported legal cases, police records, gaol reports, and newspaper accounts, the author establishes that while 'unnatural' sex acts were fairly common in western Canada in the period from 1890 to 1920, society made few attempts to come to some understanding of the Oscar Wildes in Canada, particularly in the West. Instead, homosexual encounters between males were viewed as abominable crimes, and prosecuted under the law.

274. Charbonneau, Jean-Pierre.

La filière canadienne. Montréal: Editions de l'homme, 1975.

Written by a reporter working at the time for the French-Canadian newspaper *Le Devoir*, this book is a journalistic account of organized crime in the Province of Quebec. The author relates the history, the origins, and the development of organized crime in the province, focusing on both individual members and families. A 17-page name index is provided. The book was subsequently published in English as *The Canadian Connection*, translated from the French by James Stewart (Montreal: Optimum Publishing, 1976).

275. Charland, Roger.

'Le meurtre à Montréal de 1944 à 1975: Une étude descriptive.' M.Sc. thesis, Université de Montréal, 1976.

Inspired by the cartographic techniques of the Chicago ecological school, this study provides a spatial and temporal description of the occurrence of homicides on the territory of the Island of Montreal. The author relies on first-hand police information regarding 769 homicides committed during a period of 32 years and secondary sources in an attempt to relate homicides to violent criminality, police strength, and related laws, and to compare Montreal homicide rates with those of a few other large North American cities. The author

(1) concludes that no specific pattern of homicide distribution seems to prevail although a movement of eccentric dispersion related to the growing urbanization of the territory was observed, and (2) comments on the relatively low extent of this phenomenon on the Island of Montreal.

276. Chase, Myrtle L.

'Edmund Ward and the Temperance.' *Nova Scotia Historical Quarterly*, Special Supplement (1975): 19–36.

277. Christian, Timothy J.

'The Mentally Ill and Human Rights in Alberta: A Study of the Alberta Sexual Sterilization Act.' Unpublished manuscript, Faculty of Law, University of Alberta, n.d.

In 1927 the government of Alberta introduced the *Alberta Sexual Sterilization Act*. The statute remained in effect in the province until its repeal in 1972. This study attempts to elucidate the historical events underlying the introduction of the 1927 legislation and to determine how the act was administered. Contemporary newspaper reports and archival materials are relied upon to sketch the historical events leading up to the passage of the act. Individual patient file cards developed by the Eugenics Board, appointed to decide on cases in which sexual sterilization would be carried out, are used as a data source for the statistical analysis of criteria that influenced the manner in which the act was administered. According to the author's findings, much of the impetus underlying the enactment of Alberta's sexual sterilization statute stemmed from the then accepted belief that allowing 'mentally defective' persons to produce offspring would contribute to increased criminality, vice, and pauperism. From his statistical analysis of individual patient file cards kept over a 43-year period, the author found that several factors, including the sex and age of the patient, psychiatric diagnosis, occupation, ethnic background, and marital status, influenced the Eugenics Board in deciding which individuals would be approved for sterilization and actually sterilized. He concludes that the *Alberta Sexual Sterilization Act* was an 'abhorrent statute' which was based on scientifically unsound principles, and which led to the blatant infringement of basic human rights.

278. Clemens, James M.

'Taste Not; Touch Not; Handle Not; A Study of the Social Assumptions of the Temperance Literature and Temperance Supporters in Canada West between 1839 and 1859.' *Ontario History* 64 (3, September 1972): 142–160.

There were 1990 inns and taverns in Canada West in 1851. In these drinking establishments, Upper Canadian men, women, and children consumed an average of three gallons of whiskey a year. While many Upper Canadians living in the mid-nineteenth century were consumers of alcohol, many others viewed drinking as a social evil and organized themselves into temperance societies aimed at discouraging the practice. This paper examines the social assumptions underlying the efforts of temperance workers in Upper Canada in the period 1839 to 1859. In his attempt to shed light on the social position of reformers and the methods used to discourage drinking, the author examines a wide range of temperance literature, including newspaper and magazine articles and editorials, published sermons, and pamphlets. From this examination he concludes that temperance workers of the 1840s and 1850s assumed that it was largely members of the 'poorer classes' who were guilty of drinking in excess, and who needed to be reformed.

279. Cook, Shirley Jane.

'Canadian Narcotics Legislation, 1908–1923: A Conflict Model Interpretation.' *Canadian Review of Sociology and Anthropology* 6 (1969): 36–46. Reprinted with epilogue under author name Shirley J. Small in *Law and Social Control in Canada*, pp. 28–43. Edited by William K. Greenaway and Stephen L. Brickey. Scarborough, Ont.: Prentice-Hall, 1978.

This article seeks to determine the properties of Canadian social structure which account for the decision made in the 1920s to label narcotic drug users as criminals, and to explain why a very punitive law was adopted to repress what was a relatively minor social problem. The author maintains that the emergence of Canadian narcotics legislation, which made drug addiction a crime, can best be explained in terms of a 'conflict model' of society, which stresses that punitive laws reflect the outcome of conflict between 'superordinates' who have the power to make and enforce rules and 'subordinates' whose behaviour violates those rules. In support of this theoretical model, the author presents historical evidence which indicates that while early Canadian narcotics legislation could have been directed at eliminating the widespread prescription and use of narcotics by doctors and ordinary citizens, it was in effect directed at Chinese opium dealers, who were members of a subordinate group in society. The author concludes that the discriminatory labelling of Chinese opium users as deviants and criminals reflected three properties of the Canadian social structure: (1) the prevailing stratification order, (2) the prevailing cultural attitudes and beliefs, and (3) the existence of interracial conflict.

280. Cook, Shirley Jane.

'Variations in Response to Illegal Drug Use: A Comparative Study of Official Narcotic Drug Policies in Canada, Great Britain, and the United States from 1920–1970.' M.Phil. thesis, University of Toronto, 1970.

281. Cooper, J.

'Red Lights of Winnipeg.' *Transactions of the Historical and Scientific Society of Manitoba*, Series 3 (29, 1972–3): 61–74.

282. Coulter, Rebecca.

'Alberta's Department of Neglected Children, 1909–1929: A Case Study in Child Saving.'
M.Ed. thesis, University of Alberta, 1977.

Child saving, or the care and protection of neglected, dependent, and delinquent children, was part of the larger social reform movement which was prominent in Canada from about 1880 to 1920. In order to add to the growing collection of research in the field, this thesis examines a specific child-saving endeavour which arose and developed in Alberta. The bulk of the thesis consists of a descriptive case study of the operation of the Department of Neglected Children, which from 1909 to 1929 was responsible for child protection work throughout the province. In addition, the case study is used to test the adequacy of social control theory as an explanation of the work of child savers. On the basis of her research findings, the author concludes that the hypotheses advanced by social control theorists, that middle-class reformers were motivated by self-interest and that they imposed their value system on the working class, do not provide an adequate explanation of the work of Alberta's child savers; first, because they fail to take into account the importance of ideology in human practice, and second, because they limit the role of members of the working class to that of passive recipients. In addition to utilizing government documents, reports, and statutes pertaining to Alberta, the study draws on a wide range of published secondary literature on the history of social reform and social control.

283. Coulter, Rebecca.

'"Not to Punish but to Reform": Juvenile Delinquency and Children's Protection Act in Alberta, 1909–1929.' In *Studies in Childhood History: A Canadian Perspective*, pp. 167–184. Edited by Patricia T. Rooke and R.L. Schnell. Calgary: Detselig Enterprises, Ltd., 1982.

Of the many social problems facing the new province of Alberta, juvenile delinquency was among the first to be tackled. This article examines the steps taken to deal with the problem of juvenile delinquency in Alberta. Attention is given to outlining the provisions of the province's *Children's Protection Act* of 1909, which included the juvenile delinquent within the broader category of the 'neglected child' and provided for the establishment of an administrative framework for dealing with troublesome juveniles. The author maintains that in the period from 1909 to 1929 the issue of whether juvenile delinquents should be punished along the lines of adult offenders or reformed through being placed in a 'suitable home' was the source of continuing friction between the Department of Neglected Children and the Alberta Provincial Police.

284. Crevel, Maryvonne.

'Il y a quarante ans en Gaspésie: Alambics, contrebande ... une florissante industrie.' *Revue d'histoire de la Gaspésie* 6 (1, January–March 1968): 17–22.

Alcohol has always been a chronic evil in the Province of Quebec and particularly in Gaspésie. The author uses quotations from several letters to and from Monseigneur Ross, who was appointed Bishop of Gaspésie in 1922, to describe the alcohol situation in the region: its illicit production and smuggling and the traffic in it.

285. Cross, Michael S.

'Stony Monday, 1849: The Rebellion Losses Riots in Bytown.' *Ontario History* 63 (3, September 1971): 177–190.

The planned visit of Governor General Elgin to Bytown (Ottawa) in September 1849, shortly following the granting of responsible government, precipitated a local riot in which opposing 'Tory' and 'Reform' parties battled each other in the streets. The author maintains that, although lasting only a few hours, the riot of Monday, September 17 – referred to as 'Stony Monday' because stones were the main weapon used – is historically significant, in that it reflected the manner in which long-standing 'local animosities, ethnic tensions and economic unrest combined with political differences to produce large-scale social violence.'

286. Cross, Michael S.

'The Shiner's War: Social Violence in the Ottawa Valley in the 1830's.' *Canadian Historical Review* 54 (1, March 1973): 1–26.

In the period 1835–7, the lumber community of Bytown (Ottawa) was plagued with unprecedented social violence. The instigators of the violence were Irish lumber workers who, led by their employer, Peter Aylen, indiscriminately 'swaggered the streets of Bytown, brawling and drinking on the sidewalks, savagely beating anyone who dared to challenge them.' Although the assaults perpetuated by the self-proclaimed 'Shiners' were initially based on ethnic divisions among workers and directed mainly at French Canadians, in the 1835–7 period many prominent 'upper class' members of the community became the victims of social violence. This article examines the origins of the Shiners' movement, the reasons underlying its members' propensity towards violence, and the steps taken by 'Bytown vigilantes' and authorities to deal with their threat to social order. The author maintains that the Irish workers who joined the Shiners' movement of the 1830s brought a 'tradition of violence' and a 'hatred and contempt for authority' with them from their homeland. In the absence of effective local government, adequate police forces, and generally weak institutions of social control, the Shiners were able to take control of Bytown for a short period. Only when they moved from 'group criminality' towards 'insurrection' did the community take steps to put an end to the violence.

287. Cross, Michael S.

'Violence and Authority: The Case of Bytown.' In *Law and Society in Canada in Historical Perspective*, pp. 5–22. Edited by D.J. Bercuson and L.A. Knafla. Calgary: University of Calgary, 1979.

Drawing on his previous work (see entry 286 above) the author identifies changing patterns in the nature of violence and authority in the lumbering communities of the Ottawa River in the mid-nineteenth century. Using the community of Bytown as a case example, the author points to a shift in the forms of violence perpetrated by lumber workers, from 'recreational violence' based on ethnic division among the workers, to a more 'purposive social violence' based on explicit economic motives and a genuine opposition to the established order. A concomitant shift in the response of authority, from a not-so-benign neglect to an aggressive use of the power of the state, is also noted. The different patterns of violence, and responses to violence, that evolved in the period from around 1820 to 1850 are set within the context of broader social and political events, including population growth, urbanization, and economic development.

288. Cross, Michael S.

'"The Laws Are Like Cobwebs": Popular Resistance to Authority in Mid-Nineteenth Century British North America.' *Dalhousie Law Journal* 8 (3, 1984): 103–124. Also published in *Law in a Colonial Society: The Nova Scotia Experience*, pp. 103–123. Edited by Peter Waite, Sandra Oxner, and Thomas Barnes. Toronto: Carswell, 1984.

289. Crowley, Terence.

'"Thunder Gusts": Popular Disturbances in Early French Canada.' Canadian Historical Association. *Historical Papers* (1979): 11–32.

In Canada the systematic study of popular protest and collective violence is in its infancy. The author of this paper attempts to begin to fill this gap in historical knowledge by examining available archival data on popular disturbances in French Canada prior to 1760. Research findings indicate that on at least 12 occasions 'people in New France took to the streets, paraded to the walls of towns, or otherwise assembled for direct action in defiance of the law.' Most of these demonstrations were forms of collective action used by the lower classes to protest food shortages and forced labour for the government.

290. Curtis, Bruce.

'The Political Economy of Elementary Educational Development: Comparative Perspectives on State Schooling in Upper Canada.' Ph.D. dissertation, University of Toronto, 1981.

This dissertation is primarily concerned with examining the origins of the elementary educational system in Upper Canada during its formative period from 1791 to 1851. Although by 1850, Upper Canada had a systematically organized system of public education that shared many features specific to industrial-capitalist society, the Upper Canadian economy was primarily agricultural. This 'uneven educational development,' the author contends, has not been adequately accounted for by 'social control' historians, who have tended to view educational reform in Upper Canada as a response of the urban, middle class to the social problems of vagrancy, unemployment, and juvenile delinquency. Working from a perspective informed by Marxist political economy and neo-Marxist educational theory, the author develops an alternative explanation that emphasizes the importance of considering the Upper Canadian experience with educational reform within the broader context of historically specific economic and political developments, and the colonial connection linking Upper Canada to Britain.

291. Curtis, Bruce.

'Preconditions of the Canadian State: Educational Reform and the Construction of a Public in Upper Canada, 1837–1846.' *Studies in Political Economy: A Socialist Review* (10, Winter 1983): 99–121.

This article builds on the author's Ph.D. dissertation (see entry 290 above). Here he more explicitly advances the argument that mid-nineteenth-century educational reform in Upper Canada cannot be adequately explained through adopting a 'social control' paradigm. Departing from the approach adopted by previous historians, the author focuses on examining Upper Canadian educational reform within a broader political context. He concludes that the struggle over education in the colony was in fact a struggle over political rule, and that educational reform was an important mechanism of state-building.

292. Davis, Claude Mark.

'Prohibition in New Brunswick, 1917–1927.' M.A. thesis, University of New Brunswick, 1979.

293. Decarie, Malcolm Graeme.

'The Prohibition Movement in Ontario: 1894–1916.' Ph.D. dissertation, Queen's University, 1972.

The struggle for provincial prohibition legislation in Ontario, which began in 1894, ended with the enactment of the *Ontario Temperance Act* in 1916. This dissertation examines the development, success, and eventual decline of the provincial prohibition movement in Ontario. Although the leaders of the prohibition movement were predominantly either Methodist or Presbyterian and its major base of support was in rural Ontario, the movement also attracted the support of other religious denominations, women's organizations, and the new urban middle class. The author maintains that while the movement sought to sustain a value system nurtured in rural Ontario, it was largely concerned with problems posed by urban growth. These problems included the poverty, crime, and disease which were seen to be associated with the urban working class, and attributed to lower-class drinking habits.

294. Decarie, Malcolm Graeme.

'Something Old, Something New ...: Aspects of Prohibitionism in Ontario in the 1890's.'
In *Oliver Mowat's Ontario: Papers Presented to the Oliver Mowat Colloquium, Queen's
University, November 25–26, 1970*, pp. 154–171. Edited by Donald Swainson. Toronto:
Macmillan of Canada, 1972.

Throughout the 1890s the prohibitionists of Ontario battled to preserve what they
understood to be traditional values concerning thrift, work, and morality. This essay traces
the growth of the prohibition movement in Ontario in the 1890s, and the reasons for its
gaining increased support. The author arrives at similar conclusions to those expressed in
his Ph.D. dissertation (see entry 293 above).

295. Decarie, Malcolm Graeme.

'Paved with Good Intentions: The Prohibitionists'' Road to Racism in Ontario.' *Ontario
History* 66 (1, March 1974): 15–22.

Between 1905 and 1914 the prohibition movement in Ontario broadened to include
elements of nativism and racism. In the author's view, the struggle for prohibition was a
nativist one in the sense that it entailed the opposition of church-going and middle-class
reformers to the drinking habits of a largely secular and foreign-born urban working class.
At the same time, the prohibition movement displayed certain racist tendencies, the most
widespread being the notion that Ontario's Anglo-Saxons constituted a superior race.
According to the author, this notion was supported by some prohibitionists, and lent support
by then-current scientific knowledge derived from sociology, politics, economics, and
biology. However, he concludes that racism did not become a major influence underlying
the prohibition movement in Ontario.

296. de la Broquerie, Fortier.

'Les "enfants trouvés" sous le régime français.' In *Trois siècles de médicine québécoise*.
Société historique de Québec. Cahiers d'histoire, no. 22, pp. 113–126. Québec: Société
historique de Québec, 1970.

The problem of abandoned children of illegitimate birth does not seem to have existed in
New France until the end of the seventeenth century. The first act relative to illegitimate
children in New France dates from February 6, 1722. It was rendered necessary by a greatly
felt need to protect abandoned children and to provide for their food and maintenance. The
act was followed by another dated June 9, 1736, and by a third one on March 12, 1748. A
discussion of these acts, including excerpts from them, is presented.

297. de la Broquerie, Fortier.

'Les "enfants trouvés" au Canada français (1754–1950).' *L'union médicale du Canada* 101
(4, 1972): 715–725.

The author reviews the history of the protection of abandoned children in the Province of Quebec from 1754 to 1950. Three initial periods are identified and treated separately: 1754–1800; 1801–50; 1850–68. The author then discusses the establishment of various homes and organizations dedicated to child protection. These include the Protestant Infants' Home which was opened in 1870 together with the Home and School of Industry, the Montreal Children's Bureau (1918), and the Relief Society (1932).

298. de la Broquerie, Fortier.

'La protection de l'enfance au Canada français du XVIIIe siècle au début de XXe siècle.' *La vie médicale au Canada français* 4 (6, June 1975): 732–739.

This is the text of a paper presented to the 24th International Congress on the History of Medicine (Budapest, August 1974). In it, the author reviews the history of child protection in French Canada from the eighteenth century to the beginning of the twentieth century. Two separate periods are reviewed: the French regime, 1608–1760, and the English regime, 1760–1922. The remainder is a review of pediatric hospitals and the movement to provide milk to the children.

299. Dick, Ernest.

'From Temperance to Prohibition in 19th Century Nova Scotia.' *Dalhousie Review* 61 (Autumn 1981): 530–552.

300. Douglas, Muriel H.

'A History of the Society for the Protection of Women and Children in Montreal, 1882–1966.' M.S.W. research report, McGill University, 1967.

In this research report, the history of the Society for the Protection of Women and Children is investigated in view of the concern about the adequacy of child protection services in Montreal in the 1960s. Although providing a brief overview of the history of child protection services in North America, the author concentrates mainly on examining the history of the Montreal society. Major sources of data include the minutes of directors' meetings, newspaper reports, the official records of other agencies, and personal interviews with individuals directly involved with the organization. The author concludes that at the time of writing the Society for the Protection of Women and Children in Montreal was going through a transition from its being a 'law enforcement society' to being a 'case-work agency.'

301. Dryfoos, Robert J. Jr.

'The Belcher Island Murders: An "Anti-Nativistic" Movement.' *Man in the Northeast* 2 (November 1971): 82–87.

During the winter of 1941, a group of Eskimos living in a settlement on the Belcher

Islands in Hudson Bay began to voice the belief that two of their numbers were God and Jesus Christ. Three unfortunate individuals who refused to believe that God and Jesus were living in their midst were murdered. Drawing on data obtained in the course of anthropological field-work, the author attempts to determine the factors that precipitated the 'revitalization' movement in 1941. Contrary to the view that such movements can be explained by the growing 'nativism' of individuals who feel their society is being threatened from outside, the author hypothesizes that the Belcher Eskimos developed their movement as a response to their own environment and cultural system, which they felt were unsatisfactory.

302. Duncan, Kenneth.

'Irish Famine Immigration and the Social Structure of Canada West.' *Canadian Review of Sociology and Anthropology* 2 (1, 1965): 19–40. Also published in *Studies in Canadian Social History*, pp. 140–163. Edited by Michiel Horn and Ronald Sabourin. Toronto: McClelland and Stewart, 1974.

In 1847, thousands of famine immigrants from rural Ireland arrived in Canada West. Faced with dim prospects of being able to begin a new rural life in mid-nineteenth-century Ontario, most of the immigrants settled in the urban slums and working-class areas of cities such as Toronto, London, Kingston, St. Catharines, and Hamilton: areas where 'violence and riot, disease, crime, drunkenness, and prostitution were rife.' This article examines the social and economic conditions in Canada West to which the famine immigrants had to adjust, the process of adjustment itself, and the influence of Irish peasant values and social structure upon the choices the immigrants made. The author maintains that the arrival of the famine immigrants had several consequences for Canada West. These included the subsequent introduction of controls upon overseas immigration, the creation of an Irish Catholic urban proletariat, the introduction of a tradition of violence to gain economic, religious, and political ends, and greatly increased crime and vice. He also notes that the influx of indigent persons placed a heavy burden upon existing charitable and custodial institutions, such as hospitals, prisons, and asylums. By showing that the pattern of behaviour displayed by the immigrants had its roots in Irish society, the author casts doubt on the validity of accepted explanations of immigrant adjustment that view the problems encountered by immigrants as being a result of 'a break in continuity between life in the old world and life in the new.'

303. Edmison, John Alexander.

'Eternal Problem of Crime and Criminals.' *Queen's Quarterly* 60 (Summer, 1953): 243–252.

304. Elliott, Brenda.

'The Women's Christian Temperance Union: Fifty Years of Christian Feminism and Moral Reform.' Graduate essay, Carleton University, School of Social Work, 1981.

305. Elliott, J.K.

'Crime and Punishment in Early Upper Canada.' Ontario Historical Society. *Papers and Records* 27 (1931): 335–340.

   This article discusses the nature and extent of crime and punishment in Upper Canada in the first decade of the nineteenth century. Drawing mainly on the records of the Court of Quarter Sessions for the District of London from 1800 to 1809, the author summarizes findings relating to the number of convictions registered by the court (51), the number of presentments returned by the district grand jury (92), the sentences imposed for various offences, and the provisions made for the construction of a district gaol and court house. From his study of the court's records, the author concludes that most of the crimes dealt with were of a 'very trivial character,' and that overall the penalties imposed by the court were not excessively severe, the usual punishment being a fine.

306. Fauteux, Aegidius.

Le duel au Canada. Collection du zodiaque, no. 35. Montréal: Deom, [1934]

   This is a historical study of the duel in Canada. In 1626 an Edict of Louis XIII made duels a punishable offence. The first two cases of known duels in New France were reported by Father Jêrome Lalemant in May 1646 in the *Journal des Jésuites*. One of the two cases took place in Three Rivers and the other in Quebec. Duelling seems to have ceased around 1870 although reports of incidents which supposedly took place between 1870 and 1880 may be found. The book is divided by periods. Chapter 1 covers duel cases from 1646 to 1760, Chapter 2 cases from 1760 to 1817, Chapter 3 cases from 1817 to 1833, Chapter 4 cases occurring in 1834, Chapter 5 cases from 1835 to 1836, Chapter 6 cases in the year 1837, Chapter 7 cases in the years 1838 to 1844, and the last chapter the period 1845 to 1870.

307. Fazakas, Ray.

The Donnelly Album: The Complete and Authentic Account Illustrated with Photographs of Canada's Famous Feuding Family. Toronto: Macmillan of Canada, 1977.

308. Fecteau, Jean-Marie.

'La pauvreté, le crime, l'Etat. Essai sur l'économie politique de contrôle social au Québec, 1791–1940.' Ph.D. dissertation, Université de Paris, 1983.

309. Fingard, Judith.

'The Winter's Tale: The Seasonal Contours of Pre-Industrial Poverty in British North America, 1815–1860.' Canadian Historical Association. *Historical Papers* (1974): 65–94.

310. Fingard, Judith.

'Masters and Friends, Crimps and Abstainers: Agents of Control in 19th Century Sailortown.' *Acadiensis* 8 (1, Autumn 1978): 22–46.

311. Fingard, Judith.

'The Poor in Winter: Seasonality and Society in Pre-Industrial Canada.' In *Pre-Industrial Canada, 1760–1849*, pp. 62–78. Edited by Michael S. Cross and Gregory S. Kealey. Toronto: McClelland and Stewart, 1982.

312. Foran, Max.

'The "Travis Affair".' *Alberta Historical Review* 19 (4, Autumn 1971): 1–17.

The *North-West Territories Act* of 1875 prohibited the public sale of liquor. From the onset, local Calgary authorities did not enforce the legislation strictly because they realized that the proceeds of any fines paid for contravening the act would be forwarded to Ottawa. This state of affairs changed considerably in the fall of 1885, with the appointment of Judge J. Travis (a 'transplanted Easterner' and temperance crusader) as a stipendiary magistrate. Upon his appointment, Travis launched a crusade against the 'liquor interests' (including the mayor and city councillors) that held political control in Calgary. This article chronicles the local and national political controversy that stemmed from Travis's temperance crusade, along with the final outcome of his efforts.

313. Foran, Max.

'Bob Edwards and Social Reform.' *Alberta Historical Review* 21 (3, Summer 1973): 13–17.

Bob Edwards was a controversial and widely read social reformer from Alberta. In his newspaper *The Eye Opener*, published in Calgary from 1904 to 1922, Edwards supported numerous social reform causes, including the Progressivist movement, temperance, and the rights of women to the franchise and to a place of equality in society. He was also a critic of society's hypocritical attitude towards prostitutes, of the churches 'for their myopic concept of the Sabbath observance,' and of existing hospital and educational systems. This article attempts to provide an understanding of the reasons underlying Edwards's popularity as a journalist, reform crusader, and humourist. The author maintains that his success was at least in part due to his ability to gauge the feelings and popular sentiment of people living in Alberta during the first two decades of the century.

314. Forbes, E.R.

'Prohibition and the Social Gospel in Nova Scotia.' *Acadiensis* 1 (1, Autumn 1971): 11–36. Also in *Prophecy and Protest: Social Movements in Twentieth Century Canada*, pp.

62–86. Edited by Samuel D. Clark, J. Paul Grayson, and Linda M. Grayson. Toronto: Gage, 1975.

The rise and decline of the prohibition movement in Nova Scotia was closely tied to the fate of the social gospel movement in the province. Prohibitionists, many of whom were church leaders, were motivated by a desire to 'eliminate the roots of human unhappiness' and 'create a new society in which crime, disease and social injustice would be virtually eliminated.' This article examines the closely linked rise of prohibition and social gospel movements in Nova Scotia from 1890 to 1921, and their equally closely associated decline from 1921 to 1929. The author points out that although support for prohibition was widespread prior to 1921, government attempts at enforcing prohibition legislation in the 1920s made it increasingly evident that prohibition 'did not yield the results predicted by its proponents.'

315. Fox, John, and Hartnagel, Timothy F.

'Changing Social Roles and Female Crime in Canada: A Time Series Analysis.' *The Canadian Review of Sociology and Anthropology* 16 (1, 1979): 96–104.

In this article, time-series data on female conviction rates in Canada during the period 1931 to 1968 are examined in order to evaluate the hypotheses that the female crime rate varies inversely with the rate of involvement of females in the familial role and directly with the rate of female participation in extrafamilial roles. The authors' findings support the view that changes in various aspects of women's structural position in society affect female crime rates.

316. Fraser, Alain.

'Société, criminalité et contrôle des Indiens Cris de Fort George au Nouveau-Québec.' M.A. thesis, University of Ottawa, 1977.

Since 1960 the white population has increased considerably in the various Indian villages and reserves of Quebec. The experience of the author in Fort George demonstrated that the power exercised by whites is coercive. Substantive chapters provide a historical account of white paternalism and the creation of Fort George, a description and analysis of the difficulties experienced by the Indians as a result of the white presence, a discussion of problems concerning the uncertainty and authenticity of native culture created by the James Bay hydro-electric project, and an analysis of the crime problem experienced at Fort George. The erosion of traditional Indian culture is considered as a possible explanation for rising crime rates.

317. Friesen, G.A., and Sprague, D.N.

'Applications of Modernization Theory to Crime Data in the Old World and the New.' Paper presented at the Annual Meeting of the Canadian Historical Association, Halifax, June 1981.

The jail records for the Eastern Judicial District of Manitoba, now held in the Provincial Archives of Manitoba, contain detailed biographical information on every person incarcerated in the main district jail between 1874 and 1968. This study undertakes a preliminary quantitative analysis of jail records for the period 1881 to 1931 in order to test the adequacy of hypotheses derived from modernization theory, which has been applied in explaining English and American historical crime rates. Applied in the context of Manitoba, modernization theory predicts that in its early years the district would lack a professional police force, and would be troubled by a high rate of violent crime and theft on the part of immigrants, while in later years it would have proportionately more uniformed police and a lower arrest rate for crimes against the person committed by unassimilated newcomers. Through their analysis of the Manitoba evidence, the authors found that these hypotheses lacked empirical support. They conclude that while modernization theory is too simple to be of much use as a means of interpreting the Manitoba data, conflict theory, which views social organization in terms of power relationships and class conflict, appears to provide a more fruitful means of viewing the jail records.

318. Gallacher, D.T.

'City in Depression – The Impact of the Years 1929–1939 on Greater Victoria, B.C.' M.A. thesis, University of British Columbia, 1970.

Although not primarily concerned with the history of crime, Gallacher's study does attempt to examine the impact of the depression on crime in Victoria. Based on an examination of indictments found in the B.C. Supreme Court Calendar of General Assize records, the author concludes that offences against property increased significantly with the advent of the depression.

319. Garland, M.A., and Talman, James J.

'Pioneer Drinking Habits and the Rise of the Temperance Agitation in Upper Canada Prior to 1840.' Ontario Historical Society. *Papers and Records* 27 (1931): 341–364. Also published in Ilderton, Ontario, by the author, in 1931. Also in *Aspects of Nineteenth-Century Ontario*, pp. 171–193. Edited by F.H. Armstrong, H.A. Stevenson, and J.D. Wilson. Toronto: University of Toronto Press, 1974.

The first half of the nineteenth century saw the birth of many 'liberalizing and humanitarian movements' in Upper Canada. According to the authors of this article, one of the more striking examples of 'the growth of the humanitarian movement' in the province was the rise of temperance societies aimed at reducing or eliminating the consumption of alcohol. Focusing on the period prior to 1840, the authors present evidence relating to the drinking habits of Upper Canadians, the establishment of temperance societies, and the various efforts undertaken by temperance advocates to gain support for their humanitarian crusade.

320. Gigeroff, A.K.

'The Evolution of Canadian Legislation with Respect to Homosexuality, Pedophilia and Exhibitionism.' *Criminal Law Quarterly* 8 (1965–6): 445–454.

This paper is restricted mainly to outlining statutory changes in Canadian criminal legislation governing the sexual offences of buggery, bestiality, indecent assault, gross indecency, and sexual intercourse with an underage female. Under the general headings of 'Homosexual Offences,' 'Pedophilic Offences,' and 'Exhibitionistic Offences,' the author highlights the origin of and subsequent changes to Canadian legislation concerning the noted sexual offences. He concludes that although the many amendments that have been made to the legislation create the impression that it has changed significantly, in actual fact the substance of the legislation has changed little over the last century, and has not kept pace with advances which the social and behavioural sciences have made in their knowledge of human and sexual behaviour.

321. Goff, Colin H.

'Corporate Crime in Canada.' M.A. thesis, University of Calgary, 1975.

This thesis forms the basis for the author's 1975 and 1978 co-authored published works (see entries 322 and 323 below).

322. Goff, Colin H., and Reasons, Charles E.

'Corporations in Canada: A Study of Crime and Punishment.' *Criminal Law Quarterly* 18 (1975–6): 468–498.

Few studies of the imposition of legal sanctions upon corporations have been undertaken and, in Canada, criminologists have given little attention to corporate crime. Drawing mainly on available statistical data, this study attempts to shed light on the nature and scope of corporate crime in Canada, and assess the manner in which anti-combines legislation has been enforced by the federal government. The enforcement of combines laws from 1889 to 1972 is evaluated in terms of three indices: (1) the actual enforcement record of combines laws, (2) the number of mergers and the prosecution of them by the government as well as the degree of economic concentration in various industrial sectors, and (3) the amount of financial assistance and the number of employees assigned to the Combines Branch by the federal government. The data collected suggest that over the years the Combines Branch has centred its attentions on the investigation, prosecution, and conviction of small- and medium-sized companies and corporations, leaving the very largest corporations to freely engage in their monopolistic practices.

323. Goff, Colin H., and Reasons, Charles E.

Corporate Crime in Canada: A Critical Analysis of Anti-Combines Legislation. Scarborough, Ont.: Prentice-Hall, 1978.

This book attempts to provide the reader with an initial understanding of the nature and scope of corporate crime generally, and an in-depth analysis of anti-combines legislation specifically. Since Canadian anti-combines laws have existed since 1889, they provide an excellent opportunity for the socio-historical analysis of the emergence of and changes in laws over a period of more than 80 years. Drawing on both archival and secondary data, in the historical chapters of the book, the authors provide an analysis of the emergence of anti-combines legislation within the context of 'socio-political' events in late-nineteenth-century Canada, examine the significance of the merger movement in the early 1900s and Mackenzie King's role in formulating and administering anti-combines policy since the Second World War, and provide a statistical analysis of violations of the anti-combines act by Canadian corporations. From their investigation, the authors conclude that, historically, Canadian anti-combines legislation has functioned as an 'expressive law' to convince certain segments of the public that something is being done to protect economic competition.

324. Gorman, Janine Catherine.

'Homicide in Canada: An Analysis of Trends and the Importance of Age Structure.' M.A. thesis, University of Western Ontario, 1979.

The 'conventional wisdom' in Canada is that rates of violent crime are increasing significantly and continuously. Based on McDonald's findings (see entry 384 below) that refute the 'conventional wisdom,' the present study investigates rates of homicide/murder since 1945 using multiple measures, a longer time-series analysis, multivariate statistical techniques, and 'proportion of the population aged 20 to 29' as a predictor variable. Results show that over the period 1945 to 1974, the rate of homicide/murder increased. 'The proportion of the population aged 20 to 29' is shown to be a powerful and significant predictor of rates of homicide/murder, but only for the period 1962 to 1974.

325. Graff, Harvey J.

'Crime and Punishment in the Nineteenth Century: The Experience of Middlesex County, Ontario.' *Canadian Social History Project, Report*, 5 (1973–4): 124–163.

326. Graff, Harvey J.

'Literacy and Social Structure in the Nineteenth-Century City.' Ph.D. dissertation, University of Toronto, 1975.

Contemporary investigators concerned with the history of literacy have tended to assume that increases in the level of literacy are positively related to social mobility and modernization. In addition, it has long been assumed that there is a direct relationship between illiteracy and criminality. Drawing on quantitative materials – including census data, assessment roles, employment contracts, and jail registers – supplemented by qualitative historical sources, this dissertation seeks to examine literacy's place in a variety of spheres of social life. The dissertation is divided into two parts. Part one presents a systematic exposition of the place of illiterate adults and their families in the social structure of three mid-nineteenth-century Ontario cities: Hamilton, Kingston, and London. Part two examines selected issues relating to the problem of literacy, including the alleged direct relationship between illiteracy and criminality. The author's findings bring into question the validity of prevailing assumptions concerning the nature of the relationship linking increased literacy to social mobility, modernization, and a declining level of crime.

327. Graff, Harvey J.

'Crime and Punishment in the Nineteenth Century: A New Look at the Criminal.' *Journal of Interdisciplinary History* 7 (3, Winter 1977): 477–491.

Despite the existence of source materials that make it possible to answer important quantitative questions about patterns of crime and about the criminal in the nineteenth and early twentieth centuries, historical studies of crime and punishment remain largely dependent on commission reports and anecdotal evidence. The purpose of this essay is to demonstrate that untapped source materials – the most important being jail (or gaol) registers – can be used to gain an increased understanding of the nature of crime and criminality in the last century. As an example, the author points out that jail registers for Middlesex County, Ontario, for the period 1867 to 1920, contain a wealth of information on both the individual criminal and on the offence for which he or she was detained. Through a preliminary analysis of Middlesex County jail registers for 1867–8, the author seeks to illustrate the value of the registers as a source of quantitative historical data, and the many opportunities for historical work on crime and criminals that they provide.

328. Graff, Harvey J.

'Pauperism, Misery and Vice: Illiteracy and Criminality in the Nineteenth Century.' *Journal of Social History* 11 (2, Winter 1977): 245–268. Reprinted as 'The Reality behind the Rhetoric: The Social and Economic Meanings of Literacy in the Mid-Nineteenth Century: The Example of Literacy and Criminality.' In *Egerton Ryerson and His Times*, pp. 187–220. Edited by Neil McDonald and Alf Chaiton. Toronto: Macmillan, 1978.

In the mid-nineteenth century, the promoters of compulsory schooling in Upper Canada marshalled reams of evidence to prove the perceived relationship between ignorance or lack of education and criminality. In their formulations, ignorance and crime were also associated with illiteracy, a visible and measurable sign of the lack of schooling. This essay focuses on investigating the relationship between criminality and illiteracy perceived and discussed by school promoters. First, their causal notions and their evidence is examined. These are then tested through an analysis of the manuscript jail registers of Middlesex

County, Ontario, for 1867–8, which included information concerning the literacy of convicted offenders. From his examination of the data, the author concludes that the causal connection between illiteracy and criminality assumed by school promoters was a superficial one, and that other variables such as poverty and social-structural inequality were more important determinants of criminality.

329. Grant, Barry J.

Six for the Hangman: Unforgettable New Brunswick Murders. Fredericton: Fiddlehead Poetry Books and Goose Lane Editions Ltd., 1983.

Grant recounts the story of six of New Brunswick's most famous murder cases. In each of his six short stories – the Bannister case (1936), the murder of Bernice Connors (1942), the Collins case (1906), the Paris case (1921), the case of Mr. Peck (1805), and the McKenzie murders (1857) – the author relies on newspaper accounts and available trial transcripts to reconstruct the circumstances surrounding the murders and the details of the trials which followed. The specific cases selected were chosen, the author notes, not for their 'gruesomeness alone,' but because each in its own time had an immense impact upon the general public and revealed some distinctive oddity about the workings of the judicial system.

330. Grant, Helen M.

'The Deportation of the Acadians.' *Nova Scotia Historical Quarterly* Special Supplement (1975): 101–117.

This article relates the tragic story of the Acadians deported from the Maritimes in the early 1700s. The author examines the reasons for the deportation of some 7000 French-speaking colonists, and the manner in which it was carried out. She notes that historical literature relating to the deportation of the Acadians has been divided on the question of whether their expulsion was justly undertaken, or instead 'an awful and inexcusable crime.'

331. Gray, James H.

Red Lights on the Prairies. Toronto: Macmillan, 1971.

In the early twentieth century the rapidly growing cities of western Canada were disproportionately populated by single men, many of whom patronized houses of prostitution. Focusing on the experience of prairie cities such as Winnipeg, Saskatoon, Calgary, and Drumheller, Gray provides a popular account of how prostitution was perceived and dealt with by civic authorities and the police, who recognized the futility of trying to put an end to the practice, and moral reformers, who viewed prostitution and drunkenness as the main targets of their moral crusades. The author maintains that professional historians have tended to neglect the important part played by 'ladies of ill-repute' in the settlement of the West, and have created the false impression that the West was settled by 'monks ... and vestal virgins' who were interested only in debating political and economic issues.

332. Gray, James H.

Booze: The Impact of Whiskey on the Prairie West. Toronto: Macmillan, 1972.

333. Gray, James H.

Bacchanalia Revisited: The Tradition of Alcohol in the Canadian West. Saskatoon: Western Producer Prairie Books, 1982.

334. Green, M.

'A History of Canadian Narcotics Control: The Formative Years.' *University of Toronto Faculty of Law Review* 37 (1979): 42–79.

335. Greenland, Cyril.

'L'Affaire Shortis and the Valleyfield Murders.' *Canadian Psychiatric Association Journal* 7 (5, October 1962): 261–271.

Valentine Shortis, a twenty-one-year-old immigrant from Ireland, was charged with murder and made to stand trial in Valleyfield, Quebec, in 1895. Although his legal counsel raised the defence of insanity on his behalf, and four psychiatrists voiced the opinion that Shortis was insane, he was found guilty and sentenced to death. This article examines the voluminous records relating to Shortis's trial, the subsequent commuting of his death sentence to life imprisonment, and the 42 years he spent in various penitentiaries and mental hospitals. The author maintains that throughout the years of his detention, Shortis, who was once referred to as the 'central figure in one of Canada's greatest murder cases,' retained his personality well, was able to take responsibility, and was highly regarded by staff and patients alike. Overall, he concludes that the Shortis case provides a fresh opportunity to examine, in a dispassionate way, apparently irreconcilable views on captial punishment which are as vexing today as they were a hundred years ago.

336. Greenland, Cyril.

'The History of DSO Legislation in Canada.' Appendix I, pp. 271–275, in 'Dangerous Sexual Offenders in Canada,' pp. 247–281, in Law Reform Commission of Canada. *Studies on Imprisonment*. Ottawa: Supply and Services, 1976.

This appendix provides a brief overview of the history and development of dangerous sexual offender (DSO) legislation in Canada from 1948 to 1977.

337. Greenland, Cyril.

'Dangerous Sexual Offender Legislation in Canada, 1948–1977: An Experiment That Failed.' *Canadian Journal of Criminology* 26 (1, January 1984): 1–12.

This paper provides a case study of the operation of dangerous sexual offender (DSO) legislation in Canada from 1948 to 1977. The adequacy of the legislation, which provided for the sentencing of DSOs to an indeterminate period of incarceration, is assessed in light of data on the sexual offences, victims, psychiatric diagnosis and treatment, background characteristics, and parole outcomes of 62 convicted DSOs. From his examination of available data, the author concludes that there is 'little doubt that in its twenty-nine years of existence, the DSO legislation has conspicuously failed.'

338. Greenwood, F. Murray.

'The Chartrand Murder Trial: Rebellion and Repression in Lower Canada, 1837–1839.' In *Criminal Justice History: An International Annual*, vol. 5, 1984, pp. 129–159.

In September 1838, four 'patriotes' who had participated in the 1837 Rebellion in Lower Canada were placed on trial for the murder of Joseph Armand (also called Chartrand), an ex-patriote who had joined the militia volunteers and became an informer responsible for the arrest of several suspected rebels. Drawing mainly on trial transcripts and contemporary newspaper accounts, the author examines the progress, outcome, and historical significance of the trial. Specific attention is given to documenting the backgrounds of individuals who participated in the trial, the arguments presented by the crown and defence counsel, and the evidence laid before the jury. In spite of incriminating evidence, the jury acquitted the accused, or, as the author explains, provided an early example of the practice of 'jury nullification.' The author concludes that the Chartrand murder trial is of historical significance for several reasons, including: (1) that it raised important questions concerning the powers and duties of a jury, (2) that the 'not guilty' verdict provides an explanation for the establishment of courts martial which were subsequently used to try civilians accused of participating in the Lower Canadian Rebellion of 1838, and (3) that the establishment of court martial for the trial of civilians in 1838–9 remained a grievance among French-Canadian nationalists for over half a century.

339. Hallowell, Gerald Allan.

'Prohibition in Ontario, 1919–1923.' M.A. thesis, Carleton University, 1966.

340. Hallowell, Gerald Allan.

Prohibition in Ontario, 1919–1923. Ontario Historical Society. Research Publications, no. 2. Ottawa: Love Printing Service, 1972.

341. Hamlet, Elizabeth.

'Charlotte Whitton and the Growth of the Canadian Council on Child Welfare, 1926–1941. A Study of the Role of Social Reformers in Social Policy Making in Canada.' M.S.W. thesis, Carleton University, 1978.

342. Harevan, Tamara K.

'An Ambiguous Alliance: Some Aspects of American Influences on Canadian Social Welfare.' *Histoire sociale/Social History* 3 (1969): 82–98.

343. Harris, Richard Cole.

'Of Poverty and Helplessness in Petite-Nation.' *Canadian Historical Review* 52 (1, March 1971): 23–50.

This paper deals with the French-Canadian migration to and settlement in the seigneurie of Petite-Nation, a small segment of the Quebec rim of the Canadian Shield some 40 miles east of Ottawa. It describes the coming of French Canadians to Petite-Nation, and their way of life there before approximately 1860, then considers the reasons for the extreme poverty and institutional weaknesses which were among the dominant characteristics of French-Canadian life in the seigneurie. According to the author, the 'ordinary' French-Canadian inhabitants of Petite-Nation held 'considerable disdain for authority,' lived boisterously, and enjoyed the independence that came with living in a rural society. An attempt is made to demonstrate that the extreme poverty and institutional weaknesses (i.e., lack of collective social organization at the local level) that characterized the seigneurie stemmed at least in part from the fact that the inhabitants' forebears, many of whom came to New France from Paris poorhouses, as exiled petty criminals and ordinary soldiers who had been pressed into service, were opposed to government interference in their lives and incapable of maintaining a distinct way of life. The long-term result of this was that the seigneurie of Petite-Nation became populated by subsistence farmers and underpaid labourers, who during the nineteenth century experienced extreme poverty and social isolation.

344. Hewlett, Edward Sleigh.

'The Chilcotin Uprising of 1864.' *B.C. Studies* (19, Autumn 1973): 50–72.

This article examines a case of collective violence that occurred in British Columbia in 1864. The incident involved a group of Chilcotin Indians who attacked and killed a road party on the Homathko River and, while retreating to the interior, murdered a settler and ambushed a pack train. Although officials at the time described the incident as a 'war,' the author prefers to describe it as an 'uprising,' since it involved only a small group of Indians who lacked the support of other Chilcotin.

345. Hiebert, Albert John.

'Prohibition in British Columbia.' M.A. thesis, Simon Fraser University, 1970.

Prohibition in British Columbia was in force for only a short time – 1917 to 1921 – and as a political issue it was often overshadowed by more urgent matters such as the war, or even railway construction. Nevertheless, the question of the control of the liquor traffic recurred with increasing frequency at both the local and the provincial levels, in the years following 1900. This thesis examines British Columbia's experience with prohibition. Substantive chapters are devoted to documenting the rise of temperance sentiment in the late nineteenth century, the coming of prohibition after 1900, and the circumstances leading to the repeal of the province's prohibition statute in 1921. The author concludes that although the temperance movement in British Columbia began as a movement of moral reform, the debate on the prohibition question was carried on in terms of citizenship, patriotism, justice, and economics, largely because of the war and its aftermath. While prohibitionist propaganda skilfully exploited the wartime situation by emphasizing that liquor traffic interfered with both the efficiency of the individual and the economic strength of the province, when peace returned public support for prohibition declined and prohibition legislation 'became notorious for the way in which it was either circumvented or violated rather than in the way it was enforced.'

346. Hiebert, Albert John.

'Prohibition and Social Problems in British Columbia: The Example of the Okanagan.' *B.C. Perspectives* (2, October 1972): 36–56.

This paper is restricted to investigating the prohibition movement in the Okanagan region of British Columbia. In it, the author discusses both regionally specific social problems and outside influences that resulted in 'the coming of prohibition to the Okanagan.' According to the author, the political success of the prohibition movement, particularly at the local level, can better be understood against the background of moral and democratic reform that concerned the communities of British Columbia; a concern which led to calls for the establishment of new or improved social services like hospitals, schools, juvenile courts, and workmen's compensation, as well as demands for prohibition legislation. The success of Okanagan prohibition, he maintains, was also tied to the efforts of prohibitionists from Vancouver and Victoria, who directly intervened in local politics in order to win support for their cause. As in other areas of the province, the campaign that won over Okanagan residents to the cause of prohibition was an economic one, built on an emotional foundation of patriotism.

347. Hodgins, J. George.

'Truancy and Juvenile Crime in Cities, 1859–1860. Charges of the Judges on the Subject.' In *Documentary History of Education in Upper Canada from the Passing of the*

Constitutional Act of 1791 to the Close of the Reverend Doctor Ryerson's Administration
the Education Department in 1876, vol. 15, 1860, pp. 1–5. Toronto: L.K. Cameron, 1906.

348. Houston, Susan Elizabeth.

'Politics, Schools and Social Change in Upper Canada.' *Canadian Historical Review* 53 (3, September 1972): 249–271.

During the 1830s and 1840s Upper Canadian educational reformers argued successfully for the introduction of a common school system in the province. This article examines the political, economic, and social climate in which demands for a system of public education emerged in Upper Canada, and the reasons underlying the educational-reform efforts made during the period. According to the author, one of the main influences underlying the move towards educational reform was the growing 'middle class' belief that major social problems, such as ignorance, vice, crime, and poverty, could be solved by creating a common school system that provided for the education of lower-class children.

349. Houston, Susan Elizabeth.

'Victorian Origins of Juvenile Delinquency: A Canadian Experience.' *History of Education Quarterly* 12 (1972): 254–280.

The Victorian social conscience was troubled on many accounts, and perhaps no more so than by the plight of delinquent youngsters. Focusing on the experience of the Province of Canada, the author notes that the 1850s saw an eroding of confidence in traditional methods used in dealing with neglected and delinquent children, and the emergence of new proposals for reform. One of the major proposals eventually adopted in the effort to rescue 'the hapless street arabs from certain ruin' was the juvenile reformatory, two of which were established in the province during the 1850s. The article deals with the emerging attitudes towards neglected and delinquent youth held by advocates of the juvenile reformatory and their opponents, as reflected in debates over the age until which youthful offenders should be considered juvenile delinquents, and the purposes that institutions for juveniles should serve. The author concludes that although 'progressive' legislation aimed at dealing with juvenile delinquents did not come about until decades later, 'the experience of the mid-century years had been crucial in formulating the concept of juvenile delinquency.'

350. Houston, Susan Elizabeth.

'The Impetus to Reform: Urban Crime, Poverty and Ignorance in Ontario, 1850–1875.' Ph.D. dissertation, University of Toronto, 1974.

Many Upper Canadians shared with their mid-Victorian counterparts in Britain and the United States a preoccupation with the vices of crime, poverty, and ignorance. This study analyses the transition in their perception of poverty from an acceptance of the seasonality

, transient unemployment and distress to apprehension about a permanent class of dependent urban poor. The study is divided into three major sections. Under the heading of 'Crime,' the author examines documents relating to the perception of crime, responses to crime and the emergence of a criminal class, proposals for juvenile reform, and the establishment of the juvenile reformatory at Penetanguishene. Under 'Poverty,' the author considers the perception of and response to poverty shared by Upper Canadians, and the establishment of charitable institutions for children. Finally, under the heading of 'Ignorance,' attention is given to the issue of compulsory education. The author concludes that the period from the 1850s to the 1870s witnessed a critical transition in the thinking of Upper Canadians about crime, poverty, and ignorance, and the emergence of new strategies to deal with the perceived problems.

351. Houston, Susan Elizabeth.

'School Reform and Education: The Issue of Compulsory Schooling, Toronto, 1851–1871.' In *Egerton Ryerson and His Times*, pp. 254–276. Edited by Neil McDonald and Alf Chaiton. Toronto: Macmillan, 1978.

The issue of compulsory school attendance was the focus of considerable public controversy in Toronto during the 1860s and 1870s. Cognizant of the fact that the common school system established in the 1840s did not provide a place for 'vagrant, delinquent, and incorrigible' street children, reform-minded Torontonians debated the issue of whether such children should be required by legislation to attend public schools. The author points out that although some prominent citizens believed that compulsory schooling would help solve the problem of urban delinquency, others supported the idea of establishing separate 'industrial' and 'reformatory' schools, especially suited to the 'delinquent condition' of lower-class street children. She concludes that the reluctance of Torontonians to include vagrant children in the common school reflected 'a growing apprehension of the permanent existence of a dangerous and demoralized element in urban society' that, it was believed, should be excluded from established social institutions.

352. Houston, Susan Elizabeth.

'The "Waifs and Strays" of a Late Victorian City: Juvenile Delinquents in Toronto.' In *Childhood and the Family in Canadian History*, pp. 129–142. Edited by Joy Parr. Toronto: McClelland and Stewart, 1982.

In the opinion of most respectable Canadians living in the late nineteenth century, children who disregarded the authority of the family and society were headed for a life of crime. In this chapter, the author examines the experiences of and attempts made to deal with working-class urban youth who either ran afoul of the law or, because of their extreme poverty, left school to find work as street vendors and newspaper boys. In the 1890s, juvenile delinquents were portrayed by social reformers as the product of 'vicious, degraded and neglectful parents,' who, lacking in respect for authority, engaged in various acts of truancy, vandalism, and petty thievery. In contrast to the opinion of late-nineteenth-century social reformers and moralists, the author provides evidence to suggest that juvenile delinquency was tied to structural inequalities entrenched in the institutions of Canadian society, and that the police, courts, and reform institutions tended to reinforce these inequalities.

353. Houston, Susan Elizabeth, and Prentice, Alison L., eds.

Family, School and Society in Nineteenth Century Canada. Toronto: Oxford University Press, 1975.

354. Jamieson, Stuart.

'Some Reflections on Violence and the Law in Industrial Relations.' In *Law and Society in Canada in Historical Perspective*, pp. 141–155. Edited by D.J. Bercuson and Louis A. Knafla. Calgary: University of Calgary, 1979.

In the midst of a rising tide of labour unrest in the 1960s, the federal government appointed a special 'Task Force on Labour Relations.' One of the projects commissioned was the author's study *Times of Trouble – Labour Unrest and Industrial Conflict in Canada, 1900–1966*. In this paper, the author summarizes the findings of his more detailed study, and points to areas that require further research. Particular attention is given to questions concerning the interrelationships among and between industrial conflict, violence, and the law.

355. Jarvis, Eric James.

'Mid-Victorian Toronto: Panic, Policy and Public Response, 1857–1873.' Ph.D. dissertation, University of Western Ontario, 1979.

The years from 1857 to 1873 were ones of turmoil and change in the City of Toronto. As a result of the economic panic of 1857 and subsequent depression of 1866, the city found itself in financial difficulties, and serious cutbacks were made in all branches of municipal service, including fire protection, streetlighting, and police. This was accompanied by increased destitution among many of the city's population and a corresponding strain on private charities which oversaw poor relief. Drawing primarily on the Minutes of Toronto City Council and the newspapers published in the city, the author examines the problems faced by the city corporation of Toronto and the population that lived under its jurisdiction during the period of distress and recovery, from the late 1850s to the early 1870s. Substantive chapters focus on finances; sanitation; and trade, manufacturing, and transport. The author concludes that the 'quickening pace of urban services' that came with economic recovery marked an important turning point in the history of Toronto, and the evolution of its development.

356. John, Leslie.

Legend of the Roman Line: The Donnellys of Biddulph. Hamilton, Ont.: A. Greene Pub., 1980.

357. Jolliffe, Russell.

'The History of the Children's Aid Society of Toronto, 1891–1947.' M.S.W. thesis, University of Toronto, 1952.

358. Jones, Andrew, and Rutman, Leonard.

In the Children's Aid: J.J. Kelso and Child Welfare in Ontario. Toronto: University of Toronto Press, 1981.

359. Katz, Michael B., and Mattingly, P., eds.

Education and Social History: Themes from Ontario's Past. New York: New York University Press, 1975.

360. Kelso, J.J.

Early History of the Humane and Children's Aid Movement in Ontario, 1886–1893. [Toronto]: King's Printer, 1911.

361. Klassen, Henry C.

'Social Troubles in Calgary in the Mid-1890's.' *Urban History Review/Revue d'histoire urbaine* 3 (74, February 1975): 8–16.

During the 1890s, irregular employment, inadequate housing, poverty, crime, imperfect sanitation, and disease, all played a part in giving Calgary society a dark and harsh side. In this article, the author presents some preliminary research findings concerning the darker side of Calgary's social history in the late nineteenth century. The findings indicate that as a consequence of irregular employment, a large proportion of Calgary's working-class population was unable to cope with the problem of poverty, and that poverty, coupled with the uncertainties of frontier life, generated a significant amount of social tension and criminal activity.

362. Klassen, Henry C.

'In Search of Neglected and Delinquent Children: The Calgary Children's Aid Society, 1909–1920.' In *Town and City: Aspects of Western Canadian Urban Development*, pp. 375–392. Edited by A.F.J. Artibise. Regina: University of Regina, Canadian Plains Research Centre, 1981. (Canadian Plains Studies, no. 10)

Founded in 1909, the Calgary Children's Aid Society undertook the first attempt to provide organized care for neglected and delinquent children in the city. The author documents the fact that from 1909 to 1920 the society bore the heavy responsibility of caring for the city's deprived children, through providing accommodation to meet the needs of neglected children, and through working with the juvenile court to ensure that cases involving young offenders were dealt with in a fair manner. As a result of a worsening economic and social climate, in 1920, the society found itself unable to operate effectively and gave over its work to the city council, which then created the city's children's aid department. Data sources used in the article include annual reports and minutebooks of the Children's Aid Society, City Clerk's papers, annual reports of the provincial Department of Neglected and Dependent Children, and a range of secondary literature on the history of child welfare.

363. Krasnick, Cheryl L.

'An Aristocratic Vice: The Medical Treatment of Drug Addiction at the Homewood Retreat, 1883–1900.' *Ontario History* 75 (4, December 1983): 403–427.

364. Kroll, Robert E.

'Murder and Hanging in Old New Brunswick (1808).' *Atlantic Advocate* 67 (October 1976): 34–35.

365. Lachance, André.

'La criminalité à Québec sous le régime français, étude statistique.' *Revue d'histoire de l'Amérique française* 20 (3, December 1966): 409–414.

The author presents a statistical compilation of violations of the criminal order of 1670 (Ordonnance Criminelle) which were reported to the lieutenant governor and were prosecuted before the military courts of Quebec (tribunaux de la prévote) or the Supreme Council (Conseil Souverain). Offences are divided into four categories: (1) attacks against other people's property – these include theft, possession of stolen goods, desertion of servants, and arson; (2) attacks against the person – these include murder, manslaughter, duelling, suicide, infanticide, abortion, poisoning, kidnapping, libel, and altercations; (3) offences against morality – these include sexual offences such as rape, adultery, seduction, as well as offences against morality such as drunkenness and blasphemy; (4) offences against the state – these include counterfeiting, deserting the country, disobedience, sale of liquor to Indians, etc. Fifty per cent of the offences fell under the first category. According to the author, offences against morality were severely punished. In all, 87 criminal offences were prosecuted in Quebec during the French regime (43 in the second half of the seventeenth century and 44 in the first half of the eighteenth century). A total of 110 persons (14 of them women) were convicted; 55 were offences against property.

366. Lachance, André.

'La désertion et les soldats déserteurs au Canada dans la première moitié du XVIIIe siècle.' *Revue de l'Université d'Ottawa* 47 (1–2, 1977): 151–161.

Desertion of soldiers was a real problem that greatly preoccupied the authorities in New France as it did in Europe under the old regime. The problem is difficult to study in New France because the records containing the description of deserting soldiers which were kept by the controller of the marine in Quebec do not seem to have been preserved. However, the author accidentally found, among other papers kept in the judicial documents of the National Archives of Quebec in Montreal, information on deserting soldiers and on trials for desertion. Official correspondence (series B, B^2, c 11^A, and F^3) helps complete these two sources of information. The study is limited to those soldiers who were in the service of the Government of Montreal. The author discusses the causes and circumstances of desertion, analyses the trials, and offers a general description of the deserting soldiers.

367. Lachance, André.

'Women and Crime in Canada in the Early Eighteenth Century, 1712–1759.' In *Crime and Criminal Justice in Europe and Canada*, pp. 157–168. Edited by Louis A. Knafla. Waterloo, Ont.: Wilfrid Laurier University Press, 1981.

Drawing on available criminal records of the royal courts that existed under the French regime, the author undertakes a quantitative analysis of crimes committed by women, as compared to men, in eighteenth-century Canada. Offences are divided into four categories: (1) crimes against persons, (2) crimes against property, (3) crimes against morality, and (4) offences against the state. Research findings indicate that proportionately more women than men commit crimes against property and morality, the same number commit offences against the state, and fewer women than men commit crimes against persons. The type and severity of punishment meted out for various offences committed by women is also considered. The author concludes that female crime was a daily occurrence in eighteenth-century Canada and reflected the human relationships in which women were involved.

368. Lacourcière, Luc.

'Le triple destin de Marie-Josephte Corriveau (1733–1763).' *Cahiers des dix* 33 (1968): 213–242.

(See entry 370 below.)

369. Lacourcière, Luc.

'Le destin posthume de la Corriveau.' *Cahiers des dix* 34 (1969): 239–271.

(See entry 370 below.)

370. Lacourcière, Luc.

'Présence de la Corriveau.' *Cahiers des dix* 38 (1973): 229–264.

No woman in Canadian history has had a worse reputation than Marie-Josephte Corriveau, commonly called 'La Corriveau.' Dead for more than two centuries, her memory continues to haunt the imagination. People continue to talk about her, her real crime and her fictitious crimes. In April 1763 she was convicted by a military court of killing her second husband, Louis Dodier. She was hanged and publicly exposed for over 40 days in an iron cage, a cage which, even after it disappeared, continued to spread terror among several generations. The author tells the story of La Corriveau in three parts: the first part ('Le triple destin ...' *Cahiers des dix* 33 [1968]: 213–242) is a detailed account of the case, the first trial and the second one that resulted in La Corriveau's being sentenced to death and the clearance of her father. It also contains a detailed description of the cage in which she was hanged and the history of gibbeting and hanging in chains. The second part ('Le destin posthume ...' *Cahiers des dix* 34 [1969]: 239–271) deals with La Corriveau's posthumous destiny and the formation of a legend around her, her crime, and her execution, and around the iron cage. The author discusses the treatment of the legend by different historians, novelists, and poets, in particular François Dubé, Louis Fréchette, William Kirby, and Pierre-Georges Roy, until 1947. In the third part, ('Présence de la Corriveau' *Cahiers des dix* 38 [1973]: 229–264) he continues his discussion of the treatment of the legend until 1970.

371. Lanctot, Gustave.

Filles de joie ou filles du roi? Etude sur l'émigration féminine en Nouvelle-France. Montréal: Chanteclecs, 1952.

This book is a study of female emigration to New France during two periods: 1634–62 under the Company of New France, and 1663–73 under the Royal Administration. The first group were female immigrants who came by themselves, on their own initiative. The second group were the ones recruited and transported by ministerial authority. They are the ones who can properly be called 'Les filles du Roi.' The author refutes the assertion that girls of dubious character were transported to New France. He views this to be a historical falsehood and a national defamation. Unlike Brazil, the British colonies, and the French West Indies, New France did not receive any females of loose character. This 'false allegation' is first mentioned in a poem written in 1631 by Saint Amant. Since then, the 'scandalous' rumour was propagated during the seventeenth century. The book *The Voyages of the Baron de Hontan* published in 1703 helped establish the rumour. According to Lanctot, there is no direct testimony, no facts, no documents public or private that support, closely or remotely, this assertion. He points out that it is categorically denied by persons in authority and by those who were aware of the facts. During the first period (1634–62) emigration was on private initiative and female emigrants who came to Canada were chosen with care from orphanages or were brought by parents or acquaintances. They usually travelled under the supervision of nuns or highly respectable persons. The authorities in Canada returned to France every suspect female who succeeded in entering the colony. The author concludes that the rumour incriminating female emigration prior to 1663 was due to an erroneous confusion with the West Indies and is not supported by one single element of proof. On the other hand, the accusation concerning female emigration during the decade 1663–73 seems more serious and more precise. Nevertheless it is weak and uncorroborated because none of its reporters has witnessed the events. As a result, there is no direct testimony and there are no public or private documents to prove its veracity.

372. Leach, Mary J.

'Attitudes on Crime and Poverty in Late Victorian Ontario: The Genesis of a "Social Welfare" State?' Student essay, Osgoode Hall Law School, York University, 1974.

Various historians have suggested that, through having created an administrative system and legal enactments governing the treatment of the criminal and the poor, by the late nineteenth century Ontario had become a 'welfare state.' This paper calls into question the validity of this assumption, through examining attitudes towards crime and poverty reflected in the Toronto *Globe*, in the evidence of the Royal Commission on Prisons and Reformatories in 1891, and the National Conference on Charities and Corrections in 1897. The author's findings indicate that while a great deal of attention in late Victorian Ontario was given to reforming 'the drunkard, the criminal and the pauper,' the purpose of this reform effort was to 'smooth out the wrinkles of the status quo,' rather than provide the indigent and the criminal with 'equality of opportunity' in the manner of the modern welfare state.

373. Leblond, Sylvio.

'Le drame de Kamouraska d'après les documents de l'époque.' *Cahiers des dix* 37 (1972): 239–273.

The author gives a detailed account of a murder case. Dr. George Holmes, who practised medicine in Sorel, left for Kamouraska on January 26, 1839, arriving there on January 31. There he shot and killed Lord Achille Tache, the husband of the woman Holmes loved. Holmes then returned to Sorel and afterwards crossed the border at Burlington in Vermont. Canadian authorities demanded his extradition but the request was denied because of the absence of an extradition treaty between England and the United States. Holmes never returned to Canada. Anne Hébert, the famous Quebec novelist, used this true story for one of her best known novels, *Kamouraska*.

374. Leblond, Sylvio.

'Le meutre de Pierre Dion.' In *Trois siècles de médicine québécois*. Société historique de Québec. Cahiers d'histoire, no. 22, pp. 174–181. Québec: Société historique de Québec, 1970.

The author gives an account of a case of murder committed in Quebec on January 14, 1854. The culprit, François-Xavier Julien, killed his father-in-law, Pierre Dion. Julien was sentenced to death. In the absence of the governor, the sentence was commuted to life imprisonment in the Kingston penitentiary by General Rowan, general administrator of Canada. The commutation of the sentence engendered a polemical debate on the death penalty between two newspapers: *Le Canadien* and the *Journal de Québec*.

375. Leblond, Sylvio.

'Au Québec, on volait aussi des cadavres ...' *La vie médicale au Canada* 3 (12, December 1974): 1210–1218.

376. Lee, G. Won.

'Are Crime Rates Increasing? A Study of the Impact of Demographic Shifts on Crime Rates in Canada.' *Canadian Journal of Criminology* 26 (1, January 1984): 29–42.

Relying on official crime statistics for the period 1949–68, this study provides a general picture of patterns and trends of recorded criminal activities in Canada and the extent to which age and sex variables affect the overall incidence of crime. The author's findings indicate that although Canada experienced generally a gradual increase in serious crime rates from 1949 to 1968, during the same period the crime rate for females nearly tripled.

377. Leon, Jeffrey S.

'New and Old Themes in Canadian Juvenile Justice: The Origins of Delinquency Legislation and the Prospects for Recognition of Children's Rights.' *Interchange* 8 (1–2, 1977): 151–175.

Contained in the 'Legal Issues' section of an issue of *Interchange* devoted to 'Children's Rights: Educational and Legal Issues,' this extensively footnoted paper traces the origins and evolution of juvenile delinquency legislation in Canada. Leon focuses on the difference between children's dependency upon and domination by the state, to the end of relating the necessity and opportunity of securing legal rights for children over the years. He begins with the creation of a separate juvenile justice system, which was based on the assumption that youths should not face the full rigours of the law. He also discusses the related issue of protection of children, which has as its corollary protection from children. Early approaches to child welfare are presented, when the rights of the subjects were not an issue. Reformatories and industrial schools, as well as home-centred and probation-based treatments, are discussed with the related legislation, such as *An Act Respecting the Commitment of Persons of the Tender Years* of 1890, and the influential individuals involved, such as J.J. Kelso. Leon closes by pointing out that later domination of children by the state necessitates legislation of their rights, which can be threatened by lack of access to or questionable mechanisms for enforcement of those rights.

378. Lévesque, Andrée.

'Deviant Anonymous: Single Mothers at the Hôpital de la Miséricorde in Montreal, 1929–1939.' Canadian Historical Association. *Historical Papers* (1984): 168–183.

Roughly 20 per cent of illegitimate births in Quebec during the 1930s took place at the Hôpital de la Miséricorde in Montreal. The extensive patient records of the hospital show that almost all expectant single mothers admitted to the hospital were French-Canadian Roman Catholics, that they tended to be young, and that they were often orphans themselves. Using patient records as her main source of data, the author notes that during her time in residence, the single mother 'was treated sometimes as a child, often as a criminal, and always as a sinner.' Her findings also indicate that after birth, most of the children remained within institutional care, and that a significant percentage died before their first birthdays. From her findings, the author concludes that during the 1930s single mothers were viewed as having brought shame on themselves and their families, and that the hospital served as an institution for hiding deviant behaviour and individuals.

379. Lewis, Norah.

'Physical Perfection for Spiritual Welfare: Health Care for the Urban Child 1900–1939.' In *Studies in Childhood History: A Canadian Perspective*, pp. 135–166. Edited by Patricia T. Rooke and R.L. Schnell. Calgary: Detselig Enterprises Ltd., 1982.

Early health-care professionals and reformers in British Columbia devoted considerable time and energy to improving the quality of life for children. Drawing on literature published in health-care and education journals, board-of-health reports, and school-trustee records, the author demonstrates that during the period from 1900 to 1939 children in British Columbia's urban centres had access to a growing number of programs specifically designed to meet their health-care needs. Owing to the efforts of provincial health-care advisers, who argued for a scientific approach to child health care, these programs grew and expanded to provide not only for the children's physical care, but also for their mental health and moral development.

380. Lodhi, Abdul Qaiyum.

'Urbanization, Criminality and Collective Violence: A Social Study.' Ph.D. dissertation, University of Toronto, 1971.

381. Long, W.A.

'Attitudes Towards the Poor in Toronto, 1880–1911.' M.A. thesis, University of Waterloo, 1977.

382. Lord, Fortunat.

'L'injure – Aperçu historique.' *Revue du barreau* 1 (1941): 231.

The old French law recognized three methods of 'injury': verbal insults (slander), insults in writing (libel), and assault and battery. Certain jurisdictions made a distinction between these various types. Verbal slander was thus left to the civil courts while libel and assault and battery required a complaint and a hearing before the criminal courts. In 1629, a law passed in France prohibited written criticism of the king, his councillors, and his magistrates. This law was applied to New France until the conquest. The Treaty of Paris guaranteed the right of Canadians to use their civil laws. At the time there was little difference between English and French law regarding the way they treated slander and libel. What was the situation regarding slander after the transfer of New France to Britain? The old French law continued to apply after 1763. The courts ordered the delinquent to pay damages to the victim. The oldest judgement was published in the *Gazette du Québec* in 1843 and was pronounced in Sainte-Thérèse. The author concludes that since the transfer, slander was not considered a crime but simply a fault to be corrected through the payment of money to the victim. It was regarded as an act of civil nature and the special laws passed in France did not alter this conviction.

383. McClement, Fred.

Heist: Famous Canadian Robberies. Markham, Ont.: PaperJacks, 1980.

384. McDonald, Lynn.

'Crime and Punishment in Canada: A Statistical Test of the "Conventional Wisdom".' *Canadian Review of Sociology and Anthropology* 6 (1969): 212–236.

This article explores the factual basis of 'conventional wisdom' about the rising crime rate, the effects of police force size, the trend towards leniency in sentencing, and the decline in sentencing disparities in Canada. The author's analysis of relevant statistical data for the period 1950–66 calls into question the validity of the 'conventional wisdom' concerning these issues, and the 'consensus' theory of society on which it is founded.

385. McDonald, Lynn.

The Sociology of Law and Order. Montreal: Book Centre, 1976.

Although this sociological study is international in scope, one chapter is devoted specifically to the topic 'Law and Order in Canada.' Here the author builds on her earlier work (see entry 384 above) to test the validity of opposing 'consensus' and 'conflict' theories of law and order in the Canadian setting. The author's findings, based mainly on survey research and an analysis of criminal statistics, provide greater support for the 'conflict' theory proposition that the criminal law 'very much reflects the particular interests of the holders of economic and political power.'

386. MacDougall, Heather A.

'The Genesis of Public Health Reform in Toronto, 1869–1890.' *Urban History Review/Revue d'histoire urbaine* 10 (3, February 1982): 1–10.

Although primarily concerned with examining the controversy raised by the attempts of early public-health reformers to control disease and improve the quality of urban life in Toronto, this article makes note of the fact that lay and medical reformers also became involved in 'crusades which stressed society's moral and social obligations.' Specific crusades mentioned by the author as having gained the support of early public-health reformers included temperance, sabbatarianism, women's enfranchisement, and the protection of neglected and dependent children.

387. MacFarlane, Bruce A.

Drug Offences in Canada. Toronto: Canada Law Book, 1979.

Although primarily a legal text, this book contains two chapters of historical interest: 'Drug Use and Abuse from an Historical Perspective' and 'An Historical Review of Canadian Drug Legislation."

388. McGovern, Marcia Ann.

'The Women's Christian Temperance Movement in Saskatchewan, 1886–1930: A Regional Perspective of the International White Ribbon Movement.' M.A. thesis, University of Regina, 1977.

Originally established in 1874, the Women's Christian Temperance Union (WCTU) was one of the largest and most influential women's organizations in the world for almost half a century. This study undertakes a comparative analysis of the development of the WCTU movement in Saskatchewan and the United States. Drawing on Saskatchewan-based primary sources including local newspapers, annual reports, and the minutes of WCTU meetings, as well as secondary literature on the development of the movement in the United States, the author examines the early development of the WCTU movement in Saskatchewan (1883–1912), the shifting goals of its members (1912–30), the organization's achievements and influence, and the extent to which the experience of the WCTU movement in Saskatchewan resembled that in the United States. She concludes that many of the general patterns of development that characterized the broader movement – the most evident being the gradual transition from a 'conservative, evangelical approach' to a more 'progressive' and 'professional' approach to 'handling social problems such as poverty, intemperance, injustice and crime' – can readily be detected in the Saskatchewan movement.

389. McKnight, Donald D.

'A Little Bit of Old Harry: Crime and Disorder in Victoria, 1859.' *The Register* 3 (2, September 1982): 158–183.

Drawing mainly on the 'charge books' maintained by Victoria's early police force, this article attempts to shed light on the frequency of crime and types of offences committed by the colonial population. In order to assess the type and frequency of crime, the author tabulates crime statistics contained in four monthly reports written in 1859. By selecting reports written during two summer months and two winter months, the author also attempts to determine whether there existed a seasonal variation in the amount of crime and disorder experienced in Victoria. Preliminary findings indicate that during the four months covered in the study 'victimless crimes' (including morals offences, drunkenness, and bar-room fights) constituted 61.4 per cent of all crimes reported to the Victoria police. It was also found that the incidence of crime in Victoria was no greater in the winter than in the summer months.

390. McLaren, Angus.

'Birth Control and Abortion in Canada, 1870–1920.' *Canadian Historical Review* 59 (3, September 1978): 319–340.

This article examines the debate over birth control in late– nineteenth- and early–twentieth-century Canada, as reflected in religious, medical, legal, and journalistic reports. The author attempts to account for why and how traditional contraceptive methods were employed by Canadian couples and, if these failed, how abortion was employed as a second line of defence against unwanted pregnancies. She concludes that the study of the debate over birth control reveals the extent of women's desires to control their physical functions, even in the face of attempts by the medical profession to convince women of the 'immorality of abortion,' and the law prohibiting 'criminal abortions.'

391. McLean, Robert Irwin.

'A Most Effectual Remedy: Temperance and Prohibition in Alberta, 1875–1915.' M.A. thesis, University of Calgary, 1969.

In 1915 Alberta became the first Canadian province to impose prohibition by popular vote. The purpose of this study is to describe and account for the success of the temperance and prohibition movement in Alberta, and to examine the relationship between the prohibition cause and other reform movements in the province. The author maintains that although the last three-quarters of the nineteenth century witnessed the expansion of

Protestant evangelical temperance and prohibition agitation in Canada, by the end of the century the original movement was in a state of decline. As a result of the rise of industrialization and urbanism in the early twentieth century, however, a number of new reform movements, including the social gospel movement, militant feminism, and agrarianism, emerged. According to the author, these movements 'combined in Alberta to create a reform environment conducive to the evolution of prohibition as the panacea of contemporary socio-economic problems.'

392. McLeod, D.M.

'The History of Liquor Legislation in Saskatchewan, 1870–1947.' M.A. thesis, University of Saskatchewan, Saskatoon, 1948.

393. McNaught, Kenneth.

'Violence in Canadian History.' In *Studies in Canadian Social History*, pp. 376–391. Edited by Michiel Horn and Ronald Sabourin. Toronto: McClelland and Stewart, 1974.

   Historians have tended to assume that the history of Canada has been largely free from the violence and extremism in action that have scarred American history. This article attempts to reassess this generalized version of Canadian history, in light of historical evidence relating to 'the offical uses of violence' by the police and the military. Specific cases of such violence, including the Rebellion of 1885, the 1919 Winnipeg General Strike, and the suppression of strikes in the 1930s, are discussed. The author concludes that 'today's climate of violence in Canada is no more rigorous than that which we have experienced through most of our history,' and that, unlike in the United States, the role of violence in Canadian history has been closely tied to the operation of the political system.

394. McNaught, Kenneth.

'Collective Violence in Canadian History: Some Problems of Definition and Research.' In *Report of the Proceedings [of the] Workshop on Violence in Canadian Society*, pp. 165–176. Toronto: Centre of Criminology, University of Toronto, 1975.

395. MacNutt, T.E.

'Smuggling on St. John's Island (Prince Edward Island), 1788.' *Atlantic Advocate* 50 (9, 1960): 87.

396. Malchelossé, Gérard.

'Faux sauniers, prisonniers et fils de famille en Nouvelle-France au XVIIIe siècle.' *Cahiers des dix* 9 (1944): 161–197.

   In the first part of the article the author provides a brief history of the salt trade, its regulation and its taxation. This is followed by a discussion of the prosecution in France of illegal salt traders under Louis XIV and Louis XV. The second part traces the history of transportation of prisoners, young men, and illegal salt traders to New France in the eighteenth century. The author's view is that New France was not extensively used as a penal colony, that a relatively small number of convicts were sent from France. The majority of these were not hardened or recidivist criminals but illegal salt traders and young persons from good families who were placed in prison/hospitals in France for correctional purposes. Contrary to the claims of some historians who reported that between the years 1700 and 1740 only 200 illegal salt traders were deported to Canada, the author was able to establish that between the years 1730 and 1743 alone, more than 600 were sent from France. Yet only 106 of them were identified and traced with the help of the genealogical dictionary compiled by Cyprien Tanguay. The last part is devoted to the history of the illegal salt traders who settled in Royal Island. The author concludes that France's attempt to transform its Canadian territory into a penal colony was unsuccessful due to the energetic protests of the population, their religious and civil leaders who wanted neither prisoners nor wayward libertines. Only illegal salt traders were accepted. In any case, only a small number were deported to the colony and many of them either returned to Europe or were repatriated. The 100 or so who settled down in Canada became law-abiding, respectable citizens.

397. Malcolm, Murray.

Murder in the Yukon: The Case against George O'Brien. Saskatoon: Western Producer Prairie Books, 1982.

398. Malcolmson, Patricia E.

'The Poor in Kingston, 1815–1850.' In *To Preserve and Defend: Essays on Kingston in the Nineteenth Century*, pp. 281–297. Edited by Gerald Tulchinsky. Montreal and London: McGill-Queen's University Press, 1976.

From a small settlement of some 500 people in 1800, Kingston grew to an active urban community of over 10,000 in 1850. In this chapter the author points out that Kingston, like other growing communities, 'had its share of the labouring poor, the destitute, the helpless, and the social misfits.' Drawing mainly on newspaper reports and archival materials held at the Queen's University Archives, the author describes the types of employment entered into by the labouring poor, and the provisions made for those who were either unable or unwilling to work. Particular attention is given to discussing the establishment of private charitable organizations, hospitals, and workhouses, and the efforts made by reformers to bring about the 'moral improvement' of the poor.

399. Massicotte, E.-Z.

'Duels et coups d'épée à Montréal sous le régime français.' *Bulletin des recherches historiques* 21 (12, December 1915): 353–357.

The author makes reference to a study of duels under the French regime by P.-G. Roy, published in the *Bulletin* (1907). He then reports on several cases of duelling and attacks by the sword which occurred in Montreal in the second half of the seventeenth century and the first half of the eighteenth century. The first case reported took place in Montreal in May 1677. Among the cases reported is the famous duel between Governor Perrot and Lemoyne de Saint Hélène in June 1684. The last cases reported date from 1738 and 1748. The data are collected from various sources identified in the article.

400. Massicotte, E.-Z.

'Le travesti sous le régime français.' *Bulletin des recherches historiques* 38 (1, January 1932): 60–61.

Not many cases of females disguising themselves as males were reported in the history of New France. Only two cases are known: the first is a criminal trial summarized by P.-G. Roy who describes the strange adventure of a sixteen-year-old girl from the Island of Orleans, Anne Emond, who, in 1696, disguised herself in her brother's clothes. She then went to Quebec trying to prevent Governor Frontenac from going on expedition against the Iroquois so that her lover, a soldier, would not leave her. Her disguise was discovered and she was sentenced to the lash at every intersection in the capital city. The second case occurred 42 years later when a certain Jacques Lafarge was found to be a female named Ester Brandeau who had disguised herself as a male. The details of this latter case were reported by Joseph Narmette in the Report of the Ottawa Archives (1886).

401. Massicotte, E.-Z.

'Le meutre de Jean Aubuchon.' *Bulletin des recherches historiques* 40 (11, November 1934): 681–683.

This is a brief account of a murder case that took place in Montreal in 1685. The victim was Jean Aubuchon. The killer(s) was never convicted. A brief biography of the victim is provided.

402. Maxim, Paul Stefan.

'Some Trends in Juvenile Delinquency in Canada, 1958–1973.' Ph.D. dissertation, University of Pennsylvania, 1980.

Maxim's dissertation is concerned mainly with a quantitative analysis of data on juvenile crime rates in Canada for the period 1958 to 1973. In addition to focusing attention on major substantive questions concerning the extent to which juvenile crime rates increased during the period under investigation, the author devotes attention to considering the historical development of the concept of 'delinquency' and how the present conceptualization of juvenile delinquency came to be adopted by the Canadian juvenile justice system. In his historical chapter, the author draws on published secondary sources to provide an overview of the development of Canadian juvenile delinquency legislation, the origins of juvenile probation, and the establishment of the juvenile court. Underlying these developments, the author notes, was a widespread belief that the juvenile was qualitatively different from an adult and as such ought not be held legally responsible to the same degree as an adult.

403. Miller, Hanson Orlo.

The Donnellys Must Die. Toronto: Macmillan of Canada, 1962; Laurentian Library, no. 4, Toronto: Macmillan of Canada, 1967.

404. Miller, Hanson Orlo.

Twenty Mortal Murders. Toronto: Macmillan, 1978.

405. Mitchinson, Wendy.

'Aspects of Reform: Four Women's Organizations in Nineteenth Century Canada.' Ph.D. dissertation, York University, 1977.

406. Mitchinson, Wendy.

'The Y.W.C.A. and Reform in the Nineteenth Century.' *Histoire sociale/Social History* 12 (24, November 1979): 368–384.

The Young Women's Christian Association (YWCA) was one of the many reform organizations established in Canada during the latter part of the nineteenth century. Being closely aligned with the church, the middle-class women who made up the organization were especially concerned with 'maintaining the domestic role of women' during a time of rapid social change. This article examines the historical development and reform efforts of the YWCA in Canada from 1870 to 1900. Particular attention is given to discussing the influences that affected the nature of its reform efforts and their degree of success. The author concludes that 'the YWCA, like most reform organizations, was influenced in its response to the problems of nineteenth-century Canada by many factors – its desire to improve society, vested interests, the values of society, organizational difficulties and traditional responses to new problems.' She also maintains that the experience of the YWCA underscores 'the need for historians to appreciate the sometimes conflicting and complex pressures of Canadian middle-class reformers at the turn of the century.'

407. Mitchinson, Wendy.

'The W.C.T.U.: "For God, Home, and Native Land": A Study of Nineteenth Century Feminism.' In *A Not Unreasonable Claim: Women and Reform in Canada, 1880s–1920s*, pp. 152–167. Edited by Linda Kealey. Toronto: Women's Press, 1979.

In this essay, Mitchinson focuses on examining the organization and work of the Women's Christian Temperance Union in Canada in the late-nineteenth and early-twentieth centuries. Having begun as an organization committed to promoting the cause of prohibition, over the years the concerns of the WCTU broadened to include women's suffrage, the protection of children and teenage girls, and the reform of juvenile delinquents and prisons. Attention is given to considering the reasons underlying the increasing involvement of WCTU members in various struggles to bring about a more 'moral society,' and the ironic consequence this involvement had in perpetuating conservative stereotypes of the proper role of women in society.

408. Mitchinson, Wendy.

'The Women's Christian Temperance Union: A Study in Organization.' *International Journal of Women's Studies* 4 (2, March/April 1981): 143–154.

Here Mitchinson surveys the development and organization of the WCTU in Canada. Note is made of the fact that Canadian organizers did not at first attempt to reform the drunkard, but instead unobtrusively lobbied merchants and town councils to make liquor unavailable to the public. The philosophies and major concerns of the WCTU are outlined, with reference being made to the fact that a committee was established to investigate 'Prison and Police Work and Work among Intemperate Women.'

409. Moffit, Louis W.

'Control of the Liquor Traffic in Canada.' In *Prohibition: A National Experiment*, pp. 188–196. Edited by James H.S. Bossard and Thorsten Sellin. Philadelphia: American Academy of Political Science, 1932.

410. Morel, André.

'Les crimes et les peines: Evolution des mentalités au Québec au XIXe siècle.' *Revue de droit, faculté de droit de l'Université de Sherbrooke* 8 (1977): 384–396.

The author discusses the transition from French to English law in the colony following the conquest and the passage under English rule, highlighting the differences between the two systems of criminal law. During the second half of the eighteenth century, newspapers carried little information regarding criminal justice, the exception being a brief judicial chronicle published in the *Gazette de Québec*. The situation changed at the beginning of the nineteenth century and criminal court activities were covered in detail. One rich source of information is the speeches of judges at the opening of each criminal court session. These speeches, together with newspaper reports and letters to the editor, are used by the author to discuss (1) the sources of crime and (2) the punishment for crime. Regarding the former, the stereotyped thinking of the ruling class blamed crime on alcoholism, drunkenness, immorality, and lack of moral, religious education. Regarding punishment, the full emphasis is placed on intimidation and dissuasion, on the severity of sanctions (some 200 offences being punishable by death), and the system of penalties is characterized by a lack of proportionality between the crime and the punishment.

411. Morrison, Terrence R.

'The Child and Urban Social Reform in Late Nineteenth Century Ontario.' Ph.D. dissertation, University of Toronto, 1971.

The development of social welfare in Canada has provided the subject for an increasing amount of historical research. Sparse attention, however, has been given to the social origins of provisions for the education and welfare of children. This dissertation focuses on examining the emergence of various provisions for the welfare and education of urban children in late–nineteenth-century Ontario. An attempt is made to illustrate that the child welfare crusade in Ontario existed in a reciprocal relationship with other reform movements, including the crusade for women's rights, the struggle for applied Christianity, the temperance onslaught, the sanitary movement, and the drive towards educational reform. According to the author, most of the social problems identified in the late nineteenth century – physical debilitation, poverty, delinquency, truancy, ignorance, immorality, and intemperance – were seen to affect urban children. Detailed attention is given to examining the efforts of reform groups whose primary purpose was to prevent or control the spread of these social problems, through intervening in the lives of disadvantaged and delinquent children and their families.

412. Morrison, Terrence R.

'"Their Proper Sphere": Feminism, the Family and Child Centred Social Reform in Ontario, 1875–1900.' Part I, *Ontario History* 68 (1, March 1976): 45–64; Part II, *Ontario History* 68 (2, June 1976): 65–74.

This two-part article draws heavily on the author's 1971 Ph.D. dissertation and reiterates his earlier conclusions (see entry 411 above).

413. Morton, Desmond.

'"Kicking and Complaining": Demobilization Riots in the Canadian Expeditionary Force 1918–19.' *Canadian Historical Review* 61 (3, September 1980): 334–360.

414. Muir, R.C.

'The Last Canadian Duel.' Brant Historical Society. *Papers and Records* (1930): 24–27.

415. Murphy, Emily F.

The Black Candle. Toronto: Thomas Allen, 1922. *The Black Candle: Canada's First Book on Drug Abuse*. Toronto: Coles, 1973.

416. Newell, William B.

Crime and Justice among the Iroquois Nations. Montreal: Caughnawaga Historical Society, 1965.

417. Nilsen, Deborah.

'The "Social Evil": Prostitution in Vancouver.' B.A. essay, University of British Columbia, 1976.

According to this author, prostitution has been a neglected area of research in Canadian social history. This finding is seen to stem from the fact that the historical study of prostitution is a domain plagued by source problems – particularly unreliable statistics and simple lack of information. The author's study of prostitution in Vancouver from 1900 to 1920 attempts to reduce this gap in historical knowledge. Divided into four chapters, the study examines (1) prevailing views on the causes of prostitution, (2) the local concerns of moral reformers and their response to prostitution in Vancouver, (3) changing police policy towards prostitution motivated by public intolerance of the practice, and (4) the backgrounds of some 500 Vancouver prostitutes between 1912 and 1917 as revealed in Vancouver city jail records. The author concludes that in spite of the implementation of strenuous legal measures and harsher law enforcement during the period, the repeated attempts made to curb the 'social evil' of prostitution met with little success.

418. Noel, Janet.

'Temperance Evangelism: Drink, Religion and Reform in the Province of Canada, 1840–1854.' M.A. thesis, University of Ottawa, 1978.

This thesis examines the spread of temperance as an evangelical movement in the Province of Canada from 1840 to 1854. The study attempts to explain the popularity of temperance by looking at the conditions which gave rise to the movement, the reforms which supporters envisioned, and the means they used to win and sustain converts. The immediate impact of the movement on drinking, and its broader historical significance, are also discussed. Leading mid–nineteenth-century temperance newspapers serve as the author's major primary source of information on temperance activities during the period.

419. Normore, E.L.

'Capital Crimes in Newfoundland 1750–1789.' Unpublished manuscript, Maritime History Collection, Memorial University, 1973.

Prior to 1750 capital crimes were not tried in Newfoundland. Instead the practice of transferring offenders charged with capital crimes committed in Newfoundland, along with witnesses, back to England for trial was followed. Only after 1750, when the governor of the colony was given the power to try capital offences, did the legal structure of the courts in Newfoundland begin to develop. Drawing on British Colonial Records for the period 1750 to 1787, this paper examines the manner in which persons charged with capital offences were dealt with in the years following the creation of Newfoundland's own system for trying capital crimes. A list of 32 actual cases tried by the governor of the colony is provided, along with information on the types of sentences meted out by the court.

420. Olson, Ruth A.

'Rape – An "Un-Victorian" Aspect of Life in Upper Canada.' *Ontario History* 68 (2, June 1976): 75–92.

Documentary evidence provided in this paper suggests that women living in nineteenth-century Ontario were frequently the victims of violence. Drawing on newspaper accounts and government sessional papers, the author documents several examples of cases in which men were made to stand trial on charges of rape or attempted rape. Statistics derived from government sessional papers indicate that only a small fraction of those persons charged with committing a rape or attempted rape were actually convicted. Evidence also indicates that in nineteenth-century Ontario, the onus was on the rape victim to prove she had been forced to have sexual intercourse against her will. The author concludes that proposed changes in the law 'which would institute more humane practices regarding the cross examination of rape victims' may help to eradicate some of the problems associated with modern rape trials that also existed in the nineteenth century.

421. Outerbridge, P.E.

'When Newfoundland Went Dry.' *The Atlantic Advocate* 62 (7, March 1972): 46–49.

422. Owram, Doug.

' "Conspiracy and Treason": The Red River Resistance from an Expansionist Perspective.' *Prairie Forum* 3 (2, Fall 1978): 157–174.

An attempt is made here to explain why the Red River resistance of 1869–70 became a major source of controversy between English and French Canadians. In order to do this, the author looks at the rebellion from the perspective of those English-Canadian Protestants who most opposed it, and identifies four phases, whose cumulative effect was to aggravate the rebellion and its significance to those in central Canada. In elaborating on these four phases, the author notes that: (1) by the time the resistance began, English-Canadian 'expansionists' had developed the belief that 'the Metis were simply the dupes of more powerful and dangerous forces'; (2) this belief led them to the conclusion that any attempt at conciliation was pointless; (3) the 'hard line' advocated by English-Canadian extremists led to a growing concern in French Canada; and (4) this growing French-Canadian concern 'led many expansionists to believe that the real conspiracy was centred in Quebec and its representatives in government.' According to the author, this course of events had a lasting effect on the subsequent history of antagonistic French-English relations in Canada.

423. Panzica, Norman.

'Prohibition (1919) and Marihuana (1972).' *Chitty's Law Journal* 20 (8, October 1972): 269–272.

424. Parr, G. Joy.

'The Welcome and the Wake: Attitudes in Canada West toward the Irish Famine Migration.' *Ontario History* 66 (2, June 1974): 101–113.

Between May and October 1847 over 90,000 uprooted emigrants from the British Isles arrived in Canada. The situation was most desperate for the 70,000 of these who were from Ireland. This paper examines the attitudes of Upper Canadians towards the influx of emigrants from Ireland, and the welcome they received upon arriving in Canada West. Relying mainly on newspaper accounts, the author reveals that Upper Canadians initially welcomed the Irish, thinking that they would make 'hardy and independent yeomanry.' Owing to the fact that many of the new arrivals did not find employment and establish themselves as prosperous farmers, however, observers in Canada West concluded that while those who found work in the countryside could hope for success 'the poor who hung about the cities must be idlers who lacked the initiative to seek out ready opportunities.'

425. Parr, G. Joy.

'The Home Children: British Juvenile Immigrants to Canada, 1868–1924.' Ph.D. dissertation, Yale University, 1977.

Between 1868 and 1924, 80,000 British children from refuges, workhouses, and industrial and reformatory schools were removed to Canada and indentured as agricultural labourers and domestic servants. This dissertation examines the antecedents of the British juvenile-emigration program, and the interactions between British government policy concerning pauper children and Canadian attitudes towards assisted immigration. Case records for individual immigrants are used to establish the circumstances of young emigrants and their social and economic adjustment to Canada during their apprenticeship and adulthood. Particular attention is paid to investigating the impact of the intervention of British social reformers; also investigated is the impact of the subsequent emigration on the children's kin links and upon the youngsters' role in the household economy. The author concludes that the pioneer social workers who 'dispatched youngsters to the back concessions in Canada more through practice of faith than formula, left them with less supervision than the English poor law system provided its own nearer home.'

426. Parr, G. Joy.

'"Transplanting from Dens of Iniquity": Theology and Child Emigration.' In *A Not Unreasonable Claim: Women and Reform in Canada 1880s–1920s*, pp. 169–183. Edited by Linda Kealey. Toronto: The Women's Press, 1979.

427. Parr, G. Joy.

Labouring Children: British Immigrant Apprentices to Canada 1869–1924. Montreal: McGill-Queen's University Press, 1980.

428. Paterson, Thomas W.

Outlaws of the Canadian Frontier. Langley, B.C.: Stagecoach Publishing, 1974.

429. Paterson, Thomas W., and McLean, Terry.

Outlaws of Western Canada. Langley, B.C.: Stagecoach Publishing, 1977.

430. Petryshyn, J.

'R.B. Bennett and the Communists, 1930–1935.' *Journal of Canadian Studies* 9 (November 1974): 45–48.

This article examines events surrounding the arrest and conviction of eight prominent communists on charges of sedition. It notes that the eight individuals were arrested by the Ontario Provincial Police, assisted by the RCMP, and charged under Section 98 of the Criminal Code (repealed in 1936). All of the individuals were convicted and sentenced to terms of imprisonment for being members of the Communist Party of Canada.

431. Phelan, Josephine.

'A Duel on the Island.' *Ontario History* 69 (4, December 1977): 235–238.

The author provides a brief account of a duel that took place in 1812 between William Warren Baldwin, a medical doctor, and Mr. John McDonnell, the acting attorney general of Upper Canada. The duel stemmed from a personal insult McDonnell offered Baldwin during the spring Assize held at York. It ended without bloodshed when McDonnell, at the last moment, refused to raise his gun in his own defence. Although at the time duelling was recognized as being 'contrary to the law of the land and teachings of religion,' the gentlemen were not held criminally liable for their actions.

432. Pierce, Richard.

'Nils von Schoultz – The Man They Had to Hang.' *Historic Kingston* 19 (1970): 56–65.

In November 1838, a group of Canadian expatriates and sympathizers from south of the border launched an attack on Prescott aimed at liberating Canada from the tyranny of British rule. Nils von Schoultz was one of the American-based sympathizers who, having led in the unsuccessful attack, was subsequently placed on trial and hanged. This article discusses previously undocumented aspects of von Schoultz's life and earlier career, his participation in the famous 'Battle of the Windmill,' and events leading up to his execution. The author notes that although 'the young Kingston lawyer, John A. Macdonald,' agreed to serve as von Schoultz's defence counsel, there was little he could do to save the leader of the 1838 expedition from hanging.

433. Pierson, Ruth Roach.

'The Double Bind of the Double Standard: V.D. Control and the CWAC in World War II.' *Canadian Historical Review* 62 (1, March 1981): 31–58.

434. Pinno, Erhard.

'Temperance and Prohibition in Saskatchewan.' M.A. thesis, University of Saskatchewan, Regina, 1971.

This thesis considers prohibition in Saskatchewan within the broader context of the province's temperance movement. While acknowledging that the First World War acted as a catalyst in the drive for prohibition, the author maintains that, in itself, wartime patriotism was not sufficient to account for the tremendous consensus on the subject. Rather, in his interpretation, the prohibition movement in Saskatchewan owed its success to the evangelical crusade of Protestant reformers, among whom 'liquor was considered to be evil not only in excess, but was in any degree a corruption.'

435. Pires, Alvaro A. de Oliveira.

'Crime et criminologie: Réflexions sur l'histoire d'une science et d'un objet.' M.Sc. thesis, Université de Montréal, 1978.

436. Pitsula, James.

'The Treatment of Tramps in Late Nineteenth-Century Toronto.' Canadian Historical Association. *Historical Papers* (1980): 116–132.

Due to the high rate of unemployment in late–nineteenth-century Canada and the United States, tramps became a major problem in big cities, where they were viewed by middle-class philanthropists as a 'social evil' to be contained. In Toronto, the Associated

Charities led in the effort to deal with the steadily increasing number of tramps. According to the author's account of the treatment of tramps in the city, the introduction of a labour test and more stringent hygiene requirements were two of the more successful measures employed to reduce the transient population.

437. Pollock, Sheila Joy.

'A Study of the Impact of Social Change on Developments in the Philosophy of Child Welfare in Ontario between 1891–1921.' M.S.W. thesis, University of Toronto, 1966.

438. Preece, Harold.

The Dalton Gang: End of an Outlaw Era. Toronto: New American Library of Canada, 1964.

439. Prentice, Alison.

'The School Promoters: Education and Social Class in Mid-Nineteenth Century Upper Canada.' Ph.D. dissertation, University of Toronto, 1974. Book of same title published as part of the Canadian Social History Series. Toronto: McClelland and Stewart, 1977.

Most histories of education in Ontario have emphasized the egalitarian and ameliorative aspects of free and compulsory schooling in the mid-nineteenth century. This dissertation presents a reinterpretation of the origins of the Ontario school system, which focuses on exploring the attitudes of early educators to social class. Particular attention is given to examining the ideas of Egerton Ryerson, who, as chief superintendent of schools from 1846 to 1876, was one of the major promoters of schooling in Upper Canada. The author's findings indicate that although the school promoters were optimistic about a future made better by mass education, they were exceptionally pessimistic about the present condition of their society. In particular, they believed that 'the potential for human depravity,' accentuated by the failure to educate, was reflected in increasing crime and social disorder. Through her historical analysis the author demonstrates that educational reform in Ontario was 'part of a complex interweaving of ideas, practices and events which extended far beyond the more immediate concerns of local schoolmen.'

440. Prichard, Michael J.

'1750 Crime at Sea: Admiralty Sessions and the Background to Later Colonial Jurisdiction.' *Dalhousie Law Journal* 8 (3, 1984): 43–58. Also published in *Law in a Colonial Society: The Nova Scotia Experience*, pp. 43-58. Edited by Peter Waite, Sandra Oxner, and Thomas Barnes. Toronto: Carswell, 1984.

441. Ramsey, Dean P.

'The Development of Child Welfare Legislation in Ontario: A History of Child Welfare Legislation in Ontario with Particular Reference to the Children's Protection Act, the

Adoption Act and the Children of Unmarried Parents Act and Subsequent Amendments to These Acts.' M.S.W. thesis, University of Toronto, 1949.

442. Read, Colin.

The Rising in Western Upper Canada, 1837–8: The Duncombe Revolt and After. Toronto: University of Toronto Press, 1982.

In December 1837, Charles Duncombe led some 500 men in an abortive rebellion in the southwestern region of Upper Canada. In the months following the suppression of the rebellion, hundreds of rebels and their supporters were apprehended, jailed, and tried for treason and related offences. In this book, the author documents the events and circumstances that led to the rebellion, and deals at length with its repercussions and consequences. Particular attention is given to describing the manner in which individuals accused of participating in the rebellion were dealt with by authorities, along with the nature and outcome of the ensuing treason trials.

443. Reedie, Penny B.

'The Process of Criminalization: An Examination of the Treason and Sedition Laws in Canada.' M.A. thesis, University of Ottawa, 1979.

Current writings about the evolution and function of law are dominated by opposing 'conflict' and 'consensus' schools of thought. This thesis examines the evolution of Canadian laws on sedition and treason in an effort to determine the validity of contradictory theoretical hypotheses associated with these opposing schools. Towards this end, the author analyses changes that have occurred in the Canadian laws on sedition and treason since they were brought into force, and the relationship of these changes to the social settings in which they emerged. The author found that whenever there appeared to be a threat internal or external to society, or a change in social structure, there occurred a re-examination of the laws on sedition and treason and a redefinition of the parameters of acceptable social behaviour. This is taken to support a conflict-model interpretation that changes in the law allow the powerful few in society to maintain their advantaged position by using state power to coerce the mass of the people into doing what is consistent with their own interests.

444. Reid, John G.

'Styles of Colonisation and Social Disorders in Early Acadia and Maine: A Comparative Approach.' La société historique acadienne. *Les cahiers* 7 (3, September 1976): 105–117.

445. Riddell, William Renwick.

'The Duel in Early Upper Canada.' *The Canadian Law Times* 35 (9, 1915): 726–738. Also published in *Journal of the American Institute of Criminal Law and Criminology* 6 (1915): 165–176.

The United Empire Loyalists who settled early Upper Canada brought their English laws and customs with them. The duel was a custom which was unlawful, but which continued to be used as a means of resolving some disputes. While the courts laid down the law, there was an 'unwritten law' by which participants in 'fair' duels were not always convicted. Riddell goes on to give several examples of duels which got considerable public attention, and in which concepts such as honour, justice, and fairness were implicitly enforced.

446. Riddell, William Renwick.

'Another Duel in Early Upper Canada.' *The Canadian Law Times* 36 (8, 1916): 604–610.

447. Riddell, William Renwick.

'The "Green Goods Game" in 1815.' *The Canadian Law Times* 40 (3, March 1920): 184–188.

448. Robin, Martin.

The Bad and the Lonely: Seven Stories of the Best – and Worst – Canadian Outlaws. Toronto: James Lorimer and Company, 1976.

Although written in the style of a popular account, this collection of short stories deals with factual cases involving Canadian 'outlaws,' and is based on considerable library and archival research. Each of the seven stories included in the book is followed by a select bibliography of relevant popular literature (not included in the present bibliography) and archival sources.

449. Robin, Martin.

The Saga of Red Ryan and Other Tales of Violence from Canada's Past. Saskatoon: Western Producer Prairie Books, 1982.

450. Rooke, Patricia T., and Schnell, R.L.

'Charlotte Whitton Meets "The Last Best West": The Politics of Child Welfare in Alberta, 1929–1949.' *Prairie Forum* 6 (2, 1981): 143–162.

When Charlotte Whitton was requested to come to Alberta in 1947 to undertake a personal study of the province's child welfare system, she was at the lowest point in her career. She had lost her position as director of the Canadian Welfare Council in 1941 and had failed to find an alternative vehicle to promote her ideals concerning the provision of child welfare services, and in particular her belief that child welfare agencies should be operated by 'professional' social workers. According to the authors, the confrontation that developed between Whitton and the Alberta government over her allegation that dependent children were being 'exported' from the province for adoption was carefully manipulated by Whitton to bring her public attention and support, which helped her in launching a second political career. The article relies mainly on newspaper coverage of the confrontation and primary historical documents held in the Archives of Alberta and the Public Archives of Canada.

451. Rooke, Patricia T., and Schnell, R.L.

'Child Welfare in English Canada, 1920–1948.' *Social Service Review* 55 (3, September 1981): 484–506.

The Canadian Council on Child Welfare (CCCW) was established in 1920 as a nationally based agency that would operate as 'a clearing house of child welfare.' Funded by the federal government, the original goals of the quasi-public agency included examining aspects of child hygiene, employment, education, and the special care of dependent, delinquent, and neglected children. This article examines the work carried out by the CCCW under the leadership of Charlotte Whitton. The authors maintain that in her capacity as director of the organization, Whitton exercised singular influence over the development of a professional and 'scientific' approach to child welfare in English Canada. The development of more effective provincial ministries of social welfare and the increasing direct intervention of the federal government in social-welfare matters during the depression and war years, however, resulted in the emergence of competing centres of expertise and finance in the area of child welfare that eventually matched that of the CCCW.

452. Rooke, Patricia T., and Schnell, R.L.

'The "King's Children" in English Canada: A Psychohistorical Study of Abandonment, Rejection, and Colonial Response (1869–1930).' *Journal of Psychohistory* 8 (Spring 1981): 387–420.

Between 1869 and 1930, some 80,000 young immigrants were brought over to Canada from Britain. The children were part of what is now known as the juvenile-emigration movement, which was sponsored by a score of British child-rescue agencies. This paper examines the experiences of the juvenile emigrants and the Canadian response to them by means of transactional modes developed by the psychologist Helm Stierlin to explicate the process by which parents and adolescents separate, or become relatively independent of each other. Stierlin's 'binding,' 'delegating,' and 'expelling' modes are used to analyse and interpret evidence from archives, public records, private papers, and contemporary literature. Particular attention is paid to investigating the accusations made by Canadians that the immigrants were prone to a range of abnormalities, including criminality, feeble-mindedness, and degeneracy. Attention is also given to considering the variety of possible emotional responses to their particular circumstances that children found themselves undergoing after arriving in Canada. The authors maintain that modern psychological research can assist historians in developing a more complete understanding of the pychological stresses to which the immigrant children might have been subject.

453. Rooke, Patricia T., and Schnell, R.L.

'Charlotte Whitton and the "Babies for Export" Controversy, 1947–1948.' *Alberta History* 30 (Winter 1982): 11–16.

In the late 1940s, a furore over conditions of child care in Alberta was precipitated through a number of provocative, alarming, and highly sensationalized exposés instigated by Canada's leading proponent of child welfare, Charlotte Whitton. As a consequence of her published exposés claiming that the provincial government was involved in the illicit export of babies for adoption, and that the province's child welfare system was 'tainted with authoritarianism' like that which existed in Nazi Germany and the USSR, Whitton and two associates were charged with conspiracy to commit 'defammatory libel.' In this article, the authors discuss the outcome and impact of Whitton's trial, and the much-publicized Judicial Commission of Inquiry into the operation of Alberta's child welfare system conducted in 1947. While Whitton's trial ended in a stay of proceedings, the Commission of Inquiry found that her claims concerning the extent to which dependent children were being 'exported' from the province, and the deplorable consequences that this had for the affected children, were both 'excessive and deceptive.'

454. Rooke, Patricia T., and Schnell, R.L.

'Childhood and Charity in Nineteenth Century British North America.' *Histoire sociale/ Social History* 15 (29, May 1982): 157–179.

This article traces the history of nineteenth-century child-rescue sentiment and institutions by examining the manner in which prevailing notions associated with the concept of 'childhood' – protection, segregation, dependence, and delayed responsibilities – manifest themselves in provisions for dependent and neglected children and youth in British North America. The article consists of three parts. The first part explicates dominant themes of pre-Victorian child rescue in Britain, and in particular the arguments behind the establishment of early orphan asylums, schools, houses of industry, and other charitable institutions. The second part describes the mixed forms of poor relief and child rescue available in British North America in the early nineteenth century. The third, and most developed, section seeks to demonstrate that, contrary to the view expressed by other historians, the first significant shifts in Canadian sentiment towards dependent child life had occurred well before the 1880s and that this transformation is best understood by examining the establishment and growth of children's homes. The authors draw on a variety of primary historical sources, including the annual reports of early Canadian orphan asylums, poorhouses, and benevolent societies.

455. Rooke, Patricia T., and Schnell, R.L.

'Guttersnipes and Charity Children: Nineteenth Century Child Rescue in the Atlantic Provinces.' In *Studies in Childhood History: A Canadian Perspective*, pp. 82–104. Edited by Patricia T. Rooke and R.L. Schnell. Calgary: Detselig Enterprises Ltd., 1982.

In this chapter, the authors discuss the treatment of dependent children and the rise of children's institutions in the Atlantic provinces during the nineteenth century. Included in this discussion is the common practice of 'binding out' or indenturing orphaned and destitute children to private families, which existed both before and after the establishment of specialized orphan asylums. Despite the rise of these institutions, and the efforts made to rescue children through segregating them from undesirable influences, the authors' evidence suggests that throughout the nineteenth century children continued to be confined along with adults in poorhouses, prisons, and houses of refuge. They also document the prevailing belief that homeless and destitute children who could be observed on the streets of eastern Canadian cities – commonly referred to as 'street arabs' or 'guttersnipes' – 'were destined to become the criminals of the future' unless they were 'reclaimed from [the] paths of vice, or better yet, prevented from walking them.'

456. Rooke, Patricia T., and Schnell, R.L.

'The Rise and Decline of British North American Protestant Orphan's Homes as Woman's Domain, 1850–1930.' *Atlantis* 7 (2, Spring 1982): 21–35.

Beginning in the mid-nineteenth century, at the behest of Protestant middle-class women, orphan's homes were established in most major Canadian cities. With the rise of professional social work in the early twentieth century, however, the philanthropic efforts of these women, who were identified as 'traditionalists' and 'sentimentalists,' became the object of criticism from the proponents of a more 'scientific' approach to child care. This article traces the transformation of Protestant Orphan's Homes, from being based on nineteenth-century ideas about the care of dependent and neglected children, to being guided by a professional and scientific outlook on the best methods to be followed in operating such institutions. In separate sections, the authors contrast the approach to the institutional care of children taken by nineteenth-century 'philanthropists' and twentieth-century 'professionalizers.' They conclude that the original assumptions behind the campaign to found child-rescue institutions were gradually transformed or eroded under the pressures exerted by trained child welfare professionals and by municipal and provincial child welfare departments staffed by civil servants.

457. Rooke, Patricia T., and Schnell, R.L.

'"Making the Way More Comfortable": Charlotte Whitton's Child Welfare Career, 1920–1948.' *Journal of Canadian Studies* 17 (4, Winter 1982–3): 33–45.

458. Rooke, Patricia T., and Schnell, R.L.

Discarding the Asylum: From Child Rescue to the Welfare State in English-Canada (1800–1950). Lanham, Md.: University Press of America, 1983.

Building on their previous historical work, the authors attempt to provide a national perspective on the transformation in attitudes towards children, and the transition from 'child rescue' to 'child welfare' that occurred in English Canada during the nineteenth and twentieth centuries. In ten chapters the authors describe and analyse three major organizational modes that demonstrate the transition in thinking about childhood and the treatment of children that occurred between 1800 and 1950: from philanthropy to scientific charity; from voluntarism to professionalization; and from professionalization to state welfarism. Extensive documentation is provided to substantiate the authors' thesis, and form a chronological narrative of the plight of dependent children in English Canada during the 150-year period.

459. Ross, Herman Russell.

'Juvenile Delinquency in Montreal.' M.A. thesis, McGill University, 1932.

460. Ross, Winifred Mary.

'Child Rescue: The Nova Scotia Society for the Prevention of Cruelty, 1880–1920.' M.A. thesis, Dalhousie University, 1976.

Prior to the nineteenth century, children do not appear to have been treated as a special category of individuals prized for their innocence and in need of protection from abuse. However, during the nineteenth century a growing interest in children, as reflected in the establishment of societies and organizations for the protection and welfare of children and the enactment of legislation aimed at the improvement of the conditions under which they lived, asserted itself in major western countries. This thesis focuses on determining the extent to which welfare services were made available to children in Nova Scotia, and particularly in Halifax, in the period from 1880 to 1920. The author contends that the main driving force behind the establishment of child welfare services in the province was the Nova Scotia Society for the Prevention of Cruelty (SPC). Although originally formed to lobby for the protection of animals, the SPC is recognized to have played a vital role in bringing about the enactment of provincial child protection legislation, the establishment of a juvenile court (1912), and the creation of the Department of Neglected and Dependant Children (1912). The author's major data source consists of the annual reports, minutebooks, correspondence, and other records maintained by the SPC during the period 1877 to 1920.

461. Rotenberg, Lori.

'The Wayward Worker: Toronto's Prostitute at the Turn of the Century.' In *Women at Work, Ontario, 1850–1930*, pp. 33–69. Edited by Janice Acton, Penny Goldsmith, and Bonnie Shepard. Toronto: Canadian Women's Educational Press, 1974.

Written from a feminist perspective, this paper draws on available contemporary sources in an effort to understand how prostitution operated as a social institution in Toronto in the period from 1890 to 1914. In contrast to the statements of 'moral reformers' of the period, who viewed prostitutes generally as 'fallen women,' the author recognizes prostitution as a low-status occupation entered into by women, often out of economic need. In turn, the paper examines available evidence regarding the 'physical setting' in which prostitutes 'plied the trade,' the age, ethnicity, previous occupations, and social-class origins of known Toronto prostitutes around the turn of the century, and the attempts made by police and moral reformers to control and/or reform prostitutes. The author concludes that 'in order to fully understand the role of the prostitute as a worker in Toronto' it is necessary to realize that, within a patriarchal capitalist society, the 'prostitute performed a necessary social function' by satisfying the male prerogative for pre-marital and extra-marital sex without threatening the institution of the family.

462. Rouleau, Marc Yvan Florian.

'Le Québec dans le plebiscite canadien de 1898 sur la prohibition.' M.A. thesis, Concordia University, 1979.

This paper attempts to explain the reasons underlying the Quebec anti-prohibition position in the 1898 Canadian plebiscite. Relying on primary and secondary sources, the paper recounts the course of the prohibition campaign, studies its moral and ideological stakes, and analyses the vote results in Quebec. The author draws conclusions, first, about a marked division between voting districts according to the origin of their population, the French being anti-prohibition, the British being in favour of it, and second, about the importance of individual freedom of choice in relation to the consumption of alcoholic beverages for French Quebecers.

463. Roy, Patricia.

'The Preservation of the Peace in Vancouver: The Aftermath of the Anti-Chinese Riot of 1887.' *B.C. Studies* 31 (1976): 44–59.

464. Roy, Pierre-Georges.

'Le duel sous le régime français.' *Bulletin des recherches historiques* 13 (5, 1907): 129–138.

The author reports on the punishment for duelling prescribed by a law enacted by Louis XIV, King of France, in June 1643. This is followed by an account of eight cases of duelling that were reported in New France between 1646 and 1736. The first case took place in Three Rivers in the winter of 1646. Other reported cases occurred in Three Rivers (1669 and 1736), Montreal (1684, 1689, and 1690), and Quebec (1698, 1706, and 1715). Swords were the weapons used in all these duels.

465. Roy, Pierre-Georges.

Un corsaire canadien: Jean Léger de la grange. Montréal: Lévis, 1918.

466. Roy, Pierre-Georges.

'La punition des crimes autrefois.' *Bulletin des recherches historiques* 45 (2, February 1939): 50–51.

The author reports on the punishment inflicted in 1690 on a resident of Boucherville, convicted of the murder of a Montreal merchant. The accused was sentenced to have his right hand cut in front of the door of his victim's residence and to receive six lashes on his legs, thighs, and arms on a scaffold mounted at St. Paul Street in Montreal. He was then to be placed on the wheel with his eyes facing the sky until his death. His estate was to be confiscated with a portion going to the Seigniory of Montreal and a portion going to repair the damage caused by his act. The sentence was appealed to the Supreme Council (Conseil Souverain). The council ordered that the accused be strangled without being whipped and that his body be left on the wheel for 24 hours before being buried.

467. Roy, Pierre-Georges.

'Crimes et peines sous le régime français.' *Revue canadienne* 52 (2, 1966): 707–708; (4, 1966): 250–263; (5, 1966): 314–326.

468. Rutherford, Paul.

'Tomorrow's Metropolis: The Urban Reform Movement in Canada, 1880–1920.' Canadian Historical Association. *Historical Papers* (1971): 203–224. Also published in *The Canadian City: Essays in Urban History*, pp. 368–392. The Carleton Library, 109. Edited by Gilbert A. Stelter and Alan F.J. Artibise. Toronto: McClelland and Stewart, 1977.

Between 1880 and 1920, the urban population of Canada increased in absolute terms from 1.1 million to 4.3 million, and in proportional terms from one-quarter to one-half the total population. This phenomenal urban expansion was accompanied by a growing concern with urban problems that affected Canadian cities, and the emergence of an urban-reform movement. This paper examines the development and character of the urban-reform movement in Canada, and the various efforts made by reformers to alleviate the problems associated with the 'big city.' The author notes that the urban-reform movement encompassed a broad range of concerns, including attempts at public-health reform, urban planning, tax reform, the regulation of utility corporations, and 'moral reform' crusades aimed at purifying city life by controlling vice and crime. Although drawing its leadership from the 'new middle class' concentrated mainly in central Canadian urban centres, the success of the urban-reform movement was heavily dependent upon the active support of municipal government. Along with expanding the responsibilities of municipal government, the urban-reform movement fostered the development of an increasingly professional, scientific, and bureaucratic approach to dealing with urban problems.

469. Rutherford, Paul, ed.

Saving the Canadian City: The First Phase, 1880–1920: An Anthology of Early Articles on Urban Reform. Social History of Canada, 22. Toronto: University of Toronto Press, 1974.

This anthology contains representative examples of the writings of late–nineteenth- and early–twentieth-century Canadian urban reformers, organized around four general themes: (1) the debate over the control of utility corporations, (2) the efforts made to create a healthy, moral, and equitable city, (3) the desire for a planned urban environment, and (4) the changing character of municipal-reform schemes. As well as containing a general introduction covering the development and character of the urban-reform movement in Canada, each of the four sections is prefaced with a more focused introductory essay. A supplementary bibliography of contemporary sources intended for readers interested in investigating reform mentality in greater depth is provided at the end of the book.

470. Rutman, L.

'The Importation of British Children into Canada, 1868–1916.' *Child Welfare* 52 (3, March 1973): 158–166.

About 80,000 British children crossed the Atlantic between 1868 and 1916 to begin family life in Canada. This article examines the purposes underlying the importation of 'British waifs' who came from orphanages, rescue homes, and workhouses; the arrangements made by sponsoring organizations and Canadian provincial and federal governments for their placement in Canada; and the public issues and concerns that emerged out of the practice. In addition to expressing concern about the mistreatment of the British children sent to work on farms and the fact that dependent children already living in Canada should be cared for first, critics of the movement argued that 'the importation of children taken from the reformatories, refuges and workhouses of England,' unless carried out with the utmost care and prudence, 'would swell the criminal ranks of the country.'

471. Rybak, Stephen Zachery.

'A Hasty Patching Up: An Examination of Unemployment and Relief Programs as They Affected Canada's Transient and Single Jobless, 1935–1940.' M.A. thesis, Concordia University, 1976.

Upon regaining political power in 1935, Prime Minister Mackenzie King inherited a theoretical threat to existing social and political institutions posed by an estimated 100,000 single, homeless, and unemployed adults. This group of unemployed, hardest hit by the depression, were looked upon by governments and the police as possible troops for a revolution led by communist and anarchist agitators. This thesis examines the steps taken by the Mackenzie King government to deal with the problems posed by the unemployed. Drawing on a wide range of federal government documents, it discusses 'the flurry of widely publicized studies, conferences, and commissions and programs' that were launched to cope with transients and the single unemployed. The author concludes that while Liberal policies and programs provided answers 'to the problems posed by the unemployed for governments,' they did little 'to help jobless men and women get through the depression on anything more than a mere subsistence level.'

472. Saint-Denis, Paul.

'Legislating Morality: The Case of Obscenity Legislation in Canada.' M.A. thesis, University of Ottawa, 1981.

The *Criminal Code* offence of obscenity first appeared in Canada in 1892. Since the initial introduction of the offence, Canadian legislators and the courts have been involved in a continuing controversy over the definition of 'obscene.' This thesis examines the history of Canadian obscenity law as a case study in the legislation of morality. Attention is given to tracing the historical evolution of Canadian obscenity legislation, and the manner in which the law has been interpreted by the Canadian judiciary. The author concludes that legislators' attempts to legislate morality through the use of the criminal law have been far from successful. He recommends that parliament should consider decriminalizing obscenity offences and attempt to control them through non-criminal legislation.

473. Sampson, William Rea.

'Mining Law and Social Order in the Gold Camps of California and British Columbia, 1848–1871: A Comparative Study.' Ph.D. dissertation, Washington State University, 1966.

474. Savage, Leslie.

'Perspectives on Illegitimacy: The Changing Role of the Sisters of Misericordia in Edmonton, 1900–1906.' In *Studies in Childhood History: A Canadian Perspective*, pp.

105–133. Edited by Patricia T. Rooke and R.L. Schnell. Calgary: Detselig Enterprises Ltd., 1982.

When the Order of the Sisters of Misericordia was founded in Montreal in 1848, its aim was to rescue unwed mothers from dishonour and restore them to a virtuous life. Linked to this goal was the order's focus on the rescue of the illegitimate born and unborn from the threat of death by abortion, infanticide, neglect, or abandonment. In 1900, four Sisters of the Misericordia established a mission and hospital for unwed mothers in Edmonton. This article examines the work of the order during the city's early years of rapid urban development. The author maintains that soon after having arrived in Edmonton, the central focus of the Sisters' work changed from child rescue and female reform to general medical services and hospital nursing. Evidence presented suggests that the evolution of the role of the Edmonton Misericordia was a response to the different socio-economic conditions and moral attitudes of early–twentieth-century Edmonton as opposed to those of nineteenth-century Montreal. Data sources used in the article include published law reports, census reports, parish baptismal records, and the files of the attorney general of Alberta.

475. Savoie, Gérald.

'La criminalité à Montréal.' M.A. thesis, Université de Montréal, 1961.

476. Schecter, Stephen.

'Capitalism, Class and Educational Reform in Canada.' In *The Canadian State: Political Economy and Political Power*, pp. 373–416. Edited by Leo Panitch. Toronto: University of Toronto Press, 1977.

Written from a Marxist perspective, this essay examines the formative influences underlying the establishment of a system of public education in Upper Canada, and the purposes served by educational reform during the last half of the nineteenth century. Drawing mainly on secondary sources concerned with the history of public schooling, labour, and social control, the author contends that the basic purpose of early school reform in Upper Canada 'was the social control of an emerging working class.' Without an educational system aimed at instilling habits of 'discipline, punctuality and good conduct' in the working class, school reformers feared its members would fall prey to 'crime, vice and pauperism.'

477. Scott, W.L.

'The Genesis of the Juvenile Delinquents Act.' (Typescript) n.p. [1939].

478. Séguin, Robert Lionel.

La sorcellerie au Canada français du XVIIe au XIXe siècle. Montréal Librairie Ducharme, 1961.

479. Séguin, Robert Lionel.

La sorcellerie au Québec du XVIIe au XIXe siècle. Montréal: Leméac, 1971.

This book traces the history of sorcery and witchcraft in Quebec from the seventeenth to the nineteenth century. During this period 43 cases were reported, 21 in Quebec City, 9 in Montreal, and the remainder in other parts of the 'province.' In addition to a description of the cases, various forms of repression both religious and secular are discussed.

480. Séguin, Robert Lionel.

La vie libertine en Nouvelle-France au dix-septième siècle. 2 vols. Montréal: Leméac, 1972.

481. Shaw, T.E.G.

'The Cashel Case.' *Alberta Historical Review* 8 (1, Winter 1960): 17–20.

In 1903, Ernest Cashel was convicted of and sentenced to be hanged for murder. Five days before his scheduled execution, he escaped from a NWMP guard-room in Calgary and remained at large for 46 days. This article recounts the events leading up to Cashel's arrest and conviction, the means by which he managed to escape custody, and the successful efforts made by the NWMP to recapture him. Although the author notes that the Cashel case received widespread coverage in Calgary newspapers, no references are provided in the article.

482. Sheehan, Nancy M.

'Temperance, Education and the W.C.T.U. in Alberta, 1905–1930.' *Journal of Educational Thought* 14 (2, August 1980): 108–124.

The unprecedented immigration and incipient industrialization that affected Alberta during the early decades of the twentieth century placed a tremendous burden on the province's school system, and led to various efforts at educational reform. Among the groups from outside the school system that sought to effect changes in the curriculum of Alberta schools was the Women's Christian Temperance Union (WCTU). This article examines the efforts undertaken by the WCTU in Alberta to introduce temperance education into the curriculum of Alberta schools in the period from 1905 to 1930. The author maintains that throughout the period the WCTU in Alberta considered temperance education to be one of its most important activities.

483. Sheehan, Nancy M.

'The W.C.T.U. on the Prairies, 1886–1930: An Alberta-Saskatchewan Comparison.' *Prairie Forum* 6 (1, Spring 1981): 17–34.

Here the author examines the Women's Christian Temperance Union (WCTU) in Alberta and Saskatchewan during the years 1886–1930. She argues that despite their common beginning under the territorial banner and the guidance of an international WCTU organization, the unions in the two provinces eventually emerged as distinctly different entities. The WCTU in Saskatchewan stressed charitable and benevolent activities, while its Alberta counterpart became involved in reform activities in fields such as prohibition, female suffrage, and temperance education. The author concludes that the reasons for these differences lie in factors such as local leadership, political differences, and contrasts in the economy and settlement characteristics of the two provinces.

484. Shortt, Edward.

'The Memorial Duel at Perth.' *The Law Society of Upper Canada Gazette* 5 (3, September 1971): 142–165.

485. Slattery, T.P.

They Got to Find Me Guilty Yet. Toronto: Doubleday Canada, 1972.

486. Smandych, Russell.

'Marxism and the Creation of Law: Re-Examining the "Origins" of Canadian Anti-Combines Legislation, 1890–1910.' *Canadian Criminology Forum* 6 (1, Fall 1983): 49–60.

487. Smith, Bob.

'The Liquor Question in the 1916 Election in Chilliwack.' *British Columbia Historical News* 15 (Spring 1982): 6–12.

488. Smith, James F.

'Cumberland County Hatchet Murders.' *Nova Scotia Historical Quarterly* 5 (2, June 1975): 117–129.

489. Snider, D. Laureen.

'Corporate Crime in Canada: A Preliminary Report.' *Canadian Journal of Criminology* 20 (2, April 1978): 142–168.

Marxist theory, as revised by David Stratman (1975), predicts that corporate crime and the enforcement of laws against it have tended to increase steadily over the last 30 years. However, conflict theory, as explicated by Turk (1969) and others, predicts that until and unless the power of the economic élite is decreased, the enforcement of laws against corporate crime will remain steady. The purpose of this paper is to examine key aspects of corporate crime and its enforcement in Canada in light of these different predictions. In this effort, the author presents historical and quantitative data relating to the enforcement of the Canadian *Combines Investigation Act* in the period from 1961 to 1973. She maintains that although the preliminary nature of the study makes it nearly impossible to determine whether the findings support a conflict or Marxist interpretation, evidence seems to suggest that those who control the major economic resources in Canadian society have been able to use their power to prevent the introduction of laws which threaten their position.

490.   Snider, D. Laureen.

'Revising the Combines Investigation Act: A Study in Corporate Power.' In *Structure, Law and Power: Essays in the Sociology of Law*, pp. 105–119. Edited by Paul J. Brantingham and Jack M. Kress. Beverly Hills: Sage Publications, 1979.

Canada's first *Combines Investigation Act* was passed in 1889. Focusing attention on subsequent revisions to the original 1889 act, this article examines the numerous attempts that have been made to strengthen the enforcement provisions of the legislation. The author notes that although strict 'proconsumer and procompetition' amendments to Canadian anti-combines legislation have been proposed over the years, at each stage proposals 'were weakened or eliminated in the face of business opposition.' On the basis of evidence presented, the author contends that the inability of small entrepreneurs and consumer groups to effect legislative reforms aimed at curbing illegal corporate activities is largely the result of the corporate sector's direct 'control over the life chances of most Canadians through [its] dominance over the health of the economic system,' and efforts made by government to 'defend and further the interests of the ruling class.'

491.   Snider, D. Laureen, and West, Gordon.

'A Critical Perspective on Law in the Canadian State: Delinquency and Corporate Crime.' In *Power and Change in Canada*, pp. 199–245. Edited by R.J. Ossenberg. Toronto: McClelland and Stewart, 1980.

Critical criminologists have yet to develop a distinctively relevant theoretical approach to Canadian law, crime, and delinquency. Snider and West maintain that in order to develop 'a macroscopic conflict analysis of crime and social control' that is relevant to the Canadian experience, 'we would need a theory which has an historical perspective derived from the Canadian political economy tradition, a recognition of the central role and conflicting functions of the contemporary state, and an incorporation of the best and most relevant recent criminological thinking.' As a preliminary step towards this goal, the authors attempt to illustrate the utility of employing such a theoretical approach by examining historical and quantitative data on juvenile delinquency and corporate crime in Canada.

492. Solomon, R., and Green, M.

'The First Century: The History of Nonmedical Opiate Use and Control Policies in Canada, 1870–1970.' *University of Western Ontario Law Review* 20 (December 1982): 307–336.

Prior to 1908, restrictions were imposed on the distribution or consumption of opiates, whether for medical or pleasurable purposes. The decision to prohibit non-medical opiate use stemmed not from concern about its addictive properties, but rather from a redefinition of its moral impact by some vocal reformers. This article examines the circumstances leading to the criminalization of non-medical opiate use in Canada and the strategies adopted to deal with the illicit use of drugs after 1908. Divided into five sections, the article deals with: (1) the Chinese opium question, 1870–1908, (2) the expansion of the criminal prohibition, 1909–29, (3) the continuation of the law enforcement approach, 1930–52, (4) the emergence of a treatment alternative, 1952–61, and (5) the decline and subsequent expansion of the illicit heroin trade, 1961–70. The article draws on reported legal cases, federal statutes and government documents, and published secondary literature on the history of narcotics legislation in Canada.

493. Solomon, R., and Madison, T.

'The Evolution of Non-Medical Opiate Use in Canada 1870–1908.' In *Crime in Canadian Society*, 2nd ed., pp. 22–30. Edited by R.A. Silverman and J. Teevan, Jr. Toronto: Butterworth, 1980.

494. Sprague, D.N.

'Government Lawlessness in the Administration of Manitoba Land Claims, 1870–1887.' *Manitoba Law Journal* 10 (4, 1980): 415–441.

The distribution of land in Manitoba between 1870 and 1887 was not carried out in strict accordance with the provisions outlined in the *Manitoba Act* of 1870. Among other 'promises,' the *Manitoba Act* authorized a payment in land to be distributed exclusively among partly Indian, or 'half-breed,' inhabitants of the newly created province. This article offers a detailed examination of amendments made to the *Manitoba Act* between 1873 and 1884 which, by altering substantive portions of the original statute, reduced significantly the number of partly Indian people eligible for land payments, and left them open to having their land bargained away by land speculators. The author also documents the effect of government policies aimed at protecting the land interests of white settlers, and reveals the corrupt practices of Ottawa-based bureaucrats who conspired to take advantage of Manitoba 'half-breeds' who filed land claims with the federal government.

495. Stretch, Dianne Kathryn.

'From Prohibition to Government Control: The Liquor Question in Alberta, 1909–1929.' M.A. thesis, University of Alberta, 1979.

Provincial prohibition legislation came into being in 1916 with the help of the United Farmers of Alberta (UFA), a farmers' organization traditionally allied with the social gospel, social reform groups, and strong agrarian protest. Two years after the UFA had been elected as Alberta's government in 1921, however, prohibition was defeated in a provincial referendum. This thesis examines the UFA's initial involvement and support for the prohibition cause and other social reforms and the situation the UFA found itself in when called upon to enforce prohibition after 1921. The author maintains that the problems which the new and inexperienced government faced, combined with changing public attitudes to the rigid legislation of moral issues such as prohibition, caused the UFA to abandon its traditional stance. With the defeat of prohibition in 1923, the UFA turned to problems concerning the government control of liquor sales and consumption. The thesis is based mainly on manuscript collections held in the Glenbow-Alberta Institute Archives and the Provincial Archives of Alberta, and news reports contained in local newspapers and reform periodicals.

496. Strople, Margaret J.

'Prohibition and Movements of Social Reform in Nova Scotia, 1894–1920.' M.A. thesis, Dalhousie University, 1975.

Theses concerned with examining the prohibition movement in other Canadian provinces in the late nineteenth and early twentieth centuries indicate that it was an integral part of a general movement for the reform of society, which enjoyed the support of most Protestant churches, women's groups, farmers, and a substantial segment of the urban middle class. This thesis attempts to round out our understanding of the prohibition movement in Canada by examining the success of the movement in Nova Scotia during the first two decades of the twentieth century. Separate chapters are devoted to investigating: (1) prohibition and social reform in the churches, (2) prohibition and the women's reform movement, and (3) the achievements of the prohibition movement. The author maintains that the attempt to explain the success of the prohibition movement in Nova Scotia, as in other Canadian provinces, must take into account its close relationship to other well-organized, vocal, and influential social reform movements.

497. Sutherland, John Neil.

'Children in English-Canadian Society: Framing the Twentieth-Century Consensus.' Ph.D. dissertation, University of Minnesota, 1973.

This dissertation forms the basis of the author's 1976 book published under the same title (see entry 498 below).

498. Sutherland, John Neil.

Children in English-Canadian Society: Framing the Twentieth-Century Consensus. Toronto: University of Toronto Press, 1976.

In the late nineteenth century, a new generation of reformers, believing that it was possible to free Canadian society from many of the problems of humanity, committed itself to a program of social improvement based on the more effective upbringing of children. This commitment involved changing the prevailing conception of children, from being viewed as 'inherently sinful, yet malleable into little adults by discipline and hard work,' to being thought of as 'innocent plants, requiring a great deal of careful and therefore professional nurture.' Sutherland's book examines the growth of the child-welfare reform movement in Canada and its various efforts at improving the well-being of children. Substantive sections of the book deal with: (1) changing attitudes to children in English-speaking Canada, 1870–1900, (2) children in the public-health reform movement, 1880–1920, (3) transforming the treatment of juvenile delinquents, 1885–1920, and (4) the institutional context of educational reform in Canada, 1890–1920. The author's findings indicate that the period 1880–1920 witnessed a revolution in attitudes towards and institutions aimed at dealing with children in English-Canadian society.

499. Sutherland, John Neil.

'Social Policy, "Deviant" Children and the Public Health Apparatus in British Columbia between the Wars.' *Journal of Educational Thought* 14 (2, August 1980): 80–91.

By the early 1920s, the government of British Columbia had enacted various forms of legislation aimed at promoting new child-rearing practices. Included among these was legislation that gave public-health agencies 'surprisingly broad legal powers' that could be applied in dealing with 'deviant' children, or 'youngsters whose upbringing was sharply at odds with the new social norms.' This article examines the manner in which 'deviant' children and their families were made to conform to the new social norms concerning child-health care that were being promoted by public-health agencies during the 1920s and 1930s. The author maintains that this period witnessed the increasing intervention of public-health agencies in the lives of B.C. families, as part of a concerted attempt to 'persuade or coerce' them to accept new 'scientific' ideas on child-health care.

500. Taylor, John.

'Relief from Relief: The Cities' Answer to Depression Dependency.' *Journal of Canadian Studies* 14 (1, Spring 1979): 16–23.

Relief of the unemployed was one of the major problems faced by Canadian cities during the depression. This article examines the growing problem of unemployment that affected Canadian cities during the 1930s, and the steps taken by municipal governments to deal with the problem. With the worsening of the unemployment situation in the mid-1930s, various municipal governments began calling for federal government financial assistance, using the slogan that their cities were desperate for 'Relief from Relief.'

501. Tennyson, Brian Douglas.

'Sir William Hearst and the Ontario Temperance Act.' *Ontario History* 55 (4, 1963): 233–245.

The Ontario *Temperance Act,* aimed at restricting the sale of alcohol, was passed in 1916. The person mainly responsible for the legislation was William H. Hearst, who became premier of the province in 1914. Three years after the passing of the *Temperance Act,* in 1919, Hearst was resolutely defeated in a provincial election. This article addresses the question of how it was that Hearst was able to enact the 1916 legislation, and how it was that it played a major role in destroying his career in public life. The author maintains that a major factor in bringing about Hearst's defeat in 1919 was the fact that the Conservative party entered the election badly split on the issue of prohibition, with many of its own members opposed to the 1916 act. This opposition, he concludes, discredited Hearst as a political leader, and resulted in a loss of electoral support for his party.

502. Thompson, John Herd.

'The Prohibition Question in Manitoba, 1892–1928.' M.A. thesis, University of Manitoba, 1969.

North American society has long sought a satisfactory answer to the problem of making liquor the servant, not the master, of men/women. The young province of Manitoba was in the forefront of the Canadian side of this search. This thesis examines the role of liquor control in the political and social life of the province from the year 1892, in which Manitoba became the first Canadian province to ask the opinion of its citizens on prohibitory legislation, until 1928, when the sale of beer for public consumption was legalized after an unsatisfactory experience with both total and partial prohibition. Substantive chapters focus on examining: (1) the origins and sources of prohibitionist and anti-prohibitionist support, (2) the first temperance movement, 1892–1903, (3) the 'second' temperance movement and reform coalition, 1907–16, and (4) prohibition on the defensive and in retreat, 1916–28. Research findings indicate that while the idea of prohibition found its greatest appeal among 'Manitobans of Anglo-Saxon origin and evangelical Protestant background,' it was strongly opposed by the 'non-English elements against whom it was directed.' The author concludes that in the turbulent 1920s prohibition met with opposition from new Canadians and veterans'groups, lost its reform identification, and saw its supporters become 'more blatantly nativistic and socially reactionary.'

503. Thompson, John Herd.

'"The Beginning of Our Regeneration" The Great War and Western Canadian Reform Movements.' Canadian Historical Association.*Historical Papers* (1972): 227–245. Reprinted in *Prophecy and Protest: Social Movements in Twentieth Century Canada,* pp. 87–104. Edited by Samual D. Clark, J. Paul Grayson, and Linda M. Grayson. Toronto: Gage, 1975.

Although associations advocating prohibition, women's suffrage, and economic reform had existed in Manitoba and the Northwest Territories before the turn of the century, they did not enjoy broad public support until after the onset of the 'Great War.' This article focuses on examining the manner in which the objectives of western Canadian reform movements were aided by the outbreak of the First World War, and the ensuing patriotic fervour that swept western Canada. The author maintains that the wartime experience produced 'a transformation in public attitudes to reformism,' and led to major victories in the areas of prohibition and women's suffrage.

504. Thompson, John Herd.

'The Voice of Moderation: The Defeat of Prohibition in Manitoba.' In *The Twenties in Western Canada*, pp. 170–190. Edited by Susan Mann Trofimenkoff. Ottawa: History Division, National Museums of Canada, 1972.

This article draws on the author's 1969 M.A. thesis, and reiterates his earlier conclusions (see entry 502 above).

505. Thorner, Thomas.

'The Not-So-Peaceable Kingdom: Crime and Criminal Justice in Frontier Calgary.' In *Frontier Calgary: Town, City, and Region, 1875–1914*, pp. 100–113. Edited by A.W. Rasporich and Henry C. Klassen. Calgary: McClelland and Stewart West, 1975.

This article forms part of the author's 1976 M.A. thesis (see entry 506 below).

506. Thorner, Thomas.

'The Not-So-Peaceable Kingdom: A Study of Crime in Southern Alberta, 1874–1905.' M.A. thesis, University of Calgary, 1976.

The image of the western Canadian frontier as a 'peaceable kingdom' has persisted for so long that many people accept it as historical fact. This study represents an attempt to present a more complete analysis of the nature of crime in one part of the Canadian West – southern Alberta. Judicial records, supplemented by descriptions of the conditions of the time offered by mounted policemen, Indian agents, and justices of the peace, constitute the major sources of primary historical data used in the analysis of crime. Particular attention is devoted to determining the frequency of various types of crime, the causal factors that influenced criminal behaviour, and the attitudes of the local community towards crime. The author offers the general conclusion that the common assumption concerning the prevalence of peace and order on the western Canadian frontier has shortcomings when applied to southern Alberta.

507. Thorner, Thomas.

'The Incidence of Crime in Southern Alberta.' In *Law and Society in Canada in Historical*

Perspective, pp. 53–88. Edited by D.J. Bercuson and L.A. Knafla. Calgary: University of Calgary, 1979.

In this article an attempt is made to disprove the commonly held belief that the settlement of western Canada was accompanied by a high degree of law and order, and very law-abiding behaviour. Newspapers and the records of the justices of the peace are used to gain insight into the incidence and seriousness of crime in southern Alberta in the period 1878 to 1905. The records of the justices of the peace, which provide a statistical body of information concerning criminal actions brought before the courts of southern Alberta, indicate that crime increased steadily during the period under investigation. The rising crime rate, however, did not apply equally to all offences. While assault, liquor-related offences, vagrancy, and prostitution, all increased dramatically, crimes such as fraud, false pretence, burglary, and stock theft apparently rose at a more moderate rate. In order to verify the accuracy of the justices' of the peace statistics, contemporary newspapers were examined. Through this examination evidence was brought forth that suggested the real increase in crime may have been far greater than the statistics indicate. The author concluded from his investigation that while both official records and contemporary literary evidence suggested that crime was generally on the increase in southern Alberta during the years examined, the rising crime rate could possibly be accounted for by the fact that the population of southern Alberta also increased dramatically during the period under examination. Owing to this possibility, the author stressed that the traditional interpretations of law and order in the settlement of western Canada should not be replaced with notions of lawlessness and disorder.

508.   Thorner, Thomas, and Watson, Neil Bruce.

'Patterns of Prairie Crime: Calgary, 1875–1939.' In *Crime and Criminal Justice in Europe and Canada*, pp. 219–256. Edited by Louis A. Knafla. Waterloo, Ont.: Wilfrid Laurier University Press, 1981.

This study sets out to examine the ways in which the incidence of crime in Calgary changed both in magnitude and character during the first 60 years of the city's history. The analysis of crime is based upon cases brought before the police court and local justices of the peace. Wherever possible, an attempt is made to identify the policies, institutions, and circumstances that contributed to the occurrence of crime during five distinct periods of the city's history: (1) the frontier period, 1871–91, (2) the period of immigration and reform, 1892–1913, (3) the war years, 1914–19, (4) the period of recession and growth, 1920–29, and (5) the depression, 1930–5. Contrary to the more commonly held notion which equates poverty with rising crime and disorder, the authors' findings indicate that crime in Calgary appeared to be positively related to the ebb and flow of the economy, increasing with economic prosperity and falling during times of depression.

509. Trasov, G.E.

'History of the Opium and Narcotic Drug Legislation in Canada.' *Criminal Law Quarterly* 4 (3, January 1962): 274–282.

This article examines the circumstances surrounding the enactment of Canada's earliest drug legislation (the *Opium Act* of 1908), and amendments made to it between 1911 and 1954. The author's examination of the evolution of Canadian opium and narcotic drug acts shows that penalities for trafficking and illegal possession have steadly increased over the years. He concludes that punishment as a deterrent to the problem of narcotic addiction and trafficking has failed miserably, and the punitive legislation has acted to nullify the effects of rehabilitative programs aimed at curing drug addicts.

510. Urquhart, R.

'A Survey of the Policies of the Newfoundland Government towards Poor Relief, 1860–1869.' Unpublished manuscript, Maritime History Collection, Memorial University, 1973.

During the 1860s, the colony of Newfoundland found itself deeply involved with the problem of poor relief. This study attempts to demonstrate: (1) that poor relief was viewed as an evil that was highly detrimental to the progress of the colony, and (2) that despite the efforts of authorities, attempts made to rid the colony of pauperism were futile. In support of these contentions, the author provides documentary evidence which indicates that authorities were greatly concerned that the traditional system of poor relief – which provided equally for the able-bodied and those unable to work – was being taken advantage of by able-bodied people who would rather live on relief in St. John's than work in the outports of the colony. In the course of the decade, attempts were made to eliminate this practice by revising policies to do with the distribution of poor relief, and by encouraging the development of industry and agriculture, which would provide work for the labouring classes. While these efforts acted to reduce substantially the colony's expenditure on poor relief, authorities were unable to destroy 'the evil of pauperism' with which they were apparently obsessed.

511. Ward, W. Peter.

'Unwed Motherhood in Nineteenth-Century English Canada.' Canadian Historical Association. *Historical Papers* (1981): 34–56.

512. Watson, Neil Bruce.

'Calgary: A Study of Crime, Offenders and the Police Court, 1929–1934.' M.A. thesis, University of Calgary, 1978.

The decade of the 1930s in Canada has been characterized as a period of turbulence, social unrest, and, at times, lawlessness. Unfortunately, of the commentary which exists on the general incidence of crime during the depression, the bulk consists of unsubstantiated and often contradictory personal observations. Focusing on the experience of Calgary, this study quantitatively addresses questions concerning the impact of the depression on the amount and kind of crime committed by certain types of offenders and the treatment of offenders by the police and the judiciary. Major data sources employed in the analysis consist of the arrest books of the Calgary police for the selected years 1929 and 1934 supplemented by the police court records and documents relating to civic government. Contrary to predictions based on existing commentary, the author's findings indicate that the advent of the depression did not lead to a general increase in recorded crime, or a greater judicial punitiveness.

513. Watts, R.E.

'The Trend of Crime in Canada.' *Queen's Quarterly* 39 (August 1932): 402–413.

Watts, then the chief of the Bureau of Criminal Statistics at the Dominion Bureau of Statistics, discusses trends in crime among Canadian men, largely during the 1901 to 1928 period. He starts by defining crime as 'indicated by convictions for indictable offences (as distinct from infractions of municipal by-laws and othe minor offences), whether such convictions were obtained on proceedings before a jury, or before a judge without the intervention of a jury, or summarily before a magistrate.' The effect of the war years on crime statistics is discussed as well as the variables of: immigration, spirits consumption, age groups, and urbanization. The following three principal motives of crime are indicated: malice, acquisitiveness, and lust. Criminal negligence is also considered a contributing cause, rather than a motive. Comparisons between 1881, 1891, and averages for the 1912–14, 1915–17, 1920–2, and 1926–8 periods are made based on the percentages of total crimes which can be placed under each motive and cause. Watts is not able in this short article to analyse the data in depth, but he concludes that increases in crime rates reflect quick population growth and urbanization, rather than 'any marked criminal propensities in our population.'

514. Weaver, John C.

'Crime, Violence and Immorality in a Pre-Industrial Society: Unlawful Acts and Law Enforcement in the Gore District of Upper Canada from Settlement to the Railway Era.' Paper presented at the Annual Meeting of the Canadian Historical Association, Halifax, 1981.

515. Wells, Jess.

'The Social History of Prostitution in Canada.' A Background Paper Prepared for the Canadian Advisory Council on the Status of Women (CACSW). Ottawa: CACSW, 1983.

516. Williams, David R.

Trapline Outlaw: Simon Peter Gunanoot. Victoria, B.C.: Sono Nis Press, 1982.

517. Wisdon, Jane.

'From Poor Law to Child Protection.' *Canadian Welfare* 16 (August–September 1940): 28–31.

   This brief article comments on the growth and development of modern standards of child care and protection in Nova Scotia.

518. Withers, J.W.

'Dirty, Diseased and Dangerous – And Always Exciting: St. John's in 1897.' In *The Book of Newfoundland*, vol. 5, pp. 54–71. Edited by Joseph R. Smallwood. St. John's: Newfoundland Book Publishers, 1975.

519. Wolfe, Robert D.

'Myth of the Poor Man's Country: Upper Canadian Attitudes to Immigration 1830–37.' M.A. thesis, Carleton University, 1976.

   The first great wave of immigration reached Upper Canada during the 1830s. This thesis examines attitudes on immigration, as expressed in Upper Canadian newspapers, during the years in which immigration rose to a peak and then slowly declined. The author argues that Upper Canadian attitudes to immigration form a pattern that may be termed 'the myth of the poor man's country,' within the context of which immigrants were welcomed because they would prosper in the new country and because the country would prosper with them. Despite the mounting inability of the province to provide opportunities for the newly arrived immigrants to prosper – as indicated in the proliferation of benevolent societies, the establishment of houses of industry, and the growing incidence of street-begging and crime – the author concludes that throughout most of the 1830s Upper Canadians continued to welcome massive immigration.

3

Courts and Administration of Criminal Justice

520. Aitchison, J.H.

'The Courts of Requests in Upper Canada.' *Ontario History* 41 (1949): 125–132.

Aitchison examines the origin, development, and functioning of the courts of requests in Upper Canada. He points out that the courts of requests were the lowest courts in the province, their jurisdiction being confined to dealing with 'petty civil cases,' such as those concerned with the recovery of small debts. Established by statute in 1792, these local courts existed until 1841, at which time they were abolished and replaced by division courts. The author maintains that because the courts of requests had jurisdiction over petty civil cases, they may be said to have been 'the courts closest to the lives of the people.'

521. Alberta Law Review.

'Twenty-Fifth Anniversary Issue.' *Alberta Law Review* 18 (4, Fall 1980): 1–57.

This commemorative issue of the *Alberta Law Review* contains 10 short essays that deal with various aspects of Alberta's legal history. Written by prominent Alberta judges, law professors, and members of the legal profession, the essays cover such topics as the history of the (University of Alberta) Faculty of Law, the superior courts of Alberta, the district court of Alberta, the early years of the Edmonton Bar, and the 'Emergence' of the *Alberta Law Review*.

522. Alcorn, Richard S.

'The Historical Evolution of the Court Systems in the Southwestern Ontario Region, 1800–1910.' Compiled for the Landon Project, University of Western Ontario, 1977.

523. Angus, William H.

'Judicial Selection in Canada: The Historical Perspective.' *Canadian Legal Studies* 1 (1967): 220–251.

524. Armstrong, Frederick H.

Handbook of Upper Canadian Chronology and Territorial Legislation. London, Ont.: Centennial Publication, Lawson Memorial Library, University of Western Ontario, 1967.

Although intended as a general data source for historians interested in Upper Canadian provincial and municipal affairs, this handbook contains information on various aspects of Upper Canadian legal history. Divided into six parts, the handbook consists of a preliminary collection of chronologically ordered tables covering: (1) British officials (monarchs, officials in England, governors of Canada and lieutenant governors of Upper Canada, and other officials), (2) provincial officials (the executive council and its staff, officers of the crown, and senior civil servants), (3) provincial parliaments, 1792–1840 (statistics on the duration of sessions and the statutes passed in each session, the legislative council and its staff, members of the provincial house of assembly), (4) the judiciary and the legal profession (justices and other officials associated with various courts, treasurers of the Law Society of Upper Canada, known attorneys, barristers, notaries public, solicitors, and king's counsels, and individuals appointed to special commissions), (5) miscellaneous (information relating to major figures and events associated with Anglican, Catholic, Methodist, and Presbyterian churches, the battles of the War of 1812, railway legislation, and imperial honours granted to Upper Canadians and British officials for services in Upper Canada). Each of the tables contained in the handbook is preceded by explanatory remarks, and extensive reference is made to other relevant data sources on Upper Canada.

525. Audet, Francis-Joseph.

'Le barreau et la revolte de 1837.' Royal Society of Canada. *Proceedings and Transactions* Series 3, 31, sec. 1 (1937): 85–96.

This article evaluates the attitude and behaviour of the Bar in the Province of Quebec towards the Rebellion of 1837. Since the revolt was limited to the district of Montreal, the author limits his discussion to the lawyers of the region. At the time of the upheaval there were 101 practising lawyers in the district, approximately half of whom were French-speaking and approximately half of whom were English-speaking, three of whom were Jews. The author provides a list of these lawyers and the dates of their admission to the Bar. He then divides them into three groups: the proponents of the policies of Papineau; those who were servants of, or bound to, the government; and those who were not actively involved in politics.

526. Audet, Francis-Joseph.

'Les débuts du barreau dans la province de Québec.' *Cahiers des dix* 2 (1937): 207–235.

Civil courts were created in the Province of Quebec in accordance with the *Murray Act* of September 17, 1764. The same act recognized the existence of lawyers. A 'community of lawyers' was founded in Quebec on May 11, 1779, following a meeting held at Maître Olry's, dean of the lawyers of the province. On June 29, 1779, Maître Olry presented to the court the name of a body of lawyers and an address to which complaints against the conduct of lawyers were to be sent. On April 30, 1785, Lieutenant Governor Henry Hamilton signed an act concerning 'lawyers, prosecutors, solicitors, and notaries.' According to the act those aspiring to join the profession were to work as clerks for five years in a lawyer's office or for six years in a court of justice. In 1826 a law course on the law of Canada was started in Quebec. And in 1828 the 'lawyers library' was founded under the patronage of Chief Justice James Reed. A club called 'Brothers-in-law' was formed the same year by lawyers, all of whom were English except one. In 1852 Laval University in Quebec and McGill University in Montreal obtained the powers to establish law faculties. Attempts to have the Quebec Bar incorporated were unsuccessful until 1849 when an act of the Assembly established the Bar of Lower Canada. The power to admit aspiring lawyers to the profession was removed from the governor and invested in the Bar.

527. Backhouse, Constance B.

'Involuntary Motherhood: Abortion, Birth Control and the Law in Nineteenth Century Canada.' In *The Windsor Yearbook of Access to Justice* 3 (1983): 61–130.

This article examines the various statutes passed in Canada during the nineteenth century and the patterns of prosecution and judicial analysis relating to pregnancy and abortion from a feminist and legal perspective. Prior to the nineteenth century, there were no statutes in Canada or England which prohibited the practice of abortion. The author covers the social and legal issues surrounding the introduction of abortion legislation in Canada. Infanticide was also viewed as a means of preventing unwanted motherhood. The author reviews the limited number of known abortion cases, noting the sensational professional abortionist case of *The Queen* v. *Ranson J. Andrews*. Some statistical tables on charges and verdicts relating to abortion, infanticide, and manslaughter in Ontario are provided. Backhouse gives a detailed analysis of the *Criminal Code* of 1892 which is considered to have signified the culmination of the nineteenth-century legislative drive against fertility control. The article is based on considerable research using primary and secondary sources, and includes almost 200 lengthy footnotes.

528. Backhouse, Constance B.

'Nineteenth-Century Canadian Prostitution Law: Reflection of a Discriminatory Society.' Unpublished manuscript, Faculty of Law, University of Western Ontario, 1983.

In presenting a legal-historical analysis of prostitution law in Canada the author focuses on the regulation, prohibition, and rehabilitation approaches used to control prostitution. While some statutes may have authorized sanctions against men and women, in practice the laws were directed primarily against women. Backhouse reviews early legislation, noting some differences from English precedents. The *Contagious Diseases Act* was a regulatory attempt. In the latter half of the nineteenth century a 'social purity' campaign resulted in further legislative attempts to suppress prostitution. The author provides a social profile of convicted prostitutes, statistical tables based on the Toronto Gaol Register, a comparison between decision-making by the magistrates and appellate courts, and a comparison of English and American jurisprudence. As part of the rehabilitative approach prostitutes were sent to shelters, asylums (such as the Toronto Magdalen Asylum), and prisons; alas, the recidivism continued. The involvement of various agencies of social welfare and control is apparent in the issue of prostitution, as is the undercurrent of sex discrimination in all measures to control it. Backhouse has 140 footnote references to primary and secondary materials, case reports, and statutes in the draft copy to this unpublished paper.

529. Backhouse, Constance B.

'Nineteenth-Century Canadian Rape Law 1800–92.' In *Essays in the History of Canadian Law*, vol. 2, pp. 200–247. Edited by David H. Flaherty. Toronto: The Osgoode Society and University of Toronto Press, 1983.

At the beginning of the nineteenth century rape was viewed as a crime against a species of property. As the century progressed, the law began to move away from this property concept of rape, and began to recognize women as individuals who were entitled to sexual autonomy, and who deserved protection from sexual abuse in their own right. This article examines the evolution of Canadian rape law in the nineteenth century. Drawing on relevant statutes, case law, and court documents containing information on individuals charged with rape, the author considers such matters as the early English influence on Canadian rape law (1800–60), the Canadian departure from the English legislative model (1861–80), the restrictive manner in which rape law was applied by the Canadian judiciary, and the different views held by the judiciary and legislators with regard to the intent of rape legislation. The author maintains that the history of Canadian rape law provides a wealth of rich information about the values and attitudes surrounding sexual assault in the nineteenth century, the similarities and differences between Canadian and English legal developments, continuing tensions between legislators and the judiciary, and the status and role assigned to women in a developing Canadian culture.

530. Backhouse, Constance B.

'Desperate Women and Compassionate Courts: Infanticide in Nineteenth-Century Canada.' *University of Toronto Law Journal* 34 (4, 1984): 447–478.

Many women who became pregnant in nineteenth-century Canada attempted to conceal their pregnancy and do away with their new-born children. This article examines the statutory framework relating to infanticide and the concealment of childbirth in the nineteenth century, and the manner in which women charged with these crimes were dealt with by Canadian courts. Ontario court records, covering the period 1840–1900, are used to gain insight into the social backgrounds of women charged with infanticide and concealment, the motivations that drove them to take such desperate action, and the outcome of the trials of women who were caught. The records indicate that women charged with infanticide and concealment were dealt with in a lenient and compassionate manner by the courts, which, at least in Ontario, tended to view infanticide as 'somewhat less heinous than other forms of murder' and as 'a rather common feature of daily life.'

531. Baker, G. Blaine.

'Legal Education in Upper Canada, 1789–1889: The Law Society as Educator.' In *Essays in the History of Canadian Law*, vol. 2, pp. 49–142. Edited by David H. Flaherty. Toronto: The Osgoode Society and University of Toronto Press, 1983.

The period 1785–1889 was crucial in the development of legal education in Ontario. Throughout the period the Law Society of Upper Canada existed as the only educational institution in Upper Canada, and later Ontario, that trained aspiring lawyers and set standards for the practice of law in the province. Organized along topical rather than chronological lines, this essay provides information concerning: (1) the creation of the Law Society of Upper Canada, (2) the elements of nineteenth-century legal education, (3) entrance requirements and pre-law training, (4) the apprenticeship of lawyers in training, (5) the attendance of law students at court proceedings, or 'term-keeping,' (6) the nature of law clubs, classes, and lectures, (7) scholarships and intermediate examinations, and (8) Bar admission examinations. The author concludes that in the course of the nineteenth century the Law Society of Upper Canada developed a comparatively complex and methodically administered system of legal education, which was in many respects superior to those which existed in England, in other British colonies, and in most American jurisdictions.

532. Banks, Margaret A.

'The Evolution of the Ontario Courts 1788–1981.' In *Essays in the History of Canadian Law*, vol. 2, pp. 492–572. Edited by David H. Flaherty. Toronto: The Osgoode Society and University of Toronto Press, 1983.

Drawing mainly on Upper Canada and Ontario statutes, journals of the provincial legislature, and relevant secondary literature, the author provides a detailed overview of the evolution of Ontario courts. Historical developments affecting Ontario's court system are shown in four figures, which provide a simplified picture of the system as it existed in 1800, 1860, 1910, and 1981. Throughout the essay, the author attempts to relate changes in the structure of the Ontario court system to broader political and social events of the times.

533. Banning, Magdalena.

'The History of Welfare Involvement and Its Ideology in the Development of Juvenile Justice in Canada.' M.A. thesis, University of Toronto, Centre of Criminology, 1976.

This thesis examines the history of agencies developed for the control and treatment of delinquent children. Particular reference is made to the provisions for the establishment of child welfare agencies contained in the *Juvenile Delinquents Act* (1908), the proposed *Young Offenders Act* (1965), and the proposed *Young Persons in Conflict with the Law Act* (1975). The author maintains that both early Canadian legislation and more recent reform proposals are based on the precept that 'a child in trouble is a child in need,' and that child welfare agencies have always played an important role in the juvenile court.

534. Barbe, Raoul.

'La cour du bien-être social: Son origine, son évolution.' *Canadian Bar Journal* 8 (1, February 1965): 119–123.

The Court of Social Welfare in the Province of Quebec is the equivalent to the Juvenile and Family Court in Ontario. The court did not come about spontaneously but is the outcome of various attempts to solve the problem of juvenile delinquency. The predecessor to the Court of Social Welfare is the Court for Juvenile Delinquents established in Montreal in 1910 and in Quebec in 1940. This court had three judges in Montreal and one in Quebec. All of them were appointed by the Government of Quebec. The court had jurisdiction over criminal cases involving persons under age 18. The court for juvenile delinquents was abolished in 1950 and replaced by the Court of Social Welfare, which was set up in cities having at least 50,000 inhabitants. In 1950 the maximum number of judges of the Court of Social Welfare was not to exceed 10; in 1956 the number was raised to 14 and in 1964 there were 30 judges. Information on judges' salaries is included.

535. Barreca, Ann.

'The Juvenile Court as a Method of Diversion: A Study of the Family Court in the City of Ottawa and the County of Carleton, 1940–1952.' M.A. thesis, University of Toronto, Centre of Criminology, 1977.

Recent public attention has centred on diversion as one of the most significant criminal justice reform ideas. In the past, consideration of the need for diversion and the special handling of some classes of deviants led to the establishment of the juvenile court as a means of diverting juvenile offenders from the adult criminal justice system. This thesis examines the juvenile court as a diversionary method, with particular emphasis on the Ottawa and County of Carleton Family Court during the years 1940–52. Official records of the court relating to the disposition of cases during the 12-year period constitute the major source of primary data. The author concludes from her analysis that although 'the juvenile justice system grew out of enthusiasm and reformist zeal, with talk of alternatives to criminal processing,' the juvenile court, with its vague jurisdiction, has become 'a paternalistic system paralleling the impact of the criminal courts.'

536. Beaulieu, M.-L.

'Québec et la formation d'un droit canadien.' *Revue internationale de droit comparé* 13 (1, January–March 1961): 300–306.

In 1953, M. André Taschereau, who later became a judge of the Court of Appeal, asked if Canada was in the process of creating a new system of law, a system different from both the English and the French systems, which would be to a large extent strictly Canadian though inspired by the two great systems of law. A discussion of this opinion is presented by the author.

537. Beck, James Murray.

'The Rise and Fall of Nova Scotia's Attorney General: 1749– 1983.' *Dalhousie Law Journal* 8 (3, 1984): 125–142. Also published in *Law in a Colonial Society: The Nova Scotia Experience*, pp. 125–142. Edited by Peter Waite, Sandra Oxner, and Thomas Barnes. Toronto: Carswell, 1984.

538. Bédard, T.P.

'Procès criminels à Québec au XVIIe siècle.' *Revue canadienne* (Nouvelle série, tome II) 18 (2–4, 1882): 65–78, 140–150, 216–228.

Published in three parts, this is a study of a murder trial that took place in Quebec in the second half of the seventeenth century. The trial is that of Jacques Bigion accused of killing Antoine Dupré on January 26, 1668. The analysis of the case is preceded by a review of the penal legislation which existed at the time both in France and in Canada.

539. Bell, D.G.

'A Note on the Reception of English Statutes in New Brunswick.' *University of New Brunswick Law Journal* 28 (2, Spring 1975): 195–201.

540. Bell, D.G.

'Slavery and the Judges of Loyalist New Brunswick.' *University of New Brunswick Law Journal* 31 (1982): 9–42.

541. Belley, Jean-Guy.

'Vers une sociologie historique de la justice québécoise – Réflexion en marge d'un ouvrage récent sur la justice civile sous le régime français.' *Cahiers de droit* 24 (1983): 409–417.

542. Belliveau, John Edward.

The Coffin Murder Case. Toronto: Kingswood House, 1956; reprinted with introduction and epilogue, Toronto: PaperJacks, 1979.

In February 1956 Wilbert Coffin was hanged at the Bordeaux jail in Montreal for the murder of three American hunters. The Coffin murder case raised considerable public controversy, mainly because many prominent Canadians were convinced that Coffin was innocent. This book recounts the events leading up to Coffin's trial and execution, and the public outcry it caused over the use of capital punishment.

543. Berger, Thomas R.

Fragile Freedoms: Human Rights and Dissent in Canada. Toronto: Clarke, Irwin and Co., 1981.

Written in the belief that 'by examining our history, we can understand better what kind of world must be created to foster human rights and fundamental freedoms,' this book examines the treatment of minorities and dissenters in Canada at various points in Canadian history. In eight separate historical essays, the author traces the expulsion of Acadians from the Maritimes in the 1700s and their eventual return, the destruction of the Metis as a nation and the loss of their homeland on the plains, the school crisis in Manitoba during the 1890s when French Canadians were denied the right to separate schools and that in Ontario after 1912 when French Canadians were denied the right to speak their own language in their own schools, the internment of Japanese Canadians during the Second World War and their banishment after the war, the measures taken against communists to curb their freedom of speech and of association in the 1930s, the persecution of Jehovah's Witnesses in Quebec during the Duplessis era, the internment of hundreds of dissenters in Quebec during the October Crisis in 1970, and the native rights and land-claims movement of recent years. In addition to describing the struggles, victories, and defeats of minorities and dissenters in Canada, Berger tells of the many Canadians who, over the years, have championed the ideal of tolerance and worked actively to defend their rights and freedoms. Although written in a narrative form that excludes references from the text, a bibliographic essay on the historical and legal materials consulted in preparing the essays is provided.

544. Betts, George.

'Municipal Government and Politics, 1800–1850.' In *To Preserve and Defend: Essays on Kingston in the Nineteenth Century*, pp. 223–244. Edited by G. Tulchinsky. Montreal: McGill-Queen's University Press, 1976.

This chapter examines the development of municipal government and politics in Kingston from 1800 to 1850. The author notes that whereas in 1800 '"local government" was the responsibility of the justices of the peace meeting four times a year in the court of quarter sessions,' by 1850 there had evolved a system of municipal self-government based on sound and innovative legislation. The role of early justices of the peace in the management of municipal affairs is discussed, along with the changing circumstances that led to demands for a more adequate system of local government.

545. Beullac, Pierre, and Surveyor, Edouard Fabré.

Le centenaire du barreau de Montréal, 1849–1949. Montréal: Librairie Ducharme, 1949.

This book, published on the occasion of the centennial of the Montreal Bar, is devoted to biographies of the presidents of the Bar since its foundation in 1849 up to 1899 and to profiles of some contemporary lawyers, 1902–49. The book also contains a list of the presidents since 1899, short notices on the Association of the Young Bar of Montreal and the Montreal Advocates Benevolent Association, as well as an elaborate history of the Justice Building (Palais de Justice) in Montreal.

546. Bindon, Kathryn Mae.

'Journalist and Judge: Adam Thom's British North American Career, 1833–1854.' M.A. thesis, Queen's University, 1972.

This thesis forms the basis of the author's 1981 published article (see entry 547 below).

547. Bindon, Kathryn Mae.

'Hudson's Bay Company Law: Adam Thom and the Institution of Order in Rupert's Land, 1839–1854.' In *Essays in the History of Canadian Law*, vol. 1, pp. 43–87. Edited by David H. Flaherty. Toronto: The Osgoode Society and University of Toronto Press, 1981.

The formalization of the administration of justice in Rupert's Land was a process characterized by social and commercial conflict. Most noticeably, the mid-nineteenth century witnessed a clashing of interests between the Hudson's Bay Company, which sought a more regular judicial system for the maintenance and protection of its monopoly over the fur trade, and settlers, Indians, and Metis of the Red River colony, who saw the institution of a more traditional legal administration as a means of curbing the company's authority. One of the major actors involved in the institution of order in Rupert's Land was Adam Thom, who, in 1839, became the first recorder (or legal interpreter and judge) appointed by the Hudson's Bay Company. This article examines Thom's role in the development of a more formal judicial system, and the impact of his personality on fostering hostility on the part of residents of the Red River colony towards the Hudson's Bay Company. The author maintains that while Thom's introduction of a legal code for Rupert's Land was apparently accepted by both the company and the community, his anti-French prejudices and objectionable judicial practices caused considerable controversy. She concludes that an adequate understanding of Thom's career requires that one look beyond legal codes and law reports, and recognize the social context of his judicial administration.

548. Bingaman, Sandra.

'The North-West Rebellion Trials, 1885.' M.A. thesis, University of Saskatchewan, Regina, 1971.

This thesis recounts the trials of leading figures in the 1885 North-West Rebellion, and serves as the basis for the author's subsequently published articles (see entries 549 and 550 below).

549. Bingaman, Sandra.

'The Trials of the "White Rebels," 1885.' *Saskatchewan History* 25 (2, Spring 1972): 41–54.

Among the defendants brought to trial in connection with the North-West Rebellion of 1885 were two white men, William Henry Jackson and Thomas Scott. Drawing on the transcripts of the rebellion trials, along with Department of Justice records and correspondence, the author examines the circumstances surrounding their trials, and the outcome of their cases. She concludes that while the trials of the two white defendants, both of which resulted in verdicts of not guilty, aroused considerable legal and political controversy, one cannot find in the trials any evidence of there having occurred a 'grave injustice.'

550. Bingaman, Sandra.

'The Trials of Poundmaker and Big Bear, 1885.' *Saskatchewan History* 28 (3, Autumn 1975): 81–94.

Among the other defendants brought to trial after the Rebellion of 1885 were the Cree chiefs Poundmaker and Big Bear, the acknowledged leaders of the two largest groups of Indians who had taken up arms. Rather than being charged with the capital offence of high treason upon which Riel was indicted, Poundmaker and Big Bear were charged with the crime of treason-felony. This article examines the circumstances surrounding and evidence presented at the trials of the two Indian chiefs. Attention is given to noting the similarities and differences of the trials, and discussing the appropriateness of the guilty verdicts and sentences of imprisonment imposed on the defendants.

551. Blackwell, John D.

'William Hume Blake and Judicial Reform in the United Province of Canada.' M.A. thesis, Queen's University, 1980.

William Hume Blake was a consummate law reformer. In his many roles (i.e., as the principal member of a commission appointed to serve from 1843 to 1845 to investigate the Court of Chancery in Upper Canada, as the solicitor general of the province after 1848, and as the chancellor of Upper Canada from 1849 to 1862), Blake sought to adapt English jurisprudence to the circumstances of colonial society. This thesis examines Blake's accomplishments as a legal innovator of the English liberal tradition, and in particular his role in enacting the Judicature Bills of 1849, which brought about a major reorganization of the province's judicial structure. According to the author, Blake's career provides 'an instructive and significant illustration of the interplay between the mid-nineteenth century legal system and provincial society.'

552. Blackwell, John D.

'William Hume Blake and the Judicature Acts of 1849: The Process of Legal Reform at Mid-Century in Upper Canada.' In *Essays in the History of Canadian Law*, vol. 1, pp. 132–174. Edited by David H. Flaherty. Toronto: The Osgoode Society and University of Toronto Press, 1981.

This essay draws on the author's 1980 M.A. thesis, and reiterates his earlier conclusions (see entry 551 above).

553. Bliss, Michael.

'Another Anti-Trust Tradition: Canadian Anti-Combines Policy, 1889–1910.' *Business History Review* 47 (2, Summer 1973): 177–188.

Canada's first statute relating to the general problem of preserving economic competition was passed in 1889. In the next twenty years the legislation was amended on several occasions and finally replaced by the *Combines Investigation Act* of 1910. This article examines the circumstances underlying the enactment of Canada's first anti-combines statute in 1889, and its effectiveness in fostering economic competition through eliminating unfair price-fixing, monopolies, and corporate mergers intended to place restraints on free trade. In this effort, the author draws on a range of primary historical sources, including the report of a select committee appointed to investigate alleged combines in 1889, the correspondence of and minutes of meetings held by businessmen who influenced the wording of the 1889 legislation, and House of Commons and Senate debates from 1889 to 1910 in which anti-combines policy was discussed. From his investigation, Bliss concludes that the passing of the anti-combines act of 1889 was merely a symbolic response to the concerns of small businessmen who felt threatened by the unfair price-fixing and trade-restraint practices of large combines, and did not reflect a serious desire by legislators to resist economic consolidation or restore the forces of the free market.

554. Bothwell, Robert, and Granatstein, J.L., eds.

The Gouzenko Transcripts: The Evidence Presented to the Kellock-Taschereau Royal Commission of 1946. Ottawa: Deneau Publishing Co., [1982].

In September 1945, Igor Gouzenko, a cipher clerk at the Soviet Embassy in Ottawa, defected with documents that showed the Soviet Union was engaging in espionage against Canada. In February 1946, the Canadian government created a royal commission under two justices of the Supreme Court of Canada to inquire into the evidence Gouzenko had brought and to take testimony from him and from those his material implicated. Although the royal commissioners presented their report in July 1946, the evidence they heard was not made public until 1981. This book contains over 300 pages of testimony taken from and about major figures involved in the Gouzenko affair, along with an introduction to the material by the editors.

555. Boucher, Jacques.

'Le barreau à 125 ans.' *La revue du barreau de la Province de Québec* 34 (2, March 1974): 11–16.

This is one of several articles published in a special supplement to *La revue du barreau de la Province de Québec* to pay homage to the Quebec Bar on the occasion of its 125th anniversary. The author begins with a quotation from Alexis de Tocqueville in which he recounts his observations in a Quebec court in 1831. Tocqueville is highly critical of the lawyers he saw and heard in court. The author then offers a brief history of the profession in Quebec. In 1785 lawyers were nominated by the executive branch of government. There were no law schools and no doctrine to guide or help them find the legal solutions their clients needed. Matters have changed considerably since then as shown by the author's discussion of the evolution of the profession from 1949 to 1974.

556. Bouck, John C.

'Introducing English Statute Law into the Provinces: Time for a Change?' *Canadian Bar Review* 57 (1, March 1979): 74–87.

In this article the author, a judge of the Supreme Court of British Columbia, discusses the inconsistencies and uncertainties stemming from the continued acceptance of early English statute law in the Canadian provinces, and proposes that this practice be formally ended. In presenting his argument, the author provides a historical overview of the manner in which pre-1858 English statute law came to be accepted and incorporated into the statute law of British Columbia. He then documents instances in which pre-1858 English statutes have been removed from the law of British Columbia, after they had been introduced into the province. The author's major recommendation is that the *English Law Act,* which recognizes that pre-1858 English statutes may still be in force in British Columbia, be repealed.

557. Brode, Patrick.

'Of Courts and Politics: The Growth of an Independent Judiciary in Upper Canada.' *The Law Society of Upper Canada Gazette* 12 (1978): 264–272.

558. Brode, Patrick.

'On the Matter of John Anderson: Canadian Courts and the Fugitive Slave.' *The Law Society of Upper Canada Gazette* 14 (1, March 1980): 92–97.

559. Brode, Patrick.

Sir John Beverley Robinson: Bone and Sinew of the Compact. Toronto: University of Toronto Press and The Osgoode Society, 1984.

John Beverley Robinson (1791–1863) was one of Upper Canada's foremost jurists, a dominating influence on the ruling élite of the colony, and a leading citizen of nineteenth-century Toronto. In this extensively researched biography, the author provides a detailed account of Robinson's life in Upper Canada, and his career as a prominent lawyer, politician, chief justice, and member of the 'Family Compact.' Set within the broader political and social context of the period, the author also provides insight into the nature of Upper Canadian society during the first half of the nineteenth century.

560. Brown, Desmond H.

'The Meaning of Treason in 1885.' *Saskatchewan History* 28 (2, Spring 1975): 65–73.

In the years since Louis Riel was executed as a traitor, a growing literature has discussed and debated his life and times, and the circumstances surrounding his trial. However, relatively little attention has been given to discussing the charge of treason for which Riel was placed on trial. In an effort to determine whether Riel, who was a naturalized American citizen, was properly charged with treason, the author examines the legal circumstances which led to the charge. Specific attention is devoted to assessing: (1) whether the charge of treason was properly applicable to Riel's crimes, (2) whether it was legal to lay such a charge against a U.S. citizen, and (3) whether the 1352 *Statute of Treasons* was the law in the Northwest Territories at the time of Riel's trial. The author's findings indicate that the law of treason in force in the Northwest Territories in 1885, and under which Riel was indicted, was the 1352 *Statute of Treasons* and that it was a proper charge to lay against Riel in consideration of the known facts of the 1885 Rebellion.

561. Brown, Desmond H.

'Foundations of British Policy in the Acadian Expulsion: A Discussion of Land Tenure and the Oath of Allegiance.' *Dalhousie Review* 57 (4, Winter 1977–8): 709–725.

562. Brown, Desmond H.

'Unpredictable and Uncertain: Criminal Law in the Canadian North-West before 1886.' *Alberta Law Review* 17 (3, Summer 1979): 497–512.

The development of the Canadian West and its transition from a trading territory to a settled territory produced a number of jurisdictional and administrative problems. Focusing his attention on the development of criminal law in the Northwest Territories, the author traces the process whereby a 'confused and indeterminate' body of criminal law had, by 1866, become 'the most comprehensive and up to date in Canada.'

563. Brown, Desmond H.

'The Craftsmanship of Bias: Sedition and the Winnipeg Strike Trial 1919.' *Manitoba Law Journal* 14 (1, October 1984): 1–33.

In November 1919, five months after the Winnipeg General Strike, Mr. Justice Metcalfe of the Manitoba Court of King's Bench began to hear the state trial of Robert Boyd Russell, who, being one of the strike leaders, was charged with six counts of seditious conspiracy. This article examines the biased manner in which Metcalfe presided over the accused's trial, whom he obviously disliked and thought guilty beyond question. Particular attention is given to considering the nature of Metcalfe's charge to the jury, which the author argues was based on a selective and skilful manipulation of case law on sedition, and involved directing the jury on matters of fact. Issues raised by Metcalfe's exercise of 'quasi-legislative authority' in the Russell case are considered in light of the history of sedition law in England, and the law on sedition incorporated into the 1892 Canadian *Criminal Code*. The author concludes that Russell's conviction in 1919 owed much to Metcalfe's ability to manipulate cases in such a way as 'to arrive at a pernicious definition of conspiracy, that was repugnant to the provisions of the 1892 *Criminal Code*.'

564. Buchanan, A.W. Patrick.

The Bench and the Bar of Lower Canada down to 1850. Montreal: Burton's, 1925.

565. Bucknall, Brian D.

'John Howard Sissons and the Development of Law in Northern Canada.' *Osgoode Hall Law Journal* 5 (1967): 159–171.

566. Burgoyne, R. Gordon.

Some Tragic Defects in Our Canadian Court and Prison Systems. Montreal: the author, [1945].

The author, president of the Prisoners' Aid and Welfare Association of Montreal and honorary chaplain to the Bordeaux Jail, Montreal, for 25 years, wrote these 25 essays for the Montreal *Herald*, and they have been reprinted under this title. They address problems such as the cost of recidivism, and lack of educational opportunities in prisons.

567. Cadotte, Marcel.

'Le docteur Adrien Duchesne, le premier expert médico-légal de la Nouvelle-France (1639).' *L'union médicale du Canada* 104 (2, February 1975): 276–278.

The first medico-legal investigation in New France was conducted in 1639 by Dr. Adrien Duchesne. The life and work of Dr. Duchesne are presented.

568. Canadian Advisory Council on the Status of Women.

Prostitution in Canada. Ottawa: Canadian Advisory Council on the Status of Women, 1984.

Although this report is concerned mainly with clarifying issues surrounding the debate on prostitution in contemporary Canadian society, it contains two chapters of historical interest, one prepared by Constance Backhouse, 'Canadian Prostitution Law 1839 to 1972,' and another prepared by Priscilla Platt, 'Prostitution and the Law since 1972.' The report also contains an appendix titled 'Chronology of Canadian Prostitution Law' which notes significant developments in the law relating to prostitution from 1839 to 1983.

569. Carter, Margaret A.

'The Halifax Courthouse and County Gaol.' In *Miscellaneous Historical Reports on Sites in the Atlantic Provinces*. Manuscript Report, series no. 107, pp. 247–265. Ottawa: Parks Canada, 1970.

570. Chambers, Brian William.

'Louis Riel: A Critical Examination of the Psychiatric Evidence.' M.A. thesis, University of Calgary, 1976.

This study offers a critical analysis of the psychiatric diagnosis of Louis Riel. Divided into three parts, the study: (1) provides an overview of the life of Louis Riel, and the events leading up to his trial for treason, (2) offers a review and critique of the psychiatric testimony and literature which appeared either at the time of or subsequent to Riel's trial and execution, and (3) attempts to understand the conceptualizations and generalizations of psychoanalysis which have been used in psychological studies of political personality and behaviour. The author concludes that 'the case for Riel's insanity is no way well-founded, and as a consequence the psychiatric evidence tends to obscure our understanding of Louis Riel's actions and behavior.'

571. Chisholm, Joseph.

'Our First Common Law Court.' *Dalhousie Review* (April 1921): 17–24.

572. Chisholm, Joseph.

'Our First Trial for Murder: *The King* v. *Peter Cartcel*.' *Canadian Bar Review* 18 (1940): 385–389.

The first trial for murder conducted in accordance with the procedure of the English common law in what is now Canada was held in Halifax in 1749. This article recounts the manner in which the accused, a Frenchman by the name of Peter Cartcel, was dealt with, noting that he was arrested, tried, convicted, and executed within a week of the date of the offence. The author questions whether he ought to have been found guilty of murder and executed.

573. Chunn, Dorothy E.

'Family Courts and the Dependent Poor in Ontario, 1920–1945: Intended and Unintended Consequences of Reform.' Paper presented at the Annual Meeting of the Canadian Historical Association, Learned Societies Conference, Vancouver, June 1983.

This paper examines the creation of family courts and their short-term development in Ontario from 1920 to 1945. Developments that occurred in Ontario are considered in light of competing 'functionalist' and 'social control' interpretations of the purposes served by family and juvenile courts and the consequences of social reform. The author maintains that notwithstanding the promise of Ontario reformers, juvenile and family courts could not alleviate the congestion in magistrates' courts by taking on domestic cases. The new tribunals became 'add-ons' to the existing system of lower-court justice, and served to extend the state's control over the lives of lower-class families.

574. Clement, W.H.P.

'History of the Judicial System.' In *Canada and Its Provinces: The History of the Canadian People and Their Institutions*, 23 vols. Vol. 22: *The Pacific Province*, pp. 387–397. Edited by Adam Shortt and Arthur G. Doughty. Toronto: Glasgow, Brook and Company, 1914.

575. Colgate, W.

'William Osgoode, Chief Justice.' *Canadian Bar Review* 31 (3, March 1953): 271–294.

William Osgoode arrived in Upper Canada in June 1792 to take up his appointment as the chief justice of the province. This article examines Osgoode's career in Upper Canada, and the legal system that he presided over as chief justice until his death in 1824. Particular attention is given to discussing the varied judicial and governmental duties that Osgoode assumed in Upper Canada during the first two decades of the nineteenth century.

576. Conklin, William E.

'The Origins of the Law of Sedition.' *Criminal Law Quarterly* 15 (3, May 1973): 277–300.

Lawyers have traditionally confined themselves to examining the 'ratio descendi' of prior judicial decisions. One consequence of this has been that they have sometimes neglected to inquire into the origins of particular crimes. This essay endeavours to contribute to the latter path of investigation through examining the origins of English and Canadian law on sedition. The author identifies three attributes of the law: (1) that its purpose is to protect the tranquillity of the state, (2) that it presumes a causal relationship between seditious behaviour and violence, and (3) that the intention to incite violence is an 'objective' one to be imposed by the jury on the accused. Attention is then given to tracing these attributes to their origins, and examining the peculiar political problems and thinking underlying the court's introduction of the three characteristics. The author concludes that an understanding of the origins of seditious offences provides a basis for questioning whether the political thinking underlying their inception is consistent with modern liberal-democratic values.

577. Corfield, William E.

Towers of Justice. London, Ont.: London and St. Thomas Real Estate Board, 1974.

578. Coté, J.E.

'Introduction of English Law into Alberta.' *Alberta Law Review* 3 (1964): 262–292.

At the time of the creation of each of the Canadian provinces that were at one time English colonies, statutory provisions were made for adopting the laws of England relating to civil and criminal matters. The purpose of this article is to examine the use which the courts have made of these provisions, and what implications they have for the general administration of law in the Canadian West, with particular reference to the decisions of Alberta courts. From his review of relevant English statutes and common-law rules, and the circumstances in which they have been applied in Alberta courts, the author concludes that 'in practice it is often difficult to predict which rules of law and which statutes will be held to be applicable, and most of the cases on the subject offer little guidance.' In order to help alleviate this situation, the author lists 17 general principles that offer some assistance in clarifying the matter. He also includes a 'Table of English Statutes in Force in Canada' as of the date the article was published.

579. Coté, J.E.

'The Reception of English Law.' *Alberta Law Review* 15 (1, 1977): 29–92.

Coté's second article on the subject focuses on discussing the rules and consequences inherent in the reception of English law in Commonwealth countries. After a short discussion of the distinction between Imperial laws in force *proprio vigore* and English law received in the colonies as such, the author describes differences in the manner in which English law was received in settled and conquered colonies. The parts of English law which have been received and the rules governing their applicability in former English colonies are then analysed. The article concludes with a discussion of the repeal, amendment, and reform of imported English law by the country receiving such law, and includes an appendix giving an account of the reception of English law in each of the Canadian provinces.

580. Cox, Renee.

'Juvenile Justice Process in Canada: History and Reform.' M.A. thesis, University of Toronto, Centre of Criminology, 1981.

This thesis examines the history of and attempts made to reform the *Juvenile Delinquents Act* of 1908. Attention is given initially to discussing the legal and welfare components of the 1908 act, its underlying philosophy of *parens patriae*, and the practice of the juvenile court as provided for under existing legislation. The author then turns to outlining the ongoing attempts which have been made to replace the *Juvenile Delinquents Act* and the issues addressed in ensuing debates. The thesis concludes by questioning the validity of maintaining a separate juvenile court which is based on the guiding notion that juvenile delinquency should be dealt with in a qualitatively different manner than adult criminality.

581. Craven, Paul.

'The Law of Master and Servant in Mid-Nineteenth-Century Ontario.' In *Essays in the History of Canadian Law*, vol. 1, pp. 175–211. Edited by David H. Flaherty. Toronto: The Osgoode Society and University of Toronto Press, 1981.

Mid–nineteenth-century Ontario law characterized the employment relationship as one of contract, whereby the employer (the 'master') undertook to provide wages in return for faithful and obedient service from the worker (the 'servant'). One of the mechanisms the law provided for the enforcement of employment contracts was the *Master and Servant Act* of 1847. This act gave local magistrates jurisdiction to hear and adjudicate complaints by workers that their employers had mistreated them or failed to pay wages that were due, and by employers seeking to have recalcitrant workers disciplined. According to the 'criminal provisions' of the act, a breach of contract by an employee was a criminal offence for which he/she could be arrested, summarily prosecuted, and punished by fine or imprisonment.

This essay attempts to account for the *Master and Servant Act*'s passage and eventual repeal (in 1877) and to describe the manner in which it was administered. Particular attention is given to examining the statutory and legal history of the act against the background of Ontario society in the mid-nineteenth century. Insight concerning the manner in which the act was administered on a day-to-day basis is gained through an examination of the records of the Galt police court, which from 1857 to 1870 heard close to 50 cases pertaining to the act. The author's principal finding is that the law favoured the employer and dealt harshly with the employee. He concludes that a more complete understanding of nineteenth-century employment law requires that investigators move from the study 'of law based on the statutes and the law reports' towards the study of social history.

582. Craven, Paul.

'Law and Ideology: The Toronto Police Court 1850–80.' In *Essays in the History of Canadian Law*, vol. 2, pp. 248–307. Edited by David H. Flaherty. Toronto: The Osgoode Society and University of Toronto Press, 1983.

This essay undertakes an analysis of police court reporting in Toronto newspapers in the period from 1850 to 1880. The essay begins with an institutional account of the development of the Toronto Police Court and its jurisdiction in the context of other local courts. Newspaper columns and other sources are then used to explore the ambience of the courts, employing the organizing principles of 'majesty,' 'justice,' and 'mercy.' Upon discussing the uses of metaphor in press accounts, and especially that of the court as a theatre, the author addresses the question of the function of law, and more directly the vicarious experience of being brought to law through reporting in the newspapers, in contributing to a sense of legitimation and consent in mid-Victorian Toronto.

583. Crouse, G.H.

'A Critique of Canadian Criminal Legislation.' *Canadian Bar Review* 12 (9, November 1934): 545–578.

584. Cruikshank, E.A.

'The Trials for Treason in 1814.' Ontario Historical Society. *Papers and Records* 25 (1929): 191–219.

585. d'Amours, Oscar.

'Cour supérieur, cour de bien-être social et protection de l'enfance.' *La famille: Bulletin de la fédération des services sociaux à la famille du Québec* 9 (102–103, September–October 1973): 1–52.

586. Day, Réginald.

'L'histoire judiciare de la Gaspésie.' *Revue d'histoire de la Gaspésie* 11 (3, July –September 1973) (no. 43): 121– 126; 11 (4, October–December 1973) (no. 44): 200–213; 12 (1, January–March 1974) (no. 45): 13–24; 12 (3, July–September 1974) (no. 47): 210–220; 12 (4, October–December 1974) (no. 48): 288–294; 13 (3, July–September 1975) (no. 51): 106–150.

In a series of articles published over a two-year period (1973–5), the author traces the judicial history of the region. This chronicle is divided into four distinct periods: the Indian period, the French regime, the British regime, and the century of Confederation. In the Indian period article, Day draws up an inventory of 'crimes' committed by the Indians, but shows their justification based on climatic, geographic, social, and economic conditions in which the Indians lived. In the French regime, spanning two centuries, it was impossible to apply strictly and rigorously the law that was in force in the mother country. The distances, the communication problems, the way of life, and few judicial personnel imposed certain modifications and adjustments to French law. In examining the judicial history of Gaspésie the author considers the organization of judicial powers in New France, Gaspésie as a refuge for criminals, and the functions of the seigneurs. At the end of the French regime the principal officers of justice were still the missionaries and important cases were still not heard in Gaspésie, since lawyers did not appear there until the English regime. In the third article on the British regime (1760–1867), Day describes the coming of English rule and its impact on judicial activity. There is some history of prisons and courts of justice in the region, an inventory of crimes, and some information on judicial corruption. Day includes part of the Taschereau Report which documented the inadequacy of justice administration in Gaspésie and the illustrative case of Jeannot Pauliste. Other cases from the British regime are reproduced. In the final article on the century of Confederation, Day provides a history of notaries in Gaspésie, discusses the famous Murdochville strike in 1957, and covers the Wilbert Coffin case, considered by many to be the most famous case in Canadian judicial annals.

587. Denison, G.T.

Recollections of a Police Magistrate. Toronto: Musson, 1920.

Denison's reminiscences are based on his 43 years of experience as a police magistrate in Toronto. Although the judge presided over some 650,000 cases that came before the Toronto Police Court between 1877 and 1920, his book is restricted to recounting only a selection of 'the more interesting and amusing cases.' Although autobiographical and descriptive in nature, Denison's book offers considerable insight into the kinds of work and methods of procedure involved in the operation of the Toronto Police Court during his long tenure as presiding magistrate.

588. De Salaberry, René.

'The First State Trial in Lower Canada.' *Canadian Bar Review* 5 (7, September 1927): 469–477.

The first trial for high treason in Lower Canada took place in 1797. The accused, who, among other charges, was indicted for conspiring 'to solicit the enemies of the King to invade the province of Lower Canada,' was found guilty by a jury and sentenced to die by being hanged, disemboweled, and beheaded. This article recounts the proceedings of the trial and the gruesome manner in which the sentence was carried out.

589. Deslauriers, Ignace J.

La cour supérieure du Québec et ses juges 1849 – 1er janvier 1980. Québec: Imprimerie provinciale, 1980.

590. D.G.

'La judicature en 1732.' *Bulletin des recherches historiques* 5 (7, 1899): 203–204.

The first part of this brief article is an extract from a letter sent by Mr. de Beauharnois and Mr. Hocquart to the King of France and dated October 1, 1732, explaining the situation of the judicature in the Province of Quebec. According to the senders, the poor remuneration constituted an insurmountable obstacle to the recruiting of competent personnel to fill the vacancies. The general procurator volunteered to give law lessons in French but there were no takers. One clerk was hired from Quebec to serve in Montreal, his only qualification being that he was an honest man who could write legibly. In the second part the author reports that the King of France refused to allow the officers of the Supreme Council (Conseil Souverain) to parade in public in their red robes. The red robe disappeared from the country with the transfer of the colony to Great Britain only to reappear with the creation of the Supreme Court of Canada in 1875.

591. Dickinson, John Alexander.

'Les officiers de la justice seigneuriale de Notre-Dame-des-Anges (1664–1759).' M.A. thesis, Université Laval, 1972.

The author presents a detailed analysis of one seigneurial jurisdiction, that of Notre-Dame-des-Anges during the seventeenth and eighteenth centuries. Administrative structures in New France have not retained the attention of historians. Very few historians have shown interest in seigneurial jurisdictions and certain confusion surrounds the study of such jurisdictions. This is largely due to the lack of documents. However, some small collections are available as well as a large one, namely that of Notre-Dame-des-Anges. The registers of this jurisdiction are kept in the National Archives of Quebec in the 'collection of judicial and notarial pieces.' While this collection is rich in documents, it is difficult to analyse, and there are several gaps as well. In spite of the deficiencies and gaps the documentation is complete enough to allow an analysis of the powers and functioning of one seigneurial court. The author gives a description of the nature of the cases, the way the court operated, the number of cases adjudicated by the court and its subordinates, the costs for the parties involved, and so on. The author concludes that seigneurial justice played an important role in the life of citizens and sometimes dealt with very serious cases. Seigneurial courts existed in several places in New France and functioned normally offering an alternative to the royal courts which sometimes were far away from the parties involved in disputes and which were always much more costly than seigneurial courts.

592. Dickinson, John Alexander.

'La justice seigneuriale en Nouvelle-France: Le cas de Notre-Dame-des-Anges.' *Revue d'histoire de l'Amérique française* 28 (3, December 1974): 323–346.

This article draws on the author's 1972 M.A. thesis, and reiterates his earlier conclusions (see entry 591 above).

593. Dickinson, John Alexander.

'Justice et justiciables. La procédure civile à la prévôté de Québec, 1667–1759.' Ph.D. dissertation, University of Toronto, 1977.

Interested in describing the provostship of the Quebec Court, the author tries to give the reader a general picture of the fundamental traits of the evolution and activities of this court. The author relies on primary sources from the judicial archives. The hypothesis of the author is that an institution is not a simple structure imposed on a social body, but that it is completely integrated to the world surrounding it. As a result, the institution reflects society. Since the judicial apparatus is one of the institutions which has the most influence on the population, its study is seen as contributing to a better understanding of the social structure and behaviours of modern times. The author analyses the functioning, competencies, and limits of justice. The main observation of the author is that justice is not offering, as it is meant to do, equal accessibility. Everyone can use the services of a judge but the cost of a trial and the proximity of the court are disadvantageous to the rural population. Consequently, justice is more beneficial for the rulers than for the ruled. The author examines also the activities of the court because it is seen as revealing social behaviours. This analysis resulted in the distinction of three epochs: (1) the period of the Royal regime in the colony which is characterized by turbulence; (2) the period of stabilization; (3) the period in which justice lacks its importance as a mediator of social rapports. This analysis permits the author to conclude that the superior levels of society are the ones using justice in order to maintain their position of domination.

594. Dickinson, John Alexander.

'Court Costs in France and New France in the Eighteenth Century.' Canadian Historical Association. *Historical Papers* (1977): 49–64.

595. Douville, Raymond.

'La tragédie du Chenal du Moine.' *Cahiers des dix* 35 (1970): 55–67.

The author gives a detailed account of a case of homicide that took place on March 2, 1746. The victim, Joseph Husdit Millet, age 27, died from stabbing by a sword. Two notaries were convicted for the crime: the first, Olivier-Hyacinthe Presse, sentenced to be hanged, had his sentence changed to life imprisonment; the second, Pierre-François Rigault, was sentenced to banishment from the colony then pardoned.

596. Edwards, J.Ll.J.

'The Advent of English (Not French) Criminal Law and Procedure into Canada – A Close Call in 1774.' *Criminal Law Quarterly* 26 (4, September 1984): 464–482.

In the 1770s, a major conflict emerged over whether French criminal law and procedure, as opposed to the system of English criminal justice, should serve as the model to be incorporated into the *Quebec Act* of 1774. The present essay is concerned with examining the events leading up to the watershed of 1774 and the historic choice made at that time between French and English criminal law as the organized body of principles upon which Canada has subsequently built its administration of justice. The author maintains that the historic choice made in 1774 helps to explain the existence of an essentially English system of criminal law and procedure, and a French system of civil law in modern Quebec.

597. Farr, David M.L.

'The Organization of the Judicial System of the Colonies of Vancouver Island and British Columbia, 1849–1871.' B.A. essay, University of British Columbia, 1944.

Drawing almost exclusively on previously unexamined primary historical documents, the author of this essay attempts to sketch the organization of judicial administration in the colonies of Vancouver Island and British Columbia in the period from 1849 to 1871. Chronologically, the essay deals with the organization of the judicial system of Vancouver Island (1849–66), in British Columbia (1858–66), and in the united colony of British Columbia (1866–71). Within each of these divisions, the author sketches the period of the founding of the colony, the organization of the high court of justice, the creation of the local inferior-court system, and the regulation and composition of the legal profession. The author concludes that although the organization of the judicial system of the colonies represented an attempt to transplant the English judicial system to the new colonies of the

Pacific seaboard of British North America, the unique economic and social conditions of the rough and pioneer territories modified and reshaped the institution in innumerable ways.

598. Farr, David M.L.

'The Organization of the Judicial System in the Colonies of Vancouver Island and British Columbia, 1849–1871.' *University of British Columbia Law Review* 3 (1, March 1967): 1–35.

This is a condensed version of the author's 1944 B.A. essay (see entry 597 above).

599. Fisher, Mark Winston.

'Sir James Robert Gowan: A Pioneer Judge.' M.A. thesis, University of New Brunswick, 1971.

Based primarily on the Gowan Papers held at the Ontario Archives and the Public Archives of Canada, this thesis chronicles the long and distinguished career of Sir James Robert Gowan (1815–1909). Appointed as the judge of the district of Simcoe in 1843, during the next 40 years Gowan presided over the development of Simcoe County from a pioneer outpost to a civilized society. In later life he was appointed to the Senate, and rewarded with a knighthood for his many contributions to judicial growth in Canada. In the author's view, two of Gowan's major contributions stemmed from his active involvement in the consolidation of the criminal law of Canada in 1868 and the codification of the criminal law in 1892.

600. Fitzgeorge-Parker, Ann.

Gold-Rush Justice. Don Mills, Ont.: Burns and MacEachern, 1968.

601. Flaherty, David H.

'Writing Canadian Legal History: An Introduction.' In *Essays in the History of Canadian Law*, vol. 1, pp. 3–42. Edited by D.H. Flaherty. Toronto: The Osgoode Society and University of Toronto Press, 1981.

This introductory essay seeks to promote the development of Canadian legal history both as a vehicle for research and as a method of obtaining an improved understanding of the role of law in the Canadian past. Towards this end, the author argues for the adoption of a comprehensive perspective on the appropriate scope of legal history, and for the pursuit of both broad and narrow research topics that shed light on the interaction between law and society. Reference is made to studies published by leading legal historians of the modern era, as a guide to secondary literature in the field, and as a source of positive example and inspiration for Canadian legal historians. The introduction also includes a brief excursion into the legal history of Upper Canada in order to identify issues worthy of more detailed study.

602. Flanagan, Thomas.

'The Riel "Lunacy Commission": The Report of Dr. Valade.' *Revue de l'Université d'Ottawa* 46 (1, January–March 1976): 108–127.

The story of Louis Riel's hanging has been told by several authors, and most of the documentary evidence has been examined. This article points out, however, that one unpublished report on Riel's mental condition, written by Dr. François-Xavier Valade for Sir John A. Macdonald, has long been overlooked. The report, which is 35 manuscript pages in length, provides much more detail than Valade's original one-page opinion on Riel's mental condition made public by the government. Flanagan's article includes the complete text of Valade's more lengthy report, along with an introduction explaining the circumstances under which it came to be written.

603. Flanagan, Thomas.

Riel and the Rebellion: 1885 Reconsidered. Saskatoon: Western Producer Prairie Books, 1983.

604. Flanagan, Thomas, and Watson, Neil Bruce.

'The Riel Trial Revisited: Criminal Procedure and Law in 1885.' *Saskatchewan History* 34 (2, Spring 1981): 57–73.

An attempt is made here to counter 'some false impressions' created by previous historians regarding Louis Riel's trial for high treason in 1885. The analysis presented singles out five issues which the authors claim have not been adequately studied or about which misconceptions have arisen: (1) a comparison of Riel's trial to other British and Canadian treason trials of the nineteenth century, (2) the question of whether Riel should have been charged with treason or treason-felony, (3) the issue of venue, (4) the issue of fitness to stand trial, and (5) the composition of the jury. The authors conclude that when examined in relation to the standards of contemporary 'British justice' and the prevailing rules of criminal procedure in the Northwest Territories, neither Riel's indictment for high treason nor his trial and subsequent death sentence can be said to have been improper.

605. Foster, Hamar.

'The Kamloops Outlaws and Commissions of Assize in Nineteenth-Century British Columbia.' In *Essays in the History of Canadian Law*, vol. 2, pp. 308–364. Edited by David H. Flaherty. Toronto: The Osgoode Society and University of Toronto Press, 1983.

In January 1881, four men were hanged at the prison in New Westminister, B.C. for the murder of John Ussher, a police constable. According to the author, this event 'brought to an end what may have been the most undignified espisode in the troubled and often rancorous history of British Columbia's judicial system in the nineteenth century.' One of the most remarkable aspects of the case of the 'Kamloops Outlaws' was the controversy it raised over the jurisdiction and status of the assize, and the independence of the judiciary from interference by provincial authorities. Through his examination of the unreported record of the case, and the history of commissions of assize in England and British Columbia, the author draws attention to the source of the controversey that divided the judiciary and provincial politicians, and resulted in the retrial of the 'Kamloops Outlaws.'

606. Friedland, Martin L.

'R.S. Wright's Model Criminal Code: A Forgotten Chapter in the History of the Criminal Law.' *Oxford Journal of Legal Studies* 1 (3, 1981): 307–346. Also reprinted in *A Century of Criminal Justice: Perspectives on the Development of Canadian Law* (1984) (see entry 608 below).

In 1870 R.S. Wright, a 31-year-old English barrister, was asked by the Colonial Office to draft a criminal code for Jamaica which could serve as a model for all of the colonies. Although during the 1880s and 1890s Wright's code served as the model code for the colonies, it was not adopted by any of the important ones, and has now been almost forgotten. This article outlines the background to Wright's code, discusses some of its features, and recounts its fate. The author contends that while in quality Wright's code was superior to the model criminal code drafted by his rival, James Fitzjames Stephen (which later formed the basis of the 1892 Canadian *Criminal Code*), several factors contributed to the rejection of Wright's code by the colonies. The fate of Wright's Jamaica code, the author concludes, illustrates that law reform is affected by a great number of factors apart from the merits of a particular proposal, and that in the case of Wright's code the outcome of reform was affected by a combination of politics, personalities, and pressure groups.

607. Friedland, Martin L.

'A Century of Criminal Justice.' *The Law Society of Upper Canada Gazette* 16 (3 & 4, September–December 1982): 336–349. Also reprinted in *A Century of Criminal Justice: Perspectives on the Development of Canadian Law* (1984) (see entry 608 below).

In order to show what changes have occurred in Canadian criminal law and procedure in the past century, the author analyses three murder trials which took place in Ontario in 1882, and considers how similar trials would be conducted today. The three trials, which took place in Toronto, Milton, and Napanee, were selected for analysis because of the availability of trial transcripts (which were then prepared only in capital cases involving murder and treason), and because they reflected different aspects of the criminal trial process as it existed in 1882. Upon describing the key arguments raised in the course of the 1882 trials – including the issue of the degree to which murder was 'planned and deliberate,' the admissibility of confessions, and the appropriateness of the use of the insanity defence – the author concludes that 'in the main the criminal law and trial process have not changed much in the past 100 years.'

608. Friedland, Martin L.

A Century of Criminal Justice: Perspectives on the Development of Canadian Law. Toronto: Carswell Legal Publications, 1984.

This is a collection of papers by the author which present an analysis of the development of law in Canada from a historical and comparative viewpoint. The papers include 'R.S. Wright's Model Criminal Code: A Forgotten Chapter in the History of Criminal Law' (pp. 1–45); 'Criminal Justice and the Constitutional Division of Power in Canada' (pp. 47–66); 'Pressure Groups and the Development of the Criminal Law' (pp. 67–112); 'Gun Control in Canada: Politics and Impact' (pp. 113–139); 'National Security: Some Canadian Legal Perspectives' (pp. 141–170); 'Controlling Entrapment' (pp. 171–204); 'Criminal Justice and the Charter' (pp. 205–231); and 'A Century of Criminal Justice' (pp. 233–245). Most papers were previously published.

609. Friedland, Martin L.

'Pressure Groups and the Development of the Criminal Law.' In *A Century of Criminal Justice: Perspectives on the Development of Canadian Law* (1984) (see entry 608 above), pp. 67–112. Toronto: Carswell Legal Publications, 1984.

Despite the importance of pressure groups in the development of criminal law, research by lawyers on the subject has been relatively sparse. In an attempt to illustrate the importance of pressure groups, the author examines the impact of pressure-group activity on changes made to the criminal law in Canada and Britain. Specific Canadian examples of such activity discussed by the author include the 1970s debate over gun control legislation and capital punishment. One of the principal conclusions of the essay is that 'Canadian and British governments have fostered and encouraged pressure groups and have brought them openly into the decision-making process.'

610. Gagnon, Daniele.

'Histoire de la loi sur les jeunes délinquants.' M.A. thesis, Université de Montréal, 1978.

Since 1857, laws concerning juvenile delinquency have been adopted. This study analyses the historical evolution and the underlying philosophy of these laws until 1973. Relying mainly on published government and judicial documents, this study covers the following subjects: juvenile delinquency laws and philosophy, and persons and procedures of the delinquent court. The author comments on the slow evolution of the philosophy of these laws and attributes its relative stability since 1908 mainly to the difficulties in arriving at a consensus among provinces concerning the age of criminal responsibility and to the questioning of the role and function of the juvenile court.

611. Gagnon, Philéas.

'Nos anciennes cours d'appel.' *Bulletin des recherches historiques* 26 (11–12, 1920): 342–350, 364–375.

Prior to the establishment of the Supreme Council (Conseil Souverain) in 1663, only the governor had the prerogative to hear appeals. Justice was administered by the governor assisted by his secretary, who acted simultaneously as a clerk, notary, note-keeper, and so on. The governor enjoyed ample legislative, executive, and judicial powers. The act of 1663 creating the Supreme Council provided for the organization of a court of appeal to act as final resort for all cases: civil and criminal, major or minor. The council was presided over by the governor. The system changed following the conquest and the author traces the history of the courts of appeal in the province of Quebec under the British regime, beginning with the *Murray Act* (October 31, 1760) to the foundation of the Supreme Court of Canada in 1875.

612. Gavigan, Shelley Ann-Marie.

'The Abortion Prohibition and the Liability of Women: Historical Development and Future Prospects.' LL.M. thesis, Osgoode Hall Law School, York University, 1984.

613. Gibson, Ronald Dale, and Gibson, Lee.

Substantial Justice; Law and Lawyers in Manitoba 1670–1970. Winnipeg: Peguis Publishers, 1972.

614. Gosselin, Amédée.

'La petite histoire du Canada.' Royal Society of Canada. *Proceedings and Transactions* Series 3, 33, sec. 1 (May 1939): 97–107.

This brief history of the regulations governing, among other things, the inns and the cabarets from 1663 onwards contains some information on how drunkards and sellers of alcoholic beverages were punished for violating these regulations.

615. Greenland, Cyril.

'The Life and Death of Louis Riel: II: Surrender, Trial, Appeal and Execution.' *Canadian Psychiatric Association Journal* 10 (4, 1965): 253–259.

Written as the second in a series of three articles on the psychiatric aspects of Riel's 1885 treason trial (see entries 697 and 836 below), this paper deals with the psychiatric evidence presented at the trial by witnesses for the defence and prosecution, Riel's plea to the Court of Appeal of Manitoba, and the medical commission appointed to inquire into Riel's mental state between the time of his conviction and execution.

616. Greenland, Cyril, and Griffin, John D.

'William Henry Jackson (1861–1952): Riel's Secretary, Another Case of Involuntary Commitment?' *Canadian Psychiatric Association Journal* 23 (7, November 1978): 469–477.

Although there have been many studies of the trial of Louis Riel, following the 1885 Rebellion, much less attention has been paid to the fate of his secretary, William Henry Jackson, who was charged with 'treason-felony' and found not guilty by reason of insanity. In an effort to throw some new light on this neglected aspect of medico-legal history, this paper describes the intense political and religious relationship between Riel and his secretary which culminated in the onset of Jackson's mental illness. The authors note that after a trial lasting less than half an hour, Jackson was committed to the 'Selkirk Asylum' under a warrant of the lieutenant governor, from which he later escaped to the United States where he lived until the age of 90.

617. Greenwood, F.M.

'L'insurrection appréhendée et l'administration de la justice au Canada: Le point de vue d'un historien.' *Revue d'histoire de l'Amérique française* 34 (June 1980): 57–93.

In an attempt to show Canadian historians the value of available sources and documents, the author critically examines a number of cases in which criminal prosecution was brought before the courts to prevent an apprehended insurrection. Among the cases examined are those of Louis Riel and the general strike in Winnipeg. A particular emphasis is placed on the case of McLane (1797) and the activities of the martial court that was set up in Montreal after the 1838 rebellion in Lower Canada. The author discusses the severity or leniency with which the accused in political cases were treated, the attitudes of French Canadians towards political prisoners, and the degree to which regular procedures were followed in political cases. He notes that the procedures of the Martial Court of 1838–9 in Lower Canada were probably the worst example of the abuse of the justice system in Canada. The legality of the court itself is questioned and the errors and irregularities are outlined. The author is critical of many other historians who have previously commented on the cases he examines. And to show that such cases are not something of the past, that they do not belong to a bygone era, the author concludes by examining the 'apprehended insurrection' that led to the criminal prosecution of Pierre Vallières and other members of the FLQ as well as the laws that were passed during the crisis of October 1970, laws that established guilt by association, reversed the presumption of innocence, and were enforced retroactively.

618. Gressley, Gene M.

'Lord Selkirk and the Canadian Courts.' In *Canadian History before Confederation – Essays and Interpretations*, pp. 287–304. Edited by J.M. Bumstead. Georgetown, Ont.: Irwin-Dorsey, 1972.

619. Guérin, Thomas.

Feudal Canada: The Story of the Seigniories of New France. Montreal: the author, 1926.

620. Guillet, Edwin Clarence.

[Famous Canadian Trials]. Toronto: the author, 1943–9.

The author has prepared 50 small monographs on famous Canadian trials such as '*The Queen* v. *Louis Riel*,' 'The Shooting of Thomas Scott,' and 'Sudden Death in the Arctic,' a complete listing of which appears in the *Toronto Public Library Catalogue 1921–1949*.

621. Hagan, John, and Leon, Jeffrey.

'Philosophy and Sociology of Crime Control: Canadian-American Comparisons.' *Sociological Inquiry* 47 (3, 1977): 181–207.

Drawing on material from Canada and the United States, this article undertakes a cross-national comparison of North American responses to crime. Through comparing the similarities and differences in the manner in which crime has traditionally been dealt with in the two countries, the authors attempt to show how a society's efforts to control criminal behaviour may be influenced by national values, historical conditions, and economic constraints. Substantive comparisons focus on the extent to which each of the countries has demonstrated a concern for maintaining law and order and for granting legal rights and procedural safeguards (such as the right to counsel and exclusionary rules to do with the use of illegally obtained evidence) to defendants in criminal cases. The authors conclude from their findings that, historically, Canadians have tended to place a stronger emphasis on crime control, while Americans have been more concerned with due process.

622. Hagan, John, and Leon, Jeffrey.

'Rediscovering Delinquency: Social History, Political Ideology and the Sociology of Law.' *American Sociological Review* 42 (4, August 1977): 587–598.

This paper examines a Marxian social-historical approach to the study of legal evolution. The emergence of the Marxist perspective and the logic of its premises are reviewed. Using Canadian delinquency legislation as a historical example, the authors find that the Marxist perspective 'assumes a great deal that is unconfirmed,' that it 'asserts other things that are wrong or misleading,' and that it 'ignores much that an organizational analysis helps to reveal' about the development of Canadian delinquency legislation. The authors conclude by considering the theoretical implications of these findings.

623. Hagan, John, and Leon, Jeffrey.

'The Rehabilitation of Law: A Socio-Historical Comparison of Probation in Canada and the United States.' *Canadian Journal of Sociology* 5 (3, 1980): 235–252.

This article explores similarities and differences in adult probation in Canada and the United States from the late nineteenth century to the present. The authors discuss the background to juvenile court reform in the two countries, the comparatively restrictive nature of Canadian court reforms, and the implementation of reforms as reflected in the increased use of probation as a sentencing alternative. Although the ideological shifts underlying juvenile and adult probation movements in Canada paralleled that of the United States, the authors' findings indicate that juvenile courts and their probation activities were slower to develop in Canada than in the United States, and that the informal nature of Canadian procedures was potentially more intrusive and less attentive to issues of due process. Although the article is based primarily on published secondary sources, reference is made to archival material concerning the development of juvenile courts in Canada.

624. Hamilton, James Cleland.

Osgoode Hall: Reminiscences of the Bench and Bar. Toronto: Carswell, 1904.

625. Harrington, Robert F.

'Sir Matthew Baillie Begbie.' *British Columbia Digest* 23 (1, January–February 1967): 46–50.

From his appointment as judge of the Crown Colony of British Columbia in 1858 until his death as chief justice of British Columbia in 1894, Sir Matthew Baillie Begbie dominated the courts of the province. This article relates a number of stories about Begbie, some of which are based on conjecture and others that are well documented. Although Begbie's 'frequent use of hanging as a penalty' earned him the reputation of being a merciless individual, the author provides evidence about his personal life to show that he was in many ways a gentle and humane person.

626. Harris, L.

'Pioneer Justice.' *The Advocate* 28 (1970): 265–266.

627. Harvey, Cameron, ed.

The Law Society of Manitoba, 1877–1977. Winnipeg: Peguis, 1977.

628. Harvey, Douglas A. Cameron.

'The Law of Habeas Corpus in Canada.' LL.M. thesis, Osgoode Hall Law School, York University, 1977.

629. Harvey, Horace.

'The Early Administration of Justice in the North West.' *Alberta Law Quarterly* 1 (November 1934): 1–15.

630. Harvey, Horace.

'Some Further Notes on the Early Administration of Justice in the North West.' *Alberta Law Quarterly* 2 (November 1935): 171–194.

631. Harvey, Horace.

'Some Notes on the Early Administration of Justice in Canada's Northwest.' *Alberta Historical Review* 1 (3, November 1953): 5–20.

This is the transcript of a paper the author read before the Alberta Historical Society. In it, the long-time chief justice of the Supreme Court of Alberta comments on important events and cases relating to the administration of justice in the Northwest Territories, beginning with the granting of the Hudson's Bay Charter in 1670, and ending with the murder trial of Ambroise Lépine in 1873. Although no references are provided, in his discussion the author refers to numerous primary historical sources.

632. Hassard, Albert Richard.

Famous Canadian Trials. Toronto: Carswell, 1924.

633. Hassard, Albert Richard.

Not Guilty, and Other Trials. Toronto: Lee-Collins Co., 1926.

634. Hay, Douglas.

'The Meanings of the Criminal Law in Quebec, 1764–1774.' In *Crime and Criminal Justice in Europe and Canada*, pp. 77–110. Edited by Louis A. Knafla. Waterloo, Ont.: Wilfrid Laurier University Press, 1981.

During the course of the eighteenth century, Canadiens were subject to French and English criminal law in quick succession, interrupted only by the hiatus of five years of military government from 1759 to 1764. However, Quebec did not experience the criminal justice of France, or, subsequently, that of England, in any 'pure' form. This article outlines some preliminary findings and working hypotheses about the Quebec experience with French and English criminal law, based on two kinds of comparisons. First, the author attempts to assess the reactions of the Canadiens to English criminal law between 1764 and 1774, including the degree to which they were influenced by their only standard – the French. The second comparison is of the English criminal law in Quebec with the English criminal law in England, in both its daily practice and broader social significance. Drawing on available records of the Court of King's Bench, and the lower Court of Quarter Sessions, the author explores such matters as who used the courts, the severity of the criminal law, its significance for authority, and its place in the political order.

635. Herbert, R.G.

'A Brief History of the Introduction of English Law into British Columbia.' *University of British Columbia Legal Notes* 2 (2, March 1954): 93–101.

In 1858, James Douglas, the governor of the newly created colony of British Columbia, proclaimed in an ordinance 'that the Civil and Criminal Law of England ... will remain in full force within the said Colony, till such times as they shall be altered by Her said Majesty in Her Privy Council, or by me, the said Governor; or by such other Legislative Authority, as may hereafter be legally constituted in the said Colony.' In the years following this proclamation, provincial and federal law-making bodies have greatly reduced the situations in which English law may be applied in British Columbia. This article examines the introduction of English law into the province, the subsequent emergence of Canadian case law dealing with civil and criminal matters, and the problems faced by members of the legal profession in British Columbia because of the absence of an easily accessible body of statute law. The author concludes by recommending that an ambitious program of legal research be established to address problems concerning the applicability of English law in the province.

636. Hett, Robert.

'Judge Willis and the Court of King's Bench in Upper Canada.' *Ontario History* 65 (1973): 19–30.

In 1827 the British government appointed John Walpole Willis to fill a vacancy in the Court of King's Bench of Upper Canada. Originally established in 1794, the court, which had jurisdiction over causes both civil and criminal, traditionally handed down decisions that favoured leading members of the colonial establishment. Upon his appointment to the bench, Willis began to publicly question the legality of the Court of King's Bench and its past decisions. This article, which is based primarily on colonial office correspondence held at the Public Archives of Canada, examines Willis's challenge to the legitimacy of the court and its rulings, and the action of the provincial administration in meeting his challenge. Willis's eventual removal from office, which resulted from his criticism of the court and his involvement in the political struggles of the province, served to confirm the legitimacy of the court and the manner in which it administered justice.

637. Higgins, J.G.

'How the Rule of Law Came to Newfoundland.' *Newfoundland Quarterly* 58 (1, March 1959): 7–8, 44–46.

This article attempts to shed light on the manner in which justice was administered in Newfoundland prior to the nineteenth century, and the reasons for the lack of an organized system of law courts. According to the author, the importance of the Newfoundland fishery militated against both the settlement of the colony and the development of law and legal institutions. In particular, he notes the conflict that emerged between settled inhabitants (who recognized the need for the protection of government, police, and courts of law), and adventurers and merchants (who saw no need for a permanent system of judicature). Although the early history of Newfoundland was one of 'intrigue, tyranny and lawlessness,' the author notes that the rule of law eventually came to the colony. The first signs of this were the appointment of justices of the peace and the ordering of commissions for the establishment of courts of oyer and terminer in the mid-1770s.

638. Higgins, J.G.

'How the Rule of Law Came to Newfoundland.' *Newfoundland Quarterly* 58 (2, June 1959): 13–15, 35.

This is a continuation of the author's article published under the same title in a previous issue of the *Newfoundland Quarterly* (see entry 637 above). In it, he deals with developments in the administration of civil and criminal justice in Newfoundland from 1750 to 1826. Circumstances surrounding the enactment of British legislation pertaining to the administration of justice and the courts in Newfoundland, and the role played by early judges in bringing principles of English law and tenets of British justice into the colony, are discussed.

639. Homel, Gene Howard.

'Denison's Law: Criminal Justice and the Police Court in Toronto, 1877–1921.' *Ontario History* 73 (3, September 1981): 171–186.

Between the 1880s and the 1920s Toronto's police court was the essential first level of the court system, and most cases were taken no further. Colonel George T. Denison III, who from 1877 to 1921 was Toronto's chief police court magistrate, handled most of the 650,000 cases that came before the police court, and tried 90 per cent of indictable offences. This article is concerned with investigating the process followed in trying and sentencing defendants in the court during Denison's tenure as chief magistrate. The author's findings indicate that in an era considered by most historians to be one of unprecedented humanitarian and bureaucratic court reform, traditional methods and ideas of treating criminal offenders continued to be followed by Denison. In particular, the author maintains that Denison's concern with the overt criminal act and its immediate effects in determining the sentence to be meted out, and the minimal extent to which court reforms were implemented during his tenure, bring into serious question the 'whiggish view' that the court system underwent progressive reform during the late nineteenth and early twentieth centuries.

640. Honsberger, John.

'The Honourable Mr. Justice William E. Middleton.' *The Law Society of Upper Canada Gazette* 8 (3, September 1974): 180–198.

641. Horn, Michiel.

' "Free Speech within the Law": The Letter of the Sixty-Eight Toronto Professors, 1931.' *Ontario History* 72 (1, March 1980): 27–48.

In January 1931, the editorial pages of four Toronto newspapers carried a letter signed by 68 University of Toronto professors. The letter was written to protest the action taken by the Toronto Police Commission to prohibit all political meetings held in languages other than English, and the implications this action had for the denial of the right of free speech and free assembly. This article examines the events leading up to the publication of the letter, and the ensuing controversy that it caused. In particular, the author notes that the letter became the focal point of controversy between Torontonians concerned with protecting the right to freedom of speech, and those who supported the anti-communist campaign that was launched in Toronto during the 1930s.

642. Humphreys, R.A., and Scott, S.M.

'Lord Northington and the Laws of Canada.' *Canadian Historical Review* 14 (1, March 1933): 42–61.

Prior to the introduction of the *Quebec Act* in 1774, two attempts had been made to reconstruct the legal system of Canada, one occurring in 1766, the other in 1767. This article traces the course of events leading up to these attempts at constitutional reform, and endeavours to account for their failure. According to the authors, the main actor responsible for preventing action being taken by the British government on the 'Canadian question' was Robert Henley, first Earl of Northington, lord chancellor of England, and a member of the Privy Council during the 1770s. Owing to various political and personal rivalries and disputes involving Northington and other British government officals, both attempts at changing the laws of Canada were ill-fated.

643. Jain, N.P.

'Aspects of Juvenile Justice in Toronto.' LL.M. thesis, Osgoode Hall Law School, York University, 1974.

This thesis examines distinct phases in the historical development of the juvenile court in Canada. Divided into three chapters, the thesis deals with the legislative history of the juvenile court movement, with particular reference to Toronto, the changing conceptions of both the definition of delinquency and the juvenile court during the 1960s, and the likely impact of the proposed *Young Offenders Act* (1970) with respect to the commitment of children to training school by the juvenile court of Metropolitan Toronto. The author concludes that in spite of the continuing debate over the reform of the juvenile justice system there is little doubt that the trend is towards providing additional legal safeguards to children caught up in the juvenile court process.

644. Jamieson, F.C.

'Edmonton Courts and Lawyers in Territorial Times.' *Alberta Historical Review* 4 (1, Winter 1956): 3–9.

Based mainly on personal reminiscences, this article provides information concerning lawyers who practised in Edmonton prior to 1905, and the character of the early courts established in the Northwest Territories. Attention is also given to discussing early civil and criminal cases that attracted considerable public interest.

645. Johnson, Walter S.

'The Origins of the Law of the Province of Quebec.' *Revue du droit* 13 (4, December, 1934): 218–229.

646. Johnston, G.A.

'The Law Society of Upper Canada 1797-1972.' *The Law Society of Upper Canada Gazette* 6 (4, December 1972): 1-6.

647. Jones, James Edmund.

Pioneer Crimes and Punishments in Toronto and the Home District. Toronto: George N. Morang, 1924.

Written by a local Toronto magistrate, this book provides an account of the many activities engaged in by magistrates in relation to local government and the administration of justice in Toronto and the Home District in the early nineteenth century. An attempt is made to contrast the less than satisfactory 'social, political and judicial' conditions that existed in the early nineteenth century with the much improved situation that prevailed in the 1920s. Attention is given to discussing a wide variety of subjects, including the types of punishments imposed by early magistrates on convicted criminals; the treatment of criminals, debtors, and the insane in primitive local jails; the problem of drinking and taverns; and the role of prominent citizens as justices of the peace, police constables, and the members of grand juries. Although the author does not provide a formal list of references, the book contains numerous extracts from the manuscript records of early magistrates' sessions, and other unpublished material relating to the administration of justice in Toronto and the Home District.

648. Jones, Maurice William.

'The Judges of the Court of Error and Appeal (afterwards Court of Appeal) in Upper Canada/Ontario, 1850–1881.' M.A. thesis, University of Western Ontario, 1982.

The Court of Error and Appeal in Upper Canada was created by an 1849 statute of the Province of Canada which came into force in January 1850. It continued to function as an Ontario court after Confederation, its name being changed to Court of Appeal in 1876. This thesis deals with the 25 judges who served on this court from the time it was established until it became a division of the new Supreme Court of Judicature for Ontario in 1881. While many of the judges had distinguished political, as well as judicial careers, the thesis concentrates on the latter. In addition to giving biographical sketches and assessments of their judicial careers, it presents statistical data on such matters as the country of birth, educational background, political and religious affiliations of the judges, their age when appointed to judicial office, and their age at death. The thesis draws on a wide range of primary sources, including law reports, statutes, legislative journals, the publications of judges, and newspapers.

649. Kains, John Alexander.

'How Say You?': Grand Jury System in Canada. St. Thomas, Ont.: The Journal, 1893.

The author's interest in abolition of the grand jury coincides with measures for the codification of criminal law. He reviews the need for abolition of the grand jury and cites the unanimity of the press in favour of the change and the fact that cases are being handled without using a grand jury. He claims that the government is trying to reduce costs, and recounts how in the latter half of the nineteenth century the Ontario legislature passed legislation reducing the number of jurors. Many jurists and politicians supported abolition, and quotations from their public addresses are included. Kains's pamphlet sheds light on the administration of justice. The grand jury's purpose was to certify cases for trial and was important in the development of the preliminary inquiry. He concludes that reform is slow to come, but the means of achieving it is by educating people about the need for change. He expected that an improved magistracy, an educated, experienced, and trained public prosecutor, and an 'enriched' petit jury will all go far in making the need for abolition clearer. Although the author refers to many sources of primary documentation (Hansard, statutes, etc.) and secondary sources, there are no footnotes or bibliography.

650. Kains, John Alexander.

A Review of the Movement for Abolishing the Grand Jury System in Canada. St. Thomas, Ont.: The Journal, 1893.

651. Katz, Leslie.

'Some Legal Consequences of the Winnipeg General Strike of 1919.' *Manitoba Law Journal* 4 (1, 1970): 39–52.

652. Keating, Peter.

'Psychiatry and Preventive Detention in Canada: 1948–1961.' M.A. thesis, University of Montreal, 1979.

This thesis examines the history of preventive detention in Canada mainly in the period 1948 to 1961. Divided into four chapters, the thesis deals with the legislative history of section XXI of the *Criminal Code* on preventive detention, the distinction made between the 'criminal sexual psychopath' and the 'habitual offender' prior to the Second World War, the circumstances surrounding the passage of the *Criminal Code* section on preventive detention in 1948, and the transition from 'criminal sexual psychopath' to 'dangerous sexual offender' legislation brought about by the McRuer Commission (1954–8). The author concludes that the formation of the category of 'dangerous offender' in the late 1950s provided 'a new meeting place' for the disciplines of law and psychiatry, which throughout the history of their mutual existence have shared an ongoing conflicting relationship.

653. Kinnear, Helen.

'The County Judge in Ontario.' *Canadian Bar Review* 32 (1954): 21–43, 127–160.

The attempt to make the machinery of justice more suitable to the times requires knowledge of the virtues and defects of the present judicial system. The author, herself a county court judge, maintains that judicial reform might usefully begin at the level of the county court. In support of this suggestion, the author undertakes a detailed two-part examination of the office of the county court judge in Ontario. In part one, she provides a panoramic overview of that part of the legal system in Ontario which falls under the jurisdiction of the county judge, both as a judge of the county court and in his/her many collateral capacities. Part two examines the origin and growth of the county court, discusses the place of the county judge within the total scheme for the administration of justice in the province, and provides suggestions for improving the manner in which justice is administered at the county court level. The author draws extensively on federal and provincial statutes, and primary historical documents relating to the development of the county court in Ontario.

654. Klein, William John.

'Judicial Recruitment in Manitoba, Ontario and Quebec, 1905–1970.' Ph.D. dissertation, University of Toronto, 1975.

This dissertation examines patterns in the recruitment of federally appointed judges in Manitoba, Ontario, and Quebec, from 1905 to 1970. The career paths followed by a total of 749 full-time appointees to county and superior courts are subjected to examination. Personal, professional, and political data concerning the judges were collected from published sources, interviews, and public archives. Computer-based statistical techniques are employed to determine the relative importance of the judges' professional status and political-party allegiance in affecting their initial appointment to the bench, and the subsequent chance of their being promoted to a higher court. Overall the author found that during the 65-year period covered by the study, the factors associated with the recruitment of federally appointed judges underwent significant change, with professional status eventually emerging as a more important factor than the judges' pre-appointment political activities.

655. Knafla, Louis A.

'Aspects of the Criminal Law, Crime, and Criminal Process and Punishment in Europe and Canada, 1500–1935.' In *Crime and Criminal Justice in Europe and Canada*, pp. 1–15. Edited by Louis A. Knafla. Waterloo, Ont.: Wilfrid Laurier University Press, 1981.

This introduction is designed to place the major themes of the 14 essays contained in this book within a general comparative framework. It serves to suggest the extent to which crime and justice are vital to our understanding of Continental, English, and Canadian societies and their institutions. It also serves to illustrate how the Canadian experience with crime and justice has been derived from its common- and civil-law heritage.

656. Knafla, Louis A., and Chapman, Terry L.

'Criminal Justice in Canada: A Comparative Study of the Maritimes and Lower Canada 1760–1812.' *Osgoode Hall Law Journal* 21 (2, 1983): 245–274.

The authors investigate the history of criminal justice in that area first colonized in Canada, notably the English settlements of Nova Scotia and New Brunswick, and the English-conquered colony of New France (Lower Canada) from 1760 to 1812. This study involved researching court records, legal documents, and literary sources. One objective of the study was to compare criminal justice systems in these areas for a better understanding of the interaction and conflict of law and society.

657. Knox, Olive.

'The Question of Louis Riel's Insanity.' In *The Other Native – Les Métis, vol. 1: 1700–1885*, pp. 205–224. Edited by Antoine S. Lussier and D. Bruce Sealey. Winnipeg: Editions Bois-Brulés, 1978.

658. Koester, Charles B.

'The Queen versus George Bennett: Nicholas Flood Davin's Defence of George Brown's Assassin.' *Ontario History* 64 (4, December 1972): 221–238.

On March 25, 1880, the famous Canadian politician and owner of the Toronto *Globe*, George Brown, was wounded by the shot of a pistol fired by ex-employee George Bennett. Six weeks later Brown died, and Bennett was placed on trial for his murder. The author of this article undertakes a detailed examination of Bennett's trial. Particular attention is given to examining the defences that were contemplated by Bennett's lawyer (accident, drunkenness, and insanity), and the defence he finally employed in his unsuccessful attempt to save Bennett from hanging (which involved raising doubt as to whether Bennett's pistol shot or Brown's refusal to follow medical instructions caused his death). The author's account relies mainly on evidence presented at the inquest into Brown's death, the testimony of trial witnesses recorded in the presiding judge's notebooks, and reports of the trial that appeared in the *Globe*.

659. Kos-Rabcewicz-Zubkowski, L.

'Evolution des methodes et des moyens du droit criminel au Canada.' *Revue internationale de droit pénal* 45 (1–2, 1974): 111–130.

The author discusses certain new trends in Canadian criminal law, including the decriminalization of certain acts such as deviant sex acts performed in private between consenting adults, lotteries, attempted suicide, the changes to the dispositions on abortion. They also include the creation of new offences such as those related to hate propaganda, the hijacking of aircraft, or the refusal of a motor vehicle driver to provide a blood sample for alcohol analysis when this refusal is without excuse. The author also discusses changes in penal sanctions and criminal procedures, examining, among other things, the abolition of the lash, the suspension of the death penalty, and changes to the parole system (in particular, the introduction of day parole, intermittent prison sentences, and others).

660. Kos-Rabcewicz-Zubkowski, L.

'La legislation sur la délinquance juvenile au Canada aux 19e et 20e siècles.' *Recueils de la Société Jean-Bodin pour Histoire Comparative des Institutions* 38 (1977): 235–261.

661. Lacey, E.A.

'Trials of John Montgomery.' *Ontario History* 52 (September 1960): 141–158.

John Montgomery was the proprietor of the tavern used by Upper Canadian reformers involved in the Rebellion of 1837 as a base from which to launch their assault upon Toronto. With the failure of the rebellion, Montgomery faced a spectacular trial for high treason 'which ended in his calling hell-fire down upon judge, jury and witnessess.' This article assesses the nature of Montgomery's role in the Rebellion of 1837, as revealed in reports of his trial and testimony given by Crown witnesses. Although the presiding judge, John Beverley Robinson, sentenced Montgomery to be hanged for his participation in the rebellion, his sentence was later commuted to perpetual imprisonment at Fort Henry. Montgomery eventually succeeded in escaping to the United States, and lived there until a general amnesty was granted in 1841. The author maintains that the personal and legal trials of Montgomery disclose 'the subtle play of conflicting responsibilities and loyalties, attractive and not unheroic traits of personality, and elements of a personal tragedy.'

662. Lachance, André.

'La justice criminelle du roi en Canada, 1712–1748.' Ph.D. dissertation, University of Ottawa, 1974.

The author is dissatisfied by the sources used by French-Canadian historians to describe the Canadian society under the Old Regime, namely the correspondence between Versailles and the colonialists, and the regulations, statutes, and edicts enacted by the latter. In order to present a more accurate picture of Canadian society, the author uses other primary sources, mainly sources from judicial archives. The author studies criminal justice institutions because such a study contributes to an analysis of social history. Consequently, the judicial apparatus of Canada and its members at the beginning of the eighteenth century, the types of crimes and criminals, the criminal trials, and the punishments constitute the main framework used by the author. Due to the excessive amount of documentation, the author limits his study to three periods corresponding to the three intendants in the eighteenth century (M. Bégon, C.T. Dupuis, G. Hocquart). The author observes that from the simple description of criminal justice institutions one can extract the observed rules of a society, as well as the whole social life. These conclusions are reached by using what the author considers the 'only valuable method,' the quantitative method.

663. Lachance, André.

'Le procès criminel au Canada au XVIIIe siècle (1712–1748).' *La revue de droit de l'Université de Sherbrooke* 5 (1974): 111–155.

Among all the European institutions that crossed the Atlantic, law seems to be the one which changed the least. Thus French legal institutions underwent only minor modifications in New France. Between 1712 and 1748, Canadian colonies were subject to the French 'Grande Ordonnance Criminelle' of August 1670. The inquisitorial procedure is applied and its central preoccupation is the search for a confession. The criminal trial in Canada, as in France, is divided into seven or eleven parts depending upon whether the prosecutor proceeds or not by the 'extraordinary' means. The author examines each of these in great detail. A list of different types of cases and the average cost of each is included. The author concludes that although the French act of 1670 was never registered in Canada it was followed to the letter by Canadian courts. The study reveals the extreme severity of the system of justice where the accused is almost convicted in advance, as well as the absence of legal safeguards to protect those who are innocent. Torture, however, seems to be less frequently used than in France and Canadian judges seem to acquit more often. Thus the extreme rigour of the French system seems to have been somewhat mitigated in Canada.

664. Lachance, André.

'Une étude de mentalité: Les injures verbales au Canada au XVIII siècle.' *Revue d'histoire de l'Amérique française* 31 (2, September 1977): 229–238.

This is a study of verbal insults (slander) in New France in the eighteenth century aimed at shedding light on the mentality of the society during that period. The study is based on 106 cases, which constitute almost 20 per cent of the 534 cases that were found for the period between 1712 and 1748 involving injury, slander, calumny, defamation, assault and battery, the records of which are preserved in the judicial section of the archives of Quebec, Montreal, and Three Rivers. The purpose was to analyse the ultimate language that Canadians used in crisis situations. Verbal insults reveal an active society, full of life, where human contacts are intense. People living in rural areas appear very attached to their property, their rights, and their code of honour. City dwellers are shown to spend their free time either in cabarets where alcohol is consumed or on the street. The vocabulary used in the insults is a valuable indicator of reprehensible social conduct and the cherished social values of the era.

665. Lachance, André.

La justice criminelle du roi au Canada au XVIIIe siècle: Tribunaux et officiers de justice. Québec: Les presses de l'Université Laval, 1978.

666. Lahaise, Robert.

'Le bailliage Montréalais et ses officiers de justice.' Ph.D. dissertation, Université Laval, 1968.

In order to better understand the administration of justice, the author studies the justice officers, particularly by looking at seigneurial justice or *bailliage* for the period from the foundation of Ville-Marie to 1693. The dissertation is divided into two parts: the *bailliage* and the justice officer. In part one the author examines the organization of justice in general by focusing on the judicial apparatus of Montreal, and comparing it to the general justice system of the time. In part two the author focuses on the judicial officer himself. His functions, from the time of his nomination to his resignation, destitution, or death are analysed. An effort is also made to situate the justice officer in his social class so that his behaviour and status can be better understood. The author observes that the administration of justice in Montreal was characterized by severity towards the accused. The accused had the right to appeal the decision of the justice officer to the Supreme Council (Conseil Souverain) which, in order to attenuate the sanctions imposed, sometimes substituted fines for corporal punishment. However the right of the accused to appeal the decision of the justice officer was not often used because of the costs of such appeals. The author relies on primary sources from the judicial archives of Montreal.

667. Lalonde, Paul Oliver.

'C'était hier – peut-on parler du "bon vieux temps"?' *Justice* 4 (3, May 1982): 10.

In a one-page account, the author presents a brief historical retrospective of some forms of crime and punishment which prevailed in New France and Lower Canada until the nineteenth century. The principle of 'law and order' was predominant at that time and anyone opposing it had to be punished in order to avenge society and to deter others. The punishments were extremely severe and applied for infractions which would be meaningless today. Hanging was used for crimes such as false-money fabrication, robbery, and arson. Other forms of punishment used were transportation, exile, fines, and public display. The author also gives the names of some offenders. No bibliography is provided.

668. Lamonde, Robert.

'Procès Provencher-Boisclair: Les premiers pas de la médicine légale au Québec.' *Le médecin du Québec* 13 (10, October 1978): 73, 75–79.

It was in 1867, in the region of Sorel, in a murder case that the evidence of doctors was used for the first time to prove the guilt of the accused. At the trial of Provencher-Boisclair at the Court of Queen's Bench, Boisclair was accused of murder by poisoning with strychnine. A chemical analysis, made by two groups of physicians, using different methods, led to identical results and established the existence of strychnine in the body of the victim. Despite counter-testimony from other doctors, it took the jury only five minutes to render a guilty verdict. Boisclair was sentenced to death and hanged.

669. Landon, Fred.

'Trial and Punishment of the Patriots Captured at Windsor in December 1838.' *Michigan History Magazine* 18 (Winter 1934): 25–32.

One of several unsuccessful border attacks carried out by Canadian expatriates and Americans concerned with freeing Canada from the tyranny of British rule occurred at Windsor in December 1838. This article examines the fate of 44 members of the 'patriot force' captured at Windsor and sent to London for trial by court martial. Drawing on accounts provided in local newspapers, the author describes the circumstances surrounding the trial of the captured prisoners, and the sentences imposed by the court. He notes that although all except one of the prisoners were sentenced to death, the death penalty was carried out in only six cases. Of the remaining prisoners, 14 were granted pardons, while the others were either deported to the United States or had their sentences commuted to transportation for life in Van Diemen's Land.

670. Langlois, Lyne.

'L'évolution du statut légal du malade mental au Québec et en Ontario: Une comparaison.' *L'hygiène mentale au Canada* 24 (3, September 1976): 2–6.

671. Laplante, Jacques; Grégoire-Laplante, Monique; Dandurand, Yvon; and Jayewardene, Cléo.

Evolution du concept de délinquance juvénile au Canada. Ottawa: University of Ottawa, Department of Criminology, n.d. (manuscript document)

672. Lareau, Edmond.

'La justice criminelle sous la domination française.' *Revue canadienne* 19 (1, 1883): 65–72.

In this short article the author seeks to demonstrate how severe the administration of criminal justice under the French domination was. The famous criminal statute promulgated by the king in 1670 has never been registered at the Supreme Council (Conseil Souverain) of Quebec, but, as suggested by the author, one cannot deny that it was enforced in the colony. Like the statute of Villiers-Cotterets, the statute of 1670 was secret, the accused had no defence, and torture was also used as a means of 'instruction.' The author uses primary sources, mainly the old archives of the French domination, to present the reader with 33 examples of judicial condemnation in order to demonstrate how the statute of 1670 was used.

673. Lareau, Edmond.

Histoire du droit canadien depuis les origines de la colonie jusqu'à nos jours. 2 vols. Montréal: A. Periard, 1888–9.

The author is interested in the history of the law because he sees in it one of the most important manifestations of social life. His major goal is to help the reader understand the history of Canada by looking at its legal and judicial past. The history of civil law as well as criminal, commercial, public, administrative, and even ecclesiastic law is examined. The history of Canadian law, which covers a period of approximately three centuries, is divided into two parts: the period under the French domination and the period under the English domination. Each of these parts is the object of a volume. Volume 1 presents the development of the colony, the work of the mercantile companies, the dissolution of the Royal government and the creation of the Supreme Council (Conseil Souverain) in Quebec City, the history of contentions between the state and the church, aspects of the administration of justice and the Canadian feudal system, as well as the efforts of the population to create the municipal government. Criminal, commercial, and administrative law, as well as the edicts and statutes, are treated separately. Volume 2, which deals with the English domination, starts with a description of the military regime (1759–64). The *Quebec Act* (1774), the Charter of 1791 creating the constitutional government which lasted until 1840, the unification of the two Canadas creating responsible government (1840–67), the codification, the constitution of 1867, the organization of the tribunals, the ecclesiastic government, the relationship between the church and the state, and a bibliography of Canadian law are included in volume 2. The author relies mainly on primary sources, particularly from the old archives of the French domination. Secondary sources are also used.

674. Laskin, Bora.

'The Supreme Court of Canada: The First One Hundred Years. A Capsule Institutional History.' *Canadian Bar Review* 53 (3, September 1975): 459–468.

This is the first in a series of articles written for the occasion of the centenary of the establishment of the Supreme Court of Canada, and published in two issues of the *Canadian Bar Review*. Laskin's article is restricted to providing a brief narrative of the origins and development of the Supreme Court as the highest court in Canada, avoiding any discussion of its doctrine, of its influence as a law-maker, or of its role as a constitutional adjudicator. These and related topics are the subject of subsequent articles in the series, several of which touch on the history of law, the courts, and the administration of justice in Canada.

675. Law Reform Commission of Canada.

'Theft and Fraud through History.' In *Theft and Fraud*, Working Paper 19, Appendix 1, pp. 37–73. Ottawa: Ministry of Supply and Services, 1977.

This paper examines Canadian law on theft and fraud in light of its common-law development. Divided into three sections, it deals with: (1) the English common law of theft and fraud, (2) the transition from common law to the present *Criminal Code,* and (3) theft and fraud under the present code. In each of these sections, relevant English and Canadian criminal statutes and reported legal cases are considered. Upon tracing the historical development of Canadian law on theft and fraud, and pointing out its intricacies, the paper concludes that present *Criminal Code* provisions are seriously defective.

676. Lawrence, Joseph Wilson.

The First Courts and Early Judges of New Brunswick. Paper read before the New Brunswick Historical Society, November 25, 1875. St. John, N.B.: J. & A. McMillan, 1875. Also in *Collections of the New Brunswick Historical Society* 20 (1971): 8–34.

677. Lawrence, Joseph Wilson.

The Judges of New Brunswick and Their Times. St. John, N.B.: 1907.

678. Laycock, Joseph E.

'Juvenile Courts in Canada.' *Canadian Bar Review* 21 (1, January 1943): 1–22.

In this article the author, an executive assistant of the Canadian Welfare Council, reviews the progress of Canadian efforts directed towards the prevention and treatment of juvenile delinquency. Included in the article is a discussion of the development of children's aid societies in Ontario and Quebec, the origins of the *Juvenile Delinquents Act* of 1908, and the establishment and operation of existing juvenile courts in the various provinces.

679. LeDuc, T. H.

'Critique of Canadian Criminal Legislation.' *Canadian Bar Review* 12 (11, 1934): 545–580.

680. Leon, Jeffrey S.

'The Development of Canadian Juvenile Justice: A Background for Reform.' *Osgoode Hall Law Journal* 15 (1, June 1977): 71–106.

681. Letourneau, Gilles.

'L'historique des brefs de prérogative en droit anglais et canadien.' *Revue du barreau de la Province de Québec* 35 (1975): 471–503.

This is a French translation of the first chapter of a book published in English under the title *The Prerogative Writs in Canadian Criminal Law and Procedure*. The book is published by Butterworth of Canada (see entry 682 below).

682. Letourneau, Gilles.

The Prerogative Writs in Canadian Criminal Law and Procedure. Toronto: Butterworth, 1977.

The first chapter of this legal text deals with the history of prerogative writs in English and Canadian law. Although noting that it was not until the revision of the *Criminal Code* in 1953–4 that the existence of prerogative writs in Canadian criminal law was acknowledged in a federal statute, the common-law writs of *certiorari, habeas corpus, mandamus, procedendo*, and prohibition were introduced into Canada at the same time as the laws of England. The origin of each of these prerogative writs in English common law, and their subsequent evolution in Canadian law, are dealt with on an individual basis by the author.

683. L'Heureux, Jacques.

'L'organization judiciare au Québec de 1764 à 1774.' *Revue générale de droit* (1970): 266–331.

On February 10, 1763, Canada was given to Great Britain by the Treaty of Paris. Eight months later, King George III issued a proclamation organizing the colonies acquired in America. No special regime was reserved for the Province of Quebec which was considered one of the colonies. The legality of the Royal Proclamation was challenged without success by Francis Masères. In August 1764, the Council of the Province of Quebec asked the chief justice and the general procurator of the province to prepare a judicial organization bill. The result was the *Murray Act*, adopted on September 17, 1764, which established the civil courts. The author traces the judicial organization from the *Murray Act* up to the *Quebec Act* (June 22, 1774), providing a detailed analysis of the criminal courts, the civil courts, the judges and their aids, as well as the mode for their remuneration. He concludes that the judicial organization in the province from 1764 to 1774 was not rational. Justice was slow, costly, and dispensed by incompetent judges. The system, based on English laws and conducted in English, did not take into account the presence in the province of Canadiens who constituted over 99 per cent of the population. This meant that Canadiens often went with their disputes to private arbitrators rather than taking them to the courts.

684. Loukidelis, D.

'Some Aspects of the Development of the County Courts of Ontario and the Evolution of the Office of County Court Judge, 1792–1881.' Master's essay, Laurentian University, 1978.

685. McAlister, T.G.

'The Positions and Function of the Courts in Canada.' In the Chartered Institute of Secretaries [of Joint Stock Companies and Other Public Bodies], *Addresses* [of the Season/Session 1933–4], pp. 14–20. [n.p.: The Institute, 1934?]

This was an address given before the London and District Branch of the Chartered Institute of Secretaries, at London, Ont., on January 25, 1934.

686. McCaul, C.C.

'Precursors of the Bench and Bar in the Western Provinces.' *Canadian Bar Review* 3 (January 1925): 25–40.

The charter granted to the Hudson's Bay Company in 1670 included provisions authorizing the governor and council of Rupert's Land to administer justice, whether civil or criminal, according to the laws of England. Despite these provisions, until as late as the 1830s, no person skilled in law was attached to the offices of the governor in council, as a judge, legal adviser, or assessor. This article examines the manner in which civil and criminal justice was administered in western Canada prior to the appearance of trained barristers and judges. Attention is also given to tracing the growth of the legal profession in the western provinces and the development of a judicial system distinct from that which existed in nineteenth-century Ontario.

687. McClement, Fred.

The Strange Case of Ambrose Small. Toronto: McClelland and Stewart, 1974.

688. McConnell, W.H.

'The Calder Case in Historical Perspective.' *Saskatchewan Law Review* 38 (1, 1973–74): 88–122.

689. McConnell, W.H.

Prairie Justice. Calgary: Burroughs and Company, 1980.

This book offers a descriptive account of the history of the legal profession in Sasatchewan. Divided into eight chapters, the book provides information concerning: (1) the development of legal institutions in the Northwest Territories; (2) the Law Society and the legal profession; (3) some celebrated Saskatchewan barristers; (4) legal education in Saskatchewan; (5) the magistracy and district-court judges; (6) provincial superior-court judges; (7) Saskatchewan lawyers on federal courts; and (8) legal developments and services in the post-war era.

690. MacGill, H.G.

The Juvenile Court in Canada: Origins, Underlying Principles, Governing Legislation and Practice. Ottawa: Canadian Council on Child Welfare, 1925.

691. McKay, K.W.

The Court Houses of a Century [1800–1900]: A Brief Historical Sketch of the Court Houses of the London District, the County of Middlesex and the County of Elgin. St. Thomas, Ont.: The Elgin County Council, 1901.

692. MacLeod, A.J., and Martin, J.C.

'The Revision of the Criminal Code.' *Canadian Bar Review* 33 (1, January 1955): 3–19.

This is the first in a collection of four articles designed to introduce Canadian lawyers, and other interested persons, to the revised Canadian *Criminal Code* of 1955. In their lead article, the authors discuss the background to and events preceding the enactment of Canada's first *Criminal Code* in 1892, the recognition of the need for a major revision of the *Criminal Code* in the late 1940s, and the steps taken by the government to prepare a new consolidated *Criminal Code* in the early 1950s. Specific steps included the establishment of commissions and committees to decide on the revisions to be incorporated in the new code, the drafting of the legislation and the debate in parliament leading up to the enactment of the new code in 1954. The authors' discussion of the main features of the new code, and the steps involved in its creation, is informed by their personal involvement in formulating and drafting the legislation as employees of the federal Department of Justice.

693. Macleod, Roderick Charles.

'The Shaping of the Canadian Criminal Law, 1892 to 1902.' Canadian Historical Association. *Historical Papers* (1978): 64–75.

This paper examines the forces operating to change the Canadian criminal law in the first decade after the passage of the *Criminal Code* in 1892. The main focus of attention is on examining the intentions and actions of parliament, which, it was decided, would be the principal source of change in the criminal law. The author notes that changes and innovations made during the period were 'numerous and sweeping in character,' and that the procedure introduced for handling amendments to the code in 1900 'set the pattern which prevailed until the 1950s.'

694. McNaught, Kenneth.

'Political Trials and the Canadian Political Tradition.' In *Courts and Trials: A Multi-Disciplinary Approach*, pp. 137–161. Edited by Martin L. Friedland. Toronto: University of Toronto Press, 1975.

695. MacRae, Marion, and Adamson, Anthony.

Cornerstones of Order: Courthouses and Town Halls of Ontario, 1784–1914. Agincourt, Ont.: Clarke Irwin, 1983.

696. Malchelossé, G.

'Un procès criminel aux Trois-Rivières en 1759.' *Cahiers des dix* 18 (1953): 207–226.

The author gives a very detailed account of a crime committed in Three Rivers on August

20, 1759. A slave, Marie La Sauvagesse, attacked and injured two of her ladymasters, Mme Châtelain and Mme de Niverville, with a kitchen knife that she was sharpening on a stone in the garden. The sentence of the lash, branding with hot iron, followed by permanent banishment was pronounced on September 11, 1759, just two days before the first battle of the Plains of Abraham. It was changed by the Supreme Council (Conseil Souverain) upon the prosecutor's appeal into hanging and confiscation of the estate. This is believed to be the last execution under the French regime.

697. Markson, E.R.

'The Life and Death of Louis Riel: A Study in Forensic Psychiatry. I: A Psychoanalytic Commentary.' *Canadian Psychiatric Association Journal* 10 (4, 1965): 244–252.

Written as the first in a series of three articles on the psychiatric aspects of Riel's 1885 treason trial (see entry 615 above and 836 below), this paper is mainly concerned with examining Riel's personality and mental state up to the time of his trial. Drawing on historical evidence indicative of Riel's mental condition, a psychoanalytical interpretation of the state of his mental health is offered.

698. Marston, Geoffrey.

'Historical Aspects of Colonial Criminal Legislation Applying to the Sea.' *University of British Columbia Law Review* 14 (2, 1980): 299–328.

699. Martin, Archer.

'The Rise of Law in Rupert's Land.' *The Western Law Times* 1 (June 1890): 49–59; continued in 1 (July 1890): 73–80 and 1 (August 1890): 93–100.

700. Martin, J.C.

'History in the Courts.' *RCMP Quarterly* 8 (4, April 1941): 435–442.

701. Massicotte, E.-Z.

'Les tribunaux et les officiers de justice, à Montréal, sous le régime français, 1648–1760.' La Société Royale du Canada. *Mémoires et comptes rendus* Series 3, 10, sec. 1 (1916): 273–303.

The author presents a list of the various officers of justice during the French regime compiled on the basis of data gathered from the judicial archives of Montreal. The list is divided into three periods: (1) Seigneurial justice (1648–93); (2) the First Royal Justice (1663–6); (3) the Second Royal Justice (1693–1760). The names of all officers of justice, including judges, prosecutors, clerks, sheriffs, assessors, interpreters, scriveners, prison guards, and notaries, together with the dates of their service, are provided.

702. Massicotte, E.-Z.

'Les tribunaux de police de Montréal. *Bulletin des recherches historiques* 26 (6, 1920): 180–183.

From 1642 to 1663 it was Paul de Chomédé, Sieur de Maisonneuve, founder and governor of Montreal, who dispensed justice at all levels. The year 1663, which saw the creation of the Supreme Council (Conseil Souverain), witnessed the modification of this state of affairs. In 1664 the governor set up a police court, whose judges had attributes similar to those of the justices of the peace as we know them today. These five judges were elected by the residents of the Island of Montreal. The record of this extraordinary election is kept in the archives of the Justice Building in Montreal. A hundred years later, justices of the peace emerged under English law. The first two, John Grant and Samuel Mather, were appointed on December 12, 1764. The author also provides the names of judges and magistrates who sat on the bench from 1838 to 1919 in Montreal.

703. Massicotte, E.-Z.

'Les juges de Montréal sous le régime français, 1648–1760.' *Bulletin des recherches historiques* 27 (6, 1921): 177–183.

From the founding of Montreal until the end of the French regime 12 judges presided over the courts of the city. Three different courts existed during this period. Judges enjoyed broad powers and were saddled with heavy duties going far beyond the normal judicial tasks related to civil and criminal cases. They performed functions usually performed in France itself by three persons. The author provides the names and dates of service of the 12 judges, and a brief biographical note on each. The author presents the same information in greater detail in a later article of the same title in *Cahiers des dix* 8 (1943): 235–266 (see entry 708 below).

704. Massicotte, E.-Z.

'Les greffiers de Montréal sous le régime français, 1648–1760.' *Bulletin des recherches historiques* 31 (4, April 1925): 114–119.

Under the French regime 12 judges were in charge of the administration of justice in Montreal. During the same period, 13 clerks served the three courts which existed either simultaneously or one after the other in the city. These three courts are: (1) Seigneurial Justice established by Maisonneuve in 1648, which continued to operate until 1693; (2) First Royal Justice called 'Seneschal Court,' created by the Supreme Council (Conseil Souverain) in 1663 and abolished in 1666; (3) Second Royal Justice, instituted in 1693. The author provides brief biographical notes on the 13 clerks.

705. Massicotte, E.-Z.

'Les tribunaux et les officiers de justice de Montréal sous le régime français.' *Bulletin des recherches historiques* 37 (2, February 1931): 122–128; (3, March 1931): 179–192; (4, April 1931): 252–256; (5, May 1931): 302–313.

Based on his research of the judicial archives of Montreal, the author was able to compile an index of the officers of justice in New France from 1648 to 1760. He has published various biographical notes on some of these officers. This article is a compilation of all the published and unpublished data he gathered on the officers of justice. The article is divided into four parts, each covering a different period. The first is the period of Seigneurial justice (1648–93); the second period is that of the First Royal Justice (1663–6); the third part is devoted to the Police Court 1664, while the fourth covers the period of the Second Royal Justice (1693–1760). The names of all officers including judges, prosecutors, clerks, sheriffs, assessors, interpreters, scriveners, prison guards, and notaries, together with the dates of their service, are provided.

706. Massicotte, E.-Z.

'Les pendues encagés.' *Bulletin des recherches historiques* 37 (July 1931): 427–432.

Punishments in the colony seem to have been less sanguinary than they were in the Old World. Until the nineteenth century, there were 200 crimes punishable by death in England while the number in the colony was much lower. The two persons who were hanged, then exposed in iron cages, were tried under the English regime. The first, a man named Saint Paul, killed a family of four, robbed them, and set their house on fire to hide his crime. He was hanged in 1761 in Montreal and his body was exposed in an iron cage for over a year. The second, a female called La Corriveau, was hanged for having killed her second husband in 1763. The iron cage in which her body was exposed for a long time disappeared but was found in 1850 and was later sold to the Boston Museum.

707. Massicotte, E.-Z.

'Les coroners du XVIIe et du XVIIIe siècle.' *Bulletin des recherches historiques* 40 (1934): 617–620.

From 1642 to 1760 in the cases of violent, accidental, sudden, or doubtful deaths, judicial authorities were notified. The judge of the Seigneurial or Royal court, accompanied by a clerk and a surgeon or a physician, went to the place where the body was. There, on the spot, the judge conducted an investigation. The opinion of the surgeon and the testimonies of witnesses were contained in a report deposed with the court's clerk. Whether death resulted from a crime or not, the burial was prompt since there was no morgue and the custom was to bury the dead the day of or the day after the death. When death took place outside of Montreal, the priest performed the judge's role where it was impossible to communicate with the court. Starting from 1764 there were real coroners in Montreal and a list of their names was published by the author in 1923 in the *Bulletin des recherches historiques*. Three cases – from July 5, 1667; May 20, 1693; and May 25, 1779 – are described to illustrate the procedure.

708. Massicotte, E.-Z.

'Le tribunal seigneurial de Batiscan.' *Bulletin de recherches historiques* 41 (12, 1935): 720–723.

This article is a compilation of brief biogaphical notes on some of the officers of the Seigneurial court of Batiscan, a court that operated from 1680 to 1760. It covers the judges, the prosecutors, the clerks, sheriffs, and notaries. The list is not exhaustive and the author notes that completing the list would require several days in the archives of Three Rivers. The author also reproduces an act from Jacques Raudot, King's Counsellor, ordering the judges of Batiscan and Champlain to hold their courts weekly rather than monthly.

709. Massicotte, E.-Z.

'Les juges de Montréal sous le régime français.' *Cahiers des dix* 8 (1943): 235–266.

See entry 702 above, which was a less-detailed version of this same paper.

710. Massicotte, E.-Z.

'Le tribunal seigneurial de Sorel et autres.' *Bulletin des recherches historiques* 50 (1, January, 1944): 13–14.

In this brief article, the author reports that a seigneurial court operated in Sorel in the seventeenth century and explains the difficulty of establishing a complete list of seigneurial courts that existed in New France. The location and periods of operation of some of these courts are provided.

711. Mathieu, Jacques.

'Les causes devant la prévôté de Québec en 1667.' *Histoire sociale/Social History* 3 (April 1969): 101–111.

Registers of the courts provide much information on the social history and the attitudes in New France. They reveal a reality much different from, or in contradiction to, what may be indicated by the laws and decrees. For instance, justice was rarely cost-free and the provost court of Quebec, abolished in 1674 and reinstituted in 1677, never ceased to exist despite what the decrees say. The Archives of Quebec are in possession of 113 registers of this court, covering the period of 1667 to 1760. The author conducted a small study of the court in 1667 paying particular attention to the type of cases heard, the functioning of the justice apparatus, and the parties involved in litigation. The findings presented reveal the nature of disputes; provide indices on the mentality and the way of life of Canadians, their relations to their surroundings and to Indians; and make it possible to better understand the operations of the justice machine and to determine the cost of living in the colony.

712. Matters, Diane Louise Janowski.

'A Chance to Make Good: Juvenile Males and the Law in Vancouver, B.C., 1910–1915.' M.A. thesis, University of British Columbia, 1974.

Promoters of the juvenile court in the early twentieth century claimed that it would benefit young offenders by protecting them from being subjected to the adult criminal trial and sentencing process. This thesis examines the day-to-day operation of the Vancouver Juvenile Court, with the view towards testing the validity of this assumption. In this effort, files were compiled on all juvenile males who came before the court during its first five years of operation. A computer analysis was made of the cases to determine how different variables, such as the child's home situation and who initiated his initial contact with the court, affected the handling of the cases. Findings indicate that the Vancouver Juvenile Court did not function as its promoters had intended. Children were still frequently arrested by police and held in regular police cells for varying lengths of time, and were frequently subjected to lengthy periods of detention in the Courts Detention Home. According to the author, however, the court did serve the broader economic and social functions of seeking to produce well-disciplined workers, and providing 'an important part of the machinery for extending the length of childhood.'

713. Melling, Michael W.

'Cleaning House in a Suddenly Closed Society: The Genesis, Brief Life and Untimely Death of the *Habitual Criminals Act*, 1869.' *Osgoode Hall Law Journal* 21 (2, June 1983): 315–362.

714. Mewett, Alan W.

'Criminal Law 1948–1958.' *Canadian Bar Review* 36 (4, December 1958): 445–464.

Through codifying certain common-law criminal offences and abolishing others, the revised *Criminal Code* of 1955 helped to reduce certain ambiguities in the law. In addition, judicial decisions handed down in the period 1949 to 1958 contributed to the clarification of the substantive criminal law in force in Canada. Mewett maintains that despite these recent developments, several issues in the area of substantive crimes remain to be addressed. Turning to an examination of recent court decisions, the author identifies and discusses what he considers to be 'important and controversial' issues which have arisen in relation to such matters as the requirement of *mens rea*, the defences of insanity and drunkenness, sex crimes, and the law of obscenity.

715. Mewett, Alan W.

'The Criminal Law, 1867–1967.' *Canadian Bar Review* 45 (December 1967): 725–740.

In this article, the author provides a critical overview of the process of criminal law reform in Canada from 1867 to 1967. Major efforts at consolidating, codifying, and amending the criminal law of Canada made in 1869, 1892, 1927, and 1953 are discussed. An attempt is made 'to evaluate the impact of the Code on the criminal jurisprudence of Canada and to make some estimate of the trends which appear to be emerging.' From his survey of the development of criminal law in Canada, the author pinpoints serious defects in both the law itself and in the process of criminal law reform. Noting that 'the criminal law has not progressed in one hundred years,' he offers several recommendations aimed at promoting more adequate criminal law reform.

716. Mignault, P.-B.

'L'indépendence des juges.' Royal Society of Canada. *Proceedings and Transactions* Series 3, 21, sec. 1 (1927): 29–50.

This is a historical review of the principles of the independence of judges and their tenure in England, France, and Canada. The author discusses the case of Commendams who opposed Sir Francis Bacon, then general procurator, and Sir Edward Coke, Chief Justice of the Courts of the King's Bench, the principles of common law, and the principle of equity. In Canada, it was only after the Union that judges became independent of the Crown. Lord Durham insisted that they be independent and be given the same tenure of office and security of income as existed in England. He also recommended that the principle of ministerial responsibility be extended to Canada. It was in this spirit that in 1843, under the ministry of Lefontaine-Baldwin, the legislature passed two laws: the first making judges independent; and the second depriving them of the right to vote, the right to be elected or to sit as members of the legislature. The principle of tenure was confirmed in section 99 of the *British North America Act*. Other topics discussed are the dismissal of judges, the legal situation of judges in England and Canada, and the separation of powers.

717. Montigny, Benjamin Antoine Testard de.

Histoire du droit canadien. Montréal: Eusèbe Sénécal, 1869.

718. Morel, André.

'La réaction des canadiens devant l'administration de la justice de 1764 à 1774: Une forme de résistance passive.' *Revue du barreau de la Province de Québec* 20 (2, February 1960): 53–63.

The author examines the *Murray Act* of September 17, 1764, which constituted the first application of English law in the newly acquired colony. The act remained in effect for ten years. To assess people's reaction to the transplanting of English law into their society, the author examined the records of the Montreal court from February 11, 1765, to May 1, 1775, date of entry into effect of the *Quebec Act*. There was a marked decline in the number of civil and family law cases before the court. This decline is seen as a form of passive resistance to the *Murray Act*, as a boycott of the court as a result of general dissatisfaction with Britain's attempt to impose its law upon the people of Quebec.

719. Morel, André.

'La justice criminelle en Nouvelle-France.' *Cité libre* 14 (January 1963): 26–30.

The criminal law of the Old Regime has a reputation of having been extremely severe and inspiring respect through terror. Justice is reputed to have been arbitrary and despotic, based on intimidation and repression. In the words of Von Bar, 'instead of the law controlling the judge, the judge controlled the law.' To what extent does this caricature of justice correspond to reality? The author tries to answer this question through a brief review of the penal law in New France under the French regime, examining successively the trial, the sentence, the execution of the sentence, and the appeals, both voluntary and mandatory ones.

720. Morel, André.

'Réflexions sur la justice criminelle canadienne au 18e siècle.' *Revue d'histoire de l'Amérique française* 29 (2, September 1975): 241–253.

The author presents a revised version of comments he made, as a discussant, on a paper presented by André Lachance at a meeting of the Historical Society of Canada (Edmonton, June 1975). Lachance's paper is entitled 'Crime, Criminality and Penal Repression in Canada in the 18th century 1712–1748.' After noting the lack of interest among legal historians in the history of penal law both in France and in Quebec until the 1960s, the author points out that French criminal procedures which were in effect under the French regime required (contrary to the English procedures) that everything be written. It is therefore possible to collect information on that period from the written documents containing the interrogation of the accused and the testimony of witnesses. André Lachance was able to construct an index, more or less complete, of some 800 delinquents and used it to present a collective portrait of the criminal of that era. The author uses the data compiled by Lachance to discuss the variables of gender and age in their relation to crime and sanctions. The last part of the article is devoted to a study of crimes against morality in New France concluding with a brief discussion of judges' attitudes *vis-à-vis* this type of criminality.

721. Morel, André.

'La réception du droit criminel anglais au Québec (1760–1892).' *Revue juridique thémis* 13 (1978): 449–541.

This is a detailed study, commissioned by the Law Reform Commission of Canada, of how English criminal law was received when it was introduced following the conquest (1760) and the developments that took place until codification (1892). Two barriers stood in the way of French Canadians' understanding and acceptance of English criminal law: the first was the language barrier and the second, ignorance. The laws were written, and criminal trials were conducted, in a language the majority of the population did not understand. And as late as 1793 the Legislative Assembly of Lower Canada still required that all bills related to criminal law be presented in English 'in order to preserve the unity of the texts.' Thus, for French Canadians, who did not know English, the criminal law of their country remained a closed and impenetrable universe. The study is divided into three parts, and has an introduction and a conclusion. The first part, entitled 'The Political Stage,' discusses the introduction of English criminal law into the newly acquired colony over two periods of time: 1759 to 1774 and 1774 to 1867. The second part, 'The Psychological Stage,' examines the reception of English criminal law by Canadians. This part is divided into three sections: the apparent satisfaction of Canadians; the satisfaction of Canadians – a misleading appearance; and delayed satisfaction. The third part, 'The Educative Stage,' deals with information of Canadians and the training of lawyers. The conclusion discusses the firm establishment of English criminal law in Canada through codification.

722. Morel, André.

'Canadian Legal History: Retrospect and Prospect.' *Osgoode Hall Law Journal* 21 (2, June 1983): 159–164.

723. Morrow, William G.

'Justice in the Canadian Arctic.' *Queen's Quarterly* 72 (Spring 1965): 144–149.

In 1955 the government of Canada established a territorial court in the Northwest Territories. Prior to this, justices of the peace and magistrates administered justice in the North, with judges from elsewhere in Canada being sent in for cases considered more serious. This article praises the actions of John Howard Sissons as judge of the newly constituted court. Morrow presents the knowledgeable, understanding and flexible attitude of Sissons towards the application of 'white-man's' law in the far north. Justice Sissons studied the land and its people in an effort to neither oppress nor manipulate the people of the North by laws designed for a different society in a foreign language. Examples of cases are outlined and footnoted.

724. Morrow, William G.

'Adapting Our Justice System to the Cultural Needs of Canada's North.' In *Crime and Criminal Justice in Europe and Canada*, pp. 257–271. Edited by Louis A. Knafla. Waterloo, Ont.: Wilfrid Laurier University Press, 1981.

This article examines the impact of Canadian institutions and law on the Indian, Eskimo, and white people who populate Canada's North. Based on a review of the work of the Supreme Court of the Northwest Territories from 1955 to 1971, which includes the author's own career as legal counsel and judge, the article reveals the tragic effects of alcohol on a once-proud native people. He notes that in some areas an average of one offence per capita has been registered in a single year, most of them liquor-related. Citing the details of some of the more famous criminal trials in which he was personally involved, the author shows how the court has attempted to adapt the criminal justice system to the cultural needs of Canada's North.

725. Morrow, William G.

'An Historical Examination of Alberta's Legal System: The First Seventy-Five Years.' *Alberta Law Review* 19 (1981): 148–170.

This article was written in 1980 to commemorate Alberta's seventy-fifth year as a province of Canada. Morrow maintains that the legal issues which arose in Alberta during its first 75 years, in the areas of both criminal law and civil litigation, reflected the social, economic, and political development of the province. The author provides a historical retrospective of specific legal issues that arose in Alberta from 1905 to 1980, drawing details from personal experience gained throughout his lengthy career as a lawyer and judge in Alberta and the Northwest Territories.

726. Morse, Charles.

'The Judicial Systems of the Prairie Provinces.' In *Canada and Its Provinces: The History of the Canadian People and Their Institutions*, 23 vols. Vol. 20: *The Prairie Provinces*, pp. 365–391. Edited by Adam Shortt and Arthur G. Doughty. Toronto: Glasgow, Brook and Company, 1914.

727. Morton, Desmond, ed.

The Queen vs Louis Riel. Social History of Canada Series. Toronto: University of Toronto Press, 1974.

In July 1885, Louis Riel was placed on trial at Regina for high treason. This book includes a complete transcript of the trial *The Queen* vs. *Louis Riel*, along with an introduction outlining the events leading to Riel's trial and execution, and the ensuing controversy that it raised.

728. Moyles, R.G.

British Law and Arctic Men. Saskatoon: Western Producer Prairie Books, 1979.

729. Mulvey, Thomas.

'The Judicial System.' In *Canada and Its Provinces: The History of the Canadian People and Their Institutions*, 23 vols. Vol. 18: *The Province of Ontario*, pp. 513–548. Edited by Adam Shortt and Arthur G. Doughty. Toronto: Glasgow, Brook and Company, 1914.

730. Murdoch, Beamish.

'Appendix: "Nova Scotia's Blackstone" in the Origins of Nova Scotia Law.' *Dalhousie Law Journal* 8 (3, 1984): 185–186; 'An Essay on the Origin and Sources of the Law of Nova Scotia.' *Dalhousie Law Journal* 8 (3, 1984): 187–196; also published in *Law in a Colonial Society: The Nova Scotia Experience. pp. 187–196*. Edited by Peter Waite, Sandra Oxner, and Thomas Barnes. Toronto: Carswell, 1984.

731. Nantel, Maréchal.

'Esquisse historique du barreau de la Province de Québec.' *Revue de droit pénal et de criminologie* 2 (1924): 337, 385.

732. Nantel, Maréchal.

'Les avocats à Montréal.' *Revue du barreau de la Province de Québec* 2 (10, 1942): 445–467.

The author traces the history of various lawyers' associations in Montreal. In 1828 the 'lawyers' library' was founded and held its first meeting on March 27. On December 20, 1830, the library changed its name to 'Advocates' Library and Law Institute of Montreal.' It was incorporated in June 1840 and 13 years later passed under the control of the Bar which has been incorporated by a law passed on May 30, 1849. Other associations discussed are: the Brothers-in-law Club, the law student society of Montreal, the Canadian Bar Association, the Association of the Young Bar of Montreal, the Lawyers' Circle, the Montreal Advocates Benevolent Association, the Association of French-Language Jurists. The article also examines the history of the Justice Building in Montreal.

733. Nantel, Maréchal.

'Pionniers du barreau.' *Revue du barreau de la Province de Québec* 6 (3, 1946): 97–120.

The lawyers, systematically ignored under the French regime, received from the first English governor, James Murray, the authorization to exercise their functions before the courts of the province. The restrictions imposed on French-language lawyers during the first years of the English domination were lifted in July 1766. French-language lawyers were, however, subjected to a strict control by the judges. Lawyers soon realized the need to unite to protect their interest and safeguard their professional prerogatives. They founded 'the

Advocates Community' which is the first association of this kind in the country. Because the constitution and rules have disappeared it is impossible to determine the exact date of the formation of this association. Intermittent minutes of meetings extending over the period 1779 to 1817 make it possible to reconstitute, to some degree, the life of the association. The author uses the various minutes to describe the activities of the association. He divides the period into five distinct phases. The most important extends from May 11, 1779, to June 26, 1786. There are no minutes from the latter date until November 27, 1803. This is followed by another period of silence ending on February 23, 1807. A resumption of activities on October 22, 1811, brings to an end another period of suspected inactivity. A last gap exists from November 30, 1811, to November 4, 1817, the latter the last session date for which minutes exist.

734. Neary, Hilary Bates.

'William Renwick Riddell: A Bio-bibliographical Study.' M.A. thesis, University of Western Ontario, 1977.

William Renwick Riddell was a prominent Ontario lawyer, judge, and amateur historian. His literary output, from the late 1800s to the 1930s, numbered 1258 items, many of which dealt with aspects of Ontario's legal history. This study consists of a 51-page biography of Riddell, followed by a complete bibliography of his published works.

735. Neatby, Hilda.

'The Administration of Justice under the Quebec Act.' Ph.D. dissertation, University of Minnesota, 1934.

736. Neatby, Hilda.

The Administration of Justice under the Quebec Act. Minneapolis: University of Minnesota Press, 1937.

737. Neidhardt, W.S.

'The Fenian Trials in the Province of Canada, 1866–7: A Case Study of Law and Politics in Action.' *Ontario History* 66 (1, March 1974): 23–36.

In June 1886 nearly 2000 members of the Irish Fenian Brotherhood invaded Canada from the United States in the hope of liberating their Irish homeland from British rule. After unsuccessful skirmishes with Canadian militia forces, almost 100 of the invaders were captured and placed on trial for acts of treason and lawless aggression. This study examines the attitudes that were held and the actions that were taken by the various governments and individuals involved in the Fenian trials of 1866–7. The author's findings, which are based mainly on newspaper reports of the political and judicial aspects of the trial, indicate that while the Fenian invasion elicited a remarkable amount of public controversy and anti-Irish hostility in Canada, the trials of the political prisoners 'proved to have been fair and impartial given the circumstances of the time.'

738. Newman, James Forbes.

'Reaction and Change: A Study of the Ontario Bar, 1880 to 1920.' *University of Toronto Faculty of Law Review* 33 (1, 1974): 51–74.

The four decades between 1880 and 1920 were years of profound economic and social change for Canadians. With the emergence of an urban and technological society many of the philosophical foundations on which nineteenth-century Canadians based their lives were severely challenged. This paper assesses the reaction of the Canadian legal profession to these major changes, as expressed through the pages of a major Canadian legal periodical, *The Canadian Law Times*. The author concludes that the writings of contributors to the legal periodical reflect two broad responses to the social and economic changes that swept the western world between 1880 and 1920: a conservative one, which looked favourably upon the values of a less-complex era and remained fearful of the outlines of a technological society; and a more progressive one, which accepted the changes that had occurred in society and was optimistic that the law could adapt to its needs.

739. O'Reilly, Miles.

'Middlesex County Court House.' *The Law Society of Upper Canada Gazette* 5 (4, December 1971): 233–239.

740. O'Reilly, Miles.

'Prince Edward County Court House.' *The Law Society of Upper Canada Gazette* 5 (2, June 1971): 69–72.

741. O'Reilly, Miles.

'Lennox and Addington County Court House.' *The Law Society of Upper Canada Gazette* 6 (2, June 1972): 85–89.

742. O'Reilly, Miles.

'The Oxford County Court House.' *The Law Society of Upper Canada Gazette* 7 (4, December 1973): 240–246.

743. Oxner, Sandra E.

'The Evolution of the Lower Court of Nova Scotia.' *Dalhousie Law Journal* 8 (3, 1984): 59–79; also published in *Law in a Colonial Society: The Nova Scotia Experience*, pp.

59–79. Edited by Peter Waite, Sandra Oxner, and Thomas Barnes. Toronto: Carswell, 1984.

744. Parker, Graham E.

'Some Historical Observations on the Juvenile Court.' *Criminal Law Quarterly* 9 (4, July 1967): 467–502.

During the 1960s, problems facing the juvenile court, and divergent views held of the institution, were exemplified by intensive inquiries in California, England, Scotland, and Canada. This article discusses the different views concerning the juvenile court reflected in the published reports of these inquiries, and provides a historical overview of the development of juvenile court laws. Particular attention is given to examining the historical development of the juvenile court in the United States and South Australia.

745. Parker, Graham E.

'The Evolution of Criminal Responsibility.' *Alberta Law Review* 9 (1971): 47–88.

746. Parker, Graham E.

'The Origins of the Canadian Criminal Code.' In *Essays in the History of Canadian Law*, vol. 1, pp. 249–280. Edited by David H. Flaherty. Toronto: The Osgoode Society and University of Toronto Press, 1981.

Canada's *Criminal Code* became law in 1892. With the exception of the Indian Penal Code, it was the first national 'code' of criminal law to be enacted in the British Empire. This article offers a critical discussion of the origins of the Canadian *Criminal Code*, and the extent to which it represented an original and adequate attempt at 'codification.' Specific attention is given to examining 'the climate of code reform in Canada' from 1850 to 1890, the reform efforts undertaken by leading 'Canadian codifiers,' the subsequent 'Response to the Draft Code' of 1891, the passage of the code through parliament, and the aftermath of enactment. Data sources used include nineteenth-century Canadian legal periodicals, records and correspondence of the federal Department of Justice, and documents relating to the codification of the criminal law in other countries. The author maintains that while 'Canadian codifiers' paid considerable attention to specific details of the code, they failed to consider the aims and purposes of the criminal law and the meaning of 'codification.'

747. Parker, Graham E.

'The Legal Regulation of Sexual Activity and the Protection of Females.' *Osgoode Hall Law Journal* 21 (2, June 1983): 187–244.

The law has not always been content to leave voluntary sexual behaviour free of its control. This is particularly true of the law's attempt to protect unmarried females from sexual activity. This article centres mainly on examining the attention that late–nineteenth-century legislators and social reformers in Britain and Canada gave to regulating the sexual activity of females. Historical background to the efforts of late–nineteenth-century reformers is provided through examining pre–nineteenth-century attitudes towards sexual behaviour, and the circumstances surrounding the enactment and enforcement of early English statutes pertaining to the protection of women and their property. Changing Victorian attitudes towards sexuality and the attempts made to reform laws relating to the age of consent and prostitution, in England and Canada, are then discussed. Attention is given to outlining the impact that British law reform efforts had on influencing late–nineteenth-century Canadian legislative changes, and the provisions relating to the protection of women contained in the 1892 Canadian *Criminal Code*. The author's findings indicate that although prior to 1861 there was almost no legislation that effectively controlled sexual behaviour, the last 40 years of the nineteenth century 'saw a boom in legislation' aimed at protecting females from sexual activity.

748. Patterson, G.C.

'The Establishment of the County Court in Nova Scotia.' *Canadian Bar Review* 21 (5, May 1943): 394–406.

In this article the author, a retired county court judge, examines the origins and development of the county court in Nova Scotia from the early 1700s to around 1880.

749. Pelland, L.

'Aperçu historique de notre organisation judiciaire depuis 1760.' *Revue du droit* 12 (September 1933): 14–33.

The author traces the history of judicial organization in the Province of Quebec since 1760. He discusses the various courts as well as the different laws that created them and determined their jurisdiction. The history of judicial organization is divided arbitrarily into six periods: (1) the military regime (1760–4); (2) the period from 1764 to 1774 – the period that followed the Treaty of Paris (February 10, 1763) and the Royal Proclamation of October 7, 1763, and extends from the time of the *Murray Act* (September 17, 1764) to the *Quebec Act* (June 22, 1774); (3) the period from 1774 to 1793, during which both the civil and the criminal courts were established by the acts of February 25, 1777, and March 7, 1777, respectively; (4) the period from 1793 to 1849 – during which there was abundant legislation pertaining to judicial organization, including the judicature law of 1793; (5) the period from 1849 to 1867 during which the reorganization of 1857 dividing the province into 19 judicial districts took place: (6) the period from 1867 to the date of publication (1933): with Confederation the provinces maintained the right to organize their civil and criminal courts while the federal parliament reserved the right to establish others; the first

Quebec code of civil procedures went into effect on June 28, 1867, defining the jurisdiction of each court. The second code, effective September 1, 1897, introduced some modifications to these jurisdictions.

750. Phelan, Josephine.

'The Tar and Feather Case, Gore Assizes, August 1827.' *Ontario History* 68 (1, March 1976): 17–24.

In June 1826, George Rolph, an English-born lawyer, was dragged from his house, and tarred and feathered by three disguised assailants. The ostensible reason for the assault was retribution for Rolph's living adulterously with a woman who had run away from her husband because of ill treatment. Over a year later, in August 1827, Rolph launched a civil action, seeking payment for damages from the assailants. According to the author, Rolph's case was complicated by the fact that during the same time that his lawyer, W.W. Baldwin, was pressing for a retrial of the civil cases for damages, his brother, John Rolph, also a lawyer, was seeking to have the 'perpetrators of the tar and feather outrage' indicted on a criminal charge of riot and assault. Through relating information concerning the personalities involved in, and circumstances surrounding, the tar and feather case of 1827, the author points to several oddities and anomalies that characterized the administration of justice in early-nineteenth-century Upper Canada.

751. Poultney, H.R.

'The Criminal Courts of the Province of Ontario and Their Process.' *Law Society of Upper Canada Gazette* 9 (1975): 192–237.

752. Power, John Joseph.

'The Criminal Code of Canada.' LL.D thesis, Laval University, 1924.

Written with the aim of suggesting improvements to the unrevised *Criminal Code* of Canada, this thesis offers a detailed examination of the background to and provisions contained in the *Criminal Code* of 1892. By way of background, the author devotes initial chapters to considering the history of codification, and the origin and development of the law of crimes in England and Canada. Attention is then turned to examining the evolution of the 1892 *Criminal Code*, and narrating how it has been understood and interpreted by the courts, the Judicial Committee of the Privy Council, and the House of Lords, and applied to actual concrete cases. The author concludes by pointing to the 'excellencies and defects' of the code, and suggesting improvements that might be made 'in the interests of penal justice.'

753. Proulx, Gilles.

Tribunaux et lois de Louisbourg. Manuscript Report Series, no. 303. Ottawa: Parks Canada, 1975.

754. Prud'homme, L.-A.

'Législation et administration de la justice sous le gouvernement d'Assiniboia.' *Revue canadienne* 25 (1–4, 1889): 70–73, 121–125, 229–236, 369–378.

755. Racine, Denis.

'L'ordonnance du 7 juillet 1766 et les premiers détenteurs de permis de vente d'alcool dans la province de Québec.' *L'ancêtre* 2 (10, June 1976): 479–482.

756. Racine, Denis.

'L'institution des baillis et sous-baillis au début du régime anglais.' *L'ancêtre* 4 (3, November 1977): 65–75.

757. Racine, Denis.

'Baillis et sous-baillis.' *L'ancêtre* 4 (5, January 1978): 167–177; 4 (6, February 1978): 201–205; 4 (7, March 1978): 246–251.

758. Read, D.B.

The Lives of the Judges of Upper Canada and Ontario. Toronto: Rowsell and Hutchison, 1888.

759. Read, F.

'Early History of the Manitoba Courts.' *Manitoba Bar News* 10 (1, 1937): 451–455; 10 (2, 1937): 467–471; 10 (3, 1937): 482–484.

760. Renaud, Louise.

'La cour d'appel à l'aube de l'union (1839–1849).' *Revue juridique thémis* 8 (1973): 465–499.

The origins of the court of appeal in the Province of Quebec are not well known. Using both correspondence and newspaper material the author tries to reconstruct the various steps that led to the court of appeal established in 1849. The first court of appeal can be traced to an act passed in 1777 and complemented, in 1785, by another act stipulating appeal procedures, then modified by the law on the judiciary of 1793. The court is named the Provincial Court of Appeal and is composed of the governor, the lieutenant-governor, the members of the executive council, and the chief justice. Its quorum is five. During the years that followed, the court was subject to several changes, in particular through the act of 1843 and ultimately the act of 1849. The study is divided into three chapters. In the first, the author discusses the initial period, characterized by confusion, until the separation of powers is achieved. In the second, she examines the opinion of the public at large, of parliamentarians, of professionals, as well as the criticism in the written media. The last chapter is a discussion of the repercussions on the judiciary. There are three appendices: the first contains excerpts from the Durham Report and the act of December 9, 1843, 'to establish a better court of appeal in Lower Canada"; the second contains the act of May 30, 1849, 'to establish a court with jurisdiction in appeal and in criminal matters for Lower Canada' the third lists judges who served on the court of appeal up to the nomination of Judge Dorion in 1874. A bibliography is also included.

761. Reynolds, Thomas Michael.

'Justices of the Peace in the North-West Territories 1870–1905.' M.A. thesis, University of Regina, 1978.

The magistracy was the first legal institution created in the Northwest Territories for the administration of justice, and justices of the peace handled most of the court cases there until 1905. This thesis provides a detailed examination of the role played by both appointed civilian justices of the peace and officers of the NWMP who served in a judicial capacity. Using a thematic approach to highlight the issues surrounding the magistracy, the thesis examines the legal structure within which the justices of the peace functioned, the type of men appointed and how they received their commissions, the type of assistance and advice they were provided by the government, and the wide variety of responsibilities with which they were entrusted. The author concludes that the office of the justice of the peace was admirably suited to the conditions that prevailed in the Northwest Territories between 1870 and 1905, and that the operation of the institution demonstrates that the Canadian frontier experience was markedly different from that of the United States. The thesis draws on a range of primary historical materials, including federal government records relating to the administration of justice and policing in the Northwest Territories, and manuscript collections held in the provincial archives of Manitoba and Saskatchewan.

762. Riddell, William Renwick.

The Courts and the People. [Toronto: Wm. Briggs, 1910?].

763. Riddell, William Renwick.

'The Court of King's Bench in Upper Canada, 1824–1827.' *Canadian Law Journal* 49 (3, 1913): 45–55; 49 (4, 1913): 98–103; 49 (5, 1913): 126–134.

764. Riddell, William Renwick.

'"Scandalum Magnatum" in Upper Canada.' *Journal of the American Institute of Criminal Law and Criminology* 4 (1913–14): 12–19.

The author provides statutory background to the law of slander, including reference to the Statute of Westminster, and others, and goes on to indicate that 'proceedings under these earlier statutes when they were in force were by writ of *Scandalum Magnatum*, which was both criminal and civil.' There was apparently only one attempt in Canada to bring the action of *Scandalum Magnatum* into force. Riddell describes the case of *Robert Thorpe* v. *Joseph Ryerson* with extracts from the Term Book of the King's Bench.

765. Riddell, William Renwick.

The Court of King's Bench in Upper Canada, 1824–1827. Gray v. Willcocks; An Old Cause célèbre. [Toronto? 1915?].

766. Riddell, William Renwick.

'The Early Courts of the Province.' *The Canadian Law Times* 35 (11, 1915): 879–890; 35 (12, 1915): 964–985.

767. Riddell, William Renwick.

'Canadian State Trials: The King v. David McLane.' Royal Society of Canada. *Proceedings and Transactions* Series 3, 10, sec. 2 (1916): 321–337.

768. Riddell, William Renwick.

'First English Court in (the Present) Canada on Its Criminal Side.' *Journal of the American Institute of Criminal Law and Criminology* 8 (May 1917): 8–15.

Annapolis Royal, capital of the new Province of Nova Scotia, was the seat of the First English Court of Judicature in the territory which was to become the Dominion of Canada. Created in 1721 the court was to meet annually upon the first Tuesday in May, August, November, and February. There was some overlap of the court with the council which administered the civil affairs of the province. There were continual difficulties with the French (Acadiens) and the Indians. Apparently the first criminal case to come before the court was in September 1723, when Prudane Robichau, Sr., was tried on a charge of supplying the hostile Indians, contrary to the Governor's Proclamation. Riddell goes on to document several cases which came before the court and examples of sentencing practice. It is the conclusion of the author that while this first court 'did not proceed on strictly legal lines, it seems to have done substantial justice, employing a jurisprudence suited to the place and times.'

769. Riddell, William Renwick.

'The First English Criminal Court in Canada.' *Journal of Criminal Law* 8 (1917): 8–15.

770. Riddell, William Renwick.

'A Criminal Circuit in Upper Canada: A Century Ago.' *The Canadian Law Times* 40 (9, 1920): 711–727.

771. Riddell, William Renwick.

'Criminal Law in Upper Canada a Century Ago.' *Journal of the American Institute of Criminal Law and Criminology* 10 (1920): 516–532.

This paper deals with the state of criminal law in Upper Canada as derived primarily from records of the assizes at the time of the War of 1812–14. Larceny, for example, was originally petit (petty) larceny and grand larceny, the latter of which was punishable by death by hanging. This punishment was subsequently modified, by such means as the 'benefit of clergy' privilege. Riddell relates developments in Canadian law to those of Britain. Arson, for example, was an abhorrent crime and was punished by death up until 1841. Riddell also comments on cases of perjury and forgery and instances in which pardons were granted. Offences against the person were quite common, which the author ascribes to habits of intemperance. He briefly discusses assault and battery, rape, bestiality, and murder, noting the legal status of such offences and likely punishments. The gruesome fate of those sentenced to high treason in the early nineteenth century is recounted. The article has many notes and references to primary and secondary sources.

772. Riddell, William Renwick.

'Extra-Territorial Criminal Jurisdiction in British Canada.' *The Canadian Law Times* 40 (6, 1920): 491–502.

773. Riddell, William Renwick.

'How the King's Bench Came to Toronto.' *The Canadian Law Times* 40 (4, 1920): 280–291.

774. Riddell, William Renwick.

'Trial for High Treason in 1838.' Ontario Historical Society. *Papers and Records* 18 (1920): 50–58.

775. Riddell, William Renwick.

'The Information *ex officio* in Upper Canada.' *The Canadian Law Times* 41 (2, 1921): 87–95.

776. Riddell, William Renwick.

'The Ancaster "Bloody Assize" of 1814.' Ontario Historical Society. *Papers and Records* 20 (1923): 107–125.

777. Riddell, William Renwick.

'The Criminal Law in Reference to Marriage in Upper Canada.' Ontario Historical Society. *Papers and Records* 21 (1924): 233–235.

778. Riddell, William Renwick.

'The First British Courts in Canada.' Ontario Historical Society. *Papers and Records* 21 (1924): 227–231.

779. Riddell, William Renwick.

'Criminal Courts and Law in Early [Upper] Canada.' Ontario Historical Society. *Papers and Records* 17 (1925): 210–221.

In 1788, four districts were formed out of the western portion of the Province of Quebec, which later became Upper Canada. In each district, criminal courts modelled on the English legal system were established. This article relates information concerning the establishment of various courts having jurisdiction over criminal cases in Upper Canada and the administration of criminal justice in the early years of the province. The nature of early criminal proceedings and changes in the law brought about because of the absence of adequate jail facilities to hold prisoners are also discussed. Specific attention is given to noting the various judicial and administrative duties of the court of quarter sessions in each district, and the types of punishments meted out for particular criminal offences prior to 1841.

780. Riddell, William Renwick.

'When a Few Claimed Monopoly of Spiritual Functions – Canadian State Trials – The King against Clark Burton.' Ontario Historical Society. *Papers and Records* 22 (1925): 202–209.

781. Riddell, William Renwick.

The Bar and the Courts of the Province of Upper Canada or Ontario. Toronto: Macmillan, 1928.

782. Riddell, William Renwick.

'A Day in Court in Old Niagara.' Royal Society of Canada. *Proceedings and Transactions* Series 3, 22, sec. 2 (1928): 125–130.

783. Riddell, William Renwick.

'A Philadelphia Lawyer and Early Lower Canada Law.' *Canadian Historical Review* 9 (1, 1928): 38–45.

In 1810, Philadelphia lawyer William Rawle visited Lower Canada and wrote an account of what he saw of interest in the province. Relying on the hand-written account left by Rawle, the author relates Rawle's observations concerning the laws, lawyers, and constitution of Lower Canada. The article contains lengthy extracts from Rawle's notebook, interspersed with supplementary information.

784. Riddell, William Renwick.

'Administration of Criminal Law in the Far North of Canada.' *Journal of Criminal Law and Criminology* 20 (August 1929): 294–302.

Drawing on official reports obtained from the commissioner of the RCMP, the author describes the circumstances surrounding four criminal trials that took place in the Northwest Territories between 1915 and 1925. Attention is given to noting the manner in which the Mounted Police carried out criminal investigations in the far north, and the formal and dignified manner in which the criminal trials were conducted.

785. Riddell, William Renwick.

The Jury System in Ontario. New York, 1930.

786. Riddell, William Renwick.

'Bygone Phases of Canadian Criminal Law.' *Journal of Criminal Law, Criminology, and Police Science* 23 (1, 1932): 51–66.

Riddell's article is actually composed of six smaller and somewhat unrelated 'vignettes' under the broad subject of early Canadian criminal law. Some of these parts address the matter of punishment. Riddell comments on burning at the stake in Canada, a form of execution abolished in 1730 in England and officially in Canada by the Royal Proclamation of October 7, 1763, following the cession of Canada by the Treaty of Paris in February 1762. Prior to the abolition there was one known execution by burning at the stake upon the order of the governor, which is described by Riddell. The second part or 'vignette' considers suicide and its social and legal consequences in old French Canada. In the third part Riddell uses *The Code of 1650 of Connecticut* and *La Ville de Québec sous le Régime Français* to compare punishment for crime in a typical English colony in America (Connecticut) and Canada. The fourth section covers come of the punishments under the law of old French Canada. Riddell notes that 'in 1664 the Sovereign Council at Quebec had made an agreement with some of the Indian Chiefs, whereby the Indians were to be subject to the same criminal laws as the Whites,' and provides some background on 'Indian justice' and events leading up to that decision. The fifth 'vignette' concerns one case which Riddell prosecuted, and the sixth is a brief comment on night clubs in Montreal in 1678, anecdotal in character and based upon another article on the same topic by an unnamed author. Riddell's work is without footnotes, but is based upon named sources and contributions from Pierre-Georges Roy, Archivist of the Province of Quebec.

787. Riddell, William Renwick.

'Notes on the Pre-Revolutionary Judiciary in the English Colonies.' *Canadian Bar Review* 11 (5, May 1933): 317–324; 11 (6, June 1933): 376–384.

In this two-part article, Riddell relates information concerning the pre-revolutionary judiciary in English colonies that he gained from reading the six volumes of *Acts of the Privy Council of England: Colonial Series*, published by His Majesty's Stationery Office, London. Drawing on this source, the author describes incidents involving the pre-revolutionary judiciary in Africa, Jamaica, Barbados, North and South Carolina, New York, New Hampshire, Georgia, Nova Scotia, and Quebec, during the seventeenth and eighteenth centuries.

788. Riddell, William Renwick.

'The Administration of Criminal Law in Canada.' *Journal of the American Judicature Society* 17 (2, 1933–4): 141–144.

789. Riddell, William Renwick.

'Progress of Law in the Province of Ontario or Upper Canada during the Past Century.' In *Law: A Century of Progress, 1835–1935*, pp. 27–38. Edited by New York University Law School. New York: New York University Press, 1937.

790. Riddell, William Renwick.

'The First Legal Execution for Crime in Upper Canada.' Ontario Historical Society. *Papers and Records* 27 (1931): 514–516.

In September 1792, a Negro slave named Josiah Cutten was brought before the Court of Oyer and Terminer and General Gaol Delivery in the District of Hesse to stand trial for committing a burglary. He was subsequently found guilty and sentenced to death by hanging. This article outlines the circumstances surrounding the slave's trial, and points to the fact that his was the first legal execution for crime in Upper Canada. The author notes that a full account of the trial appears in the Records of the Court, held in the Archives of Ontario.

791. Riddell, William Renwick.

'The Story of an Old Statute.' Ontario Historical Society. *Papers and Records* 27 (1931): 517–519.

In 1800, the Provincial Parliament of Upper Canada passed an act expressly declaring that the criminal law of England, as it stood in 1792, was the law of the province. This declaration meant that the traditional distinction made between the Court of King's Bench, which was charged with jurisdiction over offences against the king, and the Court of Oyer and Terminer and Goal Delivery, which was assigned to do the work of the Court of King's Bench when it was engaged upon matters of greater importance, would be maintained in practice. The author relates the fact that until 1817, when an enabling statute was enacted, the proceedings of the Court of Oyer and Terminer and Gaol Delivery were not allowed to continue once the Court of King's Bench began to hear criminal cases in the same district. The author concludes that the story of this statute provides an interesting illustration of the effect of legal tradition, and the closeness with which Upper Canadians followed the principles of English law.

792. Riddell, William Renwick, ed.

'Records of the Early Courts of Justice in Upper Canada.' In *Fourteenth Report of the Bureau of Archives for the Province of Ontario*, pp. 190–353. Toronto, 1918. Also published under same title in Ontario *Sessional Papers*, no. 51, 1918.

In 1910, previously forgotten records of the early courts of justice in Upper Canada were found in a vault at Osgoode Hall. As part of an effort to bring these records to the attention of interested scholars, the Ontario Bureau of Archives undertook the task of having them published. This volume consists of the Records of the Court of Common Pleas for the District of Hesse dating from 1789, along with a lengthy introduction by Riddell. In his introduction, Riddell discusses events leading to the establishment of early criminal and civil courts in Upper Canada, and the manner in which justice was administered in the early years of the province.

793. Ridge, Alan D.

'C.C. McCaul, Pioneer Lawyer.' *Alberta Historical Review* 21 (1, Winter 1973): 21–25.

In 1883, Charles McCaul, an Ontario lawyer, left for the Northwest Territories. This article traces McCaul's subsequent career as a practising lawyer at various locations in Alberta, the Yukon, and Vancouver. The author mentions McCaul's role as crown prosecutor in the much publicized murder trials of two Eskimos in Edmonton in 1917, and the fact that he was the first lawyer to carry a criminal appeal to the Appellate Division of the Supreme Court of Alberta.

794. Risk, R.C.B.

'Lawyers, Courts, and the Rise of the Regulatory State.' *Dalhousie Law Journal* 9 (1 November 1984): 31–54.

795. Roe, Frank Gilbert.

'A Day in Court.' *Alberta Historical Review* 20 (3, Summer 1972): 1–5.

In this article, the author, a British subject and early settler in Alberta, relates his personal experience of being charged and made to stand trial for setting a prairie fire in 1898. After describing the magistrate's court and character of the presiding judge, the author recalls the outcome of his trial and that of an American-born defendant charged with the same offence. He concludes by noting that while he was dealt with in a lenient manner, being bound over to keep the peace for six months, the American was made to pay a 25-dollar fine, considered then to be a large sum of money.

796. Romney, Paul.

'The Ordeal of William Higgins.' *Ontario History* 67 (2, June 1975): 69–89. Also published in *The Law Society of Upper Canada Gazette* 9 (4, December 1975): 265–290.

Toronto's political life in 1834 was characterized by the incessant factional strife of Tories and Reformers. This political turbulence brought the service of William Higgins, the city's first high bailiff, whose responsibilities included the supervision of the city's police force, to an abrupt and dramatic end. According to the author's account, in October 1834, Higgins was arrested on a charge of murder, stemming from the allegation that either he or one of the peace officers under his supervision stabbed and killed a Toronto citizen with a sword while engaging in a confrontation with the supporters of a Reform party political candidate. Drawing on newspaper reports containing verbatim transcripts of the subsequent coroner's inquest, an investigation into the alleged police brutality, and Higgin's murder trial, the author documents the conflicting accounts of the incident provided by various witnesses. Higgins was exonerated after the grand jury of the District Assizes found that certain witnesses had perjured themselves while testifying against the accused. The author concludes by speculating on the possible political motives underlying the decision taken by the mayor of Toronto, William Lyon Mackenzie, to have Higgins stand trial for murder.

797. Roy, Joseph-Edmond.

'Notes sur le greffe et les greffiers de Québec (1608–1648).' *Canada français* 3 (1890): 707–722.

798. Roy, Joseph-Edmond.

'L'ancien barreau au Canada.' *La revue légale – nouvelle série* 3 (1897): 231–302.

799. Roy, Pierre-Georges.

Un procès criminel au dix-septième siècle: Anne Edmond accusée de s'être travestie en homme et d'avoir répandu de fausses nouvelles. Levis: 1904.

800. Roy, Pierre-Georges.

'La prévôté de Québec.' La Société Royale du Canada. *Mémoires et comptes rendus* Series 3, 10, sec. 1 (1916): 119–128.

The Company of the West Indies, in conformity with the act that created it in 1664, established a provost court in Quebec in May 1666. The court consisted of a lieutenant-general, a prosecutor, and a clerk. The first received a yearly salary of £500, the second a salary of £300, while the clerk received a salary of £100. The court was reorganized in 1677 and continued to operate until the conquest. The author provides a list of, and some biographical notes on, the lieutenants-general, the prosecutors, and the clerks from 1666 to 1759.

801. Roy, Pierre-Georges.

'La maréchaussée de Québec sous le régime français.' La Société Royale du Canada. *Mémoires et comptes rendus* Series 3, 12, sec. 1 (1918): 189–192.

By an act signed on May 9, 1677, Louis XIV established an office of a provost of the Court of Marshalsea (Prévoté de la Maréchaussée) in New France. The attributes and functions of the provost, as mentioned in the act, are quoted. In addition, the author provides the names and periods of service of the various provosts and the clerks who assisted them.

802. Roy, Pierre-Georges.

'Les attributions des juges seigneuriaux sous l'ancien régime.' *Bulletin des recherches historiques* 32 (10, October 1926): 634–636.

This is a brief account of the attributes of the judges of seigneurial courts under the Old Regime and of the procedures followed before these courts. It was very simple to plead before these courts; the sentences were pronounced during the session and the costs paid on the spot. The collected fines were divided: half went to the hospitals and the other half to the poor of the parish.

803. Roy, Pierre-Georges.

Inventaire des jugements et délibérations du conseil supérieur de la Nouvelle France, de 1717 à 1760. 3 vols. Beauceville: L'éclaireur limitée, 1932, 1933.

804. Roy, Pierre-Georges.

Les juges de la province de Québec. Québec: Rédempti Paradis, 1933.

In this book the author presents a one-page account of all the judges of the Province of Quebec during the period of the English domination, 1760–1933. A brief historical account of the judicial organization of the Province of Quebec under the English regime is included. No bibliography or footnotes are provided.

805. Roy, Pierre-Georges.

'La punition des crimes autrefois.' *Bulletin des recherches historiques* 45 (1, January 1939): 50–51.

806. Russell, Peter.

The Supreme Court of Canada as a Bilingual and Bicultural Institution. Ottawa: Queen's Printer, 1969.

Although this book is concerned primarily with examining the manner in which the Supreme Court of Canada functions as a bilingual and bicultural institution in contemporary Canadian society, an initial chapter is devoted to providing a historical account of the Supreme Court from its inception, in 1875, to its emergence as Canada's ultimate court of appeal, in 1949. The book also contains assorted data of historical interest in other chapters, including information relating to the composition of the court (1875–1965), the nature of the court's work (1949–64), and trends in the outcome of the court's decisions in selected areas (i.e., civil liberties cases [1950–64], civil code cases [1950–64], and constitutional cases [1950–64]).

807. Schuh, Cornelia.

'Justice on the Northern Frontier: Early Murder Trials of Native Accused.' *Criminal Law Quarterly* 22 (1, December 1979): 74–111.

This article deals with a series of murder investigations and trials involving native accused, dating from the late 1890s to the early 1920s. The author argues that the enforcement of the Canadian criminal law against members of native communities who know nothing of that law posed great theoretical and practical problems. He maintains that the examination of murder cases involving natives tells us a great deal about the nature of white northern administration in general, and, in particular, the interplay between agencies like Indian Affairs, the Department of Justice, and the ever-present Mounted Police. The article is based mainly on federal government documents and reports concerning natives and the administration of justice, reported murder cases, and secondary literature relating to the opening of the Canadian North.

808. Scott, Seaman Morley.

'The Authorship of Certain Papers in the *Lower Canadian Jurist*.' *Canadian Historical Review* 10 (1929): 335–342.

809. Scott, Seaman Morley.

'Chapters in the History of the Law of Quebec, 1764–1775.' Ph.D. dissertation, University of Michigan, 1933.

810. Scott, W.L.

The Juvenile Court in Law. 4th edition. Ottawa: Canadian Welfare Council, 1952.

811. Séguin, Robert-Lionel.

'Une montréalaise devant le tribunal Bailliager.' *Cahiers des dix* 32 (1967): 109–124.

812. Shortt, Adam.

Early Records of Ontario. Being Extracts from the Records of the Court of Quarter Sessions for the District of Mecklenburg (Afterwards the Midland District) with Introduction and Notes. Kingston: Printed at the Daily News Office, 1900.

In 1789, a court of quarter sessions was established in the District of Mecklenburg, in the Province of Quebec. After the passing of the Constitutional Act of 1791, which divided the Province of Quebec into Upper and Lower Canada, the names of the districts were changed (the District of Mecklenburg becoming the Midland District) and the court of quarter sessions was required to be held at Adolphus Town on the second Tuesday of January and July, and at Kingston on the second Tuesday of April and October. This volume contains previously unpublished extracts from the records of this court, covering the period 1789 to 1818, along with an introductory essay in which the author notes events and circumstances leading to the establishment of courts of quarter sessions in early Ontario. The extracts, supplemented with explanatory notes, reveal the broad role played by the court of quarter sessions in municipal government, the settling of civil disputes, and the administration of criminal justice.

813. Sinclair, A.

'L'avocat au Québec: 209 ans d'histoire.' *Les cahiers de droit* 16 (1975): 689–702.

The year 1974 marked the 125th anniversary of the Quebec Bar as well as the 109th anniversary of the appearance of professional lawyers in Quebec. The author traces the history of the profession in the Province of Quebec. There were no professional lawyers under the French regime mainly because the authorities wanted to prevent judicial litigation and to avoid delays in the administration of justice. Notaries, clerks, and other court aids helped the parties prepare their complaints or defence. Lawyers emerged only after the British Conquest. Although the first lawyers were nominated in 1765 they were not allowed to appear before the criminal courts. This right was granted only in 1835 and only for serious offences punishable by death. The right of the accused to have a lawyer represent him in criminal cases was not recognized until 1841. In 1779 there were only 30 lawyers in the province, 10 of them in the city of Quebec. Lawyers were nominated by the governor, who proceeded by commissions, a method that led to favouritism. In 1785 a professional code was adopted and in 1849 the Quebec Bar was established. The article provides historical information on the structure and functions of the Bar, on the professional training of lawyers, admission to the Bar, the exercise of the profession, and the status of the lawyers.

814. Smith, William.

'The Struggle over the Laws of Canada, 1763–1783.' *Canadian Historical Review* 1 (June 1920): 166–186.

The most difficult problem which the acquisition of Canada presented to the government of Great Britain was to settle upon a system of municipal law for the country which would be satisfactory to the people as a whole. This article relates details concerning the struggle that raged over the form of legal system to be established in Canada in the 1770s. Particular attention is given to describing the manner in which British government instructions concerning the laws to be adopted in the country were carried out by Governor Carleton, and the discontent aroused among the British-born portion of the population when he ordered that French laws would be resorted to 'in all controversies relating to property and civil rights between His Majesty's subjects, whether Canadian or English.' Carleton's controversial tenure as governor of the colony, and the possible reasons underlying his unwillingness to adopt 'any part of the English law, beyond the English criminal law,' are also examined. (See also entry 817 below.)

815. Smout, David A.L.

'Chief Justice Osgoode.' *The Law Society of Upper Canada Gazette* 6 (4, December 1972): 11–17.

816. Snell, James G.

'Relations between the Maritimes and the Supreme Court of Canada: The Patterns of the Early Years.' *Dalhousie Law Journal* 8 (3, 1984): 143–163. Also published in *Law in a Colonial Society: The Nova Scotia Experience*, pp. 143–163. Edited by Peter Waite, Sandra Oxner, and Thomas Barnes. Toronto: Carswell, 1984.

817. Soward, F.H.

'The Struggle over the Laws of Canada, 1783–1791.' *Canadian Historical Review* 5 (4, December 1924): 314–335.

This article is intended to supplement W. Smith's article (see entry 814 above) on 'The Struggle over the Laws of Canada, 1763–1783' published in the June 1920 issue of the

Canadian Historical Review. The author argues that with the coming of the Loyalists to Quebec and the appointment of a new governor in the 1780s, political controversy again began to rage over the form of legal system to be adopted. Particular attention is given to outlining the manner in which demands put forth by the English and Loyalist portion of the population, calling for the division of the province and the introduction of English laws, were dealt with by British- and colonial-government officials. According to the author, from 1789 until the passing of the *Constitutional Act* in 1791 'the key to Canadian politics' was in London, where British politicians debated, and finally agreed upon, a plan to divide the Province of Quebec into Upper Canada and Lower Canada. This division gave French Canadians a constitution formed on the principles of French law, and the English and Loyalist settlers a constitution based on the laws of England.

818. Stanley, Della Margaret Maude.

'Pierre-Armand Landry the Judge.' *La société historique acadienne – les cahiers* 6 (2, June 1975): 82–100.

819. Stevenson, Alex.

'The Robert Janes Murder Trial at Pond Inlet.' *The Beaver* 304 (2, Autumn 1973): 16–23.

In 1923, a group of Eskimo men from Pond Inlet on Baffin Island were placed on trial for the murder of a fur trader, Robert Janes. The author, a long-time employee of the Hudson's Bay Company at Pond Inlet, discusses the circumstances surrounding the trial as told to him by Eskimos and fur traders who were living in the settlement at the time. He notes that it was during the course of the Janes trial that 'the laws of southern society' were first introduced into this remote area.

820. Stewart, V. Lorne.

'The History of the Juvenile and Family Court of Toronto.' Toronto, 1971. (Typescript)

This unpublished paper by a former judge of the Juvenile and Family Court covers attempts to deal with destitute, neglected, and delinquent children from the nineteenth century up until about 1970. Covered are the background to the *Juvenile Delinquents Act*, the Toronto Juvenile Court, the Toronto Juvenile and Family Courts, and the Provincial Court (Family Division). The author discusses the philosophy behind the law and the function of the courts, distilling it to major lines of 'civil rights vs. best interest,' and trying to reconcile the concept of social agency and court of law for the Juvenile and Family Court.

821. Stubbs, Roy St. George.

Lawyers and Laymen of Western Canada. Toronto: Ryerson Press, 1939.

822. Stubbs, Roy St. George.

Four Recorders of Rupert's Land. Winnipeg: Peguis Publishers, 1967.

823. Stubbs, Roy St. George.

'Law and Authority in Red River.' *The Beaver* 298 (Summer 1968): 17–21.

Stubbs's self-declared purpose in this article is 'to hold up the mirror of the law to give a brief reflection of life in Red River at the middle of the last century.' To this end, he offers four contemporary accounts of a trial which took place in Red River in February 1850. The parties involved included a local Metis builder, Hugh Matheson, and Adam Thom, the first recorder of Rupert's Land, who was appointed in 1839 to preside over the General Quarterly Court. Thom was not well received by the local population because of his animosity and bigotry towards French Canadians and Metis. In 1850 Thom did not hold his seat at the bench while local hostility against him, resulting from his prosecution of a Metis fur trader, subsided. However, during this time Thom was taken to court for failing to pay a builder for work done on his house. Thom presented his own weak case, using endless law books and intimidation as his defence. The four accounts of the trial differ depending on the bias of the author, and reflect the administration of justice at the time. Primary sources are quoted, but not all are fully cited.

824. Stubbs, Roy St. George.

'The First Juvenile Court Judge: Hon. T. Mayne Daly, K.C.' *Manitoba Law Journal* 10 (1, 1979): 1–21.

In 1909, Mayne Daly, a police magistrate in Winnipeg, was appointed the first juvenile court judge in Canada. Drawing on Daly's personal letters, official correspondence, and relevant secondary literature, Stubbs examines Daly's life and career as a lawyer, politician, police magistrate, and juvenile court judge. Particular attention is given to noting the enthusiastic manner in which Daly accepted the philosophy on which the juvenile court was founded, and attempted to carry out his duties in 'the best interests' of children.

825. Stubbs, Roy St. George.

The Bench and the Bar of Quebec. n.p.: Dominion Pub. Co., 1931.

826. Szabo, Denis.

'Evolution et état présent du système judiciaire pénitentiaire et policier du Canada.' *Revue de droit pénal et de criminologie* 43 (November 1962): 135–150.

This article is aimed at informing a foreign audience about the evolution of the present state of judicial, penal, and police systems in Canada. In his introduction the author gives a brief summary of the history of Canada. He then goes on to describe the Canadian criminal law as being conservative and as evolving quite slowly. The sentences handed down by Canadian courts are seen as very severe. The author describes the Canadian penal system, the parole system, and the assistance provided to parolees by after-care organizations such as the John Howard Society. The three levels of police forces in Canada (federal, provincial, and municipal) are described along with the concern about juvenile delinquency, the training of personnel for work in penal institutions, and the societies of criminology in Canada. The author concludes that in spite of its slow evolution, the Canadian penal system has progressed. In order to continue in the same direction, he calls for an increase in qualified personnel in rehabilitative methods. Some quantitative data on criminality in Canada are included.

827. Szabo, Denis.

The Evolution and Organization of the Judicial, Police and Corrective Systems in Canada. International Centre of Comparative Criminology, University of Montreal, 1974-5.

This is an updated English-language version of the author's 1962 French-language article (see entry 826 above).

828. Talbot, Charles K.

Justice in Early Ontario, 1791–1840: A Study of Crime, Courts and Prisons in Upper Canada with a description of 1,300 original unpublished letters located at the Public Archives of Canada (Upper Canada Sundries) and pertaining to the Criminal Justice System of Upper Canada. Ottawa: Crimcare, 1983.

Intended as a preliminary study of the history of criminal justice in Ontario, this document provides a descriptive overview of developments in criminal justice in early Upper Canada, and makes reference to numerous primary historical sources of potential interest to criminal justice historians. The document is divided into three main parts. In part I, 'The Judicial System of Upper Canada,' separate sections describe the character of Upper Canadian society (i.e., population, economic and social development, social problems), the criminal law, the law courts, the judiciary, the Bar and legal officials, and criminal trial procedures. Part II, 'Crime in Upper Canada,' draws on available court and jail records to discuss the extent to which crime was a social problem in the province, and the specific categories of offences of which offenders were convicted: crimes against the state, crimes against the person, and crimes against property. In part III, 'The District Jails and Provincial Penitentiary of Upper Canada, 1791–1840,' the author traces the establishment of district jails across the province, discusses the construction and management of Kingston Penitentiary, and surveys the conditions that existed within the various provincial penal institutions. In each part, the descriptive chronology of historical developments is followed with a reference collection of original letters and documents located in the Public Archives of Canada and pertaining to the criminal justice system of Upper Canada.

829. Thomas, L.H.

'A Judicial Murder – The Trial of Louis Riel.' In *The Settlement of the West*, pp. 37–59. Edited by Howard Palmer. Calgary: University of Calgary Comprint Pub. Co., 1977.

830. Thomson, Jean R.

'An Evaluation of Judicial Fees in Cases Brought before the Sovereign Council, 1663–1690.' *Revue du centre d'études du Québec* 3 (May 1969): 9–18.

831. Thorner, Thomas, and Watson, Neil B.

'Keeper of the King's Peace: Colonel G.E. Sanders and the Calgary Police Magistrate's Court, 1911–1932.' *Urban History Review/Revue d'histoire urbaine* 12 (3, February 1984): 45–55.

Canadian historians have shown limited interest in the legal development of the lower courts. In an attempt to compensate for this lack of historical knowledge, the authors focus on examining the history of Calgary's police court. They maintain that the history of the Calgary police court and in particular the administration of its presiding magistrate, G.E. Sanders, reveal much about the development of the office and urban society, since many of the issues of popular concern in Calgary came into focus through legal action. Drawing on primary historical sources, including Calgary City Police Department Annual Reports and Justice of the Peace Files, the authors present evidence indicating that as fear about crime grew with the steady influx of immigrants to Alberta, the Calgary police court assumed special significance.

832. Townsend, Charles J.

'History of the Courts of Judicature in Nova Scotia.' *Canadian Law Times* 19 (1899): 23–37, 58–72, 87–98, 142–157.

833. Tremblay, Paul.

'Le magistrat Ménalque Tremblay (1838–1911).' *Saguenayensia* 8 (2, March–April 1966): 26–31.

The author draws a profile of Judge Ménalque Tremblay who sat on the bench in the districts of Bonaventure and Gaspé from 1884.

834. Trudel, Gérard.

'Le pouvoir judiciaire au Canada.' *La revue du barreau de la Québec* 28 (4, April 1968): 193–267.

This is a study of judicial power in Canada: its organization, contents, forms, and performance. This power used to be distinct, but is becoming less and less structured, less identifiable, and less recognizable in contemporary society. The author examines the present condition of the Canadian judicial system and what can be done to improve it. In order to identify the power of the judiciary and to place it within the various institutions of the state it is necessary to refer to the political and judicial history of Canada. The author discusses various important cases, the decisions rendered, and the principles established by these decisions. This is followed by a comparative review of the judicial system in other countries, namely Mexico, Federal Republic of Germany, United States, Argentina, and Australia. The author then discusses the three powers within the state – legislative, executive, and judicial – and the separation between these powers. Other topics discussed include the independence of judges, salary suspension, retirement, and recall. The orientation and priorities of the judicial system are also discussed.

835. Tubrett, Earle Oliver.

'The Development of the New Brunswick Court System, 1784–1803.' M.A. thesis, University of New Brunswick, 1967.

This thesis examines the birth and subsequent development of New Brunswick courts during the first 20 years of their existence. Although the bulk of the thesis is concerned with highlighting the role played by civil courts in the early history of the province, initial chapters focus generally on describing the development and jurisdiction of all of New Brunswick's provincial courts, and changes made to the province's judicial structure in the period 1784–1803. The thesis draws on a wide range of primary sources, including court records, government documents, personal papers and correspondence, and newspapers published in the province.

836. Turner, R.E.

'The Life and Death of Louis Riel: III: Medico-Legal Issues.' *Canadian Psychiatric Association Journal* 10 (4, 1965): 259–264.

Written as one of a series of three articles on the psychiatric aspects of Riel's 1885 treason trial (see entries 615 and 697 above), this paper deals with some of the basic medico-legal issues arising from the trial. Specific issues addressed include the question of Riel's fitness to stand trial, the use of the defence of insanity and the application of the McNaghten Rules, and the appointment of a medical commission to inquire into Riel's mental state after he was sentenced to hang. The manner in which these issues were dealt with at the time of Riel's trial and execution is contrasted with more recent developments in forensic psychiatry.

837. Verdun-Jones, Simon N.

'The Evolution of the Defences of Insanity and Automatism in Canada from 1843 to 1979: A Saga of Judicial Reluctance to Sever the Umbilical Cord to the Mother Country?' *University of British Columbia Law Review* 14 (1, 1979): 1–73.

838. Verdun-Jones, Simon N.

'"Not Guilty by Reason of Insanity": The Historical Roots of the Canadian Insanity Defence, 1843–1920.' In *Crime and Criminal Justice in Europe and Canada*, pp. 179–218. Edited by Louis A. Knafla. Waterloo, Ont.: Wilfrid Laurier University Press, 1981.

This article examines the manner in which the defence of insanity was interpreted and applied in criminal cases in Canada during the nineteenth and early twentieth centuries. The author first outlines the circumstances surrounding the famous English case of Daniel McNaghten and the original formulation of the famous McNaghten Rules. He then examines the manner in which these common law rules were followed in Canada during the years preceding the codification of the Canadian *Criminal Code* in 1892, paying particular attention to their interpretation and application in the 1885 treason trial of Louis Riel. A third section traces the parliamentary debate leading up to the enactment of the 1892 code and the specific provisions it contained concerning the defence of insanity. The provisions are then compared to the original McNaghten Rules. Finally, the author examines the manner in which the 1892 *Criminal Code* provisions were interpreted in specific cases from 1892 to 1920. His general conclusion is that throughout the period of his study the insanity defence was interpreted in a restrictive manner, with the Canadian judiciary tending to follow the English decisions interpreting the McNaghten Rules.

839. Waite, Peter.

'An Attorney General of Nova Scotia, J.S.D. Thompson, 1878–1882: Disparate Aspects of Law and Society in Provincial Canada.' *Dalhousie Law Journal* 8 (3, 1984): 165–183. Also published in *Law in a Colonial Society: The Nova Scotia Experience*, pp. 165–183. Edited by Peter Waite, Sandra Oxner, and Thomas Barnes. Toronto: Carswell, 1984.

840. Waite, Peter; Oxner, Sandra; and Barnes, Thomas, eds.

Law in a Colonial Society: The Nova Scotia Experience. Toronto: Carswell, 1984. (Dalhousie/Berkeley Lectures on Legal History, February 25–26 and March 11–12, 1983)

This is a collection of essays presented at the Dalhousie/Berkeley Lectures on Legal History. They cover such topics as crime at sea, the evolution of the lower courts in Nova Scotia, the role of the attorney general in Nova Scotia, the influence of Nova Scotia on the

Supreme Court of Canada, and 'jailbirds' in Victorian Halifax. These articles were published in the *Dalhousie Law Journal* 8 (3, 1984).

841. Wallace, W.B.

'Progress in Criminal Legislation in Canada.' *Canada Law Journal* 38 (1902): 701–713.

842. Wallot, Jean-Pierre.

'Plaintes contre l'administration de la justice (1807).' *Revue d'histoire de l'Amérique française* 19 (4, March 1966): 551–560; 20 (1, June 1966): 28–43; 20 (2, September 1966): 281–290; 20 (3, December 1966): 366–379.

In Lower Canada, early in the nineteenth century, English and French Canadians agreed on at least one point: the administration of justice in the colony was inadequate. The former wanted to abolish all French laws, which they viewed as incomprehensible, complicated, retrograde, and contrary to the interests of commerce. French Canadians, in contrast, complained bitterly about countless delays in the courts, delays frequently attributed to the rapacity of lawyers without scruples. The author analyses the complaints against the administration of justice and to illustrate the views of the epoch he reproduces in this four-part study several articles and letters to the editor published in 1807 in the newspaper *Le Canadien*.

843. Walton, F.P.

'The Civil Code and the Judicial System.' In *Canada and Its Provinces: The History of the Canadian People and Their Institutions*, 23 vols. Vol. 15: *The Province of Quebec*, pp. 253–284. Edited by Adam Shortt and Arthur G. Doughty. Toronto: Glasgow, Brook and Company, 1914.

844. Ward, William Peter.

'The Administration of Justice in the North-West Territories, 1870–1887.' M.A. thesis, University of Alberta, 1966.

This thesis discusses the development of the judicial system in the Northwest Territories from its rude beginnings in 1870 until it reached its mature form in 1887. Prior to 1870, judicial institutions in the Northwest Territories consisted of the modest provisions for the administration of justice made by the Hudson's Bay Company. With the coming of the NWMP in 1874 and the appointment of stipendiary magistrates in 1876, however, an effective judicial system began to take shape. Relying mainly on primary sources, including sessional papers, statutes, territorial ordinances, parliamentary debates, and official correspondence, the author documents the growth of the judicial system and the problems encountered in the administration of justice during the 1870s and 1880s. He maintains that with the establishment of the Supreme Court of the Northwest Territories in 1887, the judicial system reached maturity.

845. Warren, Dorothy, and Surveyer, Edouard Fabré.

From Surgeon's Mate to Chief Justice: Adam Mabane, 1734–1792. Ottawa: Royal Society of Canada, 1930.

846. Weeks, Nancy C.

'Colonel James Morreau and "The Shorthills Affair".' Unpublished paper, Osgoode Hall Law School, York University, n.d.

In June 1838, a group of some 60 or 70 'dissaffected' Upper Canadians and American supporters encamped themselves in the Short Hills, located in the Niagara region, and took up arms against the established government. In response to this attempt at instigating a civil war, government authorities took action to quell the uprising. James Morreau, an American, was one of the reputed leaders of the 'armed rebels.' After being captured along with the other rebels, Morreau was indicted on a charge of 'felonious hostility,' tried before a Niagara court, and hanged. Drawing on official correspondence, trial records, and newspaper coverage relating to 'the Shorthills Affair,' the author of this paper examines Morreau's role in the 1838 uprising, and presents details concerning his trial and its outcome.

847. Williams, D.C.

'The Dawn of Law on the Prairies.' *Saskatchewan Bar Review* 27 (4, December 1962): 126–133; 28 (1, March 1963): 17–26; 28 (2, June 1963): 63–69.

848. Williams, D.C.

'Law and Institutions in the Northwest Territories 1869–1905.' *Saskatchewan Bar Review* 28 (3, September 1963): 109–118; 29 (2, June 1964): 51–60; 29 (3, September 1964): 83–101; 30 (2, June 1965): 51–66; 31 (1, 1966): 1–26; 31 (3, 1966): 137–161; and *Saskatchewan Law Review* 33 (2 June, 1968): 145–157.

849. Williams, David R.

'The Man for a New Country': Sir Matthew Baillie Begbie. Sidney, B.C.: Gray's Publishing, 1977.

850. Wilson, Lawrence Charles.

'Juvenile Justice in Canada: The End of the Experiment.' LL.M. thesis, University of Manitoba, 1976.

For over 60 years, judges, lawyers, and social workers have wrestled with a great experiment, the union of criminal justice and social welfare philosophy. This thesis examines the origins of this experiment and its effects on the juvenile justice system in Canada. Major substantive chapters deal with the philosophy of juvenile justice, the failure of *parens patriae*, juvenile justice and 'equality before the law,' police discretion and confessions by juveniles, judges, and lawyers in the juvenile court, the jurisdiction of the juvenile court, the trial and sentencing of juvenile delinquents, and appeals from decisions of the juvenile court. Reported legal cases involving juveniles and published government reports serve as the major sources of legal and historical data. The author concludes with a discussion of reform proposals aimed at replacing the then existing *Juvenile Delinquents Act*.

851. Winslow, J.J.F.

'The First Slander Trial in New Brunswick.' *Atlantic Advocate* 49 (3, 1958): 57–62.

852. Wodson, Harry M.

The Whirlpool: Scenes from Toronto Police Court. Toronto: n.p., 1917.

853. Wolfson, Lorne Howard.

'Juvenile Delinquents, Young Offenders and Young Persons in Conflict with the Law: A Study of Juvenile Delinquency Law Reform in Canada.' LL.M. thesis, University of British Columbia, 1976.

The purpose of this thesis is to explore both proposals for the reform of the *Juvenile Delinquents Act* and the legislation they were intended to replace. The thesis is divided into two parts. Part I consists of a retrospective analysis of the first 100 years of the juvenile court movement in Canada, with specific attention devoted to tracing the origins of Canada's first *Juvenile Delinquents Act* of 1908, and the demands for reform reflected in three major federal government reform efforts undertaken since mid-century: the Department of Justice Report (1965), the proposed *Young Offenders Act* (1970), and the proposed *Young Persons in Conflict with the Law Act* (1975). Part II of the thesis focuses on evaluating these reform efforts in light of a number of identified concerns, including the proposed scope of future legislation and its implications for practice and procedure in the juvenile court. The thesis draws on a wide range of government reports, federal and provincial statutes, reported legal cases, and comparative material on the development of the juvenile court in other jurisdictions.

854. Wright, John de Pencier.

'The Legal System in Pioneer Days.' *Law Society of Upper Canada Gazette* 13 (1979): 158–160.

855. Young, Bert.

'Corporate Interests and the State.' *Our Generation* 10 (1, 1974): 70–83.

This article examines the role of corporate interests and the state in shaping the *Combines Investigation Act* of 1910. The author contends that Canada's first anti-combines legislation, enacted in 1889, was a product of lobbying efforts by small businessmen concerned with protecting their firms from the unfair price-fixing and trade-restraint practices of developing corporate combines. However, he maintains that it was only after the movement towards corporate mergers reached a high point after 1909 that the 'ruling class called upon the state to introduce legislation' to provide for the investigation of alleged combines. From his examination of the circumstances surrounding the enactment of the *Combines Investigation Act* of 1910, subsequent enforcement of and amendments to the legislation, and the historical development of mergers and monopolies, the author concludes that rather than serving to eliminate corporate wrongdoing, anti-combines legislation provided a way for the ruling class to police its own members during times of threatening economic and social unrest.

4

Prisons and Social Welfare Institutions

856. Adamson, Christopher R.

'The Breakdown of Canadian Prison Administration: Evidence from Three Commissions of Inquiry.' *Canadian Journal of Criminology* 25 (4, October 1983): 433–446.

This paper examines the accounts of the breakdown of prison administration provided by three penitentiary commissions: the Brown Commission of 1849, the Archambault Commission of 1938, and the Parliamentary Sub-Committee of 1977. From studying the commissions' reports, the author identifies four recurrent features associated with the breakdown of prison administration: the concentration of too much power in the hands of one individual or branch of government; the lack of external supervision over the administration of the penitentiary system; a lack of public involvement; and troubled management-employee relations. The paper concludes that because prisons are intrinsically unstable organizations, historically, administrators have faced recurring problems, and the architects of prison administration (commissioners) have tended to vacillate between giving excessive power to one man or branch of government (tyranny) and checking that power by imposing bureaucratic restrictions upon administrators (anarchy).

857. Aiton, Grace.

'The Selling of Paupers by Public Auction in Sussex Parish.' *Collections of the New Brunswick Historical Society* 16 (1961): 93–110.

858. Anderson, Frank W.

'Prisons and Prison Reform in the Old Canadian West.' *Canadian Journal of Corrections* 2 (April 1960): 209–215.

This article provides a brief account of the establishment and use of various prison facilities in the Northwest Territories from 1835 to 1876. The author notes the dates of and circumstances surrounding the establishment of several local jails, lock-ups, guardhouses, and later provincial and federal prisons in the region now covering Manitoba, Saskatchewan, and Alberta. Upon surveying the conditions and practices that characterized specific institutions, the author concludes that while the conditions within various institutions improved considerably over the years, the overcrowding of prisons continued to be a problem.

859. Anderson, Frank W.

A Concise History of Capital Punishment in Canada. Calgary: Frontier Publishing, 1973.

Also known under the cover title of 'Hanging in Canada,' this book provides an account of the history of capital punishment in Canada from 1749 to 1972. The author deals with such matters as the manner in which death sentences have been carried out over the years, the reform of the criminal law which led to a reduction in the number of offences punishable by death, specific cases in which the death penalty was applied, famous Canadian executioners, and the declining use of the death penalty in the 30 years prior to 1962. Although the author draws on a range of primary historical materials, few specific references are provided.

860. Andrews, R.C.

'The Development of Public Welfare Services in Newfoundland.' *Newfoundland Journal of Commerce* 25 (October 1958): 83–89.

861. Angus, Margaret.

'Health, Emigration and Welfare in Kingston, 1820–1840.' In *Oliver Mowat's Ontario*, pp. 120–135. Edited by Donald Swainson. Toronto: Macmillan of Canada, 1972.

With very few exceptions, immigrants destined for Upper Canada in the period 1820–40 went to or through Kingston. This article examines the health and welfare problems created by the immigrants upon their arrival at Kingston, and the efforts made by established citizens to cope with these problems. The author notes that, in the absence of direct government intervention, the care of the sick and destitute immigrants was left to humanitarian individuals, churches, and benevolent societies, whose efforts led to the establishment of Kingston's first hospitals and public welfare institutions.

862. Anonymous.

La Prison de Québec, 1813–1868. n.p., n.d. (Documentation Centre, International Centre of Comparative Criminology, University of Montreal, no. M2139)

Looking at the first Quebec City common jail built in 1813 and transformed into a college in 1868 from an architectural perspective, this paper attempts to reconstruct its political, legislative, and architectural history and to analyse its design and influences on the type of confinement therein. Referring mainly to public and government papers and newspapers, this study examines the context of the jail's construction and compares its design with architectural prison designs of the same period. The author concludes (1) that the construction of the jail was an honest attempt to replicate the penitentiary design and principles of John Howard, (2) that it filled an existing gap for a common jail in Quebec City but (3) that as early as 1826 the jail was under criticism for its lack of discipline, classification and work premises, which led to its closure in 1868.

863. Baehre, Rainer Karl.

'From Pauper Lunatics to Bucke: Studies in the Management of Lunacy in 19th Century Ontario.' M.A. thesis, University of Waterloo, 1976.

Intended as a study of 'ideas on the nature of madness' which inspired the movement towards the institutionalization of the insane in nineteenth-century Ontario, this thesis examines a broad range of socio-historical factors that influenced the emergence of the insane asylum. In particular, Baehre's work reflects the notion that the movement towards the institutionalization of the insane in Upper Canada was part of a larger process of social-welfare reform, fostered in the early decades of the nineteenth century by the acceptance of the ideas of leading American and European social reformers, and the unique social pressures generated in the province after 1830. The development and nature of lunatic asylums in general, Baehre attempts to demonstrate, were typified in the establishment and operation of the London Lunatic Asylum from 1870 to 1902. In attempting to establish his thesis, the author draws on a range of published and unpublished primary material, government documents, newspapers, and Canadian and foreign secondary sources.

864. Baehre, Rainer Karl.

'Origins of the Penitentiary System in Upper Canada.' *Ontario History* 69 (September 1977): 185–207.

This article examines the ideological origins of the penitentiary in Upper Canada. The article begins with a description of the dismal state of correctional facilities in Upper Canada in the early decades of the nineteenth century, when crude jails were used to confine criminals, debtors, and the insane along with other disorderly persons. The impetus towards penal reform in Upper Canada during the 1830s was viewed as having stemmed not only from the public's recognition of the inadequacy of the province's jails, but also from changes in the English criminal law which reduced the number of crimes punishable by death, the 'discovery' of the penitentiary system in the United States, and finally, a dramatic increase in the population of Upper Canada in the years 1827–35. Primary historical documents were used to gain insight into the concerns of early Upper Canadian penal reformers, the influence of English and American penal developments on Upper Canada, the principles of punishment incorporated in the Kingston Penitentiary which was established in 1835, and the controversy over the penitentiary's system of management which arose in the late 1840s. From his study, the author concludes that while the origins of the penitentiary in Upper Canada were rooted in the reforms of the English criminal law in the 1830s, the nature of the penitentiary in Upper Canada was more importantly influenced by penal developments in the United States (especially at Auburn and Philadelphia) where emphasis was placed on the utilitarian notion that the penitentiary could serve to bring about the 'moral reformation' of criminal offenders and serve as a model to the rest of society.

865. Baehre, Rainer Karl.

'Pauper Emigration to Upper Canada in the 1830's.' *Histoire Sociale/Social History* 14 (28, November 1981): 339–367.

This paper examines the origins and impact of the unprecedented emigration of paupers from Britain to Upper Canada during the 1830s. According to Baehre, the massive increase in pauper emigration to Upper Canada in the 1830s was tied to changes in the English Poor Law which restricted poor relief to the 'deserving poor' and those confined in workhouses, or houses of industry. During this time, Upper Canadians actively encouraged emigration by portraying the colony as a land of opportunity for thousands of propertyless and impoverished individuals who made up Britain's 'surplus population.' The influx of paupers to Upper Canada is shown to have influenced, first, the establishment of voluntary charitable societies to assist the destitute, sick, and insane, and later the direct intervention of the state in creating legislation and institutions to cope with growing social problems. The author concludes that 'by virtue of the volume of destitute emigrants to Upper Canada in the 1830's, pauperism and its accompanying evils – crime, vice, disease, and disorder – ended up being exported to the colony' and that 'in attempting to help solve Great Britain's, Upper Canadians inherited many of the same problems themselves.' These conclusions are based on extensive reference to primary historical materials from Ontario-based public archives and libraries, as well as related secondary sources.

866. Baehre, Rainer Karl.

'Paupers and Poor Relief in Upper Canada.' Paper presented at the Canadian Historical Association, Learned Societies Conference, Halifax, June 4, 1981. Also in Canadian Historical Association. *Historical Papers* (1981): 57–80.

This paper examines the changing structure and ideology of poor relief in Upper Canada in the period from 1817 to 1837. An attempt is made to relate the early–nineteenth-century Poor Law debate in England to the development of various modes of relief in Upper Canada. Attention is given to examining data relating to the establishment of the Society for the Relief of Strangers in Distress (1817), the Society for the Relief of the Sick and the Destitute

(1828), the Society for the Relief of Orphans, Widows and Fatherless (1832), the Children's Friend's Society (1835), the Toronto House of Industry (1837), and other *ad hoc* measures taken to deal with the poor in Upper Canada. The paper concludes that whereas voluntary charities had been able to cope with the poor before 1828, thereafter the number of paupers and the rising cost of poor relief necessitated increased government intervention. As well, the paper argues that during the 1830s, Upper Canadian poor-relief practices underwent rationalization, reflecting, to a considerable degree, the direction taken in England after 1834.

867. Baehre, Rainer Karl.

'The Prison System in Atlantic Canada before 1880.' Paper prepared for Federal Corrections History Project, Solicitor General of Canada. Ottawa: Solicitor General of Canada, 1982.

This study provides a preliminary overview of the development of the prison system in Atlantic Canada, and the immediate steps leading to the opening of the federal Dorchester penitentiary in 1881. The study is divided into six major sections. Relying largely on published government documents (legislative journals and official reports) it examines: (1) early types of punishment in the Atlantic colonies, and the transition from a system of public punishments and congregate confinement in jails to a penitentiary system, which sought to segregate and classify inmates; (2) the rationale underlying the establishment of early Atlantic penitentiaries as defined by politicians, legislators, and prison officials; (3) the nature of prison operations in Saint John (1842) and Halifax (1844) penitentiaries during the mid-nineteenth century; (4) the character of the inmate populations incarcerated in these penitentiaries; (5) the events surrounding the opening of the federal Dorchester penitentiary; and (6) the initial structure and operation of Dorchester. The author concludes that while the 'rhetoric of the prison overseers ... confirms the use of the penitentiary as an instrument of social control,' the construction and operation of Atlantic penitentiaries also reflected humanitarian and fiscal concerns.

868. Beaudet, Céline.

Evolution de la psychiatrie anglophone au Québec: 1880–1963: Le cas de l'Hôpital de Verdun. Cahiers de l'ISSH – Etudes sur le Québec, 6. Québec: Institut supérieur des sciences humaines, Université Laval, 1976.

869. Berzins, L., and Cooper, S.

'The Political Economy of Correctional Planning for Women: The Case of the Bankrupt Bureaucracy.' *Canadian Journal of Criminology* 24 (4, October 1982): 399–416.

On December 14, 1981, a landmark decision was handed down by the Canadian Human

Rights Commission, ruling that the Correctional Service of Canada discriminates against the female prisoners in its charge. This paper examines the reasons underlying the long-standing stalemate in planning for female offenders, and suggests changes needed in order to counteract the conditions that discriminate against women in the federal prison system. These tasks are approached through providing an overview of the historical process within which previous planning attempts have repeatedly stalemated, and an analysis of the socio-political–economic factors that invariably affect the decision-making process. The authors offer a perspective which attempts to explain the apparent unwillingness and the inability of the Correctional Service of Canada to provide adequately for female offenders, and propose a blue-print for developing a new planning approach that addresses itself more effectively to the real needs of women in correctional planning.

870. Boissery, Beverley D.

'The Patriote Convicts: A Study of the 1838 Rebellion in Lower Canada and the Subsequent Transportation of Some Participants to New South Wales.' Ph.D. dissertation, Australian National University, 1977.

In February 1840, 56 Canadians from Lower Canada arrived in New South Wales after having been exiled from Lower Canada for political rebellion and social rioting during November 1838. This study examines the circumstances surrounding the 1838 Rebellion in Lower Canada and the backgrounds of the participants who were exiled to New South Wales after having had their death sentences for treason commuted. The author's findings indicate that most of the 'patriotes' who arrived in New South Wales were farmers, who though being opposed to both the autocratic political and land-tenure systems of Lower Canada and the chauvinism of the English minority, had been highly respected in their local parishes. The author maintains that because of their former respectable status in Lower Canada, the sentencing of the 56 patriotes to transportation for life in New South Wales served as an exemplary punishment for those who attempted armed rebellion against the state.

871. Boissery, Beverley D., and Greenwood, F. Murray.

'New Sources for Convict History: The Canadian Patriotes in Exile.' *Historical Studies* 18 (71, October 1978): 277–287.

Drawing in part on the first author's 1977 dissertation research, this co-authored article examines the eventual fate of the 56 'patriotes' exiled to New South Wales after the 1838 Rebellion in Lower Canada. After being confined in a stockade near Sydney, and forced to work building roads, the exiles were granted pardons in early 1844 and allowed to return to Lower Canada. The authors maintain that the experience of the 'patriotes' exiled to New South Wales is worthy of more scholarly attention, since 'they left a surprisingly rich literary legacy relating to the convict system.' This is demonstrated in the books published by some of the 'patriotes' on their return to North America (for which references are provided) and the daily journals they kept while in exile. Translated extracts from the daily journal written by one of the 'patriotes,' Maurice Lepailleur, are included at the end of the article.

872. Borthwick, John Douglas.

History of the Montreal Prison from 1784 to 1886 Containing a Complete Record of the Troubles of 1837–1838, Burning of the Parliament Buildings, in 1849, the St. Alban's Raiders, 1864, the Two Fenian Raids of 1866 and 1870, and a Chronological Digest of all the principal events for the past hundred years. Valuable statistical tables from the Police and Recorder's Courts. Curious Proclamations, Warrants and other documents never before printed, relating to the Patiots of '37, and the administration of justice from the commencement of the Courts in 1784. With descriptions of Branding on the hand, Standing in the Pillory, the Stocks, Whipping, &c. Montreal: A. Periard, 1886.

Drawing on available historical records, and his knowledge of the political and social history of Quebec, Borthwick provides an account of the history of prisons that existed in Montreal, the administration of justice in the province, and significant political events that occurred between 1784 and 1886. The specific contents of the book are reflected in its lengthy title.

873. Borthwick, John Douglas.

Rébellion de 37–38: Précis complet de cette périod, rôle d'honneur ou liste complète des patriotes détenus dans les prisons de Montréal en 1837, 1838, 1839, date et lieux des arrestations et autres détails intéressants et inédits sur ce sujet. Montréal: Imprimerie du 'Cultivateur,' L.J. Tarte & frère, props., 1898.

874. Borthwick, John Douglas.

From Darkness to Light; History of the Eight Prisons Which Have Been, or Are Now in Montreal, from A.D. 1760 to A.D. 1907 – 'Civil and Military.' Montreal: Gazette Printing Company, 1907.

875. Bowers, Gregory Martin.

'Juvenile Correctional Services in Nova Scotia: A Study Tracing the Development of Juvenile Correctional Services from 1867–1967, with a Critical Analysis of Present Day Services.' M.S.W. thesis, St. Mary's University, 1969.

876. Boyd, Neil.

'An Examination of Probation.' *Criminal Law Quarterly* 20 (1977–8): 355–381.

The purpose of this article is to critically examine the substance of probation as a sentencing measure. Towards this end, the article deals with current criminal law and practice relating to the use of probation, the evolution of probation as a sentencing option in

Canada, and the official justifications offered for the increased use of probation: avoidance of incarceration, offender rehabilitation, deterrence, and economy. The author concludes that despite the realities of its application, probation will continue to flourish as a sentencing option, because 'it is erroneously *perceived* as both a more lenient and more productive alternative to incarceration.'

877. Boyd, Neil.

'The Release of Children from Ontario Training Schools: A Critical Analysis.' LL.M. thesis, York University, 1978.

This thesis takes a critical look at procedures for the release of juveniles from Ontario training schools. The author approaches this task by way of a critical analysis of pertinent contemporary and historical literature. In turn, he examines: (1) the rationale underlying the present legal response to juvenile delinquency ('the notion of coerced rehabilitation'), (2) the history of practices governing the release of juveniles from Ontario training schools from 1874 to 1978, (3) contemporary release practices, and (4) the move towards fixed sentencing within the juvenile justice system. From this examination, the author concludes that the substance of Ontario's efforts to control juvenile criminality has not changed in over 100 years, and that present (1978) release practices cannot be justified. Furthermore, the author reasons that although training schools are 'ostensibly designed to curb delinquency,' they 'in fact function as a vehicle for socio-economic and socio-cultural indoctrination.'

878. Boyd, Neil.

'The Circularity of Punishment and Treatment: Some Notes on the Legal Response to Juvenile Delinquency.' *Canadian Journal of Family Law* 3 (1980): 419–438.

879. Boyd, Neil.

'The Cruelty of Benevolence: The Release of Delinquents from Ontario's Training Schools.' *Osgoode Hall Law Journal* 19 (1981): 237–266.

880. Boyer, Raymond.

'Histoire de la torture à travers les âges.' *Cité libre* 14 (59, August/September 1963): 1–12.

The 'question' is the legal term that was used to describe the torture to which accused or convicted persons were subjected, to extract from them confessions or information. The author reviews the history of torture, paying special attention to Ancient Rome and France. He describes the various methods of torture and cites comments made by various French philosophers of the Age of Enlightenment on the issue. In New France, the question seems to have been ordered in few cases. Since the Supreme Council (Conseil Souverain) was created in 1663 and until the Conquest, 96 years later, only 29 persons were subjected to the question. Among them were five women and two black slaves. Out of the 29 only 9 death sentences were confirmed after the question whereas 20 were commuted to less severe sentences including 4 acquittals. A summary of the cases is provided. The last person to be subjected to the question in New France was a man named André Malaguen. Accused of complicity in a theft committed in 1758 in the house of a Montreal surgeon, Dr. Viger, Malaguen was sentenced to death but had his sentence commuted to the lash, branding with hot iron, and banishment for three years from the colony.

881. Boyer, Raymond.

'The Question: Judicial Torture in New France.' *Canadian Journal of Criminology and Corrections* 5 (1963): 284–291.

The content of this article varies only slightly from that of entry 880.

882. Boyer, Raymond.

'La peine capitale en Nouvelle-France.' *Cité libre* 4 (55, March 1963): 13–20.

To study the death penalty in the early days of New France one needs to ascertain the attitude of the native Indians towards this extreme punishment and to see whether this attitude has had any influence on the French population. Indian customs are briefly discussed and this is followed by an examination of the death penalty in the laws of New France. These laws punish several crimes by death, including: conspiracy, sale of alcoholic beverages to Indians, counterfeiting, arson, duel, rape, murder, abortion, infanticide, and desertion. Actual cases for each of these offences are cited. The first death sentence pronounced in Montreal dates from 1648. It was for a crime against nature and was ultimately commuted. But the next year, 1649, a young female thief, aged 15 or 16, was executed.

883. Boyer, Raymond.

'The Hangman in Canada.' *Canadian Psychiatric Association Journal* 9 (6, 1964): 521–532.

884. Boyer, Raymond.

Barreaux de fer, hommes de chair. Montréal: Du Jour, 1972.

885. Branca, A.E.

'Capital Punishment.' *Chitty's Law Journal* 24 (2, 1976): 37–43.

886. Briggs, Asa.

'The Welfare State in Historical Perspective.' In *The Welfare State: Selected Essays*, pp. 25–45. Edited by Charles I. Schottland. New York: Harper and Row, 1967.

887. Brown, Lorne A.

'Unemployment Relief Camps in Saskatchewan, 1933–1936.' *Saskatchewan History* 23 (3, August 1970): 81–104. Also in *Law and Social Control in Canada*, pp. 191–218. Edited by William K. Greenaway and Stephen L. Brickey. Scarborough: Prentice-Hall, 1978.

The efforts of the federal government to deal with the problem of the single, homeless, and unemployed in Saskatchewan from 1933 to 1936 were based on federal policies which were applied on a nation-wide basis. In Saskatchewan, as elsewhere, one of the methods used to deal with the problem of the single unemployed was to establish unemployment relief camps. This article examines the circumstances surrounding the establishment of such camps in Saskatchewan, and the purposes that they apparently served. The author contends that the primary purpose of the camps, which 'were compulsory for thousands of single unemployed who were cut off relief,' was to keep young men with 'radical political potential' out of the cities, where it was feared they would cause labour and social unrest. The author concludes that although the fear of violence and insurrection which prompted authorities to establish unemployment relief camps was exaggerated for political and economic reasons, it was not entirely unfounded.

888. Brown, M. Jennifer.

'Influences Affecting the Treatment of Women Prisoners in Toronto, 1880 to 1890.' M.A. thesis, Wilfrid Laurier University, 1975.

Set within the context of late-nineteenth-century urban reform, this thesis examines influences affecting the treatment of women prisoners incarcerated in Toronto penal institutions in the 1880s. As a preliminary step in this effort, statistics relating to the backgrounds and lifestyles of women prisoners held in the Andrew Mercer Reformatory for Women (established in 1880) and census data for the period 1881–90 are used to establish that the female prison population was disproportionately made up of 'lower class' women, whose activities, the most often being prostitution, were considered 'most threatening to the institution of the family.' In subsequent chapters, the author examines the character of the 'rehabilitative institutions and programmes' established for women prisoners, the 'lack of success' of programs aimed at reforming women inmates, and the consequent 'tactical realignment' of the efforts of reformers. The author submits that the treatment afforded women prisoners in the 1880s was largely dependent on general attitudes towards the importance of their role in society, and especially the part they played as 'wife and mother within the home.' According to her argument, in the late 1880s, the evident failure of penal reformers to create programs capable of teaching women prisoners to conform to this role led to a shift in the attention of reformers away from adult female offenders and towards child-saving efforts. The author concludes that the shift in emphasis from a focus on the adult offender to one on the juvenile delinquent reflected an increased desire on the part of middle-class reformers to control all deviant members of a rapidly changing society.

889. Brown, Thomas Edward.

'"Living with God's Afflicted": A History of the Provincial Lunatic Asylum at Toronto, 1830–1911.' Ph.D. dissertation, Queen's University, 1980.

No formal legislative provision was made for the care and treatment of the insane in early Upper Canada. Rather, prior to 1830, the insane were left to be cared for by their friends and families or, on occasion, subjected to short-term confinement in district jails. In the 1830s, however, a small but influential group of Upper Canadians championed a new institutional panacea, a provincial lunatic asylum. This dissertation is guided by a twofold purpose. First, the author attempts to explain why a 'revolution' in the care and treatment of the insane took place in Upper Canada in the 1830s. Second, an attempt is made to explain why the great promise of the asylum – the provision of humane care and the cure of the insane – was never to be realized in the Toronto Asylum in the nineteenth century. In carrying out these tasks, the author draws extensively on the correspondence and papers of leading Upper Canadian social reformers, published government documents and reports, contemporary medical journals, and secondary literature on the history of psychiatry and the asylum in the nineteenth century.

890. Brown, Thomas Edward.

'Architecture as Therapy.' *Archivaria* (10, Summer 1980): 99–123.

This article attempts to show, through a brief examination of the architecture of the Toronto Asylum in the nineteenth century, that the history of mental institutions can be a rewarding area of investigation for social historians. The article also provides an overview of recent European and American literature on the asylum, and calls attention to documentary sources (mainly institutional records) of particular value to social historians.

891. Brown, Thomas Edward.

'The Origins of the Asylum in Upper Canada, 1830–1839: Towards an Interpretation.' *Canadian Bulletin of Medical History* 1 (1, Summer 1984): 27–58.

In this article, Brown offers a critical re-interpretation of the origins of the insane asylum in Upper Canada. Drawing heavily on ideas advanced by Scull (1979) in his work on the nineteenth-century English experience with 'lunacy reform,' and citing documents relating to the emergence of the demand for such reform in Upper Canada, the author argues that the insane asylum was one of a number of 'new social-control institutions' set into place by a 'new middle class' in order to 'establish its hegemony' over propertyless wage-labourers. The author further maintains that the movement towards 'lunacy reform' in Upper Canada 'was both a product of and a response to the shift to the capitalist mode of production which Upper Canada, however hesitatingly, had begun to undergo in the 1830s.'

892. Burgess, T.J.W.

'A Historical Sketch of Our Canadian Institutions for the Insane.' Royal Society of Canada. *Proceedings and Transactions* Series 2, 4, sec. 2 (1898): 3–122.

Originally presented as a presidential address before members of the Royal Society of Canada, this extended paper reviews the progress made in the treatment of the insane in nineteenth-century Canada. At various points, the author notes that prior to the establishment of specialized institutions for the insane, they were often left to the care of their families, or confined in district jails along with criminals and debtors. The author traces the progress of institutional developments in each of the Canadian provinces during the nineteenth century. Overall he argues that such changes as did occur in the treatment of the insane were the result of the growth of medical knowledge regarding the causes and treatment of insanity, and the humanitarian reform efforts of dedicated social reformers. The paper is based mostly on the author's own knowledge of events and experiences as a leading nineteenth-century psychiatrist and asylum medical superintendent.

893. Burroughs, Peter.

'Tackling Army Desertion in British North America.' *Canadian Historical Review* 61 (1, March 1980): 28–68.

In the period from 1815 to 1865, numerous British soldiers stationed in British North America deserted their regiments and took up civilian life. This article examines the motives which spurred soldiers to 'flee the colours' in British North America, and the consequences that befell those who were caught. The author maintains that discontent with the monotony of military life, wages and allowances, and the desire by 'inveterate tipplers' to avoid having to pay money owed to the proprietors of regimental canteens, led many a soldier to attempt desertion. Note is made of the fact that before the construction of purpose-built military prisons in the 1840s, British army deserters unfortunate enough to be caught were punished by flogging and/or sentenced to terms of imprisonment in civilian jails and prisons. Attempts on the part of military authorities to deal with the problem of desertion through improving living conditions and introducing financial incentives for the ordinary soldier are given detailed attention.

894. Calder, William Arnold.

'The Federal Penitentiary System in Canada, 1867–1899: A Social and Institutional History.' Ph.D. dissertation, University of Toronto, 1979.

The purpose of this dissertation is threefold: to examine the essential features of the late–nineteenth-century penitentiary, to outline its evolution, and to identify the forces promoting change and stability within the penal sphere. In pursuit of these aims, the author first outlines the pre-Confederation penal heritage of the federal penitentiary system. Subsequent chapters deal in turn with: (1) the establishment and operation of federal penitentiaries, and the character of prison staffs, 1867–89; (2) the aim of convict reformation and its impact on penitentiary inmates; (3) the punitive measures inflicted on those in confinement, and the justifications offered for their use; (4) the aim of economy in prison matters, and the search for productive prison industries; and (5) the convict penitentiary reality, and the reaction of convicts to imprisonment. The dissertation draws on a wide range of primary sources, including internal penitentiary records, official correspondence, private papers, and published government reports.

895. Calder, William Arnold.

'Convict Life in Canadian Federal Penitentiaries, 1867–1900.' In *Crime and Criminal Justice in Europe and Canada*, pp. 297–318. Edited by Louis A. Knafla. Waterloo, Ont.: Wilfrid Laurier University Press, 1981.

This article provides a descriptive account of convict life in Canadian federal penitentiaries towards the end of the nineteenth century. At the onset, the author reasons that while 'it is probably not possible to make definitive statements' concerning the nature of convict life, 'a useful indication of the quality of the prison experience' felt by inmates can be obtained by exploring 'the main features of the prison environment,' and 'the convict reaction to imprisonment.' In relation to the main features of the prison environment, the author examines institutional records and official reports containing information on penitentiary architecture, the rules and regulations governing inmate life, the enforcement of discipline, the quality of food, conditions of health and sanitation, convict labour, and the abuse of power by prison officials. With regard to the convict reaction to imprisonment, the author explores data relating to the impact of imprisonment on different categories of inmates (particularly insane, female, and Indian prisoners), and the range of inmate responses to imprisonment (from co-operation to convict strikes and revolt). The author concludes that although 'convicts in many cases successfully broke, disregarded, or evaded the rules' governing their existence, late–nineteenth-century convict life was none the less a harsh experience. This harsh reality was reflected in the 'persistent convict quest for freedom,' through conforming to institutional rules thereby increasing the possibility of early release, or simply by means of escape.

896. Campbell, George A.

'Social Life and Institutions of Nova Scotia in the 1830's.' M.A. thesis, Dalhousie University, 1949.

This thesis provides a broadly based account of the nature of social life and the development of social institutions in Nova Scotia during the 1830s. The central theme underlying this account is the argument that, in the decade from 1830 to 1840, Nova Scotia experienced an 'intellectual awakening,' which by placing emphasis on the need for 'self-improvement' among the colonial population, led to the founding of many new and unique social institutions. Drawing on a variety of primary and secondary source materials held in the Public Archives of Nova Scotia, the author surveys the development of major 'cultural institutions' (schools and colleges, societies, mechanics' institutes, libraries, newspapers, and magazines) and institutions concerned with 'moral order' (religious institutions, temperance societies, and penal and welfare institutions). The author concludes that although Nova Scotia had its share of crime, poverty, and immorality, 'these evils' were 'subordinated to a lesser importance by the good work that was being done in the social and cultural life' of the colony by reformers.

897. Chandler, David.

Capital Punishment in Canada: A Sociological Study in Repressive Law. Carleton Library Series. Toronto: McClelland and Stewart, 1976.

Although this is mainly a sociological study concerned with pointing out the repressive nature of Canada's capital punishment law, it deals with the historical background to the legislation. Particular attention is given to considering the legislative history of the death penalty in France, the United States, England, and Canada. The author also provides evidence concerning public opinion about the death penalty in Canada, and the parliamentary debates on capital punishment that took place between 1967 and 1973.

898. Christie, Hugh G.

'Treatment in Provincial Institutions.' *Canadian Bar Review* 27 (9, November 1949): 1052–1066.

The author of this article critically examines the treatment of inmates in provincial penal institutions. Drawing on federal criminal statistics and royal commission reports and his experience as the director of corrections for Saskatchewan, the author argues that little progress has been made in the scientific treatment of provincial offenders during the last century. He maintains that 'outdated Dominion legislation, the lack of resources ... and the absence of understanding of the problem and its solution by the average citizen' have inhibited the progress of penal reform, and contributed to the 'chaotic condition' of provincial institutions.

899. Chunn, Dorothy.

'Good Men Work Hard: Convict Labour in Kingston Penitentiary, 1835–1850.' *Canadian Criminology Forum* 4 (1, Fall 1981): 13–22.

From its inception in 1835, convict labour was a key component of the operation of the penitentiary at Kingston. Drawing on penitentiary documents and newspaper accounts for the period 1835 to 1850, along with secondary source material relating to Upper Canadian economic and demographic developments, the author examines the rhetoric and reality surrounding the use of convict labour in Kingston Penitentiary. Although advocated by penal reformers as a method for ensuring that Kingston would be a reformative and self-sufficient institution, the author found that the penitentiary failed to meet these objectives. Despite the 'unmitigated failure' of the penitentiary as a reformative and cost-effective institution, the author contends that, when viewed as a mechanism for the punishment and discipline of the 'less eligible,' the penitentiary was an unqualified success.

900. Clarke, Ian Hope.

'Public Provisions for the Mentally Ill in Alberta, 1907–1936.' M.A. thesis, University of Calgary, 1973.

This thesis provides an initial look at provisions made for the care and treatment of the insane and the 'mentally defective' in Alberta from 1907 to 1936. Divided into four chapters, the study examines archival data relating to: (1) early legal provisions concerning the confinement of 'dangerous lunatics' (1870–1911) and the establishment of the province's first mental institution at Ponoka (1911); (2) the consolidation, operation, and expansion of the senior provincial mental hospital at Ponoka, and auxiliary institutions at Oliver, Red Deer, and Charesholm (1912–28); (3) the growing eugenics movement and the use of sexual sterilization in dealing with the 'mentally defective' (1919–35), and; (4) the breakdown, reform, and reorganization of Albert's mental-health system (1928–35). The study found that prior to 1911, 'dangerous lunatics' from the Northwest Territories and Alberta were transfered to Manitoba, where they were housed first in the Stony Mountain Penitentiary, and later in the Brandon mental asylum. After 1911, these individuals were turned over to the Ponoka institution, which, along with other admissions, led to serious overcrowding and the need for auxiliary institutions. The problem of overcrowding, especially in the case of the 'mentally defective,' served eventually to justify the sexual sterilization of individuals who it was believed would produce deviant and criminal offspring. The author further found that as late as the 1930s, mechanical restraints were used on individuals held in provincial mental institutions. Consequently, the author concluded that regardless of the many 'progressive' innovations that were implemented during the period from 1911 to 1936, Alberta's mental-health system was unable to escape its original limitations – the major one being the commitment to building massive custodial institutions.

901. Coles, D.

Nova Scotia Corrections – An Historical Perspective. Halifax: Communications Project in Criminal Justice, Correctional Services Division, 1979.

902. Coughlan, D.W.F.

'The History and Function of Probation.' *Canadian Bar Journal* 6 (1963): 198–213.

The author, then director of Probation Services for the Province of Ontario, provides a review of the history and function of probation in Canada. The development of probation as a sentencing alternative in Canada in the period 1908 to 1961 is compared with developments that have occurred in other jurisdictions such as Britain and the United States. The author argues the need for a change in public attitudes towards probation, and the assistance of the legal profession in gaining public support for its increased use.

903. Cross, Michael S.

'Imprisonment in Canada: An Historical Perspective.' Toronto: John Howard Society of Ontario, 1975. (Community Education Series 1, no. 6)

Written for the John Howard Society as an educational service to the community, this paper examines the formative period of Canadian penal institutions in the mid-nineteenth century. The author compares the underlying assumptions and policies on imprisonment voiced in the mid-nineteenth century with the assumptions reflected in the more recent Law Reform Commission of Canada position on penal reform. He concludes that members of society involved with penal reform shared much the same concerns and goals in the mid-nineteenth century as they do now.

904. Curry, Starr.

'Early Efforts to Improve Services for the Mentally Retarded in Nova Scotia.' *Nova Scotia Historical Quarterly* 5 (4, December 1975): 381–390.

During the early decades of the twentieth century, the improvement of services for the mentally retarded in Nova Scotia became an important provincial concern. This concern led to the appointment of a royal commission to inquire into the nature and causes of mental retardation, which reported its findings in 1927. The present article examines the manner in which the 1927 Royal Commission approached the problem of mental retardation in Nova Scotia, and the solutions it proposed. The author notes that the Royal Commission included within its definition of 'feebleminded' all 'mentally deficient persons' and those with 'undesirable temperamental qualities which render a person unfit to take his place in society.' Comment is made on research carried out at the time which indicated that the 'mentally deficient tend to reproduce their own kind and contribute to illegitimacy, delinquency and immorality.' The main solution proposed for dealing with the problem of the mentally retarded in the province was to have 'feebleminded' individuals placed in training schools and custodial institutions.

905. Curtis, Bruce, and Edginton, Barry.

'Uneven Institutional Development and the "Staple" Approach: A Problem of Method.'
Canadian Journal of Sociology 4 (3, 1979): 257–273.

Intended as a contribution to Marxist historical sociology, this paper attempts to account for the anomalous character of the development of social welfare institutions in Upper Canada prior to 1851. Referring to supporting primary and secondary historical sources, the authors note that, in Upper Canada, institutions usually associated with industrialization appeared prior to substantial industrialization in the province. In addition to witnessing the advent of a state system of public education (1843), prior to 1851, 'specialized institutions' developed in Upper Canada for the punishment of criminals (Provincial Penitentiary, 1835), for disciplining the unemployed (Toronto House of Industry, 1837), for the separate confinement of the insane (Toronto Lunatic Asylum, 1841), and for the care of the indigent sick (Kingston Hospital, 1832). In attempting to account for the apparent 'lack of correspondence between forms of production and types of institutions' that came to characterize pre-1851 Upper Canada, the authors turn to an examination of the 'staple' approach to Canadian development, variations of which are reflected in the writings of early economic historians (Innis, Fowke, Lower) and more recent proponents of 'neo-Marxist dependency theory.' On the basis of this examination, they argue that 'the peculiar character of the colonial economy' (the focus of the 'staple' approach) forms only part of the analysis necessary to explain the phenomenon of uneven institutional development. More importantly, the authors conclude that the emergence of social welfare institutions in Upper Canada must also be considered in relation to 'the structure of capitalist development' that was emerging in major western countries, and its impact on institutional development in Upper Canada.

906. Dawe, Jane-Alice Kathleen.

'The Impact of Social Change on the Development of Welfare Services in Ontario, 1891–1921: "A Historical Study of the Transition from Institutional to Foster Care for Children in Ontario, 1891–1921".' M.S.W. thesis, University of Toronto, 1966.

907. Delisle, Dominique.

'La prison de Bordeaux et sa population (de 1912 à 1940).' *Criminologie* 9 (1–2, 1976): 23–59.

This is a quantitative study of the inmate population at the Bordeaux prison in Montreal from 1912 to 1940. These three decades of operation are divided into two distinct periods, 1912– 30 and 1931–40. Most of the admissions (50–80 per cent) are for short terms of imprisonment of less than two months. The offences committed by those admitted are minor, neither offences against property nor against the person. Between 30 per cent and 60 per cent of these offences can be classified as public nuisance offences, and 30–50 per cent are related to drunkenness. While most of those admitted are under the age of 30, a relatively large percentage (15–20 per cent) are older offenders over 50 years old, while one-third of the inmate population are over 40 years old. The inmate population has very little education and is composed primarily of workers and labourers. Several statistical tables illustrate and complete the written text.

908. DeLottinville, Carl B.

'The Asylum for the Insane: A Study of the History of Institutional Care and Treatment of the Mentally Ill in Ontario, 1820–1900.' M.S.W. research report, McGill University, 1976.

This research report examines the emergence and perpetuation of the 'custodial asylum' in nineteenth-century Ontario. According to the researcher, the tremendous influx of immigrants to Canada during the period 1820–50 created 'staggering social problems' for colonial citizens, and led to the creation of various institutions of social control, including the penitentiary, the house of industry, and the insane asylum. The author finds support for his claim that the insane asylum in particular functioned as a mechanism of social control in an analysis of the first 100 admissions to the Hamilton Lunatic Asylum in 1875. He concludes that long after the asylum's ineffectiveness as a therapeutic institution was recognized, it continued to function as a place of confinement of economically and socially dependent individuals.

909. Dempsey, Hugh Aylmer.

'Penal Colonies in Alberta.' *Alberta Historical Review* 8 (Winter 1960): 15–16.

In 1888, Sam Bedson, the warden of the Stony Mountain Penitentiary in Manitoba, suggested in his annual report that the Canadian government take steps to establish a penal colony in the Peace River area of what is now the province of Alberta. This brief article consists largely of extracts from Bedson's report, in which he proposes a plan for the establishment of such a penal colony. Dempsey notes that Bedson's idea was not well received and never went beyond the talking stage.

910. Desaulniers, Claude.

'La peine de mort dans la législation criminelle de 1760 à 1892.' *Revue générale de droit* 8 (1, 1977): 141–184.

When English laws were introduced in the colony, approximately 200 crimes were punishable by death, whereas when the first Canadian *Criminal Code* was enacted in 1892, it contained only three capital offences. The author examines the history of Canadian criminal laws through the application of the death penalty. In the introduction he discusses the implementation of English law following the conquest and the state of both French and English criminal laws at that time. In the first part he examines the state of public opinion *vis-à-vis* the death penalty at the time of the conquest. This is followed by a discussion of the ideas that emerged in Europe with the publication of Beccaria's *On Crimes and Punishments* and the influence these ideas had in Canada, as well as the heated debates between the retentionists and abolitionists as appeared in newspaper articles. The second part examines the attitude of parliament and the various legislative efforts from the conquest to the reform of Black, and then from the reform of Black to the codification of 1892. In the last section, entitled 'The British Influence,' the author compares the evolution of British and Canadian legislation and tries to explain the motives behind the gap between the two legislations.

911. Desaulniers, Claude.

'La peine de mort et la législation canadienne de 1760 à 1892.' LL.M. thesis, Université d'Ottawa, 1977.

This thesis forms the basis of the author's 1977 published article (see entry 910 above).

912. Dillon, Richard.

'Convict Colonies for the Pacific-Northwest.' *B.C. Historical Quarterly* 19 (1–2, January/April 1955): 93–102.

The author relates evidence concerning early plans for the settlement of convicts as colonists in the Pacific Northwest. In 1788, the idea of colonizing nascent British Columbia with felons and debtors was advanced in letters written to Sir Joseph Banks, president of the Royal Society and a 'prime mover in many of Britain's eighteenth-century voyages and expeditions.' Further evidence of interest in the idea of establishing convict colonies in the Pacific Northwest is revealed in two letters written in 1789, copies of which are contained in the Banks Papers (Sutro Branch of the California State Library) and reproduced at the end of the article. The first letter gave support to a plan for 'disposing of convicts in some settlement to be made about *Nootka*,' while the second 'expressed high hopes for convict settlement of the western portion of British North America.' The author concludes that while none of the plans for convict settlements ever came to pass, they serve to reflect the state of knowledge concerning the northwestern portions of the American continent towards the end of the eighteenth century, and the imagination with which the potential development of the region was projected.

913. Dixon, W.G.

History of the Penitentiaries Branch of the Canadian Department of Justice. Chicago: School of Social Service Administration, 1947.

914. Drapeau, S.

Histoire des institutions de charité, de bienfaisance et d'éducation du Canada depuis leur fondation jusqu'à nos jours. 7 vols. Ottawa: Foyer Domestique, 1877.

In seven volumes the author presents a chronological historical account of the principal charitable institutions of Canada from the arrival of the first colonialists to 1877. The author wants to make public the numerous efforts, heroic sufferings, and self-sacrifice the members of these religious institutions demonstrated. A historical overview of the main activities of the religious charitable institutions in Canada is offered in volume 1. The main topic of discussion is, however, the hospitals created by these institutions. Of particular note is volume 2, which focuses on asylums for the insane, and volume 3 on orphan-homes. Volume 4 is on the education of the young, volume 5 on the philanthropic actions of the Saint-Vincent de Paul Society, and volume 6 describes public and private welfare during disasters such as epidemics which occurred in Canada. An appendix containing statistical tables which summarize the information of the previous volumes constitutes volume 7. The author uses primary sources from various institutions of charities he studied.

915. Driedger, Otto.

'The Canadian Experience: The System of Crime Control in Saskatchewan.' In *Alternative Strategies for Coping with Crime*, pp. 120–136. Edited by Norman Tutt. London: Basil Blackwell and Mott Ltd., 1978.

Focusing on the experience of Saskatchewan, the author examines the development of alternative strategies for coping with juvenile and adult offenders. Under the heading 'Juvenile Services,' he discusses the major shift in approach reflected in the province's 1959 child welfare legislation, and the subsequent development of community-based treatment alternatives for children and youth. With respect to 'Adult Services,' he reviews the development and status of alternative coping strategies such as diversion, probation services, legal aid, fine-option programs, and special police and court services for the province's native population. He concludes that while in Saskatchewan 'the shift to a community-based service has been accomplished in the juvenile field,' the adult system is still institutionally based.

916. Duguay, Roger.

L'échafaud: J'ai vu les dernières pendaisons à la prison de Bordeaux. Montréal: Editions Québecor, 1979.

917. Edginton, Barry.

'Formation of the Asylum in Upper Canada.' Ph.D. dissertation, University of Toronto, 1981.

Edginton's dissertation addresses the question: 'Why in the period 1841–53 did the government of Upper Canada provide for the separate institutionalization of the mad in asylums?' Guided by 'the general principles of Marxist political economy,' the author attempts to explain the formation of the asylum in Upper Canada by way of examining the colony's relationship to Britain as a producer of raw materials and a 'dumping ground' for its 'surplus population.' Following closely on the thesis developed by Andrew Scull (1979) in his attempt to account for the rise of the insane asylum in Britain, Edginton argues that the formation of the asylum in Upper Canada was tied to the development of public-welfare institutions (workhouses or houses of industry) and the increasing emphasis placed on the need to distinguish between, and confine separately, the 'able-bodied' and the 'non–able-bodied' poor. The dissertation is based mainly on secondary sources and published contemporary materials.

918. Edmison, John Alexander.

'Civil Rehabilitation.' *Canadian Bar Review* 27 (9, November 1949): 1091–1110.

Included in a special issue of the *Canadian Bar Review* devoted to 'Penal Reform in Canada,' Edmison's article focuses on considering the problems faced by 'reformed and reformable' offenders after they are released from prison. In addition to noting various immediate needs and problems that affect ex-prisoners, the author discusses the historical development and operation of prisoner rehabilitation agencies and services in Canada. He concludes that although the prisoner-aid movement in Canada has made considerable progress over the years, it has still 'a long way to go before it reaches maximum efficiency.'

919. Edmison, John Alexander.

'The Eternal Problem of Crime and Criminals.' *Queen's Quarterly* 60 (Summer 1953): 243–252.

First presented as a paper to the Canadian Psychological Association in the spring of 1953, this article relates early prison discipline methods at Kingston Penitentiary. Edmison describes the sadistic and brutal treatment afforded male, female, and child inmates during the early years of the penitentiary. Unfootnoted passages are taken from the *Rules and Regulations* of the Penitentiary and the Report of the Brown Commission of 1849 as evidence of the harsh treatment received by inmates. Note is made of the much improved conditions of penal institutions, and more humane treatment of inmates, in more recent years.

920. Edmison, John Alexander.

'The History of Kingston Penitentiary.' *Historic Kingston* 3 (November 1954): 26–35. Also in Kingston Historical Society. *Historic Kingston: Transactions of the Kingston Historical Society*, vols. 1–10. Belleville: Mika, 1974.

In this article, Edmison takes a retrospective look at the history of Kingston Penitentiary. In it he compares the harsh conditions experienced by nineteenth-century inmates to the more humane treatment of inmates in the mid-twentieth century. Quoting extensively from early correspondence, inspectors' reports, and the reports of the Brown (1849) and Archambault (1938) commissions, Edmison discusses the early use of convict labour, changes in the rules and regulations governing the institution and its inmates, the backgrounds of inmates imprisoned at Kingston, and the use of corporal punishment. The paper concludes that whereas the early history of Kingston Penitentiary was characterized by 'repression,' 'corruption,' and 'inefficiency,' in more recent years inmates have been treated according to a 'new and more civilized' approach.

921. Edmison, John Alexander.

'Kingston Penitentiary and Charles Dickens.' *Chitty's Law Journal* 13 (1965): 255–257.

922. Edmison, John Alexander.

'First Steps in Canadian Aftercare.' *Canadian Journal of Corrections* 10 (April 1968): 272–281. Also reprinted in *Prison Journal* 56 (1, Spring/Summer 1976): 44–52.

In an attempt to cast fresh light on the history of prison after-care services in Canada, the author chronicles the early efforts of Ontario penal reformers to establish and maintain a society for the assistance of discharged prisoners. Formed in 1874, the Prisoner's Aid Association in Ontario worked actively on behalf of ex-prisoners and their families, and, prior to ceasing operation in 1915, advocated numerous progressive penal-reform proposals. Citing extracts from the minutes of the National Prison Congress held in Toronto in 1887, the Royal Commission appointed to inquire into the Prison and Reformatory System of Ontario (1891), and the writings and correspondence of leading penal reformers, the author describes the motivating concerns, achievements, and obstacles encountered by Canadian pioneers in the field of prison after-care services. He concludes that '[f]ortunately for the future of our prisoner-aid movement' the provision of after-care services continued to be of concern to John Kidman who, after 1918, 'was destined to become the first truly national leader of prison reform and prisoner rehabilitation in Canada.'

923. Edmison, John Alexander.

'Perspective in Corrections.' *Canadian Journal of Corrections* 12 (1970): 534–548.

Drawing on his personal experience as a leading Canadian penal reformer, Edmison recalls the founding of the Canadian Penal Association at a congress held in 1935, subsequent meetings of the CPA in 1946 and 1949, and the merging of the CPA and the Canadian Welfare Council into the Canadian Corrections Association in 1956. The issues and concerns addressed by Canadian penal reformers after 1935, along with other significant aspects of the recent history of Canadian corrections, are discussed.

924. Edmison, John Alexander.

'Some Aspects of Nineteenth-Century Canadian Prisons.' In *Crime and Its Treatment in Canada*. 2nd ed., pp. 347–369. Edited by W.T. McGrath. Toronto: Macmillan, 1976.

This chapter deals with several aspects of the history of Canadian corrections in the nineteenth century. Focusing mainly on the period from 1830 to 1880, the author examines the nature of and conditions that characterized early 'pioneer prisons' in central and western Canada; the use made of alternatives to imprisonment such as the stocks, branding, banishment, and transportation; the establishment of Kingston Penitentiary and issues surrounding its operation and management (i.e., the corruption of early officials and the excessive use of corporal punishment); and the period of 'major penitentiary expansion' which occurred with the opening of new federal penitentiaries in Quebec, Manitoba, British Columbia, and New Brunswick from 1873 to 1880. Among other data sources, Edminson makes use of early magistrates' reports, annual penitentiary records, the correspondence of leading penitentiary officials and federal politicians, newspapers, and contemporary published accounts. Overall, he concludes that while 'prison reform as we now understand the term was not a continuing major issue' in nineteenth-century Canada, the treatment of juvenile and adult offenders took a more progressive turn as the century drew to a close.

925. Edmison, John Alexander, and Turner, Walter.

'Kingston Penitentiary a Century Ago.' *Canadian Welfare* 25 (October 1949): 29–32.

926. Edwards, John Ll.J.

'Penal Reform and the Machinery of Criminal Justice in Canada.' *Criminal Law Quarterly* 8 (4, July 1966): 408–426.

Although the author of this article is primarily concerned with discussing contemporary penal-reform efforts in Canada in the 1960s, attention is given to noting important developments and events in the history of English and Canadian criminal justice since the early twentieth century. Several recommendations are made for improving the machinery of criminal justice in the various Canadian provinces.

927. Ekstedt, John W.

'History of Juvenile Containment Policy in British Columbia.' In *Issues in Juvenile Justice*, pp. 285–301. Edited by R.R. Corrado, M. Le Blanc, and J. Trépanier. Toronto: Butterworth, 1983.

928. Ekstedt, John W., and Griffiths, Curt T.

Corrections in Canada: Policy and Practice. Toronto: Butterworth, 1984.

Although aimed primarily at providing an overview of the present Canadian correctional system, this text devotes substantial attention to discussing the history of corrections in Canada. In a major chapter on the 'history of Canadian corrections,' the authors draw on published and unpublished secondary sources, government documents, and commissioned reports in an attempt 'to highlight the events, personalities and legislative acts which had an impact on the development of corrections in Canada.' Attention is given to examining the nature of crime and punishment in early Canada, the origins and operation of the penitentiary in the pre-Confederation era, and major developments in Canadian corrections from the late 1880s through to the 1970s. Noting the existence of competing 'conservative,' 'liberal-pluralist,' and 'radical-élitist' interpretations of correctional change, the authors contend that it is important to consider the history of Canadian corrections within a larger societal context, and to recognize that in addition to 'humanitarian spirit' various political, social, and economic factors may play a role in correctional developments. This historical chapter sets the background to and is used to inform the authors' subsequent discussion of contemporary corrections policy and practice.

929. Ernst, Fred.

'The Treatment of the Criminally Insane in Ontario, 1830–1900.' Unpublished paper, Osgoode Hall Law School, York University, 1980.

This paper examines the treatment accorded the criminally insane in nineteenth-century Ontario. To this end, the author provides brief accounts of the development of Ontario's prison and asylum systems, traces the history of legislative provisions governing the care and custody of individuals defined as 'criminal lunatics,' and considers the treatment meted out to the criminally insane in nineteenth-century Ontario prisons and asylums. Extensive reference is made to provincial and later federal statutes concerning the criminally insane, and the records and reports of provincial mental and penal institutions. The author concludes that the treatment received by the criminal lunatic was no different in prisons and asylums. In both types of institutions, the history of the criminally insane was one of mistreatment, rejection, and avoidance.

930. Evans, Marvin Keith.

'The Prerogative of Pardon in Canada: Its Development, 1864–1894.' M.A. thesis, Carleton University, 1971.

This is a study of the development of the prerogative of pardon in Canada (from just prior to Confederation to the early 1890s), constructed primarily from correspondence and government documents. During this period, the pardon was transformed from a power vested solely in the central government and ultimately exercised by the governor general to one administered by both the federal and provincial governments, subject to cabinet control. Substantial attention is given to examining the 1860s disputes between the fathers of Confederation and the British Colonial Office over vesting pardons in the lieutenant-governors, as well as the litigation, later known as the *Executive Power* case, which resolved that pardons be administered at both levels of government. Later confusion regarding the cabinet's role in pardoning around the time of the Red River Rebellion, and negotiations with the Colonial Office which resulted in cabinet control of pardons in Canada, are also discussed.

931. Fagan, John.

'Early Prison Customs in Newfoundland.' *RCMP Quarterly* 28 (1, July 1962): 5–9.

932. Fattah, Ezzat A.

'Canada's Successful Experience with the Abolition of the Death Penalty.' *Canadian Journal of Criminology* 25 (1983): 421–431.

933. Fay, C.R.

'Newfoundland and Convict Settlement.' *Newfoundland Quarterly* 59 (4, Winter 1960): 34–35.

In 1789, 80 convicts were confined in St. John's, Nfld., after a ship's captain forced prisoners being transported from Ireland to land on the island. This short article consists mainly of extracts from correspondence between W.W. Grenville, the British Home Secretary, and Lord Fitz-Gibbon, the Lord Chancellor of Ireland, concerning the issue of whether the convicts should be allowed to remain in Newfoundland or be returned to Ireland. Grenville argued that since it was the policy of the British government to discourage permanent settlement in Newfoundland, the convicts should be (and were) returned.

934. Fingard, Judith.

'The Relief of the Unemployed: The Poor in Saint John, Halifax and St. John's, 1815–1860.' *Acadiensis* 5 (1, 1975): 32–53. Also in *The Canadian City: Essays in Urban History*, pp 341– 367. Edited by Gilbert A. Stelter and Alan F.J. Artibise. Toronto: McClelland and Stewart, 1977.

In the years following the Napoleonic Wars, overseas immigration, economic recession, and other factors forced urban poverty to the forefront of public attention in the major centres of eastern British North America. The response to the unemployed poor in Saint John, Halifax, and St. John's was guided by public concerns with 'economy, order, and the wider welfare of the town.' Consequently, in order to qualify for relief, the unemployed were required to perform heavy outdoor labour, such as stone-breaking, or work indoors in factories. The author maintains that the requirement that the unemployed poor perform useful work in return for relief enabled capitalists of the period to exploit patterns of unemployment to their advantage.

935. Fingard, Judith.

'Jailbirds in Mid-Victorian Halifax.' *Dalhousie Law Journal* 8 (3, 1984): 81–102. Also published in *Law in a Colonial Society: The Nova Scotia Experience*, pp. 81–102. Edited by Peter Waite, Sandra Oxner, and Thomas Barnes. Toronto: Carswell, 1984.

936. Fiser, Vladimir.

'Development of Services for the Juvenile Delinquent in Ontario, 1891–1921.' M.S.W. thesis, University of Toronto, 1966.

937. Foucauld, Deirdre.

'Prison Labour, Punishment or Reform: The Canadian Penitentiary System, 1867–1960.' M.A. thesis, University of Ottawa, 1982.

The intent of this study is to examine the social process within which the Canadian penitentiary system has evolved, changed, and continued to survive through the conduct of prison labour. The history of the use of prison labour in the Canadian penitentiary system is approached through examining changes that have occurred in the occupation of the general labour force as well as the occupations of the prison labour force. The study covers five distinct periods from 1867 to 1960. The author hypothesizes that if prison labour was in practice guided by the 'principle of reform,' changes in prison labour would parallel those in the general labour force; and conversely, if prison labour was guided by the 'principle of punishment,' there would be no parallel changes. Evidence presented by the author indicates that throughout the period of the study, prison labour in the Canadian penitentiary system served as a form of punishment, rather than as a method of reforming inmates.

938. Francis, Daniel.

'That Prison on the Hill: The Historical Origins of the Lunatic Asylum in the Maritime Provinces.' M.A. thesis, Carleton University, Ottawa, 1975.

This thesis examines the development and operation of institutions for the insane in the Maritime provinces during the nineteenth century. The author maintains that although in both Nova Scotia and New Brunswick asylums were originally intended as a place where the insane could receive care and treatment, almost from the day their doors were opened the asylums were overcrowded and little treatment was given. The author's analysis of institutional records and reports further indicates that the inmates of asylums were largely paupers or immigrants, and that legislators were not called upon to improve the conditions of institutions. On the basis of these findings, he concludes that 'whatever the intentions of its founders, the nineteenth century asylum was as much a correctional institution as the prison or the poorhouse. Its primary purpose became the protection of society, not the treatment of its sick members.'

939. Francis, Daniel.

'The Development of the Lunatic Asylum in the Maritime Provinces.' *Acadiensis* 6 (2, Spring 1977): 23–38.

This article is a condensed version of the author's (1975) M.A. thesis (see entry 938 above).

940. Gagon-Pratte, France.

'L'architecture des prisons du régime français.' M.A. thesis, Université Laval, 1977.

This thesis studies the architectural design of different places of confinement in New France. Relying on primary and secondary sources and paintings, the architecture of the Montreal, Three Rivers, Quebec City, and Louisbourg jails, of military redoubts and barracks, and of asylums used for confinement purposes under the French regime is considered in order to analyse the underlying organizational concepts and to determine the conditions of detention therein. The author concludes that these buildings are always adjacent to military or judicial facilities, in a perpetual state of decay and insalubrity, and architecturally similar to those existing in France during the same period.

941. Gaucher, Robert.

'Class and State in Lower and Upper Canada, 1760 to 1873: Groundwork for the Analysis of Criminal Justice in Pre-Confederation Canada.' Ph.D. dissertation, University of Sheffield, 1982.

This dissertation provides a Marxist analysis of the creation of state disciplinary institutions in Upper and Lower Canada (1760 to 1873), with particular emphasis on the penitentiary. First, Marxist theoretical arguments about disciplinary institutions and their relationship to the state and civil society are addressed. Following from this a political economic analysis of the development of the Canadian social formation, civil society, and the Canadian nation-state (which constitutes the bulk of the thesis) is provided. Finally, the author undertakes an analysis of the creation of state disciplinary institutions, locating this analysis within the larger context of Canadian society. The dissertation draws primarily on published secondary sources and recent Marxist theoretical and historical literature concerned with the development of state disciplinary institutions in Europe and the United States.

942. Gaucher, Robert.

'On the Need for Specificity in Marxist Criminology: An Illustration.' *Canadian Criminology Forum* 6 (1, Fall 1983): 35–47.

This essay outlines some of the major findings stemming from the author's doctoral dissertation research (see entry 941 above). He stresses the need for Canadian criminologists and historians to avoid the uncritical application of arguments and explanations concerning the development of disciplinary institutions advanced by European authors.

943. Gauquelin, M.

'L'abolition de la peine de mort au Canada en 1967 pour une périod d'essai de 5 ans.' *Québec Science* 11 (7, April 1973): 22–25.

In 1967, Canada suspended the death penalty for a trial period of five years. The studies conducted between 1967 and 1972 make it possible to draw some clear-cut conclusions: the death penalty is useless when it comes to deterring future killers. The studies point to the need to pass a final law, a law abolishing capital punishment.

944. Gibson, James A.

'Political Prisoners, Transportation for Life, and Responsible Government in Canada.' *Ontario History* 67 (4, December 1975): 185–198.

In the aftermath of the rebellions in Upper and Lower Canada (1838–9) 150 political prisoners were transported from Canada to penal colonies in Australia. Drawing primarily on the official correspondence of colonial officials in Britain, Canada, and Australia, this article considers the effect that mounting animosity against the system of penal transportation may have had on other facets of colonial policy, and in particular the eventual granting of responsible government. Findings indicate that the use of transportation as a method of punishment in the case of Canadian political prisoners raised important issues concerning the administration of government and the authority vested in various colonial officials. The author concludes that animosity over and reaction against the system of penal transportation in part induced the British Colonial Office to more warmly embrace the principles of responsible government.

945. Gibson, R.B.

'Treatment in Federal Institutions.' *Canadian Bar Review* 27 (9, November 1949): 1041–1051.

The purpose of this article is to describe briefly some of the steps taken in the late 1940s to develop convict rehabilitation programs in Canadian federal penitentiaries that would give effect to the recommendations contained in the 1938 Report of the Royal Commission to Investigate the Penal System in Canada. The author discusses the 'philosophy of the purpose of imprisonment' advanced in the Royal Commission Report, and recent trends in the treatment of federal penitentiary convicts.

946. Gigeroff, A.K.

'The Evolution of Suspended Sentence and Probation Legislation in Canada.' *Chitty's Law Journal* 16 (7, September 1968): 230–235.

947. Girouard-Décarie, Jeanne.

'Une page de notre histoire ... aux Bermudes.' *Québec – Histoire* 2 (1, Autumn 1972): 41–44.

In 1838, by order of Lord Durham, representative of her Majesty the Queen of England in Canada, eight Canadians, charged with treason, were deported to Bermuda. The case received wide coverage in the papers of the island. Objections to Lord Durham's decision centred around the fact that the accused were not convicted and that the island was not a penal colony. After four long days of negotiations between the governor and his privy council, the eight Canadians were allowed to disembark after having given their word of honour not to go beyond certain boundaries. The governor put them up in a small cottage (which continued to be called 'the exiles' cottage'). Durham was forced to resign, the deportation order was rescinded by the British parliament, and the exiled were free to leave the island.

948. Goldring, Philip.

The Manitoba Penitentiary and Asylum. Manuscript Report Series, no. 28. Ottawa: Parks Canada, 1970.

949. Gosselin, Luc.

Prisons in Canada. Montreal: Black Rose Books, 1982.

Originally written in response to a strike by prisoners at the Archambault Penitentiary in 1977, Goselin's book offers a stinging indictment of the penitentiary system in Canada. The book is divided into three parts. In part one, entitled 'The Great Contradiction,' Gosselin draws on the reports of major commissions of inquiry into the penitentiary system in Canada, and recent criminological literature on the effects of and prisoners' reactions to incarceration, to document 'the gap between authorities' justifications for penitentiaries and their observed effects.' The second part of the book, entitled 'The Historical Link,' sketches the birth and evolution of the penitentiary system throughout the world and in Canada, with particular attention being given to documenting the inhumane conditions and treatment prison inmates have been forced to endure throughout the history of the penitentiary in Canada. Part three of the book, 'The Political Role of the Penitentiary,' provides a Marxist analysis of the political functions served by the penitentiary in capitalist societies such the United States and Canada. It is the author's general contention that the penitentiary evolved as a key element in the 'web of coercion' used by the state to establish and 'maintain physical and psychological control, and/or the threat of such control, over millions of Canadian workers.'

950. Gouett, Paul M.

'The Halifax Orphan House, 1752–87.' *Nova Scotia Historical Quarterly* 6 (3, September 1976): 281–291.

951. Grant, M.H.L.

'Historical Sketches of Hospitals and Almshouses in Halifax, 1749 to 1859.' *Nova Scotia Medical Bulletin* 27 (4, April 1938): 229–238; 27 (5, May 1938): 294–304; 27 (8, August 1938): 491–512.

In this series of three articles, the author chronicles the development of hospitals and almshouses in Halifax in the eighteenth and nineteenth centuries. The circumstances leading to the establishment of various institutions for the care of the sick and poor, along with the conditions that existed in these institutions, are discussed. The articles also contain information on early medical and poor-relief practices that were followed in Nova Scotia.

952. Greenhous, Brereton.

'Paupers and Poorhouses: The Development of Poor Relief in Early New Brunswick.' *Histoire sociale/Social History* 1 (April 1968): 103–126.

New Brunswick was the last British colony in North America to attempt a system of poor relief copied from that of the mother country. The pattern of New Brunswick's poor relief was established at the first session of the province's first legislature in 1786, with the passage of 'An Act for preventing Idleness and Disorders and for punishing Rogues, Vagabonds and other Idle and Disorderly Persons,' which was very similar in its essential aspects to the Elizabethan Poor Law statute. This article, which is based primarily on newspaper reports and the journals of the provincial legislature, examines the problems faced by authorities in attempting to adapt the English poor-law system to the conditions of the colony. Among the major problems confronted were the widespread lack of prisons and workhouses in the early decades of the province's existence, and the reluctance or inability of people to pay the taxes that were levied for the purpose of maintaining the system. Faced with having to deal with increasing numbers of pauper-emigrants after 1812, several private charitable organizations were established to provide relief to the poor, and the government began to assume responsibility for establishing poorhouses, in which people seeking relief would be compelled to live and work.

953. Greenland, Cyril.

'Services for the Mentally Retarded in Ontario, 1870–1930.' *Ontario History* 54 (1962): 267–274.

The aim of this paper is to trace the history of services for the retarded in Ontario and describe their vicissitudes over a period of 60 years. The author notes that until the 1870s it was believed that nothing could be done to help individuals suffering from 'mental deficiency' or 'idiocy' except to confine them in institutions. He then goes on to chronicle the progressive steps taken by mental-health reformers to establish separate facilities and services for the mentally retarded in the province. These steps included the opening of a training school for 'feeble-minded' children at Orillia in 1888, the establishment of special classes for retarded pupils by the Toronto School Board in 1910, and the ongoing work of committees and organizations concerned with improving services for the mentally retarded.

954. Greenland, Cyril.

'The Compleat Psychiatrist: Dr. R.M. Bucke's Twenty-five Years as Medical Superintendent, Asylum for the Insane, London, Ontario, 1877–1902.' *Canadian Psychiatric Association Journal* 17 (1, February 1972):71–77.

955. Greenwood, F. Murray, ed.

Land of a Thousand Sorrows: The Australian Prison Journal, 1840–1842, of the Exiled Canadien Patriote, François Maurice Lepailleur. Vancouver: University of British Columbia Press, 1980.

In 1839, François Maurice Lepailleur was sentenced to death for participating in the 1838 rebellion in Lower Canada. After spending nearly a year in a Montreal jail, his sentence was commuted to transportation to New South Wales. During the two years he spent in Australia, Lepailleur kept a daily journal giving his account of life in a prison settlement and the personal hardships he endured. Greenwood provides an English translation of Lepailleur's journal, along with an introduction outlining the events in Lower Canada that led to his exile. The editor points out that Lepailleur's journal is 'the only comprehensive account written day to day of life in a prison settlement left by a convict,' and, as such, is an important historical document.

956. Griffin, John D.

'Planning Psychiatric Service – Historical Perspective.' *Medical Services Journal – Canada* 23 (10, November 1967): 1245–1260.

The author, then general director of the Canadian Mental Health Association, endeavours to place in historical perspective the story of the involvement of local groups of professional and lay people in planning community and regional psychiatric services in Canada. The planning and development of psychiatric services for the care and treatment of the mentally ill in selected Canadian provinces from the 1830s to the 1960s are discussed, and recommendations concerning the direction that future developments should take are offered. The author maintains that whereas in the early nineteenth century the public tended to identify 'lunatics' with the criminal and the poor, and to press for 'some sort of custodial care to protect the community,' over the years 'this public attitude of fear, avoidance and hostility changed to one of sympathy, intelligent interest and dedicated determination to plan ... sensible services within the community.'

957. Griffin, John D., and Greenland, Cyril.

'The Asylum at Lower Fort Garry.' *The Beaver* (Summer, 1980) 18–23.

The confinement of lunatics in penitentiaries was a serious problem in nineteenth-century Canada. The establishment of a temporary asylum at Lower Fort Garry in 1885 was a desperate measure taken by authorities to contain the problem until a provincial asylum was built in 1886. In this article, the authors describe the conditions that prevailed in institutions in which insane persons were held in Manitoba prior to the construction of a provincial asylum. From 1871 to 1876 insane persons were held in a former warehouse that had been converted for use as the Lower Fort Garry penitentiary and from 1877 to 1885 in the Stony Mountain Penitentiary, where they were forced to endure the same conditions as convicted criminals. According to the authors, however, after the establishment of the temporary asylum at Lower Fort Garry in 1885, the quality of treatment received by the unfortunate insane improved significantly.

958. Guérin, T.

The Gaol in New France. Montreal, 1916.

959. Hackett, Gerald Thomas.

'The History of Public Education for Mentally Retarded Children in the Province of Ontario, 1867–1964.' Ph.D. dissertation, University of Toronto, 1969.

Although concerned mainly with the history of public education for the mentally retarded in Ontario, this study also provides an overview of the manner in which the mentally retarded (who were considered to be insane) were treated in custodial institutions during the nineteenth century. Particular note is made of the nineteenth-century practice of confining the mentally retarded and the insane, along with criminals and the indigent, in local jails. According to the institutional documents and reports examined by the author, this practice persisted even after the establishment of the Orillia hospital for the mentally retarded in 1876, because of overcrowding in the institution. Nevertheless, even at this early stage in the modern care of the mentally retarded, attempts were being made to provide them with a rudimentary education.

960. Happy, Barbara M.

'A Study of the History and Philosophy of Penal Reform in Canadian Federal Penitentiaries.' M.S.W. research report, McGill University, 1962.

Written from a progressive viewpoint, this research report surveys historic and philosophical changes that have affected the treatment of prisoners in Canadian federal penitentiaries. Focusing mainly on the period from 1920 to 1960, the author maintains that prior to the late 1930s federal penitentiary inmates were subjected to 'barbaric treatment,' and that Canadians failed to keep pace with progressive changes in penal philosophy that were occurring in Britain. However, as a consequence of the efforts of Canadian prison reformers such as Agnes Macphail, and the publication of the Archambault Report of 1938, a drastic shift in the philosophy underlying the treatment of prisoners occurred. Upon outlining the recommendations contained in the Archambault Report, the author goes on to describe the new classification procedures and treatment techniques employed in federal penitentiaries during the 1940s and 1950s, concluding that this period witnessed the beginning of a more humane approach to dealing with the criminal offender.

961. Hart, George E.

'The Halifax Poor Man's Friend Society, 1820–1827: An Early Social Experiment.' *Canadian Historical Review* 34 (2, 1953): 109–123.

962. Harvey, Janice.

'Upper Class Reaction to Poverty in Mid-Nineteenth Century Montreal: A Protestant Example.' M.A. thesis, McGill University, 1978.

In 1850 Montreal was entering a period of extensive industrialization and urbanization. Faced with the resulting problems of a growing population, seasonal unemployment, and increased poverty, the upper class was forced to fill the vacuum created by the lack of state relief programs by creating private charities to relieve destitution. This thesis is a study of the five main Protestant charities which existed in Montreal in the period 1850–67 and the upper-class attitudes represented by their form of organization. From her examination of archival materials relating to five charities, the author contends that the wealthy saw poverty as a result of immorality, not underemployment, and oriented charity towards moral reform. The main themes running through the thesis are: the Victorian emphasis on morality and work, the question of institutional versus outdoor poor relief, and the extension of relief to the able-bodied unemployed.

963. Hedwige, S.G.C.

'The Evolution of Institutional Services for Dependent Children.' Ottawa: University of Ottawa, 1962.

964. Hooper, Tom.

'The St. John's Gibbet.' In *Miscellaneous Historical Reports on the Sites in the Atlantic Provinces,* pp. 155–167. Manuscript Report, Series no. 107. Ottawa: Parks Canada, 1968.

965. Hurd, H.M., ed.

The Institutional Care of the Insane in the United States and Canada, 4 vols. Baltimore, Md.: Arno Press, 1917.

Although this survey of the development of institutional care for the insane deals mainly with developments that occurred in the United States during the nineteenth century, one volume is partly devoted to reviewing the progress made in Canada. The section on the institutional care of the insane in Canada draws extensively on the 1898 work of T.J.W. Burgess (see entry 892 above).

966. Jackson, Michael.

Prisoners of Isolation: Solitary Confinement in Canada. Toronto: University of Toronto Press, 1983.

This book has as its focus the practice of solitary confinement in Canada's maximum-security penitentiaries. Although concerned primarily with relating the facts and legal issues surrounding the challenge to solitary confinement in the case of *McCann* vs *Her Majesty The Queen and Dragan Cernetic* (1975), the book devotes an initial chapter to examining the evolution of penitentiary discipline and the origin of the use of solitary confinement in nineteenth-century Canada. Here the author draws on published and unpublished secondary sources, legislative journals (of Upper Canada), and annual penitentiary and royal commission reports to describe the penitentiary regime that emerged in nineteenth-century Canada and the use made of solitary confinement as a method of punishment for incorrigible inmates. In developing his subsequent analysis of issues surrounding the contemporary use of solitary confinement, the author notes the striking similarities in the practice of solitary confinement in the nineteenth and twentieth centuries.

967. Jaffary, Stuart K.

Sentencing of Adults in Canada. Toronto: University of Toronto Press, 1963.

An effort is made in this book to examine the structure of criminal justice in Canada, its background, aims, and practice, with emphasis on the sentencing process. Towards this end, the author analyses the role of magistrates in the sentencing process, the English and American experience with penal reform, and the need for changes in Canadian sentencing practices along the lines of those already implemented in other countries. Historical and contemporary quantitative data are used to support the argument that the courts must play a substantial part in implementing much-needed penal and sentencing reforms in the various Canadian provinces.

968. James, J.T.L.

'Gaols and Their Goals in Manitoba, 1870–1970.' *Canadian Journal of Criminology* 20 (January 1978): 34–42.

There have been few attempts to analyse the history of Canadian penology to see how the past has – or could have – influenced the present. This article attempts to overcome this lack of historical perspective by examining the treatment afforded offenders in the Red River colony in the years following the establishment of the Province of Manitoba in 1870. Particular attention is given to noting the progressive penal philosophy and practices advanced by Samual Lawrence Bedson, the first warden of the Lower Fort Garry penitentiary and the provincial inspector of prisons and asylums. The author concludes that had the goals of successive provincial and federal gaolers in Manitoba built on the ideas advanced by the 'province's pioneer penologist' the history of Manitoba corrections over the last century would have been considerably different.

969.   Jobson, Keith Berton.

'Sentencing in Canada: Historical Aspects, 1892–1965.' LL.M. thesis, Columbia University, 1966.

In this thesis, an attempt is made to set in historical perspective the sentencing laws established by the Canadian *Criminal Code* of 1892 and related statutes. Towards this end, the thesis deals with the history of Canadian sentencing laws before 1892, the origin of and philosophy reflected in the 1892 *Criminal Code*, the use of imprisonment as a sentencing option, release procedures (remission, ticket of leave, provincial pardon, and extra-mural employment), the sentence of preventive detention for habitual criminals and sexual psychopaths, and alternatives to imprisonment (suspended sentences, probation, fines, and corporal punishment). The author concludes that because of the slow pace of sentencing reform in Canada, changes in Canadian sentencing law have not kept pace with the changing needs of society and the growing recognition of the success of alternatives to the sentence of imprisonment.

970.   Johnson, Cornelia Brusse.

'A History of Mental Health Care in Manitoba: A Local Manifestation of an International Social Movement.' M.A. thesis, University of Manitoba, 1980.

Although the history of the mental hospital has received considerable attention in both the United States and Britain, the historical literature on the development of the asylum in Canada has been fragmentary. This thesis sets out to examine the history of the development of Manitoba's mental-health system, in order to document a portion of the Canadian experience more fully. Substantive chapters examine the beginnings of 'lunacy reform' as an international social movement, the history of mental-health care in Manitoba from 1870 to 1885, the expansion of Manitoba's asylum system after 1885, the search for alternatives to institutional treatment which began in the 1930s, and recent efforts to provide 'community care' for the mentally ill. The author concludes that while in the period 1870–85 'lunatics' were treated in the same manner as 'prisoners,' as the years progressed social policies developed in response to 'changing psychiatric solutions' for dealing with the mentally ill were introduced. Primary sources used include sessional papers and statutes of the Province of Manitoba, newspapers, and papers held in the Brandon Mental Hospital Archives.

971. Johnstone, Walter F., and Henheffer, B.W.

'History of Treatment in Canadian Penitentiaries.' In *Social Problems: A Canadian Profile*, pp. 449–454. Edited by Richard Laskin. Toronto: McGraw-Hill, 1964. Also in *Canadian Welfare* 29 (September 1953): 5–9.

This brief article argues that Canada has developed through four main stages of penal thought: pre-Confederation, 1867–1938, 1938–46, and 1946–53. The authors maintain that during the pre-Confederation era treatment in Canadian penitentiaries was guided by the general principle 'that incarceration meant punishment only, and if an individual could be reformed it was only by repressive and barbaric techniques.' Although the period 1867–1938 witnessed a shift towards more humane treatment, it was not until after the 'quiescent period' from 1938 to 1946 that programs aimed at reforming inmates through individual and humane treatment were introduced. The article concludes by recommending additional reforms directed at creating an effective system of inmate rehabilitation.

972. Jolliffe, Charles Kyle.

'An Examination of Medical Services at the Kingston Penitentiary, 1835–1856.' M.A. thesis, Queen's University, 1983.

This thesis examines the early history of medical services at Kingston Penitentiary. Divided into seven chapters, the thesis deals with: (1) the reasons behind the founding and strict regime of the Kingston Penitentiary, including why health care was regarded by its promoters as a priority in the prison's operation, (2) Dr. James Sampson, the long-time doctor at the penitentiary, and his staff, (3) living conditions in the institution and the general health of the convicts, (4) the care of infirm convicts, (5) cholera and other dangerous epidemics that frequently beset the penitentiary, (6) the treatment of insane convicts to 1851, and (7) the controversy surrounding the confinement of insane convicts and events leading to the opening of the Rockwood asylum for the criminally insane, 1851–65. The thesis is based almost exlusively on primary historical sources, including annual penitentiary reports, official correspondence, and internal penitentiary records. The author concludes that throughout the early history of Kingston Penitentiary, medical treatment was subordinated to the ultimate custodial needs of the institution.

973. Jolliffe, Charles Kyle.

'Penitentiary Medical Services, 1835–1983.' [Paper prepared for Federal Corrections History Project, Solicitor General of Canada.] Ottawa: Solicitor General of Canada, 1984. User Report Series 1984–19.

974. Jones, Andrew.

'Closing Penetanguishene Reformatory: An Attempt to Deinstitutionalize Treatment of Juvenile Offenders in Early Twentieth Century Ontario.' *Ontario History* 70 (4, December 1978): 227–244.

From 1882 to 1903 the Ontario Reformatory for Boys at Penetanguishene was an institution in a state of decline. There was considerable pressure to close the reformatory based on the recognized unsuitability of the reformatory's location and buildings, and the growing movement towards placing juvenile offenders in industrial schools and foster homes. Relying mainly on archival materials and provincial legislative papers, this article examines the origins and early years of the institution, the pressures that led to its closing, and the efforts of various groups of child-welfare reformers to reform, create alternatives to, or abolish institutions for juvenile offenders altogether. Although the closure of the Penetanguishene Reformatory in 1904 represented the high point of efforts to deinstitution- alize the treatment of juvenile offenders, the apparent victory of the advocates of deinstitutionalization was short-lived. The continuing belief that institutions could reform delinquent boys is evidenced in the revival of the reformatory system in Ontario after the First World War.

975. Julien, Ghislaine.

'Equisse historique de l'univers carcéral à Montréal.' M.A. thesis, Université de Montréal, 1976.

This thesis attempts to relate the transformations within the penal institutions of the Montreal region to the changing penal philosophy through the nineteenth century until 1913. Drawing on government documents and secondary sources, the thesis provides a comprehensive reconstitution of the context and concepts (punishment; penal reform; role, architecture, and daily reality of common jails) of the prison universe. The author concludes: (1) that political indifference accounts for the delays in considering prison problems, (2) that transformations implemented have to adapt to the prison setting and their program rather than the opposite, and (3) that the lack of knowledge and training of the administrative authorities and personnel of the jails is evident.

976. Kellough, Darlene Gail.

'Incarceration as a Response to Political and Economic Conditions.' M.A. thesis, University of Manitoba, 1977.

Traditional criminological theories regard capture and punishment as a more or less direct response to criminality. Conflict theories of social control suggest that political and economic conditions rather than crime per se are principal factors influencing state control efforts. Using jail records as the basis for investigation, this study looks at variations in patterns of incarceration in the Eastern Judicial District of Manitoba during the period 1918–39. Data give some qualified support to the proposition that the law is a tool in the hands of ruling élites used to pursue repressive ends in times when the social order may appear to be in greatest jeopardy.

977. Kellough, Darlene Gail; Greenaway, William K.; and Brickey, Stephen L.
'The Politics of Incarceration: Manitoba, 1919–1939.' *Canadian Journal of Sociology* 5 (3, Summer 1980): 253–271.

This article provides a summary of the theoretical perspective, historical data, research design, and findings and conclusions underlying the first author's more detailed work on the political and economic conditions affecting incarceration rates in the Eastern Judicial District of Manitoba during the period 1919–39.

978. Kenny, Wilma Loreen Gossage.
'The Impact of Social Change on the Organization of Welfare Services in Ontario, 1891–1921; Adult Correctional Institutions in Ontario, 1891–1921.' M.S.W. thesis, University of Toronto, 1966.

979. Kidman, John.
The Canadian Prison: The Story of a Tragedy. Toronto: Ryerson Press, 1947.

Written by a leading Canadian prison reformer, this book outlines the history of penal-reform efforts undertaken in Canada from the 1870s to the 1940s. Specific topics dealt with include the early history of the prisoners' aid associations in major Canadian cities, reform efforts undertaken with respect to the introduction of adult probation and parole systems, the abolition of capital punishment, the provision of after-care services for discharged prisoners, and the growing acceptance of the view that the aim of imprisonment is to 'correct and rehabilitate' the inmate. Despite the humanitarian efforts of reformers, the author maintains that several obstacles, including the secrecy surrounding the operation of Dominion penitentiaries, the failure of officials to deal with prisoners' grievances, and the failure of federal and provincial governments to act on the recommendations of various royal commissions, have tended to hinder the progress of penal reform.

980. Kirkpatrick, A.M.
'The Birth of Prison Reform.' *Canadian Welfare* 33 (May 1959): 3–11.

981. Kirkpatrick, A.M.
'Jails in Historical Perspective.' *Canadian Journal of Corrections* 6 (October 1964): 405–418.

The jail was the earliest form of prison. To its original purpose of temporary restraint the function of punishment was added in England as a result of the changing sentencing practices of the eighteenth and nineteenth centuries. This article examines the emergence of the jail as a custodial institution. Particular reference is made throughout to the historical development and contemporary problems of municipal and provincial jails in Ontario. Lengthy extracts from various primary sources, including the correspondence of early Upper Canadian colonial officials and sheriffs, and the report of the commission appointed to study the prisons and reformatories in Ontario in 1891, are included in the text. Considered from a modern standpoint, the author concludes that while 'the jail is the oldest penal institution,' it has been the least changed and affected by contemporary correctional philosophy and practice.

982. Kirkpatrick, A.M.

'Penal Reform and Corrections.' In *Crime and Its Treatment in Canada*, pp. 465–486. Edited by W.T. McGrath. Toronto: Macmillan of Canada, 1965; 2nd ed., Toronto: Maclean-Hunter, 1976, pp. 569–591.

In this chapter, the author surveys the progress in penal reform and corrections from the time of the writings of Howard, Bentham, and other eighteenth-century penal reformers, through to more recent efforts at improving the treatment of criminal offenders in the 1960s and 1970s. Particular attention is given to noting the manner in which progressive changes in penal philosophy, and the growth of social-scientific knowledge pertaining to the treatment of criminal offenders, have influenced the active development of more enlightened correctional policies and programs in Canada.

983. Krasnick, Cheryl L.

'The London, Ontario Asylum for the Insane, 1870–1902.' M.A. thesis, University of Western Ontario, 1981.

This examination of the London, Ontario, Asylum for the Insane (London Psychiatric Hospital) from its opening in 1870 until the end of the nineteenth century is one of the first analytical studies of a Canadian mental institution, particularly from an inmate's perspective. The thesis attempts to describe the types of people who were committed to asylums in the late nineteenth century through an analysis of the patients admitted to the London Asylum between 1870 and 1877. Primary sources consulted include patients' casebooks, court records, and the papers of R.M. Bucke, an early superintendent. The administrations of the first two superintendents, Henry Landor and Richard Maurice Bucke, are compared. Because their position required an authoritative outlook, they experienced difficulties in dealing with their employer, the provincial government, and their own subordinates. Their attempts to apply moral treatment in an institution which, because of serious overcrowding, inevitably became custodial are discussed. Nineteenth-century ideas about insanity are examined, and the extent to which definitions of insanity and prescriptions for treatment reflected the moral norms of the time. Particular attention is given to the treatment of the 'disease' of masturbatory insanity. Other primary sources, such as government documents, sessional papers, were consulted in the preparation of the thesis.

984. Krasnick, Cheryl L.

' "In Charge of the Loons": A Portrait of the London, Ontario, Asylum for the Insane in the Nineteenth Century.' *Ontario History* 74 (3, September 1982): 138–184.

This article is a condensed version of the author's 1981 M.A. thesis (see entry 983 above).

985. Kroll, Robert E.

'Confines, Wards and Dungeons.' *Collections of the Nova Scotia Historical Society* 40: 93–108.

986. Lachance, André.

'L'exécuteur de la haute justice au Canada sous le régime français.' M.A. thesis, Université Laval, 1964.

This thesis forms the basis of the author's 1966 book (see entry 987 below).

987. Lachance, André.

Le bourreau au Canada sous le régime français. Québec: Société historique de Québec, 1966.

This is a study of the executioner in Canada under the French regime. In the introduction the author offers an overview of the judicial administration in New France: the beginnings, the reorganization of 1663, the act of 1670. The first chapter reviews the use of torture in the process of interrogation while the second chapter discusses torture as a means of punishment. Chapter 3 deals with those executioners who were employed to carry out death sentences, many of whom were criminals granted a reprieve in exchange for their services. Use of criminals for this task was mainly a result of the difficulty of finding someone willing to perform the duty of executioner. Chapter 4 deals with those who carried out the death penalty from 1642 to 1759, where they came from, the circumstances in which they were appointed, etc. Chapter 5 discusses the social and material life of the executioners. There are four appendices: the first is a statistical study of crime in Quebec under the French regime; the second contains excerpts from the act of 1670; the third gives the age of the various executioners; and the fourth is a list of the executioners and the period during which they served, starting with 1648 and ending with 1759.

988. Lachance, André.

'Les prisons au Canada sous le régime français.' *Revue d'histoire de l'Amérique française* 19 (1966): 561–565.

In New France, the prison was not used, as it is being used today, to punish criminals. It was a place where accused and convicted persons could be kept secure while awaiting either trial or the execution of their sentence. The security in the prisons left much to be desired. Escapes were common and the conditions were unhealthy. In winter, the situation was even worse because the prisons were not heated. Because of the difficulty of recruiting executioners, some prisoners were pardoned if they agreed to execute death sentences.

989. Lachance, André.

'Le Bureau des Pauvres de Montréal, 1698–1699: Contribution à l'étude de la société montréalaise de la fin du XVIIe siècle.' *Histoire sociale/Social History* 4 (November 1969): 99–112.

Around 1688 poverty and misery became more and more widespread following the Iroquoian attacks and the expeditions organized by the colonial authorities to put an end to those raids. The number of those in need increased and they began to invade the cities of Quebec, Three Rivers, and Montreal. The hospitals, overcrowded with patients, were unable to cope simultaneously with the care of the sick and the assistance for the poor. To alleviate this alarming situation the Supreme Council (Conseil Souverain) established on April 8, 1688, an office for the poor in each of the three cities. This office was modelled after the ones which existed in the principal cities in France in the middle of the sixteenth century.

990. La Grenade-Meunier, Monique.

La prison des plaines d'Abraham. Québec: Ministère des affaires culturelles, Direction générale du patrimoine, 1977.

This pamphlet is based on a three-volume document entitled *La Prison de Québec* (Ministry of Cultural Affairs 33 20–1414 12.96). The pamphlet contains information concerning the proposed prison, its architect Charles Bailliarge, its location, the influence of the Auburn prison in New York on it, a description of its functional and modern architecture, and its closing in 1967. After closing, the prison came to be used as a youth hostel, an artists' village, and finally a museum.

991. Landreville, Pierre.

La prison de Montréal (Bordeaux) 1913–1940. Rapport no. 1: Inventaire des documents. Rapport no. 2: Le mouvement de la population de la prison de Bordeaux 1912–1940. Rapport no. 3: Histoire et évolution des prisons de Montréal. Montréal: Conseil des Arts, 1974.

992. Landreville, Pierre, and Carrière, Pierre.

'Release Measures in Canada.' In Law Reform Commission of Canada. *Studies on Imprisonment*, pp. 79–152. Ottawa: Supply and Services, 1976.

This contribution consists of three separate papers dealing respectively with 'remission,' 'parole,' and 'day parole and temporary absence' programs. In each paper, the authors include a discussion of the historical origins and legislative history of the specific release measure under review. Particular attention is given to examining the history and contemporary use made of the three release measures in Canada.

993. Landreville, Pierre, and Julien, Ghislaine.

'Les origines de la prison de Bordeaux.' *Criminologie* 9 (1–2, 1976): 5–22.

The authors trace the history of the Bordeaux prison in Montreal. The prison was built from 1908 to 1912 after the Pennsylvanian model and received its first 100 inmates on November 18, 1912. The authors begin by examining the penological context in the nineteenth century. This is followed by a review of the situation of the old prison located at Pied-du-Courant. The various steps that led to the construction of the Bordeaux prison are discussed. The views of M.J.A. Vallee, warden of the old prison and one of the planners of the new prison, are summarized, and brief notes are provided on each of the two architects who designed the prison: Marchand and Barassard. The article ends with a review of the state of the Bordeaux prison in 1913.

994. Laurencelle, Ulric-G.

'Le shérif et les malades mentaux qui lui sont confiés.' *La Revue du barreau de la Province de Québec* 20 (2, 1960): 63–71.

The functions, tasks, duties, and responsibilities of the sheriffs in the Province of Quebec are outlined and the respective sections of the sheriff's law are reproduced. Among other duties, sheriffs were in charge of prisons and correctional institutions and were responsible for their good administration and also for the conduct of prison guards in their district. The sheriff was also responsible for the custody of accused persons suffering from (or suspected of suffering from) mental illness. The role of the sheriff *vis-à-vis* these mentally sick clients of the system of criminal justice is outlined.

995. Lavell, Alfred E.

The Convicted Criminal and His Re-Establishment as a Citizen. Toronto: Ryerson Press, 1926.

996. Lavell, Alfred E.

'The Beginnings of Ontario Mental Hospitals.' *Queen's Quarterly* 49 (1942): 59–67.

Prior to 1841, there existed no specialized institution for the care and treatment of the insane in Upper Canada. Rather, such unfortunate individuals were either 'boarded out' at public or private expense, or confined in district jails along with criminals and debtors. This article examines the treatment afforded the insane in Upper Canada during the early decades of the nineteenth century, and the efforts made by 'progressive' reformers to bring about the establishment of a provincial lunatic asylum in the 1830s and 1840s. Reference is made to several primary sources, including the minutes of the Court of Quarter Sessions for the Home District, grand jury presentments, the Duncombe Report of 1836, and official reports of the 'temporary' lunatic asylum, which operated in Toronto from 1841 to 1850.

997. Lavell, Alfred E.

'The Penal and Reformatory Institutions in Upper Canada, Canada West and Ontario, 1792–1932.' Unpublished manuscript. Queen's University Archives, n.d.

998. Lawton, Alma.

'Relief Administration in Saskatoon during the Depression.' *Saskatchewan History* 22 (2, Spring 1969): 41–59.

This article describes the poor-relief efforts undertaken in Saskatoon during the depression of the 1930s. The author notes that the primary responsibility for the provision and administration of relief in the urban municipalities of Saskatchewan lay with the local authority, although during the depression financial help was received from both provincial and federal governments. Different types of unemployment relief administered by the urban municipality – public-works schemes and direct relief – are examined, along with the administrative role played by various city officials.

999. Lefèbvre, Fernand.

'La vie à la prison de Montréal au XIXe siècle.' *Revue de histoire de l'Amérique française* 7 (4, March 1954): 524–537.

Under British rule, prisoners in Montreal seem to have been held in an old residence of the Jesuits which was converted into a prison. The first real prison was constructed in 1808 and then replaced by another in 1836. The first women's prison, at the time called 'asylum of Sainte-Darie,' was opened in Montreal in 1876 and had 85 prisoners. On May 9, 1890, the government handed the women's prison over to the nuns who added to it another wing in 1894. In 1836 a committee was set up to inquire into the penitentiary system in Lower Canada. The author uses various documents to describe the conditions in the Montreal prison during that period. The rules of the prison, consisting of 10 sections, are reproduced.

1000. Lemon, Donald Percy.

'Public Relief Policy in Moncton: The Depression Years, 1929–1939.' M.A. thesis, University of New Brunswick, 1978.

The major question during the 1930s was the provision of aid for the numerous unemployed throughout New Brunswick. This thesis examines the development of relief policy in Moncton during the 1930s. At the beginning of the decade, care of the needy was provided for through the Poor Law dating from 1786. However, the inability of municipal government to handle the problem of unemployment during the depression led to calls for provincial- and federal-government financial assistance. In attempting to trace the development of relief policy, the author outlines the dealings between Moncton and the province and attempts to show how dominion-provincial relief agreements were translated into actual policy at the municipal level. He concludes that rather than solving the problems of the unemployed, Moncton's relief program merely provided for their most urgent necessities.

1001. Levy, J.C.

'The Poor Laws in Early Upper Canada.' In *Law and Society in Canada in Historical Perspective*, pp. 23–44. Edited by D.J. Bercuson and L.A. Knafla. Calgary: University of Calgary, 1979.

In this admittedly speculative essay the author explores various possible reasons for Upper Canada's failure to enact a poor law, modelled on that of England, in 1792. In opposition to the view that practical obstacles, such as the absence of local government and a viable tax base, led Upper Canadians to legislate against adopting an English-style poor law, the author suggests that Upper Canadians rejected a legal solution to poverty because of their faith in voluntarism and the belief that Upper Canada offered ample opportunities to individuals who were sufficiently self-reliant and industrious. In support of this contention, the author examines the analogous case of Upper Canada's rejection of English bankruptcy legislation, the English poor-law experience, prevailing Upper Canadian attitudes towards taxation, and the poor-law experience in other North American jurisdictions.

1002. Lysne, David Edgar.

'Welfare in Alberta, 1905–1936.' M.A. thesis, University of Alberta, 1966.

This study is concerned with examining the response of the government of Alberta to various welfare needs in the period from 1905 to 1936. The author notes that aside from constructing a 'provincial prison' and an 'insane asylum,' in the first years of the province's existence 'there was no conscious design to have the provincial government assume a major role for welfare services.' Rather, it was commonly accepted that voluntary organizations would undertake the bulk of the task of providing relief to the destitute and the disabled, and the provincial government lent considerable encouragement to their efforts. While not concerned with introducing legislation to create a centralized welfare system, the author points out that the government enacted numerous individual statutes to do with the provision of workmen's compensation (1908), the establishment of industrial schools (1908), child protection (1909), the establishment of a juvenile court (1913), and the provision of mothers' allowances (1919). Despite these developments, the author maintains that it was not until the depression of the 1930s that the government took on a major role in providing welfare services.

1003. MacDonald, John A.

'Juvenile Training Schools and Juvenile Justice Policy in B.C.' *Canadian Journal of Criminology* 20 (4, October 1978): 418–436.

In an effort to provide guidance in determining future juvenile justice policy in British Columbia, the author turns to examining the history of juvenile training schools in the province. The major elements of past policies are identified through exploring the legislative history of juvenile training schools, and the background characteristics of the clientele traditionally contained in the province's juvenile correctional institutions. Special emphasis is placed on examining the factors which prompted the provincial government to repeal the *Training Schools Act* in 1969, and the results of ensuing juvenile justice policy in the period 1969 to 1975. The author concludes that between 1969 and 1975 the thrust of juvenile justice policy in British Columbia was towards reducing the institutional confinement of juvenile offenders, and that persons in the corrections field should continue pressing for alternatives to juvenile detention.

1004. McFarlane, G.G.; Coughlan, D.W.F.; and Sumpter, A.H.

The Development of Probation Services in Ontario. Toronto: Ontario Probation Services, 1966.

1005. McIlraith, George J.

'Developments in Federal Corrections in Canada.' *Canadian Journal of Corrections* 12 (4, 1970): 526–533.

This is the published text of a speech given by the solicitor general of Canada. In it he reviews major recent developments in federal corrections, including the establishment of the Department of the Solicitor General, the expansion of the National Parole Board, the construction of new institutions, and the then forthcoming Report of the Canadian Committee on Corrections.

1006. McKenzie, Betty Ann.

'The Impact of Social Change on the Organization of Welfare Services in Ontario, 1891–1921: Care of the Poor in Toronto.' M.S.W. thesis, University of Toronto, 1966.

1007. Martin, Jed.

'Convict Transportation to Newfoundland in 1789.' *Acadiensis* 5 (Autumn 1975): 84–99.

1008. Massicotte, E.-Z.

'La détention préventive à Montréal au XVIIe siècle.' *Bulletin des recherches historiques* 30 (3, March 1924): 106–107.

The author gives a brief account of an incident which occurred in July 1679 in the prison of Montreal where François Quintal was awaiting trial. Wine was consumed and an assault ensued. Quintal, the aggressor, stabbed and injured the victim in the left arm. He was sentenced to a fine and to pay £45 plus legal costs as compensation to the victim.

1009. Massicotte, E.-Z.

'Peines et châtiments sous M. de Maisonneuve.' *Bulletin des recherches historiques* 45 (3, April 1939): 115–116.

The first court in Montreal dates from 1648 and was presided over by M. de Maisonneuve. The court dealt with all cases, criminal and civil. The punishments imposed were fines, confiscation, and banishment from Montreal. There was one single death sentence and since there were no gallows and no executioner the condemned person was sent to Quebec City. There is no record of any prison sentence in the city of Montreal prior to 1663 when Maisonneuve pronounced, for the first time, a sentence of fine and imprisonment. That same year two courts of justice operated in the city: one was the seigneurial court and the other was a royal court (a senechal court) set up by the Supreme Council (Conseil Souverain).

1010. Massicotte, E.-Z.

'Premières prisons des femmes à Montréal.' *Bulletin des recherches historiques* 46 (2, February 1940): 40–43.

Under the French regime, deprivation of liberty with or without labour does not seem to have been one of the penalties used as the administrators had neither the personnel nor the money necessary to house, clothe, and feed the criminals for weeks, months, or years. Yet, there was a desire to punish women differently. A decision was made to set up a place to detain convicted women and certain documents indicate that such a place existed already in 1689. It is not possible to establish the exact location of that prison. It seems to have been closed in 1693. Following its closure a certain number of rooms in the general hospital of the 'Soeurs Grises' seem to have been used for the same purpose.

1011. Matters, Diane L.

'The Development of Public Welfare Institutions in Vancouver, 1900–1920.' B.A. essay, University of Victoria, 1973.

1012. Matters, Diane L.

'Public Welfare Vancouver Style 1910–1920.' *Journal of Canadian Studies* 14 (1, Spring 1979): 3–15.

Greater Vancouver experienced a phenomenal growth rate during the first decades of the twentieth century. As the population soared, the provision of welfare services was one area that experienced the greatest changes. During the period 1910–20, the piecemeal voluntary approach to dealing with the destitute and the poor began to give way to a more comprehensive, government-supported welfare system. Relying mainly on local newspaper reports and provincial government documents, the author examines various welfare developments, including the provision of social assistance to neglected and dependent children, deserted wives and widows with young children, the elderly and the sick, and unemployed women and men. The author notes that one group that did not benefit from the development of welfare services was orphans and abandoned children, who were on occasion taken before the juvenile court for being disobedient and attempting to 'escape' from orphanages.

1013. Matters, Diane L.

'The Boys' Industrial School: Education for Juvenile Offenders.' In *Schooling and Society in Twentieth Century British Columbia*, pp. 53–70. Edited by J. Donald Wilson and David Jones. Calgary: Detselig Enterprises Ltd., 1980.

1014. Maxwell, Lillian M.B.

'A History of Fredericton Gaols.' *Maritime Advocate and Busy East* 34 (1943): 5–8, 29.

1015. Miller, F.P.

'Parole.' In *Crime and Its Treatment in Canada*, 2nd ed., pp. 376–442. Edited by W.T. McGrath. Toronto: Macmillan, 1976.

Although concerned mainly with an examination of the organization and function of Canada's current parole system, this chapter provides an overview of the history of parole in Canada. In it, the author surveys the history of the early release of offenders from Canadian prisons from the enactment of the federal *Ticket of Leave Act* in 1898 through to the mid-1970s. Miller notes several significant developments that occurred after 1898, including the appointment of the first Dominion parole officer (1905), the creation of the remission service within the federal Department of Justice (1913), the development of offender after-care services in the post-Second World War period, the publication of the Fauteux Report recommending the establishment of a national parole board (1956), and the expansion of federal parole services in the 1960s and 1970s. The inception of the National Parole Board in 1959 is viewed as a major turning point in the history of parole in Canada.

1016. Mitchinson, Wendy.

'R.M. Bucke, A Victorian Asylum Superintendent.' *Ontario History* 73 (4, December 1981): 239–254.

Care of the insane was still rudimentary in the last quarter of the nineteenth century in Canada. This paper examines the operation of the London, Ontario, Lunatic Asylum under the superintendence of R.M. Bucke from 1877 to 1902. Drawing on Bucke's correspondence and writings on insanity, along with institutional records and contemporary medical literature, the author notes that throughout his career Bucke tried to raise the status of medical superintendents from that of being the custodians of institutions to being a recognized specialization within the profession of medicine.

1017. Morel, André.

'L'imposition et le côntrole des peines au Bailliage de Montréal (1666–1693).' In *Etudes juridiques en hommage à Monsieur le Juge Bernard Bissonette*, pp. 411–432. Edited by 'Un groupe de professeurs et d'amis.' Montréal: Les presses de l'Université de Montréal, 1963.

1018. Morrison, J.S.

'A Short Summary of the History of Parole Development in Ontario.' Unpublished paper (draft) prepared for the Chairman of the Ontario Board of Parole, 1983.

This draft provides an outline of the development of parole in Ontario. The author notes that although various forms of parole or conditional release from custody were employed in the nineteenth century, Ontario's experience with parole began with the establishment of the Ontario Board of Parole in 1910 and the enactment of the *Ontario Parole Act* in 1917. Brief note is also made of the attention given to parole in the Archambault Report (1938), the Fauteux Report (1956), and the Ouimet Report (1969). No references are included.

1019. Munro, Donald Richard.

'The Care of the Dependent Poor in Ontario, 1891–1921: A Study of the Impact of Social Change on the Organization of Welfare Services in Ontario for the Dependent Poor, Especially the Unemployed, the Aged, and the Mother Raising Children Herself, between 1891–1921.' M.S.W. thesis, University of Toronto, 1966.

1020. Neatby, Blair.

'The Saskatchewan Relief Commission, 1931–1934.' In *Historical Essays on the Prairie Provinces*, pp. 267–288. Edited by D. Swainson. Toronto: McClelland and Stewart, 1970.

1021. Needham, H.G.

'Historical Perspectives on the Federal-Provincial Split in Jurisdiction in Corrections.' *Canadian Journal of Criminology* 22 (3, July 1980): 298–306.

This article examines the origin of a periodic debate surrounding the federal-provincial split in jurisdiction in Canadian corrections. The author traces the origin of the split to legislation enacted in the Province of Canada in 1842, which required that offenders sentenced to terms of imprisonment for two years or more be transferred to a 'penitentiary,' while those sentenced to less than two years be incarcerated in a 'prison.' Although reaffirmed in post-confederation consolidations of the criminal law, the author notes that since the late nineteenth century the appropriateness of the two-year split in jurisdiction has become the object of debate at several federal-provincial conferences and in major commissioned reports on correctional reform. Drawing on the minutes of interprovincial conferences held in 1887, 1902, and 1906, and later reports such as the Archambault Report (1938), the Fauteux Report (1956), the Ouimet Report (1968), and a report of the Law Reform Commission of Canada (1976), the author outlines the various arguments that have been advanced regarding the appropriateness of maintaining the present federal-provincial jurisdictional split in corrections. Based on this examination, he concludes that although there have been periodic disputes over the matter, obstacles to change, the paramount one being the financial costs involved, have contributed to federal and provincial governments' maintaining the split as it was originally constituted.

1022. Nicolas, Michel.

'Un rappel historique de la libération conditionnelle: Deux volets d'une évolution.' *Criminologie* 14 (2, 1981): 73–80.

In this brief article, Nicolas presents a historical account of the parole system in Canada. His main focus is on the evolution of parole. Basing his analysis on secondary sources, the author examines two aspects of the evolution of parole: the criminological nature of parole and the judicial nature of parole. The criminological nature of parole evolved in three steps. First, parole was a reward instrument for inmates showing collaboration. Second, parole became a helping instrument for inmates in need of help, assistance, or surveillance. Finally, parole is now seen as an instrument of transition, the idea behind transition being the necessity of surveying the return of inmates in the community. The author goes on to contrast the criminological nature of parole with its judicial nature being solely a privilege. As a conclusion, Nicolas questions seriously the future of parole.

1023. Noble, Joey.

'Class-ifying the Poor: Toronto Charities, 1850–1880.' *Studies in Political Economy: A Socialist Review* (2, Autumn 1979): 109–128.

1024. Noppen, Luc.

'La prison du Pied-du-Courant à Montréal: Une étape dans l'évolution de l'architecture pénitentiaire au Bas-Canada et au Québec.' *RACAR; Revue d'art canadienne* 3 (1, 1976): 36–50.

The old Montreal prison located at Pied-du-Courant was used from 1836 to 1912 when the Bordeaux prison was opened. Recently the old prison has been declared a protected monument by the Quebec Ministry of Cultural Affairs which recognized the innovative role it played in the field of prison architecture in Lower Canada. The history of the Pied-du-Courant prison is presented with an emphasis on its architectural characteristics. The study is divided into five sections. In the first, the author traces the evolution of prison architecture in Europe and North America. The second is a discussion of the project to construct the prison in the years from 1824 to 1831. The third deals with the actual construction of the prison from 1831 to 1836. Section four is devoted to the modifications that were made to the original construction in 1852. The last section covers the history of the prison from 1852 to 1912.

1025. Norman, William George Christian.

'A Chapter of Canadian Penal History: The Early Years of the Provincial Penitentiary at Kingston, and the Commission of Inquiry into Its Management, 1835–1851.' M.A. thesis, Queen's University, 1979.

This thesis deals with the development and operation of Kingston Penitentiary during the 1830s and 1840s. Particular attention is given to examining the operation of the institution under Warden Henry Smith, and the immediate and long-term repercussions of the Commission of Inquiry of 1848–9. The author's findings indicate that while 'the initiation of a costly penitentiary system reflected significant changes in attitudes toward crime and punishment,' in its early years Kingston Penitentiary 'was plagued by recurring staff quarrels, and problems with funding, discipline and convict reformation.' The study draws on a wide range of government reports, statutes, official and private correspondence, and newspapers.

1026. O'Gallagher, Marianna.

'Care of the Orphan and the Aged by the Irish Community of Quebec City, 1847 and the Years Following.' Canadian Catholic Historical Association. *Study Sessions* 43 (1976): 39–56.

This article describes the work of the Catholic church in caring for Irish immigrants and the poor in Quebec City from 1847 to 1972. Particular attention is given to outlining the history and development of the St. Bridget's Home, which was established in 1856 to provide shelter for destitute children and the elderly poor. Note is made of changes in the manner of operation, location, and clientele of the home that occurred prior to 1972.

1027. O'Gallagher, Marianna.

'The Sisters of Charity of Halifax – The Early and Middle Years.' Canadian Catholic Historical Association. *Study Sessions* 47 (1980): 57–68.

In this article, the author provides an account of the establishment and early work of the Sisters of Charity of Halifax. After being granted permission to operate as an independent congregation in 1849, the Sisters of Charity of Halifax took on several duties, including teaching school, providing for the sick and poor, and caring for orphans. The author traces the substantial growth of and additional responsibilities assumed by the Sisters of Charity during its first 75 years of existence.

1028. Oliver, Peter.

'From Jails to Penitentiary: The Demise of Community Corrections in Early Ontario.' *Correctional Options* 4 (1984): 1–10.

1029. Palmer, Bryan.

'Kingston Mechanics and the Rise of the Penitentiary, 1833–1836.' *Histoire sociale/ Social History* 13 (May 1980): 7–32.

Plans for the establishment of Kingston Penitentiary were not welcomed by all the residents of Kingston. Between 1833 and 1836 local mechanics or skilled workers organized a series of agitations in opposition to the proposed use of convict labour in the penitentiary, on the grounds that the practice of teaching inmates a trade debased craft skills and threatened the economic well-being of skilled workers. This article examines this early example of vehement opposition to the penitentiary. The author reveals that despite the concerted efforts of working-class and politically reform-minded opponents of the penitentiary, they were unable to stop the establishment of a prison system based on convict labour. Possible reasons for the failure of opposition to the use of convict labour in Kingston Penitentiary to persist after 1836 are discussed.

1030. Paradis, André.

'L'émergence de l'asile québécoise au XIXe siècle.' *Santé mentale au Québec* 2 (2, November 1977): 1–44.

1031. Paradis, André.

'L'asile temporaire de Toronto (1841–1850) ou l'impossibilité provisoire de l'utopie asilaire.' *Santé mentale au Québec* 3 (1, June 1978): 18–35.

1032. Parker, Graham E.

'Corporal Punishment in Canada.' *Criminal Law Quarterly* 7 (1964–5): 193–211.

In the 1960s, Canadian courts and penal reformers were concerned with re-assessing the efficacy of corporal punishment. At the time the issue of whether corporal punishment should be retained aroused considerable debate. This article addresses the question: 'How real is the concern for the retention of what is generally thought to be a brutal and senseless punishment, in light of its present application?' In answering this question, the author undertakes a critical examination of *Criminal Code* provisions and reported judicial decisions relating to the imposition of corporal punishment. On the basis of his analysis of the present state of the law, the author concludes that if corporal punishment is to be retained, its utility should be proved conclusively. Otherwise it would be best to repeal or revise substantially the law providing for corporal punishment.

1033. Pentland, Harry C.

Labour and Capital in Canada 1650–1860, edited and with an introduction by Paul Phillips. Toronto: James Lorimer and Co., 1981; originally 'Labour and the Development of Industrial Capitalism in Canada.' Ph.D. dissertation, University of Toronto, 1961.

Although this book is concerned with the broad historical aspects of economic development and social change in Canada, considerable attention is given to examining different forms of labour that existed in the eighteenth and nineteenth centuries. Specific labour practices, including Indian and Negro slavery, the indenturing of servants, and convict labour (in New France and Upper Canada), are discussed. In the course of succeeding chapters on pre-industrial labour relations, population growth and migration, and the transformation of Canada's economic structure, an attempt is made to relate the changing labour practices followed in Canada to changes in economic and social structure.

1034. Pitsula, James Michael.

'The Emergence of Social Work in Toronto.' *Journal of Canadian Studies* 14 (1, Spring 1979): 35–42.

In nineteenth-century Toronto charity was provided largely through various private charitable societies and organizations which, in addition to raising their own funds, received municipal and provincial support. The Toronto House of Industry, founded in 1837, was typical of the types of efforts sponsored by private charitable organizations and operated by unpaid volunteers. This article traces the steps, from the 1880s to the 1920s, by which the provision of charity in Toronto changed from being a concern of private citizens to being a task carried out by professional social workers employed at public expense. The author concludes that the history of the emergence of social work in Toronto supports the interpretation offered by historians, that the late–nineteenth-century urban-reform movement in Canada marked the beginning of the age of professionalism.

1035. Pitsula, James Michael.

'The Relief of Poverty in Toronto, 1880–1930.' Ph.D. dissertation, York University, 1979.

Significant changes overtook the outdoor poor-relief system in Toronto between 1880 and 1930. What had been a hodge-podge of private charities was transformed into a reasonably well co-ordinated system of public and private welfare. This dissertation documents the major changes that affected Toronto's outdoor poor-relief system. In separate chapters, the author considers (1) the provision of outdoor relief in late–nineteenth-century Toronto, (2) prevailing ideas concerning the causes of poverty, (3) the establishment of Toronto's Associated Charities and their battle against pauperism, (4) the attempt to organize charity (1880–1912), (5) the emergence of bureaucratic social-welfare organizations (1912–30), and (6) the emergence of professional social work. The author concludes that although the poor-relief system in 1930 was more coherent than it had been in 1880, the fundamental approach to poverty had not altered. The essential purpose of charity organizations was to repress pauperism, which was attributed, for the most part, to individual shortcomings.

1036. Pollock, Sheila Joy Godfrey.

'Social Policy for Mental Health in Ontario, 1930–1967.' D.S.W. dissertation, University of Toronto, 1974.

Although this dissertation is primarily concerned with mental-health policy in Ontario after 1930, initial chapters deal with attitudes towards the mentally ill and the development of provincial mental institutions in the nineteenth century.

1037. Pratten, J.S.

'Early History of the Rockwood Hospital.' *Historic Kingston* 17 (1968): 50–68.

In 1856, plans were undertaken for the construction of a criminal lunatic asylum near Kingston, intended for the purpose of receiving insane inmates from the provincial penitentiary and persons who were certified as being too 'dangerous' to be at large. Until 1877, the Rockwood Criminal Lunatic Asylum remained under the jurisdiction of the federal government, at which time it was purchased by the Ontario government to serve as a provincial insane asylum for the eastern part of the province. This article traces the history of the Rockwood asylum from the time of its establishment until the 1890s. The author notes that although the asylum was originally intended to be for insane inmates and dangerous lunatics, soon after it opened it began to receive insane persons whose relatives and friends preferred having them committed to the institution under the pretext of their being 'dangerous,' to incurring the expense of having them transferred to the provincial lunatic asylum in Toronto. Although the article contains no references to primary materials, lengthy extracts from the diary of one of the institution's medical superintendents are included.

1038. Price, Gifford.

'A History of the Toronto Hospital for the Insane.' M.S.W. thesis, University of Toronto, 1950.

Price's historical sketch of the Toronto Hospital for the Insane (also known as the Toronto Lunatic Asylum) attempts to show the 'gradual evolution' of the institution from being a place of custodial care to being a place of medical care and treatment. Conditions that prevailed in the institution during the nineteenth century, along with advances made in the treatment of the insane during the period, are discussed.

1039. Prince, Ellen.

'A History of the John Howard Society of Quebec, 1892–1955.' M.S.W. thesis, McGill University, 1956.

This thesis traces the growth of the John Howard Society of Quebec from its inception as a voluntary Anglican prisoners' aid association in 1892 to its position as a professional case-work agency and member of the Welfare Federation of Montreal in 1955. The history of the society is divided into three main periods, which correspond to changes in its name: (1) the Prisoners' Aid Association of Montreal, 1892–1931; (2) the Prisoners' Aid and Welfare Association of Montreal Incorporated, 1931–47; and (3) the John Howard Society of Quebec Incorporated, 1947–55. The author's account is based mainly on an examination of the minutes and records kept by the society throughout its history.

1040. Quiblier, J.

'L'ancienne prison de Montréal.' *Bulletin des recherches historiques* 26 (10, October 1920): 310.

This brief historical note indicates that the first mass was offered in the new prison of Montreal, situated in the convent of St. Mary, on February 23, 1840.

1041. Quinsey, Vernon L.

'The Ontario Reformatory at Penetanguishene: 1882.' *Canada's Mental Health* 30 (4, December 1982): 14–15.

The present administration building of the Mental Health Centre in Penetanguishene, Ont., was once a boy's reformatory. The author, who is now the director of research at the centre, notes that a number of documents from the old reformatory have survived and are of considerable historical interest. The bulk of his two-page article consists of extracts from the 1882 Annual Report Upon Common Gaols, Prisons and Reformatories for Ontario, which illustrate how similar the reformatory's situation was to that of contemporary institutions.

1042. Racine, Denis.

'Quelques évasions de la prison de Québec en 1786.' *L'ancêtre* 2 (7, March 1976): 349.

1043. Rains, Prue.

'Juvenile Justice and the Boys' Farm: Surviving a Court Created Population Crisis, 1909–1948.' *Social Problems* 31 (5, June 1984): 500–513.

Reform schools for juvenile delinquents have shown remarkable resilience and adaptability in the face of changing public policy about how children who break the law should be treated. This paper is a case study of one Canadian reform school which has survived four serious population crises since 1909: the Boys' Farm and Training School in Shawbridge, Quebec. The author focuses on examining the first population crisis, from 1921 to 1930, showing how it arose and the strategies adopted by the board of directors at the Boys' Farm to deal with it. Other strategies which the board used subsequently to deal with the ongoing problem of dwindling population at the reform school are then considered. The author concludes by discussing the implications of the study for the ongoing debate over juvenile justice policy.

1044. Rappak, Mary.

['History of Alberta Corrections.'] A Series of articles in *Focus* [a quarterly journal of news and events for the Alberta Correctional Service] 2 (February 1982): 8–9; 2 (June 1982): 14; 2 (October 1982): 14; 2 (December 1982): 14; 3 (April 1983): 14; 3 (July 1983): 14; 3 (October 1983): 14; 3 (December 1983: 14; 4 (April 1984): 14; 4 (July 1984): 12–13.

These articles are exerpts from a 'History of Alberta Corrections' currently being written by the author. Articles include (in order of publication): 'A Tale of Two Jails,' a background piece on the Lethbridge and Fort Saskatchewan gaols; 'The Prosperous Twenties,' including some information on the use of inmates as farm labourers; 'The Thirties – Depression Years,' documenting the effect of the depression on incarceration in the province; 'The 1940s – A Time of Re-evaluation,' in which the effects of the federal Archambault Report, the Second World War, changes in government administration of corrections, and custodial care for young offenders all brought about re-evaluation of correctional services; 'Bowden Institution – Expansion during the 1950's'; 'The Belmont Rehabilitation Centre – Continued Expansion during the 1950's,' describing a centre for professional care and assistance to alcoholic offenders; 'The 1960's – Treatment for the Offender,' documenting the increasing use of probation; 'History of Alberta Corrections – Facility Expansion during the 1960's'; 'History of Alberta Corrections'; and the final instalment 'The History of Corrections: Alberta during the 1970's.'

1045. Reid, Allana G.

'The First Poor Relief System in Canada.' *Canadian Historical Review* 27 (4, December 1946): 424–431.

Even in the days of Champlain there were 'unworthy souls who lay about the Quebec fort in a drunken daze until they were shipped back to France by the disgusted governor.' As the population of the colony of New France grew and the iron hand of Champlain was removed, there developed the problem of the poor of Quebec. This article traces the origin and early development of Canada's first poor-relief system, established in the town of Quebec in the seventeenth century. According to the author, although the 'evils of beggary and destitution' first became the subject of public attention in the 1670s, it was not until 1688 that a committee, named the 'Bureau de Pauvres,' was established to look after poor-relief in the town. The committee continued in its poor-relief efforts, which included the establishment of a temporary almshouse, until 1701, at which time an order of nuns at the General Hospital of Quebec took over the task of caring for the poor. The author concludes by commenting on the historical significance of the 'Bureau de Pauvres,' noting that because it was the first poor-relief system of any kind in Canada, it is worthy of a place in the social history of the country.

1046. Rice, William.

'The History and Development of Child Reformatories in Ontario.' Unpublished paper, Osgoode Hall Law School, York University, 1970.

The aim of this paper is to outline the early development of reformatory construction and legislation in Britain and the United States, and to demonstrate how Ontario reformatories and their managers carried on from the English and American leads. The paper describes the manner in which children were confined along with criminals and the insane in early Upper Canadian penal institutions, and attempts to show how and why separate institutions for children were established. Attention is given to tracing the growth of various Ontario reformatories, industrial schools, and refuges; the quest for efficient treatment; and the development of pertinent legislation from 1857 to 1970.

1047. Riddell, William Renwick.

'The First Legal Execution for Crime in Canada.' Ontario Historical Society. *Papers and Records* 27 (1931): 514–516.

1048. Robert, Jacques.

'L'architecture des prisons du Québec (1900–1950).' Travail presénté dans le cadre d'un seminaire sur: L'architecture des prisons du Québec (1600–1940). Québec: Université Laval, Ecole des Gradués, 1978.

This paper attempts to place the architectural design of Quebec jails between 1900 and 1950 in its historical, theoretical, and international contexts. Referring to the well-known Auburnian and Pennsylvanian penitentiary designs in the study of the blueprints of the province's jails and relying on secondary sources, the author examines: (1) the Pennsylvanian influence on the design of the Montreal common jail, (2) the use of the Auburnian model in the construction of the province's jails prior to the twentieth century, and (3) the influence of the early–twentieth-century American prison architect A. Hopkins on the mostly Pennsylvanian design of the 1900–50 Quebec jails. The author concludes that if differences between institutions may be accounted for by the discretionary powers of district sheriffs, the architecture of the Montreal common jail demonstrates the international shift in prison design.

1049. Roy, Huguette-Lapointe.

'Paupérisme et assistance sociale à Montréal, 1832–1865.' M.A. thesis, McGill University, 1972.

1050. Roy, Pierre-Georges.

'Les bourreaux de Québec sous le régime français.' *Bulletin des recherches historiques* 29 (1, January 1923): 3–12.

Hanging was quite frequent under the French regime. Until 1658 there were no regular executioners but only ones who were picked for the occasion. The first death sentence in Montreal was given in 1648. The convicted person, whose name is unknown, had his sentence commuted and agreed to serve as an executioner. An official executioner seems to have been operating in 1665 as the records show that in that year the Supreme Council (Conseil Souverain) had decided to provide the executioner with a house. The house was located at Cap Rouge on the main road leading to Quebec. The author provides the names, periods of operation of, as well as brief biographical notes on, the executioners in New France. They were recruited mostly from among criminals and agreed to serve in exchange for being pardoned or having the charges against them dropped. They were ridiculed and mistreated by the general public and several of them suffered a violent death. The difficulty in recruiting executioners led to the importation in 1731 of a black man named Malgein from Martinique to perform this function. He died in 1743.

1051. Roy, Pierre-Georges.

'Une exécution capitale dans le Porte de Québec en 1663.' *Bulletin des recherches historiques* 29 (5, May 1923): 137–140.

This brief article is the story of a capital execution carried out in 1663 on a raft erected in the St. Lawrence River within viewing distance from the city of Quebec. The execution took place on the order of a certain Captain Gargot, a ship commander who refused to surrender those accused of two murders to the authorities, choosing rather to subject them to maritime justice. One of the accused performed the duties of the executioner. No mention of the trial was found in the records of the Supreme Council (Conseil Souverain) but the story is told in a brochure entitled 'Mémoire de la vie et des aventures de Nicolas Gargot ...'

1052. Saunders, Catherine Estelle.

'Social Conditions and Legislation in Nova Scotia (1815–1851).' M.A. thesis, Dalhousie University, 1949.

Although concerned generally with the social conditions and social legislation that affected Nova Scotians in the first half of the nineteenth century, this thesis devotes particular attention to detailing the manner in which specific social problems were dealt with in the colony. According to the author, three of the most pressing social concerns that attracted the attention of colonial citizens were physical and mental illness, poverty, and crime. In separate chapters on public health, poor relief, and penal institutions, the author documents the legislative provisions enacted and practical steps taken towards the establishment and improvement of purpose-built hospitals, insane asylums, poorhouses, orphan asylums, a provincial penitentiary, and county jails. She notes that although a provincial penitentiary or 'Bridewell' was opened in 1844, it was not until the late 1850s that a general hospital and insane asylum were established. Until these facilities were completed, the established poorhouse continued to serve as a multipurpose institution. The thesis is based mainly on primary sources, the two most referred to being the Statutes of Nova Scotia and the Journals of the House of Assembly of Nova Scotia for the period 1815–1951.

1053. Sauvant, G.L.

'Historical Sketch on Canadian Penitentiaries.' *CPS [Canadian Penitentiary Service] Bulletin* 1 (3): 2–8.

1054. Sheridan, A.K.B., and Konrad, J.

'Probation.' In *Crime and Its Treatment in Canada*, 2nd ed., pp. 249–302. Edited by W.T. McGrath. Toronto: Macmillan, 1976.

Although concerned mainly with an examination of the use of probation as a sentence disposition and the nature of probation work as a specialized field within contemporary Canadian corrections, this chapter touches on the history of probation in Canada. The authors trace 'the statutory birth of probation in Canada' to the passage of *An Act for the More Speedy Trial and Punishment of Juvenile Offenders* in 1857. This act, which allowed for the dismissal of charges against children with or without sureties, was followed 32 years later by an *Act to Permit the Conditional Release of First Offenders in Certain Cases* (1889), which specified that in certain cases the sentences of first-time offenders could be suspended 'on probation for good conduct.' Despite these statutes, it was not until 1921, after amendments to the *Criminal Code* were made, that release on probation required that the offender report to an officer designated by the court. From this beginning, the development of probation services was gradually taken up by the provinces. Dates of the enactment of provincial probation acts are noted, and the 'phenomenal growth' in probation services during the 1960s is exemplified in the case of British Columbia. Data sources referred to by the authors include published secondary literature and major royal commission reports on correctional reform.

1055. Shoom, Sidney.

'Kingston Penitentiary ... The Early Decades.' *Canadian Journal of Corrections* 8 (3, 1966): 215–220.

This article provides a descriptive account of the punishments meted out to prisoners in Kingston Penitentiary from 1835 to 1848. On the basis of evidence contained in the institution's Punishment Book, annual reports, and the reports of the Brown Commission (1849), the author documents several cases in which juvenile offenders confined in the penitentiary were subjected to corporal punishment. The author concludes that 'the early years of the penitentiary saw little evidence of humane treatment of prisoners,' and that only after the Brown Commission presented its findings did 'the first and perhaps most degrading chapter in the history of Canadian penal institutions' come to an end.

1056. Shoom, Sidney.

'The Upper Canada Reformatory, Penetanguishene: The Dawn of Prison Reform in Canada.' *Canadian Journal of Corrections* 14 (1972): 260–267.

During the early years of the operation of the provincial penitentiary at Kingston, juvenile offenders were incarcerated along with adult criminals in the general prison population. In the second of its reports, the Brown Commission of 1849 recommended the establishment of separate institutional facilities for young prisoners. This article examines the various steps leading to the establishment of the Upper Canada Reformatory in Penetanguishene, Ont., in 1859, and describes the rehabilitative programs applied during the first years of its operation. The author concludes that the administration of the reformatory appears to have been popular with the inmates, whose activities included attending school, learning trades, and participating in military drills.

1057. Simard, Michel.

Répertoire des documents parlementaires québécois relatifs à la justice pénale 1867–1900. Montréal: Université de Montréal, Centre international de criminologie comparée, 1981. (Les cahiers de l'Ecole de Criminologie, no. 6)

Aimed at filling a gap, this study was undertaken to facilitate the consultation of provincial parliamentary documents concerning criminal justice in Quebec from 1867 to 1900. Divided under four headings (police; judicial; correctional; miscellaneous), this repertory indexes Quebec's statutes and the debates and journals of the legislative assembly related to the criminal justice system and includes a thematic index of places and proper names. The author hopes this paper will be useful to researchers and that it will stimulate historical studies of the criminal justice system.

1058. Simmons, Harvey G.

From Asylum to Welfare: The Evolution of Mental Retardation Policy in Ontario from 1831–1980. Downsview, Ont.: National Institute on Mental Retardation, 1982.

Drawing on extensive archival research, Simmons analyses the development of social policy with respect to mental retardation in Ontario from the early nineteenth century to 1980. Divided into three major parts, the book deals with: the institutional treatment of mentally retarded persons and the evolution of mental-retardation policy from 1831 to 1900; the influence of the English eugenics movement and the 'myth of the menace of the feeble-minded' on mental-retardation policy in Ontario between 1900 and 1945; and the impact that parents of the mentally retarded and the advocates of deinstitutionalization had on policy changes that occurred between 1945 and 1980. The author maintains that although during each of these periods particular and unique combinations of influences impinged on policy, since 1831 it has tried to achieve four overall objectives: to provide asylum for mentally retarded people; to educate those defined as being educable; to impose some kind of social control on mentally retarded people labelled as being delinquent or immoral; and to provide social welfare for individuals whose personality and behaviour traits have led the community to reject them.

1059. Simms, C.A.

'An Institutional History of the Asylum for the Insane (the Rockwood Asylum) at Kingston, 1856–1885.' M.A. thesis, Queen's University, 1981.

1060. Skinner, Shirley J.; Driedger, Otto; and Grainger, Brian.

Corrections: An Historical Perspective of the Saskatchewan Experience. Regina: Canadian Plains Research Centre, University of Regina, 1981.

The primary focus of this book is on historical developments in the Saskatchewan provincial system of adult corrections between 1905 and 1975. Developments in adult corrections are considered in terms of three time periods: the first, from 1905 to 1945, in which concepts of retribution and deterrence predominated correction practices; the second, from 1946 to 1966, during which emphasis was placed on reform, treatment, and rehabilitation; and the third, from 1967 to 1975, which was dominated by a community corrections approach. The book is almost exclusively based on primary sources, including materials obtained from provincial and national archives, correctional centres, private agencies, and private individuals. As well, in-depth interviews were conducted with 20 individuals, employed at various times and in various positions in the provincial correctional system. Although the book is primarily descriptive, some analysis and interpretation of events are offered.

1061. Smandych, Russell C.

'The Rise of the Asylum in Upper Canada, 1830–1875: An Analysis of Competing Perspectives on Institutional Development in the Nineteenth Century.' M.A. thesis, Simon Fraser University, 1981.

In this thesis, the utility of competing 'conventional liberal' and 'social control' perspectives on the rise of the insane asylum is assessed in light of historical evidence concerning the Upper Canadian experience with institutional reform. Particular attention is given to examining materials relating to the origins and early development of the insane asylum, the penitentiary, and the house of industry in Upper Canada (and Ontario) in the period 1830 to 1875. On the basis of evidence which suggests that common threads underscored the development of these institutions, the author concludes that while none of the perspectives on institutional reform produced to date can, on their own, account for the rise of the insane asylum in Upper Canada, the potential exists for the development of a more adequate 'comparative macro-sociological' approach.

1062. Smandych, Russell C.

'The Rise of the Asylum in Upper Canada: An Application of Scull's "Macro-Sociological" Perspective.' *Canadian Criminology Forum* 4 (2, Spring 1982): 142–148.

This article draws on the author's 1981 M.A. thesis, and points to similar conclusions (see entry 1061 above).

1063. Speisman, Stephen A.

'Munificent Parsons and Municipal Parsimony: Voluntary vs. Public Poor Relief in Nineteenth Century Toronto.' *Ontario History* 65 (1, March 1973): 33–49.

Torontonians in the early decades of the nineteenth century desired to fulfil their responsibilities towards their unfortunate fellow citizens and to do so as a religious community. In fact, prior to 1900, the very religious character of Toronto militated against the assumption of social welfare responsibilities by the city government. This article examines the manner in which poor relief was administered by various voluntary relief organizations in nineteenth-century Toronto. The author argues that, with the exception of cases involving the establishment of the York hospital (1820) and the Toronto House of Industry (1837), the 'multiplicity of relief organizations' established and operated by different religious denominations prevented the development of a unified private approach to charity. At the same time, the 'virtually endless' list of charities that existed in Toronto resulted in city officials adopting the attitude 'that charity was a private matter.' The author concludes that '[a]s a result of this municipal attitude, the lack of government machinery, and the enormous number of unco-ordinated private charities,' the needs of the poor of Toronto were not adequately met.

1064. Splane, Richard Beverly.

'The Development of Social Welfare in Ontario, 1791–1893: The Role of the Province.' D.S.W. dissertation, University of Toronto, 1961.

This dissertation forms the basis of the author's 1965 book (see entry 1065 below).

1065. Splane, Richard Beverly.

Social Welfare in Ontario, 1791–1893: A Study of Public Welfare Administration. Toronto: University of Toronto Press, 1965.

This recognized standard text offers a broad coverage of the history of social welfare developments in Upper Canada and Ontario. Divided into seven chapters, the author deals in turn with: (1) prevailing ideas and their influence on social welfare, (2) the development of the administrative structure of provincial and municipal governments, (3) the care of the poor, (4) the development of correctional programs, (5) the development of health services, (6) the welfare of children, and (7) the role of public welfare in a century of social welfare development. The author draws extensively on unpublished manuscript materials held in provincial and federal public archives, government documents and reports, contemporary newspapers, and published books and pamphlets.

1066. Stalwick, Harvey.

'A History of Asylum Administration in Canada before Confederation.' Ph.D. dissertation, University of London, 1969.

This dissertation offers an account of the origin of mental hospital care in Canada. Through his investigation of the circumstances surrounding the emergence of mental institutions in New Brunswick, Nova Scotia, Prince Edward Island, Newfoundland, Quebec, and Ontario, the author attempts to shed light on the sources of inspiration responsible for the establishment of Canada's first mental hospitals, the values and assumptions which supported this social reform, the manner in which the institutions were to be financed, and the reasons why the pre-Confederation attempt to meet the needs of the mentally disordered appeared to be given priority over other social problems, such as public health, physical illness, and poverty. According to the author, the humanitarian ideal of caring for the mentally disordered by applying 'moral methods of treatment' within institutions designed to perform a therapeutic rather than a custodial function was one of the major factors underlying the rise of Canada's first mental hospitals. Despite the well-meaning attempts at reform undertaken during the 1840s and 1850s, the author concludes, by the 1860s established mental hospitals began to take on custodial characteristics.

1067. Stansbury, W.T.

'Penalties and Remedies under "the Combines Investigation Act" 1899–1976.' *Osgoode Hall Law Journal* 14 (1976): 571–631.

1068. Stevenson, D.

'Colonial Sanctions: A Historical Essay.' *Justice of the Peace* 139 (29, 1975): 414–415.

1069. Stewart, V. Lorne.

'Capital Punishment in Canada 1867–1967.' Paper prepared for Dr. Thorsten Sellin, Department of Sociology, University of Pennsylvania, 1968.

This paper examines the history of the use of capital punishment in Canada and the continuing debate over whether the sentence of death by hanging should be abolished. The author documents specific cases in which the sentence was imposed in the nineteenth and twentieth centuries, the number of condemned prisoners who were either executed or had their sentences commuted, and the efforts of abolitionists in parliament to restrict and eventually abolish the use of capital punishment.

1070. Strong, M.K.

Public Welfare Administration in Canada. Social Service Monographs, no. 10. Chicago: University of Chicago Press, 1930. Paterson Smith Reprint Series in Criminology, Law Enforcement and Social Problems, no. 94. Montclair, N.J.: Paterson Smith, 1969.

Intended as an introduction to the subject of public-welfare administration in Canada, this book surveys the development of public-welfare measures and institutions from the beginning of the French regime (1600s) to modern times (1920s). The book is divided into three major parts. In part I, the author deals with poor-relief practices and the development of private and religious charitable organizations in Upper and Lower Canada prior to 1840, and the development of public-welfare institutions (i.e., houses of industry, the penitentiary, insane asylums, juvenile reformatories, and orphanages) in the Province of Canada from 1840 to 1867. In part II, attention is given to examining the organization of public welfare at the federal government level, and the activities engaged in by the Department of Justice – Penitentiary Branch, the Dominion Council of Health, the Department of Health and Soldier's Civil Re-establishment, and the Department of Immigration and Colonization. Part III focuses on outlining the organization of public welfare in selected Canadian provinces, and provincial developments relating to the treatment of poverty, delinquency, the insane, the feeble-minded, the deaf and blind, and children in need of protection.

1071. Stuart, Ernest Donald.

'The Purpose and Practice of the Penal System.' M.A. thesis, University of Toronto, 1940.

1072. Taylor, C.J.

'The Kingston, Ontario Penitentiary and Moral Architecture.' *Histoire sociale/Social History* 12 (November 1979): 385–408.

When planned in 1832, the Kingston penitentiary incorporated one of the most advanced prison designs in the world. This article is concerned with exploring the ideas which prompted the building of the provincial penitentiary, and gave rise to its specific 'moral architecture.' In this effort, the author examines documents on the events leading up to the construction of the penitentiary, the relative influence that American and British penal reformers had on the eventual design of Kingston Penitentiary, and the various concerns that prompted Upper Canadians to adopt the penitentiary model. Although Upper Canadians apparently drew heavily on plans advanced by American proponents of the Auburn model, Taylor notes that the architecture of Kingston Penitentiary also incorporated some of the recommendations of the British penal reformers, John Howard and Jeremy Bentham. Considered within the broader social context, the author concludes that Kingston Penitentiary was created in response to both particular concerns for a more rational system of punishment and more general concerns about growing social disorder in the province.

1073. Taylor, D.A.

'A Study of Adult Probation in Ontario.' M.S.W. thesis, University of Toronto, 1952.

1074. Théorêt, Bruno.

'Inventaire des archives localisées dans les prisons du Québec.' Université de Montréal, Ecole de Criminologie, 1982. (Cahiers de l'Ecole de Criminologie)

1075. Thomas, Charles Humbert.

'The Administration of the Poor Law in Nova Scotia, 1749–1937.' M.A. thesis, Dalhousie University, 1938.

This thesis surveys the history of poor-law administration in Nova Scotia from the early days of the province through to 'the modern period.' The author notes that although the province originally assumed responsibility for poor relief, over the years it increasingly began to delegate its responsibility to smaller and more localized units of poor-law administration which eventually became known as 'poor districts.' Specific attention is devoted to outlining the methods used in dealing with the poor in these districts, including the provision of indoor and outdoor poor relief. The author maintains that at the time of the writing of the thesis the movement towards the decentralization of poor relief had reached its climax, and that the province was divided into a great number of poor districts, many of which were financially unable to support their poor. On the basis of this evidence, he suggests that the province take steps to reverse this trend and move towards centralizing the administration of poor-relief services.

1076. Thompson, Frederic.

'Transportation of Convicts to Newfoundland, 1789–1793.' *Newfoundland Quarterly* 59 (1, March 1960): 30–31.

In July 1789, some 114 convicts being transported from Ireland on a brig clandestinely landed in Newfoundland. The fact that the ship's captain used Newfoundland as a 'dumping ground' for convicts aroused considerable concern in the colony and led to an investigation by British government officials. This article recounts the incident, noting the concerns raised by colonial officials and residents of the colony, and the steps taken in dealing with the unwelcome immigrants. After being confined for a month at St. John's, 80 prisoners were shipped back to Ireland. The author speculates that some of the 34 convicts not accounted for may have hidden in Newfoundland, while others may have died during the voyage.

1077. Topping, Coral Wesley.

'Canadian Penal Institutions.' Ph.D. dissertation, Columbia University, 1929.

This dissertation forms the basis of the author's 1929 [revised edition, 1943] book (see entry 1078 below).

1078. Topping, Coral Wesley.

Canadian Penal Institutions. Toronto: Ryerson Press, 1929; rev. ed., 1943.

The aim of this volume is to describe and evaluate the state of Canadian penal and reformative institutions. On the basis of information derived from numerous personal prison visits, interviews with prison officials, and a range of published government reports, the author deals in turn with the historic rise and present organization of the federal penitentiary system, the policies and programs being implemented in Kingston Penitentiary and other federal penal institutions, the organization and operation of provincial institutions (including local jails, industrial farms, and juvenile reformatories), and existing practices and programs aimed at returning convicted persons to society (probation, remission, parole). The state of Canadian penal and reformative institutions is evaluated in light of the 'modern standards' for the treatment of inmates being followed in other countries. In addition to providing a bibliography of primary and secondary sources, the book contains the text of an article written by Dr. M. MacEachern on 'The Care of the Sick in Canadian Penal Institutions.'

1079. Tremblay, Pierre.

'La punition du crime: Le comportement de la justice pénale de Montréal de 1845 à 1913.' Unpublished paper, Université de Montréal, Ecole de Criminologie, 1983.

In this article the author attempts to determine the quantity of punishment inflicted on delinquents in Montreal during the second half of the nineteenth century. The main goal of the author is to demonstrate how the criminal justice system contributed to the regulation of moral anxieties and social conflicts during the period. This particular period was chosen because it corresponds to the time in which the fundamental rules of the Canadian contemporary system of punishment emerged. The period is also characterized by identifiable economic cycles, which permit the author to examine hypotheses linking criminality to industrialization, social disorganization, and modernization. Various forms of punishment employed in the nineteenth century, including fines, prison and penitentiary incarceration, and capital punishment, are examined, with special attention being given to tracing the development of reformatories for the incarceration of juvenile delinquents.

1080. Tuke, Daniel H.

The Insane in the United States and Canada. London: H.K. Lewis, 1885.

Written by a member of the famous Tuke family of mental-health reformers, this book examines the state of mental institutions and the care of the insane in the United States and Canada. In the chapter devoted specifically to Canada, the author surveys the state of public and private lunatic asylums in the provinces of Quebec, Ontario, New Brunswick, Nova Scotia, Prince Edward Island, and in Newfoundland. The author's observations are based on correspondence and interviews with the officials of various institutions, and historical documents and reports relating to the operation of nineteenth-century Canadian mental institutions.

1081. Verdun-Jones, Simon N., and Smandych, Russell C.

'Catch-22 in the Nineteenth Century: The Evolution of Therapeutic Confinement for the Criminally Insane in Canada, 1840–1900.' In *Criminal Justice History: An International Annual*, pp. 85–108. New York: John Jay Press, 1981.

This article investigates the treatment of the 'criminally insane' in Canada during the nineteenth century. The authors provide an outline of the development of Canadian legislation relating to the disposition of the criminally insane, an overview of the history of the institutional care of the insane in Canada during the nineteenth cenutury, and an analysis of the specific provision made for the treatment of the criminally insane. Primary historical documents, including statutes, government sessional papers, and published contemporary material, are used as sources of information on the legislative provisions and institutional conditions associated with the treatment of the criminally insane in Canada during the nineteenth century. The authors conclude that while the criminally insane were spared the 'formal' punishment meted out by the criminal justice system in the nineteenth century, they nevertheless suffered the 'pains of imprisonment' in asylum conditions that were either similar to, or worse than, those that existed within the prisons of the day.

1082. Walker, J., and Glasner, A.

'The Process of Juvenile Detention: The Training School Act, The Child Welfare Act.' *Osgoode Hall Law Journal* 3 (2, April 1965): 343–361.

1083. Wallace, Elisabeth.

'The Origin of the Social Welfare State in Canada, 1867– 1900.' *Canadian Journal of Economics and Political Science* 15 (1950): 383–393.

1084. Wallot, Hubert.

'A View on the Socio-Political History of Psychiatric Care in French-Canada with Particular Reference to Quebec Asylums.' *Social Science and Medicine* 14 (6, December, 1980): 485–494.

This paper examines the history of psychiatric care at the Robert Giffard Hospital in Quebec, which the author states as having been 'the oldest psychiatric hospital in Lower Canada.' The study covers six periods: (1) the 'politico-religious' period (before 1845); (2) the asylum period (1845–93); (3) the 'French-religious' period (1893–1940); (4) the psychiatric period (1940–71); (5) the 'technocratic rationalization social period' (1971–8); and (6) the beginning of the new period 'toward uncertain outcomes' (since 1978). From his survey of the changing attitudes towards and types of treatment afforded institutionalized individuals during these periods, the author offers the general observation that 'the goals of organizations which take responsibility for madness vary according to the social definition of madness at a given time and according to the interests of the social groups in power at that time.'

1085. Wallot, Jean-Pierre.

'La querelle des prisons (Bas-Canada) 1805–1807.' *Revue d'histoire de l'Amérique française* 14 (1–4, 1960–1): 61– 86, 259–276, 395–407, 559–585.

The author's Master's thesis, presented to the University of Montreal in 1957, is published in four parts. The conflict between Canadians of French origin and the English, dormant during the years 1791 to 1805, was re-ignited by the dispute surrounding the 'gaols Bills' passed by the legislative assembly in 1805. The method of taxation, necessary to finance two proposed new prisons (one in the district of Montreal and the other in the district of Quebec), opposed the two ethnic groups. Canadians of French origin, mainly involved in agriculture, were vehemently opposed to any tax on the land, while Canadians of English origin, mostly involved in commerce, were strongly opposed to the proposed tax on imported goods. The legislation on prisons, apparently without importance, set in motion an acute crisis the causes of which should be sought elsewhere. The crisis seems to have opened a sore point in the relations between the two sides. The constitutional dispute, engendered by the gaols bills, involved not only individuals and political parties but also newspapers such as the *Mercury* of Quebec and the newly established paper *Le Canadien*. From 1805 on, it was impossible to administer the country without taking into account the struggle between the two groups both entrenched behind their positions and prejudices. The thesis is divided into seven chapters, an introduction, and a conclusion. Subjects covered in the chapters are: the need for new prisons, the act of the legislature, the petitions of English merchants, the incident of the *Gazette* of Montreal and the *Mercury* of Quebec, statement of Canadians, the founding of the newspaper *Le Canadien*, and the war of pens.

1086. Wallot, Jean-Pierre.

Un Québec qui bougeait: Trame socio-politique au Québec au tournant du XIXe siècle. Montréal: Boréal Express, 1973.

1087. Ward, C.

'Punishments of Seventy Years Ago.' *New Brunswick Magazine* 3 (1899): 81–87.

1088. Weiler, Karen M.

'Section Eight of the Training Schools Act, R.S.O. 1970 Chapter 467.' LL.M. thesis, York University, 1974.

Although this study is devoted mainly to examining the legal concerns and problems arising from the application of Section 8 of the Ontario *Training Schools Act*, 1970, it includes a historical overview of the development of Ontario legislation which has allowed for the placing of 'unmanageable' children in industrial and training schools. In addition, the author offers a critical comparison of the provisions for the detention of children contained in 'old' and 'new' legislation. From her historical and legal analyses, the author concludes that the *Training Schools Act* of 1970 is a good example of how little thought concerning the 'rehabilitation' of 'unmanageable' children has changed since the turn of the century.

1089. Welling, B., and Hipfer, L.A.

'Cruel and Unusual? Capital Punishment in Canada.' *University of Toronto Law Journal* 26 (1976): 55–83.

1090. Wetherell, Donald Grant.

'To Discipline and Train: Adult Rehabilitation Programs in Ontario Prisons, 1874–1900.' *Histoire sociale/Social History* 12 (May 1979): 145–165.

After 1874 there were three categories of prisons to which adult offenders were sentenced in Ontario: county or common jails for men and women convicted of minor offences or awaiting trial, and the Central Prison for men and the Mercer Reformatory for Women for those sentenced to between two months and two years. This article examines the purposes underlying the development of adult rehabilitation programs in Ontario's provincial penal institutions in the late nineteenth century. Attention is given to discussing the perceived causes of crime, the objectives of Ontario prison reformers and officials, the types of rehabilitation programs that were implemented, and the impediments which hindered their success. The author maintains that '[i]n the last quarter of the nineteenth century Ontario penal institutions were one element in the struggle to preserve social order by deterring deviance and by changing the behaviour of those who had been imprisoned.'

1091. Weatherell, Donald Grant.

'Rehabilitation Programmes in Canadian Penitentiaries, 1867–1914: A Study of Official Opinion.' Ph.D. dissertation, Queen's University, 1980.

In his dissertation, the author examines rehabilitation programs in federal penitentiaries from 1867 to 1914. Organized along topical as opposed to chronological lines, substantive chapters deal with: official views concerning the causes of crime, the search for an 'ideal environment' for reforming criminals, the methods used in disciplining inmates and maintaining institutional order, the use of pardons, remission and parole, prison labour and inmate training, inmate educational programs, and the problem of recidivism. The annual reports of the inspector of penitentiaries serve as the author's major source of primary historical data. He concludes that the rehabilitation programs developed in Canadian penitentiaries reflected a number of elements of Canadian thinking during the period, and in particular the belief that education and religion were the two institutions that 'provided the child and the adult with guidance, learning and direction in life.'

1092. Whalen, James Murray.

'New Brunswick Poor Law Policy in the Nineteenth Century.' M.A. thesis, University of New Brunswick, 1968.

This thesis is primarily concerned with investigating the role poor-law authorities and public and private welfare schemes played in providing for the destitute in Saint John County, New Brunswick, during the nineteenth century. The author maintains that because of its industrial and commercial character, Saint John County had a disproportionate number of paupers and consequently more benevolent institutions than other areas of the province. Substantive chapters focus on examining: (1) the New Brunswick Poor Law of the nineteenth century, (2) immigration and its effect on welfare policy, (3) the almshouse system in Saint John County, (4) poor relief in Kings County, and (5) the development of public and private welfare institutions in Saint John. The author's findings indicate that the institutional care of the poor in almshouses, although slow in coming to New Brunswick, eventually became common in the more heavily populated areas of the province. In addition, he notes that public and private groups supplemented the efforts of poor-law authorities through establishing orphanages, a public hospital, and institutions offering specialized care to the insane, aged, and delinquent. These institutions, however, were not enough to prevent the almshouse from remaining a 'catch-all' for paupers of all ages and conditions.

1093. Whalen, James Murray.

'The Nineteenth-Century Almshouse System in Saint John County.' *Histoire sociale/ Social History* 7 (April 1971): 5–27.

This article draws heavily on the author's 1968 M.A. thesis, and reiterates his earlier conclusions (see entry 1092 above).

1094. Whalen, James Murray.

'Social Welfare in New Brunswick 1784–1900.' *Acadiensis* 2 (1, Autumn 1972): 54–64.

1095. Whittingham, Michael D.

'Criminality and Correctional Reformism in Ontario, 1831 to 1954.' Ph.D. dissertation, York University, 1980.

In this dissertation, the incidence of crime and correctional problems in Ontario and the institutional response to them in the area of correctional policy and practice are analysed with particular reference to the period 1831–1954. Although correctional royal commission documents constitute the central focus of the research, sources such as jail registers, penitentiary statistics, and prison inspectors' reports are also used. Substantive chapters deal with the rise of the 'institutional state,' the social reaction to crime, the work of 15 Canadian correctional commissions appointed between 1831 and 1954, and the social characteristics and 'reform mission' of correctional commission members. The author's findings indicate that social control and reform responses were conditioned, in part, by factors other than simply the level of serious crime itself. While reflecting differing notions of criminal responsibility, social values, and ideologies, the author maintains that correctional commissions may commonly be viewed as 'the primary political response to crime,' and the main means of 'crisis rationalization or containment' within corrections.

1096. Whittingham, Michael D.

'The Role of Reformers and Volunteers in the Advance of Correctional Reform in Canada, since Confederation.' Paper prepared for Federal Corrections History Project, Solicitor General of Canada. Ottawa: Solicitor General of Canada, 1984. User Report Series 1984–70.

In this study, the advance of correctional reform in Canada, and in particular Ontario since 1867, is traced through a critical analysis of governmental commissions and the activities of prison after-care societies. The author contends that the historical development of social welfare programs such as corrections reflects the increasing emphasis placed on the use of formal mechanisms of social control by various levels of government, which began in earnest in the mid-nineteenth century. In addition to providing a general overview of the evolution of Canadian correctional reform, the author discusses the reform role of governmental commissions, the development of voluntary after-care agencies, and the influence of international prison societies and congresses on correctional reform in Canada. The study draws mainly on the reports of governmental commissions, and published secondary literature.

1097. Williams, R.

'Poor Relief and Medicine in Nova Scotia, 1749–1783.' *Collections of the Nova Scotia Historical Society* 24 (1938): 33–56. Reprinted in *Medicine in Canadian Society: Historical Perspectives*, pp. 75–92. Edited by S.E.D. Shortt. Montreal: McGill-Queen's University Press, 1981.

During the mid-1770s, Nova Scotia became inundated by persons who were thought to be 'not only useless but very burdensome to the community.' These persons included 'not only those of the most dissolute manners, and void of all Sentiments of honest Industry, but also Infirm, decrepit, and insane.' This article provides an account of the manner in which established residents of Nova Scotia attempted to deal with the problems posed by poverty and sickness in the province during the last half of the eighteenth century. Particular attention is given to examining the poor-relief system that existed in the province, and the public institutions that were established to cope with the poor and the sick. The author notes that three public institutions were established during the period: a 'Bridewell or Workhouse ... where able-bodied dependants could be made to work for their keep instead of being a burden to the community,' an orphanage which provided shelter for poor children, and a hospital established to provide care for the sick and the infirm.

1098. Wilson, Harry Leonard.

'The Use of the Prerogative of Mercy in Canada.' M.S.W. thesis, University of Toronto, 1954.

1099. Wilson, Thomas H.

'An Historical Study of the Relationship of the Anglican Church of Canada to Kingston Penitentiary 1835–1913.' Ph.D. dissertation, University of Ottawa, 1980.

The dissertation traces the work and involvement of the Anglican Church of Canada in Kingston Penitentiary from 1835 to 1913. Particular attention is given to examining the work carried out by Anglican chaplains in the areas of religious services, spiritual guidance, education, and penal reform. The author relies mainly on primary data sources (including inspectors' and wardens' letterbooks, penitentiary records, and annual chaplains' reports) held at the Canadian Penitentiary Service Museum, Kingston.

1100. Wilton, Jean B.

May I Talk to John Howard? The Story of J.D. Hobden – A Friend to Prisoners. Vancouver: Wilton, 1973.

1101. Wines, Enoch Cobb.

The State of Prisons and of Child-Saving Institutions in the Civilised World. Cambridge, Mass.: University Press, 1880. [Paterson Smith Reprint Series in Criminology, Law Enforcement and Social Problems, no. 24. Montclair, N.J.: Paterson Smith, 1968]

Intended as an encompassing review of the state of penal and reformative institutions in the civilized world, this volume includes a section on developments that have occurred in 'Great Britain and Her Dependencies.' Under the sub-heading 'Colonial Possessions,' brief mention is made of the state of prisons and penitentiaries in Ontario, Newfoundland, Nova Scotia, New Brunswick, Prince Edward Island, and British Columbia.

1102. Withrow, Oswald C.J.

Shackling the Transgressor: An Indictment of the Canadian Penal System. Toronto: Thomas Nelson, 1933.

1103. Wright, John De Pencier.

'Capital Punishment in Ontario.' *The Law Society of Upper Canada Gazette* 14 (1980): 203–204.

1104. Zubrycki, Richard M.

The Establishment of Canada's Penitentiary System: Federal Correctional Policy, 1867–1900. Toronto: Faculty of Social Work, University of Toronto, 1980. (Working Papers on Social Welfare in Canada, no. 2, 1980)

This paper traces Canadian federal correctional policy and developments during the period 1867 to 1900, and discusses some of the social and economic forces underlying those developments. Special attention is given to penitentiaries which were then the major manifestation of federal correctional policy, and to Kingston Penitentiary, which was the physical and operational model for all subsequent federal penitentiaries for a full century. The author argues that the history of the federal penitentiary system in the period 1867 to 1900 reflects three major policy themes: (1) the creation of a social control system to augment the Dominion's task of nation building, (2) the establishment of the dominance of central Canadian social patterns by the federal government, and (3) the gradual acceptance and legislative recognition of 'scientific penology.'

Sources Searched

GENERAL AND REGIONAL BIBLIOGRAPHIES

Aitken, Barbara B.
Local Histories of Ontario Municipalities, 1951–1977: A Bibliography: With Representative Trans-Canada Locations of Copies. Toronto: Ontario Library Association, 1978.

Amtmann, Bernard.
Contributions to a Short-Title Catalogue of Canadiana. 4 vols. Montreal: Bernard Amtmann Inc., 1971–3.

Artibise, Alan F.J.
Western Canada since 1870: A Select Bibliography and Guide. Vancouver: University of British Columbia Press, 1978.

Atlantic Provinces Library Association.
Atlantic Provinces Checklist: A Guide to Current Information in Books, Pamphlets, Government Publications, Magazine Articles and Documentary Films Relating to the Four Atlantic Provinces. vol. 1 (1957) to vol. 9 (1965), and vol. 16 (1972); vols. 10–15 (1966–71) not published. Halifax: Atlantic Provinces Economic Council, 1957–72.

Bibliographic Index: A Cumulative Bibliography of Bibliographies.
New York: H.W. Wilson, 1938–.

Bibliographie du Québec.
Montréal: Bibliothèque nationale du Québec, 1969–.

Bibliographie du Québec, 1821–1967.
Québec: Editeur officiel du Québec, 1980–.

Bishop, Olga B., assisted by Barbara I. Irwin and Clara G. Miller.
Bibliography of Ontario History, 1867–1976: Cultural, Economic, Political, Social. 2 vols. 2nd ed., enl. and updated, of *Ontario since 1867: A Bibliography.* Ontario Historical Studies Series. Toronto: University of Toronto Press, 1980.

Canada. Public Archives.
Union List of Manuscripts in Canadian Repositories / Catalogue collectif des manuscrits des archives canadiennes. Rev. ed. 2 vols. Ottawa: The Archives, 1975. Supplements: 1976, 1977/8, 1979/80.

Canadian Local Histories to 1950: A Bibliography.
3 vols. Toronto: University of Toronto Press, 1967–78.
Vol. 1: *The Atlantic Provinces: Newfoundland, Nova Scotia, New Brunswick, Prince Edward Island.* Edited by William Felix Edmund Morley.
Vol. 2: *La Province de Québec.* Edited by André Beaulieu and William Felix Edmund Morley.
Vol. 3: *Ontario and the Canadian North.* Edited by William Felix Edmund Morley.

Canadiana.
Ottawa, 1951–. Issues for 1951–2 published by the Canadian Bibliographic Centre; 1953– by the National Library of Canada.

Canadiana 1867–1900 Monographs.
Ottawa: National Library of Canada, 1980–. Microfiche ed.

Dionne, N.E.
Inventaire chronologique. 5 vols. Québec: Sociéte royale du Canada, 1905–9. Supplement: 1904–11, published 1912.

Edwards, Margaret H., and Lort, C.R., with the assistance of Wendy J. Carmichael.
A Bibliography of British Columbia: Years of Growth 1900–1950. Victoria: Social Sciences Research Centre, University of Victoria, 1975.

Friesen, Gerald, and Potyondi, Barry.
A Guide to the Study of Manitoba Local History. Winnipeg: Published by the University of Manitoba Press for the Manitoba Historical Society, 1981.

Haight, Willet Ricketson.
Canadian Catalogue of Books, 1791–1897; 1791–1895 and the Two Annual Supplements for 1896 and 1897. London: H. Pordes, 1958.

Lochhead, Douglas Grant, ed.
Bibliography of Canadian Bibliographies. 2nd ed., rev. and enl. Toronto: Published in association with the Bibliographical Society of Canada by the University of Toronto Press, 1972.

Lotz, J.R., comp.
Yukon Bibliography. Ottawa: Northern Co-ordination and Research Centre, Department of Northern Affairs and National Resources, 1964. Supplements: 1963–70, 1971–3, 1974–5, 1975– 7, 1978–9, 1980, 1981, 1982. Authors and imprints vary.

Lowther, Barbara J., with the assistance of Muriel Laing.
A Bibliography of British Columbia: Laying the Foundations, 1848–1899. Victoria: University of Victoria, 1968.

Mailloux, Pierre, comp.
Bibliographie annotée d'ouvrages de référence en usage au bureau de la bibliographie rétrospective. Montréal: Ministère des Affaires culturelles, 1973.

Matthews, Keith.
Check List of Research Studies Pertaining to the History of Newfoundland in the Archives of the Maritime History Group. St. John's: Memorial University of Newfoundland, 1974.

McGill University, Montreal. Library. Lawrence Lande Collection of Canadiana.
The Lawrence Lande Collection of Canadiana in the Redpath Library of McGill University: A Bibliography Collected, Arranged and Annotated by Lawrence Lande. Montreal: Lawrence Lande Foundation for Canadian Historical Research, 1965. Also: *Rare and Unusual Canadiana: Supplement to the Lande Bibliography*. Montreal: McGill University, 1971.

Notices en langue français du Canadian Catalogue of Books 1921–1949.
Montréal: Bibliothèque nationale du Québec, 1975.

O'Dea, Agnes C., comp.
A Newfoundland Bibliography: Preliminary List. St. John's: Memorial University of Newfoundland, 1960.

Peel, Bruce Braden, comp.
A Bibliography of the Prairie Provinces to 1953, with Biographical Index. 2nd ed. Toronto: University of Toronto Press, 1973.

Québec. Bibliothèque nationale.
Les ouvrages de référence du Québec, bibliographie analytique compilée sous la direction

de Réal Bosa. Montréal: Ministère des Affaires culturelles, 1969. Supplement: 1967–74, published 1975.

Québec. Bibliothèque nationale.
Bibliographie de bibliographies québécoises. 2 vols. Montréal: Ministère des Affaires culturelles, 1979. Supplements: 1980, 1981.

Recent Publications Relating to the Atlantic Region: Bibliography. Fredericton: Spring 1975–. Title varies. Xerographically reprinted from *Acadiensis*, periodical of the Department of History, University of New Brunswick.

Review of Historical Publications Relating to Canada.
22 vols. Toronto: University of Toronto Press, 1897–1918. Superseded by: *Canadian Historical Review*.

Ryder, Dorothy E., ed.
Canadian Reference Sources: A Selective Guide. 2nd ed. Ottawa: Canadian Library Association, 1981.

Strathern, Gloria M., comp.
Alberta, 1954–1979: A Provincial Bibliography. Edmonton: University of Alberta, Department of Print Services, 1982.

Taylor, Hugh A., comp.
New Brunswick History: A Checklist of Secondary Sources / Guide en histoire du Nouveau-Brunswick: une liste de controle des sources secondaires. Fredericton: Provincial Archives of New Brunswick, Historical Resources Administration, 1971. Supplement: 1974, compiled by Eric L. Swanick.

Thibault, Claude.
Bibliographia Canadiana. Don Mills, Ont.: Longman Canada, 1973.

Tod, Dorothea Douglas, and Cordingley, Audrey, eds.
A Check List of Canadian Imprints, 1900–1925 / Catalogue d'ouvrages imprimés au Canada. Ottawa: Canadian Bibliographic Centre, Public Archives of Canada, 1950.

Toronto. Public Library.
The Canadian Catalogue of Books Published in Canada, about Canada, as well as those written by Canadians, with imprint 1921–1949. 2 vols. Toronto: The Library, 1959.

Viaison, Robert, comp.
Studying Nova Scotia: Its History and Present State, Its Politics and Economy: A Bibliography and Guide. Halifax: Mount Saint Vincent University, 1974.

SUBJECT BIBLIOGRAPHIES

Artibise, Alan F.J., and Stelter, Gilbert A.
Canada's Urban Past: A Bibliography to 1980 and Guide to Canadian Urban Studies. Vancouver: University of British Columbia Press, 1981.

Aubin, Paul, and Linteau, Paul-André.
Bibliographie de l'histoire du Québec et du Canada, 1966–1975. 2 vols. Québec: Institut québécois de recherche sur la culture, 1981.

Beaulieu, André; Hamelin, Jean; and Bernier, Benôit.
Guide d'histoire du Canada. Les cahiers de l'institut d'histoire, no. 13. Québec: Presses de l'Université Laval, 1969.

Betke, Carl.
The Development of Non-RCMP Policing in Canada: A Preliminary Bibliography. Ottawa: RCMP Historical Section, 1977.

A Bibliography of the Royal Canadian Mounted Police.
Ottawa: RCMP Historical Section, 1979.

Boult, Reynald.
A Bibliography of Canadian Law. New ed. Ottawa: Canadian Law Information Council, 1977. First Supplement published 1982.

Chunn, Dorothy.
Bibliography on Sentencing in Canada. Toronto: University of Toronto, Centre of Criminology, 1975.

Durocher, René, and Linteau, Paul-André.
Histoire du Québec: bibiographie selective 1867–1970. Trois Rivières, Québec: Editions Boréal Express, 1970.

Findlay, Joanna, comp.
White Collar Crime: A Bibliography. Ottawa: RCMP Headquarters Library, 1980.

Garigue, Philippe, and Savard, Raymonde.
Bibliographie du Québec, 1955–1965. Montréal: Presses de l'Université de Montréal, 1967.

Knafla, Louis A.
'Crime, Criminal Law and Justice in Canadian History: A Select Bibliography, Origins to 1940.' In *Law and Society in Historical Perspective*, pp. 157-171. Edited by D.J. Bercuson and L.A. Knafla. Calgary: University of Calgary, 1979.

Law Books 1876–1981: Books and Serials on Law and Its Related Subjects.
New York: R.R. Bowker, 1981. Supplemented by: *Law Information 1982*, and *Law Information Update*, 1983–.

Linteau, Paul-André; Thivierge, Jean; and Beauséjour, Hugette.
Montréal au 19e siècle: bibliographie. Montréal: Groupe de recherche sur la société montréalaise au 19e siècle, 1972.

Maddaugh, Peter D.
A Bibliography of Canadian Legal History. Toronto: York University Law Library, 1972.

Martin, Gérard.
Bibliographie sommaire du Canada français 1854–1954. Québec: Secrétariat de la Province de Québec, 1954.

Moscovitch, Allan, with the assistance of Theresa Jennissen and Peter Findlay.
The Welfare State in Canada: A Selected Bibliography, 1840–1978. Waterloo, Ont.: Wilfrid Laurier University Press, 1983.

A Reader's Guide to Canadian History.
2 vols. Toronto: University of Toronto Press, 1982.
Vol. 1: *Beginnings to Confederation*. Edited by D.A. Muise.
Vol. 2: *Confederation to the Present*. Edited by J.L. Granatstein and Paul Stevens.

Rosenberg, Gertrude; Mayer, Katia Luce; and Brunet-Aubry, Lise.
Criminologie canadienne: bibliographie commentée: la criminalité et l'administration de la justice criminelle au Canada / Canadian Criminology: Annotated Bibliography: Crime and the Administration of Criminal Justice in Canada. Ottawa: Solicitor General Canada, Research Division, 1977.

Schlesinger, Benjamin.
Poverty in Canada and the United States: Overview and Annotated Bibliography. Toronto: University of Toronto Press, 1966.

Wilkins, James L.; Rogers, Judith; and Greer, Marbeth.
Legal Aid in Criminal Matters: A Bibliography. Toronto: University of Toronto, Centre of Criminology, 1971.

Woods, Gerry.
Bibliography of Canadian Criminal Justice History. Programs Branch User Report, no. 1984–71. Ottawa: Ministry of the Solicitor General, Programs Branch, 1984.

PERIODICAL INDEXES

The Canadian Abridgement Index to Canadian Legal Literature. 2nd ed. Toronto: Carswell, 1981. Supplements: *Canadian Abridgement Appendix*, December 1981 and December 1982. Updated in: *Canadian Current Law*. Toronto: Carswell, monthly.

Canadian Periodical Index / Index de périodiques canadiens. Ottawa: Canadian Library Association, 1964–. Supersedes: *Canadian Periodical Index*. Windsor, Ont.: Public Library, 1928–32. Toronto: Public Libraries Branch, Ontario Department of Education, 1938–47. *Canadian Index to Periodicals and Documentary Films*. Ottawa: Canadian Library Association, 1948–1963.

Criminal Justice Abstracts.
New York: National Council on Crime and Delinquency, 1977–. Supersedes: *Selected Highlights of Crime and Delinquency Literature*, and *Information Review on Crime and Delinquency*. New York: NCCD, 1968–9. *Crime and Delinquency Literature*. New York: NCCD, 1970–6.

Criminal Justice Periodical Index.
Ann Arbor, Mich.: University Microfilms International, 1975–.

Criminology and Penology Abstracts.
Leiden, The Netherlands: The Criminologica Foundation, 1980–. Supersedes: *Excerpta Criminologica*. Amsterdam: Excerpta Criminologica Foundation, 1961–8. *Abstracts on Criminology and Penology*. Leiden, The Netherlands: The Criminologica Foundation, 1969–79.

Cumulated Magazine Subject Index, 1907–1949.
2 vols. Boston: G.K. Hall & Co., 1964.

Current Law Index: Multiple Access to Legal Periodicals.
New York: Information Access Corporation and American Association of Law Libraries, 1980–.

Cushing, Helen Grant, and Morris, Adah V.
Nineteenth Century Reader's Guide to Periodical Literature, 1890–1899, with Supplementary Indexing 1900–1922. New York: H.W. Wilson Company, 1944.

Index to Canadian Legal Periodical Literature.
Montreal: The Canadian Association of Law Libraries, 1961–.

Index to Commonwealth Legal Periodicals.
Halifax: Sir James Dunn Law Library, 1974–8. Toronto: Carswell, 1978–81.

Index to Foreign Legal Periodicals.
London: Published by the Institute of Advanced Legal Studies, University of London in co-operation with the American Association of Law Libraries, 1960–.

An Index to Legal Periodical Literature.
Boston: The Boston Book Company, 1888–1939. Publishers vary.

Index to Legal Periodicals.
New York: American Association of Law Libraries and H.W. Wilson, 1908–.

Index to Periodical Articles Related to Law.
New York: Glanville Publications Inc., 1958–. Publishers vary.

Périodex: Index analytique de périodiques de langue français.
Montréal: La centrale des bibliothèques, 1972–. Supersedes: *Index analytique*. Québec: Les Presses de l'Université Laval, 1966–72.

Police Science Abstracts.
Leiden, The Netherlands: The Criminologica Foundation, 1980–. Supersedes: *Abstracts on Police Science*. Leiden, The Netherlands: The Criminologica Foundation, 1973–9.

Poole, William Frederick.
Poole's Index to Periodical Literature, 1802–1906. Gloucester, Mass.: Peter Smith, 1963.

RADAR: répertoire analytique d'articles de revues du Québec.
Montréal: Ministère des Affaires culturelles, 1972–83.

Répertoire bibliographique.
31 vols. Québec, 1940–70.

Social Sciences Index.
New York: H.W. Wilson, 1974–. Supersedes: *International Index to Periodicals: A Guide to Periodical Literature in the Social Sciences and Humanities.* New York: H.W. Wilson, 1907–65. *Social Sciences and Humanities Index.* New York: H.W. Wilson, 1965–74.

DISSERTATION INDEXES

Canadian Graduate Theses in the Humanities and Social Sciences, 1921–46.
Ottawa: Canadian Bibliographic Centre, 1951.

Canadian Theses / Thèses canadiennes.
Ottawa: National Library of Canada, 1952–.

Dissertation Abstracts International.
Ann Arbor, Mich.: University Microfilms International, 1980–. Supersedes: *Comprehensive Dissertation Index 1861–1972.* Ann Arbor, Mich.: Xerox University Microfilms, 1973. Supplements: 1973–7, 1978, 1979.

Jacobs, P.M., comp.
History Theses 1901–70: Historical Research for Higher Degrees in the Universities of the United Kingdom. London: University of London, Institute of Historical Research, 1976.

Kuehl, Warren F.
Dissertations in History: An Index to Dissertations completed in History Departments of United States and Canadian Universities, 1873–1960. 2 vols. Lexington, KY: University of Kentucky Press, 1965–72.

McGill University Thesis Directory.
2 vols. Montreal: The Faculty of Graduate Studies and Research, 1976–.

Mills, Judy, and Dombra, Irene, comps.
University of Toronto Doctoral Theses, 1897–1967: A Bibliography. Toronto: University of Toronto Press, 1968.
Supplement: 1968–75, published 1977.

Register of Post-Graduate Dissertations in Progress in History and Related Subjects.
Ottawa: Canadian Historical Association, 1966–.

Tupling, Donald M., ed.
Canada: A Dissertation Bibliography / Une bibliographie de dissertations. Ann Arbor, Mich.: University Microfilms International, 1980. Supplement: 1983.

University of Alberta Theses.
Edmonton: The Library, University of Alberta, 1971–.

Woodward, Frances.
Theses on British Columbia History and Related Subjects in the Library of the University of British Columbia. Rev. and enl. ed. Reference Publication, no. 35. Vancouver: The Library, 1971.

JOURNALS COMPREHENSIVELY SEARCHED

Le bulletin des recherches historiques.
Lévis, Québec. vol. 1 (1895) – vol. 70 (2, 1968).

Canadian Bar Review / La revue du barreau canadienne. Ottawa. vol. 1 (January 1923) –.

Canadian Journal of Criminology / *Revue canadienne de criminologie.*
Ottawa. vol. 20 (January 1978) –. Supersedes: *Canadian Journal of Corrections* / *La revue canadienne de criminologie.* Ottawa. vol. 1 (October 1958) – vol. 12 (October 1970). *Canadian Journal of Criminology and Corrections* / *Revue canadienne de criminologie.* Ottawa. vol. 13 (January 1971) – vol. 19 (October 1977).

Canadian Historical Review.
Toronto. vol. 1 (1920) –.

Criminologie.
Montréal. vol. 8 (1975) –. Supersedes: *Acta Criminologica.* Montréal. vol. 1 (January 1968) – vol. 7 (January 1974).

Histoire sociale / *Social history.*
Ottawa. vol. 1 (April 1968) –.

Journal of Canadian Studies / *Revue d' études canadiennes.*
Peterborough, Ont. vol. 1 (May 1966) –.

RCMP Quarterly.
Ottawa. vol. 1 (July 1933) –.

Revue d' histoire de l'Amérique française.
Montréal. vol. 1 (1947/8) –.

Urban History Review.
Ottawa. vol. 1 (February 1972) –.

Author Index

Subject Index

ABANDONED CHILDREN. See
ORPHANS AND ORPHANAGES
ABORTION. See BIRTH CONTROL
AND ABORTION
ADMINISTRATION OF JUSTICE 338,
524, 566, 601, 607, 608, 636, 642,
655, 686, 788, 789, 794, 817, 826, 827,
828, 834; ALBERTA 578, 579, 725,
795; BRITISH COLUMBIA 597, 598;
ENGLISH INFLUENCE 410, 419,
556, 634, 673, 718, 721, 779, 789, 814;
FEDERAL ISSUES AND RESPON-
SIBILITIES 97, 913, 930, 1005, 1021,
1070, 1104; FRENCH INFLUENCE
410, 634, 672, 673, 720, 801; NEW
BRUNSWICK 656; NEWFOUND-
LAND 637, 638; NORTHWEST TER-
RITORIES 562, 565, 629, 630, 631,
761, 807, 844, 849; NOVA SCOTIA
656, 840; ONTARIO 782, 792;
PROVINCIAL ISSUES AND RE-
SPONSIBILITIES 97, 839, 930,
1021, 1044, 1057, 1070; QUEBEC 590,
593, 645, 656, 702, 705, 711, 721,
735, 736, 749, 783, 809, 813, 825, 842,
843, 1009, 1057, 1085; QUEBEC –
ENGLISH REGIME 175, 586, 634,
804; QUEBEC – FRENCH RE-

GIME 175, 586, 634, 662, 663, 672,
701, 703, 709, 719, 801, 987, 988,
1010; SASKATCHEWAN 689. See also
Chapter 3 and relevant specific sub-
jects relating to the Administration of
justice (e.g., COURTS; POLICE)
ALBERTA PROVINCIAL POLICE 113,
220
ALCOHOL-RELATED ISSUES. See
PROHIBITION AND TEMPERAN-
CE; WOMEN'S CHRISTIAN TEM-
PERANCE UNION; POLICE –
LIQUOR CONTROL; ROYAL CANA-
DIAN MOUNTED POLICE – LI-
QUOR CONTROL
ALMSHOUSES. See RELIGIOUS AND
CHARITABLE INSTITUTIONS;
ORPHANS AND ORPHANAGES;
WELFARE SERVICES
APPEAL COURTS 611, 648, 760
ARCHAMBAULT REPORT (1938). See
COMMISSIONS OF INQUIRY
ASYLUMS 863, 889, 890, 891, 892, 900,
904, 908, 914, 917, 929, 938, 939,
948, 957, 965, 970, 996, 1030, 1031,
1036, 1037, 1038, 1052, 1061,
1062, 1066, 1080, 1081, 1084. See also
names of specific asylums